Operations and Supply Chain Management 13e

F. Robert Jacobs
Indiana University, Bloomington

Richard B. Chase
University of Southern California

Professor Rex Cutshall
P370 Operations Management
Kelley School of Business

 **Learning Solutions**

Boston   Burr Ridge, IL   Dubuque, IA   New York   San Francisco   St. Louis
Bangkok   Bogotá   Caracas   Lisbon   London   Madrid
Mexico City   Milan   New Delhi   Seoul   Singapore   Sydney   Taipei   Toronto

The **McGraw·Hill** Companies

Operations and Supply Chain Management, Thirteenth Edition
Professor Rex Cutshall
P370 Operations Management
Kelley School of Business

This book is a McGraw-Hill Learning Solutions textbook and contains select material from *Operations and Supply Chain Management*, Thirteenth Edition by F. Robert Jacobs and Richard B. Chase. Copyright © 2011 by The McGraw-Hill Companies, Inc. Reprinted with permission of the publisher. Many custom published texts are modified versions or adaptations of our best-selling textbooks. Some adaptations are printed in black and white to keep prices at a minimum, while others are in color

1 2 3 4 5 6 7 8 9 0 BRP BRP 13 12 11

ISBN-13: 978-0-07-758362-0
ISBN-10: 0-07-758362-0

Learning Solutions Representative: Ann Hayes
Production Editor: Nichole Birkenholz
Printer/Binder: BR Printers

*To my parents Joan and Jake and my children
Jennifer and Suzy*

*To my wife Harriet and to our children
Laurie, Andy, Glenn, Robb, and Christine*

Contents
in Brief

Contents

APPENDICES

section 1

STRATEGY AND SUSTAINABILITY

TWENTY-FIRST-CENTURY OPERATIONS AND SUPPLY MANAGEMENT

Managing a modern supply chain involves specialists in manufacturing, purchasing, and distribution, of course. However, today it is also vital to the work of chief financial officers, chief information officers, operations and customer service executives, and chief executives. Changes in operations and supply management have been truly revolutionary, and the pace of progress shows no sign of moderating. In our increasingly interconnected and interdependent global economy, the process of delivering supplies and finished goods from one place to another is accomplished by means of mind-boggling technological innovation, clever new applications of old ideas, seemingly magical mathematics, powerful software, and old-fashioned concrete, steel, and muscle.

In the first section of *Operations and Supply Management,* we lay a foundation for understanding the dynamic field of operations and supply management. This book is about designing and operating processes that deliver a firm's goods and services in a manner that matches customers' expectations. Really successful firms have a clear and unambiguous idea of how they intend to make money. Be it high-end products or services that are custom-tailored to the needs of a single customer or generic inexpensive commodities that are bought largely on the basis of cost, competitively producing and distributing these products is a great challenge.

chapter 1

OPERATIONS AND SUPPLY CHAIN MANAGEMENT

QUICK SUPPLY CHAINS ENABLE RETAILERS TO GET FASHIONS TO MARKET QUICKLY

Retailers now know that to keep earnings high they need to get the latest fashions into their stores as quickly as possible. Chains ranging from JC Penney to J. Crew scramble to make their orders more precise, so they can stock just enough of the hottest styles for today's increasingly fickle and tight-fisted consumers. Advances in software and technology allow stores to offer the latest trends weeks or even months faster than before and give these retailers more stable profitability. The analysts at Piper Jaffray, a consulting company, say that profit margins have improved at such retailers as Abercrombie & Fitch, Gap, Aéropostale, and Kohl's due to these technology advances.

After reading this chapter you will:

1. Understand why it is important to study operations and supply chain management.

2. Define efficient and effective operations.

3. Categorize operations and supply chain processes.

4. Contrast differences between services and goods producing processes.

5. Identify operations and supply chain management career opportunities.

6. Describe how the field has developed over time.

Efficient logistics have taken on a whole new level of importance. Until recently, many stores were still using the phone and fax machines to place big orders, a very manual and slow, error-prone process. Now, software lets designers, buyers, and manufacturers view the same fabric swatch or color at the same time, thereby eliminating the need to fly designers around the globe or to send overnight packages. By quickly moving the most desirable items into stores, retailers can also ease their reliance on price markdowns, which cut into earnings. They can also order less merchandise and order more often. This lets them adjust orders more easily once certain styles or sizes fail to sell.

SOURCE: ADAPTED FROM JAYNE O'DONNELL, "STORES GET FASHIONS TO MARKET LICKETY-SPLIT," *USA TODAY*, MAY 29, 2008, P. 1B.

The goal is to have the right product at the right place at the right time. In these competitive times, fashion retailers, in particular, need to be agile and flexible. They cannot afford to carry excess inventory, and thus the ability to react to what is selling is as important as customers demand the most innovative and current products. So today's leading retailers are using operations and supply chain management techniques to match supply and demand as closely and quickly as possible. They refer to the strategy as minimizing "concept-to-cash" time and work to minimize the time between the appearance of a fashion concept and the time they start receiving revenue from the sales of that concept.

WHAT IS OPERATIONS AND SUPPLY CHAIN MANAGEMENT?

Operations and supply chain management (OSCM)

Service

Operations and supply chain management (OSCM) is defined as the design, operation, and improvement of the systems that create and deliver the firm's primary products and services. Like marketing and finance, OSCM is a functional field of business with clear line management responsibilities. OSCM is concerned with the management of the entire system that produces a good or delivers a service. Producing a product such as the Men's Nylon Supplex Parka or providing a service such as a cellular phone account involves a complex series of transformation processes.

Exhibit 1.1 shows a supply network for a Men's Nylon Supplex Parka sold on Web sites such as L.L. Bean or Land's End. We can understand the network by looking at the four color-coded paths. The blue path traces the activities needed to produce the Polartec insulation material used in the parkas. Polartec insulation is purchased in bulk, processed to get the proper finish, and then dyed prior to being checked for consistency—or grading—and color. It is then stored in a warehouse. The red path traces the production of the nylon Supplex used in the parkas. Using petroleum-based polymer, the nylon is extruded and drawn into a yarnlike material. From here the green path traces the many steps required to fabricate the clothlike Supplex used to make the parkas. The yellow path shows the Supplex and Polartec material coming together and used to assemble the lightweight and warm parka. The completed parkas are sent to a warehouse and then on to the retailer's distribution center. The parkas are then picked and packed for shipment to individual customers. Think of the supply network as a pipeline through which material and information flows. There are key locations in the pipeline where material and information is stored for future use: Polartec is stored near the end of the blue pipeline; Supplex is stored near the end of the red pipeline. In both cases, fabric is cut prior to merging with the yellow pipeline. At the beginning of the yellow path, bundles of Supplex and Polartec are stored prior to their use in the fabrication of the parkas. At the end of the yellow path are the distribution steps which involve storing to await orders, picking according to actual customer order, packing, and finally shipping to the final customer.

Networks such as this can be constructed for any product or service. Typically each part of the network is controlled by different companies including the nylon Supplex producer, the Polartec producer, the parka manufacturer, and the catalog sales retailer. All of the material is moved using transportation providers, ships

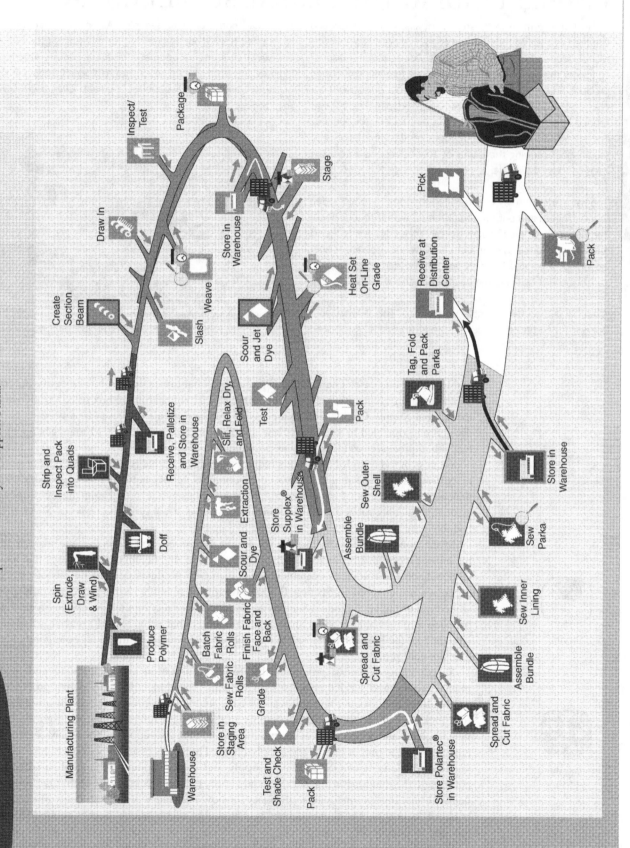

exhibit 1.1   Process Steps for Men's Nylon Supplex Parka

UNDERSTANDING THE GLOBAL SUPPLY CHAIN

At an iron-ore mine in Western Australia, I once stood and watched as a young man worked an excavator to claw bucketfuls of deep-red ore from the ground. For a project, I wanted to follow the ore on its journey from raw material to finished product. So I went on a train that took it to a port, then traveled on the Chinese ship that carried it to Japan. There it was refined into steel ingots, which were sent to a factory outside Tokyo and fashioned into a Toyota Corolla. Next I got on a mighty ship carrying thousands of Toyota imports across the Pacific Ocean to Seattle.

The car made from my ore—small, red, sporty—was unloaded in Washington and put on a truck. I rode with it to a dealer in San Francisco, where I bought the car. Then I drove it to a port and put it, and me as well, onto a Norwegian passenger liner bound for Australia. Ten days later, I unloaded and drove the car to the cliff face and the young excavator operator.

"Here," I said to him, pointing at the car. "This is what your bucketful of iron ore made." He was astonished. Astonished that I had come back to see him. Astonished that his pile of ore had been made into a car. But most astonished of all to learn that so many people—Chinese, Japanese, American, Norwegian—from so many countries had been involved in the process. "I guess we are all linked," he said. "Even if we never think we are."

SOURCE: ADAPTED FROM SIMON WINCHESTER, "HOW AMERICA CAN MAINTAIN ITS EDGE," *PARADE*, DECEMBER 21, 2008, P. 8.

and trucks in this case. The network also has a global dimension with each entity potentially located in a different country. Trace the origin of a Toyota car in the box titled "Understanding the Global Supply Chain." For a successful transaction, all of these steps need to be coordinated and operated to keep costs low and to minimize waste. OSCM manages all of these individual processes as effectively as possible.

Success in today's global markets requires a business strategy that matches the preferences of customers with the realities imposed by complex supply networks. A sustainable strategy that meets the needs of shareholders and employees while preserving the environment is critical. Concepts related to developing this type of strategy is the topic of Section I (see Exhibit 1.2).

In the context of our discussion, the terms *operations* and *supply chain* take on special meaning. *Operations* refers to manufacturing, service, and health care processes that are used to transform the resources employed by a firm into products desired by customers. These processes are covered in Section II. For example, a manufacturing process would produce some type of physical product such as an automobile or a computer. A service process would produce an intangible product such as a call center that provides information to customers stranded on the highway. A hospital that services accident victims in an emergency room is a health care process.

Supply chain refers to processes that move information and material to and from the manufacturing and service processes of the firm. These include the logistics processes that physically move product and the warehousing and storage processes that position products for quick delivery to the customer. Supply in this context refers to providing goods and service to plants and warehouses at the input end, and also the supply of goods and service to the customer on the output end of the supply chain. These processes are covered in Section III.

Another element of OSCM is the supply and demand planning needed to manage and coordinate the manufacturing, service, and supply chain processes. These involve forecasting demand, making intermediate-term plans for how demand will be met, controlling different types of inventory, and detailed weekly scheduling of processes. Topics related to this are covered in Section IV.

All managers should understand the basic principles that guide the design of transformation processes. This includes understanding how different types of processes are organized,

Service

Supply Chain

Organization of OSCM: The Integration of Strategy, Processes and Planning

exhibit 1.2

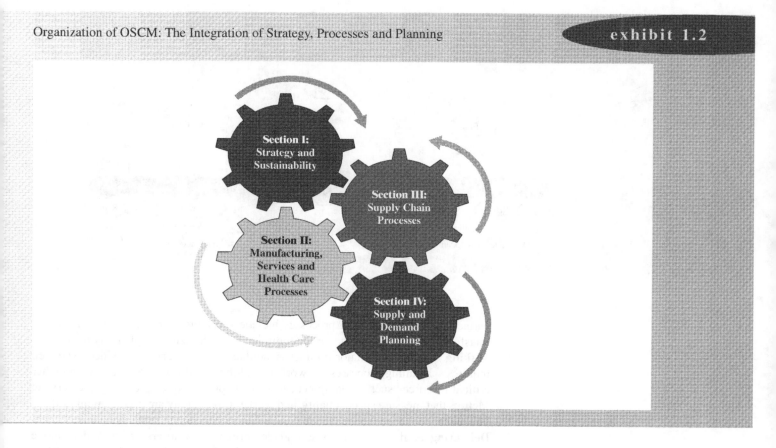

how to determine the capacity of a process, how long it should take a process to make a unit, how the quality of a process is monitored, and how planning information systems are used to coordinate these processes.

The field of operations and supply management is ever changing due to the dynamic nature of competing in global business and the constant evolution of information technology. So while many of the basic concepts have been around for many years, their application in new and innovative ways is exciting. Internet technology has made the sharing of reliable real-time information inexpensive. Capturing information directly from the source through such systems as point-of-sale, radio-frequency identification tags, bar-code scanners, and automatic recognition has changed the focus to one of understanding what all the information is saying and how good decisions can be made using it.

OPERATIONS AND SUPPLY CHAIN PROCESSES

Operations and supply chain processes can be conveniently categorized, particularly from the view of a producer of consumer products and services, as planning, sourcing, making, delivering, and returning. Exhibit 1.3 depicts where the processes are used in different parts of a supply chain. The following describes the work involved in each type of process.

1. **Planning** consists of the processes needed to operate an existing supply chain strategically. Here a firm must determine how anticipated demand will be met with available resources. A major aspect of planning is developing a set of metrics to monitor the supply chain so that it is efficient and delivers high quality and value to customers.
2. **Sourcing** involves the selection of suppliers that will deliver the goods and services needed to create the firm's product. A set of pricing, delivery, and payment processes is needed together with metrics for monitoring and improving the relationships between

exhibit 1.3   Supply Chain Processes

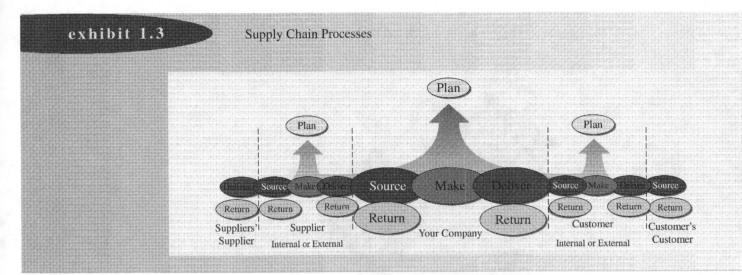

partners of the firm. These processes include receiving shipments, verifying them, transferring them to manufacturing facilities, and authorizing supplier payments.

3. **Making** is where the major product is produced or the service provided. The step requires scheduling processes for workers and the coordination of material and other critical resources such as equipment to support producing or providing the service. Metrics that measure speed, quality, and worker productivity are used to monitor these processes.

4. **Delivering** is also referred to as logistics processes. Carriers are picked to move products to warehouses and customers, coordinate and schedule the movement of goods and information through the supply network, develop and operate a network of warehouses, and run the information systems that manage the receipt of orders from customers, and invoicing systems to collect payments from customers.

5. **Returning** involves the processes for receiving worn-out, defective, and excess products back from customers and support for customers who have problems with delivered products. In the case of services, this may involve all types of follow-up activities that are required for after-sales support.

Service

To understand the topic it is important to consider the many different players that need to coordinate work in a typical supply chain. The aforementioned steps of planning, sourcing, making, delivering, and returning are fine for manufacturing and can also be used for the many processes that do not involve the discrete movement and production of parts. In the case of a service firm such as a hospital, for example, supplies are typically delivered on a daily basis from drug and health care suppliers and require coordination between drug companies, local warehouse operations, local delivery services, and hospital receiving. Patients need to be scheduled into the services provided by the hospital such as operations and blood tests. Other areas, such as the emergency room, need to be staffed to provide service on demand. The orchestration of all of these activities is critical to providing quality service at a reasonable cost.

DIFFERENCES BETWEEN SERVICES AND GOODS

Service

There are five essential differences between services and goods. The first is that a service is an *intangible* process that cannot be weighed or measured, whereas a good is a tangible output of a process that has physical dimensions. This distinction has important business implications since a service innovation, unlike a product innovation, cannot be patented. Thus, a company with a new concept must expand rapidly before competitors copy its procedures. Service intangibility also presents a problem for customers since, unlike with a physical product, they cannot try it out and test it before purchase.

The second is that a service requires some degree of *interaction with the customer* for it to be a service. The interaction may be brief, but it must exist for the service to be complete. Where face-to-face service is required, the service facility must be designed to handle the customer's presence. Goods, on the other hand, are generally produced in a facility separate from the customer. They can be made according to a production schedule that is efficient for the company.

The third is that services, with the big exception of hard technologies such as ATMs and information technologies such as answering machines and automated Internet exchanges, are inherently *heterogeneous*—they vary from day to day and even hour by hour as a function of the attitudes of the customer and the servers. Thus, even highly scripted work such as found in call centers can produce unpredictable outcomes. Goods, in contrast, can be produced to meet very tight specifications day-in and day-out with essentially zero variability. In those cases where a defective good is produced, it can be reworked or scrapped.

The fourth is that services as a process are *perishable and time dependent,* and unlike goods, they can't be stored. You cannot "come back last week" for an air flight or a day on campus.

And fifth, the specifications of a service are defined and evaluated as a *package of features* that affect the five senses. These features are

- Supporting facility (location, decoration, layout, architectural appropriateness, supporting equipment).
- Facilitating goods (variety, consistency, quantity of the physical goods that go with the service; for example, the food items that accompany a meal service).
- Explicit services (training of service personnel, consistency of service performance, availability and access to the service, and comprehensiveness of the service).
- Implicit services (attitude of the servers, atmosphere, waiting time, status, privacy and security, and convenience).

THE GOODS–SERVICES CONTINUUM

Most any product offering is a combination of goods and services. In Exhibit 1.4, we show this arrayed along a continuum of "pure goods" to "pure services." The continuum captures the main focus of the business and spans from firms that just produce products to those that only provide services. Pure goods industries have become low-margin commodity businesses, and in order to differentiate, they are often adding some services. Some examples are providing help with logistical aspects of stocking items, maintaining extensive information databases, and providing consulting advice.

Service

The Goods–Services Continuum

exhibit 1.4

Pure Goods	Core Goods	Core Services	Pure Services
Food products	Appliances	Hotels	Teaching
Chemicals	Data storage systems	Airlines	Medical advice
Book publishing	Automobiles	Internet service providers	Financial consulting

Goods ◄───► Services

SOURCE: ANDERS GUSTOFSSON AND MICHAEL D. JOHNSON, *COMPETING IN A SERVICE ECONOMY* (SAN FRANCISCO: JOSSEY-BASS, 2003), P. 7.

Core goods providers already provide a significant service component as part of their businesses. For example, automobile manufacturers provide extensive spare parts distribution services to support repair centers at dealers.

Core service providers must integrate tangible goods. For example, your cable television company must provide cable hookup and repair services and also high-definition cable boxes. Pure services, such as may be offered by a financial consulting firm, may need little in the way of facilitating goods, but what they do use—such as textbooks, professional references, and spreadsheets—are critical to their performance.

SERVITIZATION STRATEGIES

Service

Servitization refers to a company building service activities into its product offerings for its current users, that is, its installed base. Such services include maintenance, spare part provisioning, training, and in some cases, total systems design and R&D. A well-known pioneer in this area is IBM, which treats its business as a service business and views physical goods as a small part of the "business solutions" it provides its customers. Companies that are most successful in implementing this strategy start by drawing together the service aspects of the business under one roof in order to create a consolidated service organization. The service evolves from a focus on enhancing the product's performance to developing systems and product modifications that support the company's move up the "value stream" into new markets. A servitization strategy might not be the best approach for all product companies, however. A recent study found that while servitized firms generate higher revenues, they tend to generate lower profits as a percentage of revenues when compared to focused firms. This is because they are often unable to generate revenues or margins high enough to cover the additional investment required to cover service-related costs.

GROWTH OF SERVICES

Service

The dominance of services throughout the world economies is clearly evident in Exhibit 1.5. Looking first at the United States, in 1800, 90 percent of the labor force was working on farms doing agriculture production. Today only 3 percent of the U.S. labor force is involved in agriculture production. This represents over a one-million-times productivity increase in about 200 years. Manufacturing peaked in the 1950s and, due to automation and outsourcing, now employs only about 27 percent of the U.S. labor force.

The shift toward services is not simply a U.S. phenomenon, or a developed nation's phenomenon—the chart shows the top 10 nations of the world by size of their labor force: China is 21 percent of the world's labor force, and Germany is 1.4 percent of the world's labor force. China has seen its service sector grow by 191 percent in the last 25 years. Germany has seen its service sector grow by 44 percent in the last 25 years. The shift to services represents the single largest labor force migration in human history. Global communications, business and technology growth, urbanization, and low labor costs in the developing world are all responsible for this dramatic shift. The world is becoming a giant service system, composed of six billion people, millions of businesses, and millions of technology products connected into service networks.

TWO OF THE LEADING EUROPEAN BANKS EXEMPLIFY THE GROWTH OF THE SERVICE INDUSTRY WORLDWIDE.

International Growth in Service

exhibit 1.5

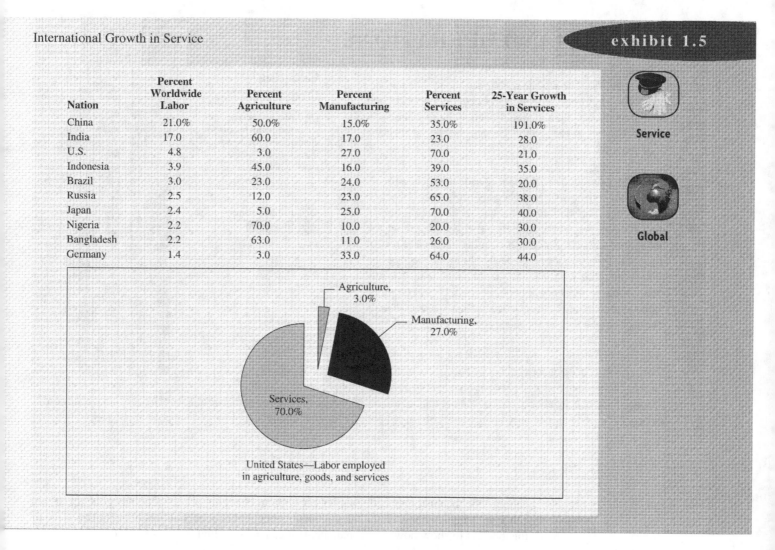

Nation	Percent Worldwide Labor	Percent Agriculture	Percent Manufacturing	Percent Services	25-Year Growth in Services
China	21.0%	50.0%	15.0%	35.0%	191.0%
India	17.0	60.0	17.0	23.0	28.0
U.S.	4.8	3.0	27.0	70.0	21.0
Indonesia	3.9	45.0	16.0	39.0	35.0
Brazil	3.0	23.0	24.0	53.0	20.0
Russia	2.5	12.0	23.0	65.0	38.0
Japan	2.4	5.0	25.0	70.0	40.0
Nigeria	2.2	70.0	10.0	20.0	30.0
Bangladesh	2.2	63.0	11.0	26.0	30.0
Germany	1.4	3.0	33.0	64.0	44.0

Agriculture, 3.0%

Manufacturing, 27.0%

Services, 70.0%

United States—Labor employed in agriculture, goods, and services

Service

Global

EFFICIENCY, EFFECTIVENESS, AND VALUE

Compared with most of the other ways managers try to stimulate growth—technology investments, acquisitions, and major market campaigns, for example—innovations in operations are relatively reliable and low cost. As a business student, you are perfectly positioned to come up with innovative operations-related ideas. You understand the big picture of all the processes that generate the costs and support the cash flow essential to the firm's long-term viability.

Through this book, you will become aware of the concepts and tools now being employed by companies around the world as they craft efficient and effective operations. Efficiency means doing something at the lowest possible cost. Later in the book we define this more thoroughly, but roughly speaking the goal of an efficient process is to produce a good or provide a service by using the smallest input of resources. Effectiveness means doing the right things to create the most value for the company. Often maximizing effectiveness and efficiency at the same time creates conflict between the two goals. We see this trade-off every day in our lives. At the customer service counter at a local store or bank, being efficient means using the fewest people possible at the counter. Being effective, though, means minimizing the amount of time customers need to wait in line. Related to efficiency and effectiveness is the concept of value, which can be metaphorically defined as quality divided by price. If you

Efficiency

Effectiveness

Service

Value

UNDERSTAND OPERATIONS

EFFICIENCY: IT'S THE DETAILS THAT COUNT

Getting passengers on a plane quickly can greatly affect an airline's costs. Southwest says that if its boarding times increased by 10 minutes per flight, it would need 40 more planes at a cost of $40 million each to run the same number of flights it does currently.

Not all the innovation in the airline industry is from Southwest. US Airways, working with researchers at Arizona State University, has developed an innovative boarding system called "reverse pyramid." The first economy-class passengers to get on the plane are those with window seats in the middle and rear of the plane. Then US Airways gradually fills in the plane, giving priority to those with window or rear seats, until it finally boards those seated along aisles in the front. This is in contrast to the approach used by many airlines of just boarding all seats starting from the back of the plane and working forward.

The time it takes for passengers to board has more than doubled since 1970, according to studies by Boeing Co. A study in the mid-1960s found that 20 passengers boarded the plane per minute. Today that figure is down to nine per minute as passengers bring along heftier carry-on luggage. Both Boeing and

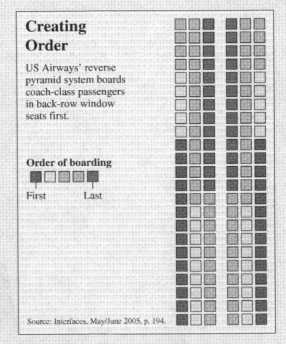

Creating Order

US Airways' reverse pyramid system boards coach-class passengers in back-row window seats first.

Order of boarding

First　　　Last

Source: Interfaces, May/June 2005, p. 194.

Airbus, the two top commercial-aircraft makers, are working on improving boarding time as a selling point to airlines.

can provide the customer with a better car without changing price, value has gone up. If you can give the customer a better car at a *lower* price, value goes way up. A major objective of this book is to show how smart management can achieve high levels of value.

CAREERS IN OPERATIONS AND SUPPLY CHAIN MANAGEMENT

Service

So what do people who pursue careers in operations and supply chain management do? Quite simply, they specialize in managing the production of goods and services. Jobs abound for people who can do this well since every organization is dependent on effective performance of this fundamental activity for its long-term success.

It is interesting to contrast entry-level jobs in operations and supply management to marketing and finance jobs. Many marketing entry-level jobs focus on actually selling products or managing the sales of products. These individuals are out on the front line trying to push product to potential customers. Often a significant part of your income will depend on commissions from these sales. Entry-level finance (and accounting) jobs are often in large public accounting firms. These jobs often involve working at a desk auditing transactions to ensure the accuracy of financial statements. Other assignments often involve the analysis of transactions to better understand the costs associated with the business.

Contrast the marketing and finance jobs to operations and supply chain management jobs. The operations and supply chain manager is out working with people to figure out the best way to deliver the goods and services of the firm. Sure, they work with the marketing folks, but rather than being on the selling side, they are on the buying side: trying to select the best materials and hiring the greatest talent. They will use the data generated by the finance people and analyze processes to figure out the best way to do things. Operations and supply chain management jobs are hands-on, working with people and figuring out the best way to do things.

The following are some typical management and staff jobs in operations and supply chain management:

- Plant manager—Oversees the workforce and physical resources (inventory, equipment, and information technology) required to produce the organization's product.
- Hospital administrator—Oversees human resource management, staffing, and finances at a health care facility.
- Branch manager (bank)—Oversees all aspects of financial transactions at a branch.
- Department store manager—Oversees all aspects of staffing and customer service at a store.
- Call center manager—Oversees staffing and customer service activities at a call center.
- Supply chain manager—Negotiates contracts with vendors and coordinates the flow of material inputs to the production process and the shipping of finished products to customers.
- Purchasing manager—Manages the day-to-day aspects of purchasing such as invoicing and follow-up.
- Business process improvement analyst—Applies the tools of lean production to reduce cycle time and eliminate waste in a process.
- Quality control manager—Applies techniques of statistical quality control such as acceptance sampling and control charts to the firm's products.
- Lean improvement manager—Trains organizational members in lean production and continuous improvement methods.

BREAKTHROUGH BIO

TIMOTHY D. COOK, CHIEF OPERATING OFFICER, APPLE

Timothy D. Cook is Apple's chief operating officer and reports to Apple's CEO. Cook is responsible for all of the company's worldwide sales and operations, including end-to-end management of Apple's supply chain, sales activities, and service and support in all markets and countries. He also heads Apple's Macintosh division and plays a key role in the continued development of strategic reseller and supplier relationships, ensuring flexibility in response to an increasingly demanding marketplace.

Before joining Apple, Cook was vice president of corporate materials for Compaq and was responsible for procuring and managing all of Compaq's product inventory. Previous to his work at Compaq, Cook was the chief operating officer of the reseller division at Intelligent Electronics.

Cook also spent 12 years with IBM, most recently as director of North American fulfillment, where he led manufacturing and distribution functions for IBM's Personal Computer Company in North and Latin America. Cook earned an M.B.A. from Duke University, where he was a Fuqua Scholar, and a Bachelor of Science degree in Industrial Engineering from Auburn University.

SOURCE: HTTP://WWW.APPLE.COM/PR/BIOS/COOK.HTML.

- Project manager—Plans and coordinates staff activities such as new-product development, new-technology deployment, and new-facility location.
- Production control analyst—Plans and schedules day-to-day production.
- Facilities manager—Assures that the building facility design, layout, furniture, and other equipment are operating at peak efficiency.

CHIEF OPERATING OFFICER

So how far can you go in a career in operations and supply management? One goal would be to become the chief operating officer of a company. The chief operating officer (COO) works with the CEO and company president to determine the company's competitive strategy. The COO's ideas are filtered down through the rest of the company. COOs determine an organization's location, its facilities, which vendors to use, and how the hiring policy will be implemented. Once the key decisions are made, lower-level operations personnel carry them out. Operations personnel work to find solutions and then set about fixing the problems.

Managing the supply chain, service, and support are particularly challenging aspects of a chief operating officer's job at such innovative companies as Apple Computer. (See Breakthrough Bio on Timothy D. Cook of Apple.) Career opportunities in operations and supply management are plentiful today as companies strive to improve profitability by improving quality and productivity and reducing costs. The hands-on work of managing people is combined with great opportunities to leverage the latest technologies in getting the job done at companies around the world. No matter what you might do for a final career, your knowledge of operations and supply management will prove to be a great asset.

HISTORICAL DEVELOPMENT OF OPERATIONS AND SUPPLY CHAIN MANAGEMENT

Our purpose in this section is not to go through all the details of OSCM; that would require us to recount the entire Industrial Revolution. Rather, the focus is on major OSCM-related concepts that have been popular since the 1980s. Where appropriate, how a supposedly new idea relates to an older idea is discussed. (We seem to keep rediscovering the past.)

Lean Manufacturing, JIT, and TQC The 1980s saw a revolution in the management philosophies and technologies by which production is carried out. Just-in-time (JIT) production was the major breakthrough in manufacturing philosophy. Pioneered by the Japanese, JIT is an integrated set of activities designed to achieve high-volume production using minimal inventories of parts that arrive at the workstation exactly when they are needed. The philosophy—coupled with total quality control (TQC), which aggressively seeks to eliminate causes of production defects—is now a cornerstone in many manufacturers' production practices, and the term "lean manufacturing" is used to refer to the set of concepts.

Of course, the Japanese were not the first to develop a highly integrated, efficient production system. In 1913, Henry Ford developed an assembly line to make the Model-T automobile. Ford developed a system for making the Model-T that was constrained only by the capabilities of the workforce and existing technology. Quality was a critical prerequisite for Ford: The line could not run steadily at speed without consistently good components. On-time delivery was also critical for Ford; the desire to keep workers and machines busy with materials flowing constantly made scheduling critical. Product, processes, material, logistics, and people were well integrated and balanced in the design and operation of the plant.[1]

Manufacturing Strategy Paradigm   The late 1970s and early 1980s saw the development of the manufacturing strategy paradigm by researchers at the Harvard Business School. This work by professors William Abernathy, Kim Clark, Robert Hayes, and Steven Wheelwright (built on earlier efforts by Wickham Skinner) emphasized how manufacturing executives could use their factories' capabilities as strategic competitive weapons. Central to their thinking was the notion of factory focus and manufacturing trade-offs. They argued that because a factory cannot excel on all performance measures, its management must devise a focused strategy, creating a focused factory that performs a limited set of tasks extremely well. This required trade-offs among such performance measures as low cost, high quality, and high flexibility in designing and managing factories. Ford seems to have realized this about 60 years before the Harvard professors.

Service Quality and Productivity   The great diversity of service industries—ranging from airlines to zoos, with many different types in between—precludes identifying any single pioneer or developer that has made a major impact in these areas. However, McDonald's unique approach to quality and productivity has been so successful that it stands as a reference point in thinking about how to deliver high-volume standardized services.

Total Quality Management and Quality Certification   Another major development was the focus on total quality management (TQM) in the late 1980s and 1990s. All operations executives are aware of the quality message put forth by the so-called quality gurus: W. Edwards Deming, Joseph M. Juran, and Philip Crosby. It's interesting that these individuals were students of Shewhart, Dodge, and Romig in the 1930s (sometimes it takes a generation for things to catch on). Helping the quality movement along is the Baldrige National Quality Award, which was started in 1987 under the direction of the National Institute of Standards and Technology. The Baldrige Award recognizes companies each year for outstanding quality management systems.

Service

The ISO 9000 certification standards, created by the International Organization for Standardization, now plays a major role in setting quality standards for global manufacturers. Many European companies require that their vendors meet these standards as a condition for obtaining contracts.

Global

Business Process Reengineering   The need to become lean to remain competitive in the global economic recession in the 1990s pushed companies to seek innovations in the processes by which they run their operations. The flavor of business process reengineering (BPR) is conveyed in the title of Michael Hammer's influential article in *Harvard Business Review:* "Reengineering Work: Don't Automate, Obliterate." The approach seeks to make revolutionary changes as opposed to evolutionary changes (which are commonly advocated in TQM). It does this by taking a fresh look at what the organization is trying to do in all its business processes, and then eliminating non–value-added steps and computerizing the remaining ones to achieve the desired outcome.

Hammer actually was not the first consultant to advocate eliminating non–value-added steps and reengineering processes. In the early 1900s, Frederick W. Taylor developed principles of scientific management that applied scientific analysis to eliminating wasted effort from manual labor. Around the same time, Frank and Lillian Gilbreth used the new technology of the time, motion pictures, to analyze such diverse operations as bricklaying and medical surgery procedures. Many of the innovations this husband-and-wife team developed, such as time and motion study, are widely used today.

Six-Sigma Quality   Originally developed in the 1980s as part of total quality management, six-sigma quality in the 1990s saw a dramatic expansion as an extensive set of diagnostic tools was developed. These tools have been taught to managers as part of "Green and Black Belt Programs" at many corporations. The tools are now applied to not only the well-known manufacturing applications, but also to nonmanufacturing processes such as accounts receivable, sales, and research and development. Six-sigma has been applied to

**Supply
Chain**

Mass customization

environmental, health, and safety services at companies and is now being applied to research and development, finance, information systems, legal, marketing, public affairs, and human resources processes.

Supply Chain Management   The central idea of supply chain management is to apply a total system approach to managing the flow of information, materials, and services from raw material suppliers through factories and warehouses to the end customer. Recent trends such as outsourcing and mass customization are forcing companies to find flexible ways to meet customer demand. The focus is on optimizing core activities to maximize the speed of response to changes in customer expectations.

Electronic Commerce   The quick adoption of the Internet and the World Wide Web during the late 1990s was remarkable. The term *electronic commerce* refers to the use of the Internet as an essential element of business activity. The Internet is an outgrowth of a government network called ARPANET, which was created in 1969 by the Department of Defense of the U.S. government. The use of Web pages, forms, and interactive search engines has changed the way people collect information, shop, and communicate. It has changed the way operations managers coordinate and execute production and distribution functions.

Service

Service Science   A direct response to the growth of services is the development of a major industry and university program called Service Science Management and Engineering (SSME). SSME aims to apply the latest concepts in information technology to continue to improve service productivity of technology-based organizations. An interesting question raised by Jim Spohrer, leader of the IBM team that started the effort, is where will the labor go, once productivity improves in the service sector? "The short answer is new service sector industries and business—recall the service sector is very diverse and becoming more so every day. Consider the growth of retail (franchises, ecommerce, Amazon, eBay), communication (telephones, T-Mobile, Skype), transportation (airlines, FedEx), financial (discount ebrokers, Schwab), as well as information (television, CNN, Google) services. Not to mention all the new services in developing nations of the world. The creative capacity of the service sector for new industries and business has scarcely been tapped."[2]

CURRENT ISSUES IN OPERATIONS AND SUPPLY CHAIN MANAGEMENT

**Supply
Chain**

Operations and supply chain management is a dynamic field, and challenges presented by global enterprise suggest exciting new issues for operations managers. Looking forward to the future, we believe the major challenges in the field will be as follows:

1. **Coordinating the relationships between mutually supportive but separate organizations.** Recently there has been a dramatic surge in the outsourcing of parts and services that had previously been produced internally. This has been encouraged by the availability of fast, inexpensive communications. A new breed of *contract manufacturers* that specialize in performing focused manufacturing activities now exists. The success of this kind of traditional outsourcing has led companies to consider outsourcing other major corporate functions such as information systems, product development and design, engineering services, packaging, testing, and distribution. The ability to coordinate these activities is a significant challenge for the operations manager of the future.

2. **Optimizing global supplier, production, and distribution networks.** The implementation of global enterprise resource planning systems, now common in large

companies, has challenged managers to use all of this information. This requires a careful understanding of where control should be centralized and where autonomy is important, among other issues. Companies have only begun to take advantage of the information from these systems to optimally control such resources as inventory, transportation, and production equipment.

Global

3. **Managing customer touch points.** As companies strive to become superefficient, they often scrimp on customer support personnel (and training) required to effectively staff service departments, help lines, and checkout counters. This leads to the frustrations we have all experienced such as being placed in call-center limbo seemingly for hours, getting bad advice when finally interacting with a company rep, and so on. The issue here is to recognize that making resource utilization decisions must capture the implicit costs of lost customers as well as the direct costs of staffing.

4. **Raising senior management awareness of operations and supply chain management as a significant competitive weapon.** As we stated earlier, many senior executives entered the organization through finance, strategy, or marketing and built their reputations on work in these areas and, as a result, often take operations for granted. As we will demonstrate in this book, this can be a critical mistake when we realize how profitable companies such as Toyota, Dell, Taco Bell, and Southwest Airlines are. These are companies where executives have creatively used operations and supply chain management for competitive advantage.

5. **Sustainability and the triple bottom line.** Sustainability is the ability to maintain balance in a system. Management must now consider the mandates related to the ongoing economic, employee, and environmental viability of the firm (the triple bottom line). Economically the firm must be profitable. Employee job security, positive working conditions, and development opportunities are essential. Nonpolluting and non–resource-depleting products and processes bring new challenges to operations and supply managers.

Sustainability

Triple bottom line

KEY TERMS

Operations and supply chain management (OSCM) Design, operation, and improvement of the systems that create and deliver the firm's primary products and services.

Servitization Building service activities to support a firm's product offerings.

Efficiency Doing something at the lowest possible cost.

Effectiveness Doing the right things to create the most value for the company.

Value Ratio of quality to price paid. Competitive "happiness" is being able to increase quality and reduce price while maintaining or improving profit margins. (This is a way that operations can directly increase customer retention and gain market share.)

Mass customization Producing products to order in lot sizes of one.

Sustainability The ability to maintain balance in a system.

Triple bottom line Relates to the economic, employee, and environmental impact of the firm's strategy.

REVIEW AND DISCUSSION QUESTIONS

1 Look at the want ads in *The Wall Street Journal* and evaluate the opportunities for an OSCM major with several years of experience.
2 What factors account for the resurgence of interest in OSCM today?
3 Using Exhibit 1.3 as a model, describe the source-make-deliver-return relationships in the following systems:
   a. An airline.
   b. An automobile manufacturer.
   c. A hospital.
   d. An insurance company.

INTERNET EXERCISE: HARLEY-DAVIDSON MOTORCYCLES

Harley-Davidson has developed a Web site that allows potential customers to customize their new motorcycles. Working from a "basic" model, the customer can choose from an assortment of bags, chrome covers, color schemes, exhausts, foot controls, mirrors, and other accessories. The Web-based application is set up so that the customer cannot only select from the extensive list of accessories but also see exactly what the motorcycle will look like. These unique designs can be shared with friends and family by printing the final picture or transferring it via e-mail. What a slick way to sell motorcycles!

Go to the Harley-Davidson (HD) Web site (*www.Harley-Davidson.com*). From there select "Parts & Apparel" and "Genuine Motor Accessories," then select "The Customizer." This should get you into the application.

1. How many different bike configurations do you think are possible? Could every customer have a different bike? To make this a little simpler, what if HD had only two types of bikes, three handlebar choices, four saddlebag combinations, and two exhaust pipe choices? How many combinations are possible in this case (assume they need to select one item from each set of options)?
2. To keep things simple, HD has the dealer install virtually all these options. What would be the trade-off involved if HD installed these options at the factory instead of having the dealers install the options?
3. How important is this customization to HD's marketing strategy? Concisely describe HD's operations and supply strategy.

CASE: FAST-FOOD FEAST

Visit at least two different fast-food restaurants that make hamburgers. For example, in the United States McDonald's, Wendy's, and Burger King are good choices. For some of you fast-food junkies, this will not be difficult; vegans may have to take a friend for product testing. Observe the basic operational differences between these stores. Note the differences in the following processes:

QUESTIONS

1 How are in-store orders taken?
2 Are the hamburgers prepared to order, or are they prepared ahead of time and delivered from a storage bin?
3 How are special orders handled?
4 How are the hamburgers cooked?
5 How are the hamburgers assembled?
6 Is a microwave oven used in the process?
7 How are other common items, such as french fries and drinks, handled?

SUPER QUIZ

1 The pipelinelike movement of the materials and information needed to produce a good or service.
2 A strategy that meets the needs of shareholders, employees, and preserves the environment.
3 The processes needed to determine the set of future actions required to operate an existing supply chain.
4 The selection of suppliers.
5 A type of process where the major product is produced or service provided.
6 A type of process that moves products to warehouses or customers.
7 Processes that involve the receiving of wornout, defective, and excess products back from customers and support for customers who have problems.
8 A business where the major product is intangible, so that it cannot be weighed or measured.
9 Refers to when a company builds service activities into its product offerings.
10 Means doing something at the lowest possible cost.
11 Means doing the right things to create the most value for the company.
12 Metaphorically defined as quality divided by price.
13 A philosophy which aggressively seeks to eliminate causes of production defects.
14 An approach that seeks to make revolutionary changes as opposed to evolutionary changes (which is advocated by total quality management).

15 An approach that combines TQM and JIT.

16 Tools that are taught to managers in "Green and Black Belt Programs."

17 A program to apply the latest concepts in information technology to improve service productivity.

1. Supply (chain) network 2. Triple bottom line strategy 3. Planning 4. Sourcing 5. Making 6. Delivery 7. Returning 8. Service 9. Servitization 10. Efficiently 11. Effectively 12. Value 13. Total quality control 14. Business process reengineering 15. Lean manufacturing 16. Six-Sigma Quality 17. Service science management and engineering.

SELECTED BIBLIOGRAPHY

APICS The Association for Operations Management. www.APICS.org.

Journal of Operations Management. Washington, DC: American Production and Inventory Control Society, 1980–current.

Manufacturing & Service Operations Management: M&SOM. Linthicum, MD: Institute for Operations Research and the Management Sciences, 1999–current.

Production and Operations Management: An International Journal of the Production and Operations Management Society/POMS. Baltimore: Production and Operations Management Society, 1992–current.

Production and Operations Management Society. www.poms.org.

FOOTNOTES

1 See J. Wilson, "Henry Ford: A Just-in-Time Pioneer," *Production & Inventory Management Journal* 37 (1996), pp. 26–31.

2 Jim Spohrer, "Service Science, Management, and Engineering (SSME): A Next Frontier in Education, Employment, Innovation, and Economic Growth," IBM India, teleconference to India from Santa Clara, CA, December 2006.

chapter 2

STRATEGY AND SUSTAINABILITY

HOW IKEA DESIGNS ITS SEXY PRICES

Global

Competitive strategy is about being different. It means deliberately choosing a different set of activities to deliver a unique mix of value. IKEA, the Swedish retailer of home products, dominates markets in 43 countries, and is poised to conquer North America.

Above all else, one factor accounts for IKEA's success: good quality at a low price. IKEA sells household items that are cheap but not cheapo, with prices that typically run 30 to 50 percent below those of the competition. While the price of other companies' products tends to rise over time, IKEA says it has reduced its retail prices by a total of about 20 percent during the last four years. At IKEA the process of driving down costs starts the moment a new item is conceived and continues relentlessly throughout the life of the product.

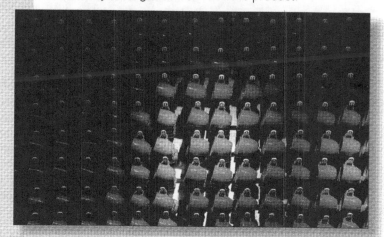

IKEA has always had a 50-cent coffee mug. Prior to the new TROFÉ mug, the company offered the "Bang" mug, which had been redesigned three times, in ways to maximize the number of mugs that could be stored on a pallet. Originally, only 864 mugs would fit. A redesign added a rim such as you would find on a flowerpot so that each pallet could hold 1,280 mugs. Another redesign created a shorter mug with a new handle, allowing 2,024 to squeeze onto a pallet. These changes reduced shipping costs by 60 percent.

The latest version of the 50-cent coffee mug has been made even more useful with a simple notch on the bottom that prevents water from pooling up around the base during a dishwasher run. Further refinements have optimized the speed at which the cup can pass through the machines forming the cups and enable IKEA to fit the maximum number into kilns, saving on the expensive firing process. Simple changes in the

After reading the chapter you will:

1. Compare how operations and supply chain strategy relates to marketing and finance.
2. Understand the competitive dimensions of operations and supply chain strategy.
3. Identify order winners and order qualifiers.
4. Understand the concept of strategic fit.
5. Describe how productivity is measured and how it relates to operations and supply chain processes.
6. Explain how the financial markets evaluate a firm's operations and supply chain performance.

shape of the mug have reduced the cost to produce the mug significantly while creating more value for customers purchasing this simple 50-cent coffee mug.

This is the essence of operations supply chain management: creating great value to the customer while reducing the cost of delivering the good or service.

A SUSTAINABLE STRATEGY

Strategy should describe how a firm intends to create and sustain value for its current shareholders. By adding "sustainability" to the concept, we add the requirement to meet these current needs without compromising the ability of future generations to meet their own needs. *Shareholders* are those individuals or companies that legally own one or more shares of stock in the company. Many companies today have expanded the scope of their strategy to include stakeholders. *Stakeholders* are those individuals or organizations who are influenced, either directly or indirectly, by the actions of the firm. This expanded view means that the scope of the firm's strategy must not only focus on the economic viability of its shareholders but should also consider the environmental and social impact on key stakeholders.

Triple bottom line

To capture this expanded view the phrase triple bottom line has been coined.[1] The triple bottom line, Exhibit 2.1, considers evaluating the firm against social, economic, and environmental criteria. Many companies have developed this expanded view through goals that relate to sustainability along each of these dimensions. Some alternative phrases for the same concept are "People, Planet, and Profit" used by Shell Oil Company, and "Folk, Work, and Place" which originated with the 20th-century writer Patrick Geddes. The following expands on the meaning of each dimension of the triple bottom line framework.

- **Social** Pertains to fair and beneficial business practices toward labor, the community, and the region in which a firm conducts its business. A triple bottom line company seeks to benefit its employees, the community, and other social entities that are impacted by the firm's existence. A company should not use child labor, should pay fair salaries to its workers, maintain a safe work environment with tolerable working hours, and not otherwise exploit a community or its labor force. A business can also give back by contributing to the strength and growth of its community through health care, education, and other special programs.

exhibit 2.1   The Triple Bottom Line

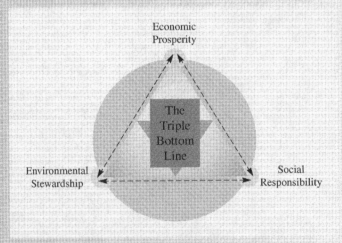

- **Economic** The firm is obligated to compensate shareholders who provide capital through stock purchases and other financial instruments via a competitive return on investment. Company strategies should promote growth and grow long-term value to this group in the form of profit. Within a sustainability framework, this dimension goes beyond just profit for the firm but also provides lasting economic benefit to society.
- **Environmental** This refers to the firm's impact on the environment. The company should protect the environment as much as possible—or at least cause no harm. Managers should move to reduce a company's ecological footprint by carefully managing its consumption of natural resources and by reducing waste, as well as ensuring that the waste is less toxic before disposing of it in a safe and legal manner. Many businesses now conduct "cradle-to-grave" assessments of products to determine what the true environmental costs are—from processing the raw material to manufacture to distribution to eventual disposal by the final customer.

Conventional strategy focuses on the economic part of this framework. Because many of the processes that fall under the domain of operations and supply chain management have social and environment impact, it is important these criteria be considered as well. Some proponents argue that in many ways European Union countries are more advanced due to the standardized reporting of ecological and social losses that came with the adoption of the euro.

Although many company planners agree with the goals of improving society and preserving the environment, many others disagree. Dissenting arguments relate to the potential loss of efficiency due to the focus on conflicting criteria. Others argue that these goals may be appropriate for rich societies that can afford to contribute to society and the environment. A company in a poor or developing society/nation must focus on survival. The economic benefit derived from the use of abundant local resources may be viewed as worth their destruction.

In this chapter we take a customer-centered focus; issues associated with people and the environment are left to an individual case approach. Depending on the country, industry, and scope of the firm, these other issues vary widely and thus are not amenable to a general approach for analysis. The issues and their relationship to operations and supply chain management are very real, however, and we anticipate they will become even more relevant in the future.

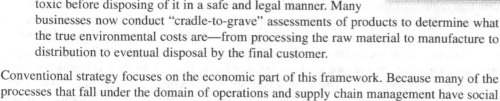

WHAT IS OPERATIONS AND SUPPLY CHAIN STRATEGY?

Operations and supply chain strategy is concerned with setting broad policies and plans for using the resources of a firm and must be integrated with corporate strategy. So, for example, if the high-level corporate strategy includes goals related to the environment and social responsibility, then the operations and supply chain strategy must consider this. A major focus to the operations and supply chain strategy is operations effectiveness. *Operations effectiveness* relates to the core business processes needed to run the business. The processes span all the business functions from taking customer orders, handling returns, manufacturing, managing the updating of the Web site, to shipping products. Operational effectiveness is reflected directly in the costs associated with doing business. Strategies associated with operational effectiveness, such as quality assurance and control initiatives, process redesign, planning and control systems, and technology investments, can show quick, near-term (12 to 24 months) results.

Operations and supply chain strategy

Operations and supply chain strategy can be viewed as part of a planning process that coordinates operational goals with those of the larger organization. Since the goals of the larger organization change over time, the operations strategy must be designed to anticipate future needs. A firm's operations and supply chain capabilities can be viewed as a portfolio best suited to adapt to the changing product and/or service needs of the firm's customers.

Planning strategy is a process just like making a product or delivering a service. The process involves a set of activities that are repeated at different intervals over time. Just as products are made over and over, the strategy planning activities are repeated. A big difference is that these activities are done by executives in the board room!

Exhibit 2.2 shows the major activities of a typical strategic planning process. Activity 1 is performed at least yearly and is where the overall strategy is developed. A key part of this step is the "strategic analysis," which involves looking out and forecasting how business conditions that impact the firm's strategy are going to change in the future. Here such things as changes in customer preferences, the impact of new technologies, changes in population demographics, and the anticipation of new competitors are considered. A successful strategy will anticipate change and formulate new initiatives in response. *Initiatives* are the major steps that need to be taken to drive success in the firm. Many of these initiatives are repeated from year to year such as the updating of existing product designs and the operation of manufacturing plants in different regions of the world. New initiatives that innovatively respond to market dynamics are extremely important to company success. Initiatives that develop innovative new products or open new markets, for example, drive future revenue growth. Other initiatives that reduce costs directly impact the profitability of the firm. Companies with triple bottom line strategies may have initiatives that reduce waste or enhance the welfare of the local communities.

Activity 2 in Exhibit 2.2 is where the overall strategy is refined and updated as often as four times a year. Here each initiative is evaluated and appropriate budget estimates for the next year or more are developed. Measures that relate to the performance of each initiative are needed so that success or failure can be gauged in an unbiased and objective way. Because of the quickly changing nature of global business, many businesses must revise plans several times per year.

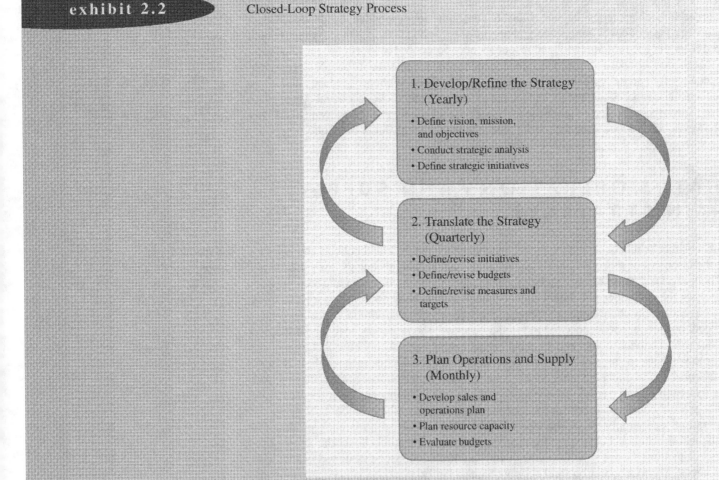

exhibit 2.2   Closed-Loop Strategy Process

1. Develop/Refine the Strategy (Yearly)
   - Define vision, mission, and objectives
   - Conduct strategic analysis
   - Define strategic initiatives

2. Translate the Strategy (Quarterly)
   - Define/revise initiatives
   - Define/revise budgets
   - Define/revise measures and targets

3. Plan Operations and Supply (Monthly)
   - Develop sales and operations plan
   - Plan resource capacity
   - Evaluate budgets

The operations and supply chain planning activity shown in the third box is where operational plans that relate to functional areas such as marketing, manufacturing, warehousing, transportation, and purchasing are coordinated for six months up to a year and a half. The functional areas involved in the coordination can vary greatly depending on the needs of the firm. A hospital requires coordination across the operating room, intensive care units, and auxiliary units such as radiation and chemotherapy. Similarly, the coordination for a retailer such as Walmart may be very different compared to an automobile manufacturer such as Ford. These coordination efforts are largely focused on adjusting capacity and resource availability based on anticipated demand scenarios.

In the next section, we focus on integrating operations and supply chain strategy with a firm's operations capabilities. This involves decisions that relate to the design of the processes and infrastructure needed to support these processes. Process design includes selecting the appropriate technology, sizing the process over time, determining the role of inventory in the process, and locating the process. The infrastructure decisions involve the logic associated with the planning and control systems, quality assurance and control approaches, work payment structure, and organization of the operations and supply chain functions. A firm's operations capabilities can be viewed as a portfolio best suited to adapt to the changing product and/or service needs of a firm's customers.

COMPETITIVE DIMENSIONS

Given the choices customers face today, how do they decide which product or service to buy? Different customers are attracted by different attributes. Some customers are interested primarily in the cost of a product or service and, correspondingly, some companies attempt to position themselves to offer the lowest prices. The major competitive dimensions that form the competitive position of a firm include the following.

Cost or Price: "Make the Product or Deliver the Service Cheap"   Every industry usually includes a segment of the market that buys solely on the basis of low cost. To successfully compete in this niche, a firm must be the low-cost producer, but even this does not always guarantee profitability and success. Products and services sold strictly on the basis of cost are typically commoditylike; in other words, customers cannot distinguish the product or service of one firm from those of another. This segment of the market is frequently very large, and many companies are lured by the potential for significant profits, which they associate with the large unit volumes. As a consequence, however, competition in this segment is fierce—and so is the failure rate. After all, there can be only one lowest-cost producer, who usually establishes the selling price in the market.

Price, however, is not the only basis on which a firm can compete. Other companies, such as BMW, seek to attract those who want *higher quality*—in terms of performance, appearance, or features—than that available in competing products and services, even though accompanied by a higher price.

Quality: "Make a Great Product or Deliver a Great Service"   Two characteristics of a product or service define quality: design quality and process quality. Design quality relates to the set of features the product or service contains. This relates directly to the design of the product or service. Obviously a child's first two-wheel bicycle is of significantly different quality than the bicycle of a world-class cyclist. The use of special aluminum alloys and special lightweight sprockets and chains is important to the performance needs of the advanced cyclist. These two types of bicycle are designed for different customers' needs. The higher-quality cyclist product commands a higher price in the marketplace due to its special features. The goal in establishing the proper level of design quality is to focus on the requirements of the customer. Overdesigned products and services with too many or inappropriate features will be viewed as prohibitively expensive.

In comparison, underdesigned products and services will lose customers to products that cost a little more but are perceived by customers as offering greater value.

Process quality, the second characteristic of quality, is critical because it relates directly to the reliability of the product or service. Regardless of whether the product is a child's first two-wheeler or a bicycle for an international cyclist, customers want products without defects. Thus, the goal of process quality is to produce defect-free products and services. Product and service specifications, given in dimensional tolerances and/or service error rates, define how the product or service is to be made. Adherence to these specifications is critical to ensure the reliability of the product or service as defined by its intended use.

Delivery Speed: "Make the Product or Deliver the Service Quickly"   In some markets, a firm's ability to deliver more quickly than its competitors is critical. A company that can offer an on-site repair service in only 1 or 2 hours has a significant advantage over a competing firm that guarantees service only within 24 hours.

Service

Delivery Reliability: "Deliver It When Promised"   This dimension relates to the firm's ability to supply the product or service on or before a promised delivery due date. For an automobile manufacturer, it is very important that its supplier of tires provide the needed quantity and types for each day's car production. If the tires needed for a particular car are not available when the car reaches the point on the assembly line where the tires are installed, the whole assembly line may have to be shut down until they arrive. For a service firm such as Federal Express, delivery reliability is the cornerstone of its strategy.

Coping with Changes in Demand: "Change Its Volume"   In many markets, a company's ability to respond to increases and decreases in demand is important to its ability to compete. It is well known that a company with increasing demand can do little wrong. When demand is strong and increasing, costs are continuously reduced due to economies of scale, and investments in new technologies can be easily justified. But scaling back when demand decreases may require many difficult decisions about laying off employees and related reductions in assets. The ability to effectively deal with dynamic market demand over the long term is an essential element of operations strategy.

Flexibility and New-Product Introduction Speed: "Change It"   Flexibility, from a strategic perspective, refers to the ability of a company to offer a wide variety of products to its customers. An important element of this ability to offer different products is the time required for a company to develop a new product and to convert its processes to offer the new product.

Service

Other Product-Specific Criteria: "Support It"   The competitive dimensions just described are the most common. However, other dimensions often relate to specific products or situations. Notice that most of the dimensions listed next are primarily service in nature. Often special services are provided to augment the sales of manufactured products.

1. **Technical liaison and support.** A supplier may be expected to provide technical assistance for product development, particularly during the early stages of design and manufacturing.
2. **Meeting a launch date.** A firm may be required to coordinate with other firms on a complex project. In such cases, manufacturing may take place while development work is still being completed. Coordinating work between firms and working simultaneously on a project will reduce the total time required to complete the project.
3. **Supplier after-sale support.** An important competitive dimension may be the ability of a firm to support its product after the sale. This involves availability of replacement parts and, possibly, modification of older, existing products to new performance levels. Speed of response to these after-sale needs is often important as well.

4. **Environmental impact.** A dimension related to criteria such as carbon dioxide emissions, use of nonrenewable resources, or other factors that relate to sustainability.

5. **Other dimensions.** These typically include such factors as colors available, size, weight, location of the fabrication site, customization available, and product mix options.

THE NOTION OF TRADE-OFFS

Central to the concept of operations and supply chain strategy is the notion of operations focus and trade-offs. The underlying logic is that an operation cannot excel simultaneously on all competitive dimensions. Consequently, management has to decide which parameters of performance are critical to the firm's success and then concentrate the resources of the firm on these particular characteristics.

For example, if a company wants to focus on speed of delivery, it cannot be very flexible in its ability to offer a wide range of products. Similarly, a low-cost strategy is not compatible with either speed of delivery or flexibility. High quality also is viewed as a trade-off to low cost.

A strategic position is not sustainable unless there are compromises with other positions. Trade-offs occur when activities are incompatible so that more of one thing necessitates less of another. An airline can choose to serve meals—adding cost and slowing turnaround time at the gate—or it can choose not to, but it cannot do both without bearing major inefficiencies.

Straddling occurs when a company seeks to match the benefits of a successful position while maintaining its existing position. It adds new features, services, or technologies onto the activities it already performs. The risky nature of this strategy is shown by Continental Airlines' ill-fated attempt to compete with Southwest Airlines. While maintaining its position as a full-service airline, Continental set out to match Southwest on a number of point-to-point routes. The airline dubbed the new service Continental Lite. It eliminated meals and first-class service, increased departure frequency, lowered fares, and shortened gate turnaround time. Because Continental remained a full-service airline on other routes, it continued to use travel agents and its mixed fleet of planes and to provide baggage checking and seat assignments.

Straddling

Service

Trade-offs ultimately grounded Continental Lite. The airline lost hundreds of millions of dollars, and the chief executive officer lost his job. Its planes were delayed leaving congested hub cities or slowed at the gate by baggage transfers. Late flights and cancellations generated a thousand complaints a day. Continental Lite could not afford to compete on price and still pay standard travel agent commissions, but neither could it do without agents for its full-service business. The airline compromised by cutting commissions for all Continental flights. Similarly, it could not afford to offer the same frequent-flier benefits to travelers paying the much lower ticket prices for Lite service. It compromised again by lowering the rewards of Continental's entire frequent-flier program. The results: angry travel agents and full-service customers. Continental tried to compete in two ways at once and paid an enormous straddling penalty.

ORDER WINNERS AND ORDER QUALIFIERS: THE MARKETING–OPERATIONS LINK

A well-designed interface between marketing and operations is necessary to provide a business with an understanding of its markets from both perspectives. The terms *order winner* and *order qualifier* describe marketing-oriented dimensions that are key to competitive success. An *order winner* is a criterion that differentiates the products or services of one firm from those of another. Depending on the situation, the order-winning criterion may be the cost of the product (price), product quality and reliability, or any of the other dimensions developed earlier. An *order qualifier* is a screening criterion that permits a firm's products to even be considered as possible candidates for purchase. Oxford

Order winner

Order qualifier

Global

Professor Terry Hill states that a firm must "requalify the order qualifiers" every day it is in business.

It is important to remember that the order-winning and order-qualifying criteria may change over time. For example, when Japanese companies entered the world automobile markets in the 1970s, they changed the way these products won orders, from predominantly price to product quality and reliability. American automobile producers were losing orders through quality to the Japanese companies. By the late 1980s, product quality was raised by Ford, General Motors, and Chrysler; today they are "qualified" to be in the market. Consumer groups continually monitor the quality and reliability criteria, thus requalifying the top-performing companies. Today the order winners for automobiles vary greatly depending on the model. Customers know the set of features they want (such as reliability, design features, and gas mileage), and they want to purchase a particular combination at the lowest price, thus maximizing value.

STRATEGIC FIT: FITTING OPERATIONAL ACTIVITIES TO STRATEGY

Service

All the activities that make up a firm's operation relate to one another. To make these activities efficient, the firm must minimize its total cost without compromising customers' needs. IKEA targets young furniture buyers who want style at a low cost. IKEA has chosen to perform activities differently from its rivals.

Consider the typical furniture store, where showrooms display samples of the merchandise. One area may contain many sofas, another area displays dining tables, and many other areas focus on particular types of furniture. Dozens of books displaying fabric swatches or wood samples or alternative styles offer customers thousands of product varieties from which to choose. Salespeople escort customers through the store, answering their questions

and helping them navigate through the maze of choices. Once a customer decides what he or she wants, the order is relayed to a third-party manufacturer. With a lot of luck, the furniture will be delivered to the customer's home within six to eight weeks. This is a supply chain that maximizes customization and service but does so at a high cost.

In contrast, IKEA serves customers who are happy to trade service for cost. Instead of using sales associates, IKEA uses a self-service model with roomlike displays where furniture is shown in familiar settings. Rather than relying on third-party manufacturers, IKEA designs its own low-cost, modular, ready-to-assemble furniture. In the store there is a warehouse section with the products in boxes ready for delivery. Customers do their own picking from inventory and delivery. Much of its low-cost operation comes from having customers service themselves, yet IKEA offers extra services such as in-store child care and extended hours. Those services align well with the needs of its customers, who are young, not wealthy, and likely to have children, and who need to shop at odd hours.

Exhibit 2.3 shows how IKEA's strategy is implemented through a set of activities designed to deliver it. Activity-system maps such as the one for IKEA show how a company's strategy is delivered through a set of tailored activities. In companies with a clear strategy, a number of higher-order strategic themes (in darker green) can be identified and implemented through clusters of tightly linked activities. This type of map can be useful in understanding how good the fit is between the system of activities and the company's strategy. Competitive advantage comes from the way a firm's activities fit with and reinforce one another.

Activity-system maps

Mapping Activity Systems

exhibit 2.3

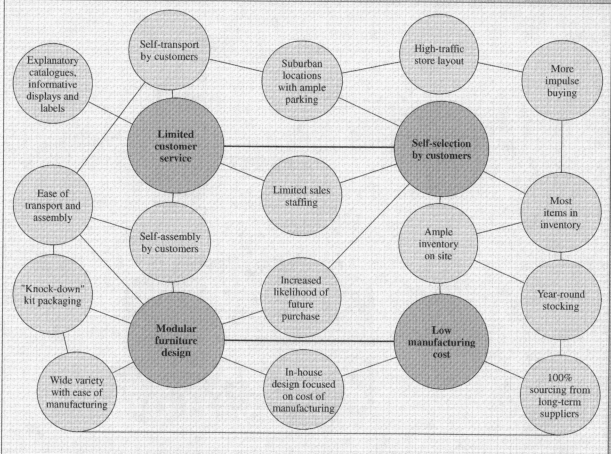

Activity-system maps, such as this one for IKEA, show how a company's strategic position is contained in a set of tailored activities designed to deliver it. In companies with a clear strategic position, a number of higher-order strategic themes (in darker green circles) can be identified and implemented through clusters of tightly linked activities (in lighter circles).

SOURCE: M. E. PORTER, *ON COMPETITION* (BOSTON: HBS, 1998), P. 50.

A FRAMEWORK FOR OPERATIONS AND SUPPLY CHAIN STRATEGY

Operations strategy cannot be designed in a vacuum. It must be linked vertically to the customer and horizontally to other parts of the enterprise. Exhibit 2.4 shows these linkages among customer needs, their performance priorities and requirements for manufacturing operations, and the operations and related enterprise resource capabilities to satisfy those needs. Overlying this framework is senior management's strategic vision of the firm. The vision identifies, in general terms, the target market, the firm's product line, and its core enterprise and operations capabilities.

The choice of a target market can be difficult, but it must be made. Indeed, it may lead to turning away business—ruling out a customer segment that would simply be unprofitable or too hard to serve given the firm's capabilities. An example here is clothing manufacturers not making half-sizes in their dress lines. Core capabilities (or competencies) are the skills that differentiate the service or manufacturing firm from its competitors.

Core capabilities

exhibit 2.4   Operations and Supply Chain Strategy Framework: From Customer Needs to Order Fulfillment

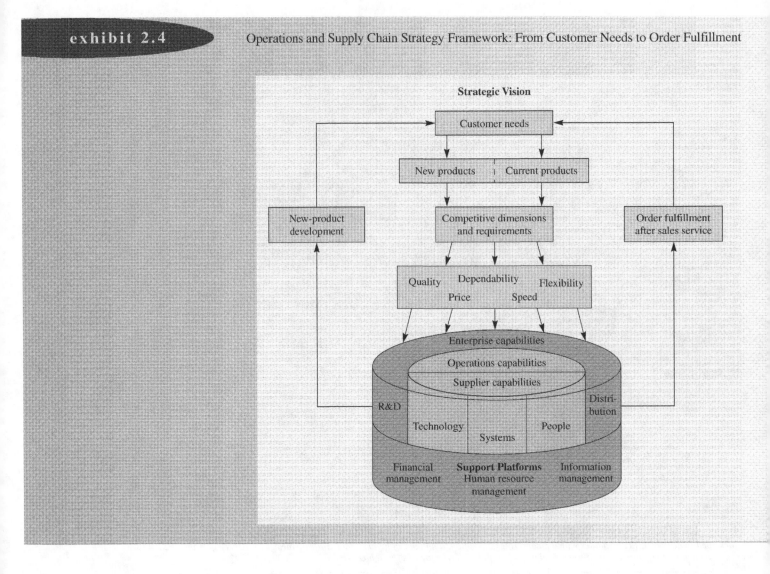

Possibly the most difficult thing for a firm to do is part with tradition. Top-level managers often make their mark based on innovations made 15 to 20 years ago. These managers are often too comfortable just tinkering with the current system. All the new advanced technologies present themselves as quick fixes. It is easy to patch these technologies into the current system with great enthusiasm. While doing this may be exciting to managers and engineers working for the firm, they may not be creating a distinctive core competence—a competence that wins future customers. What companies need in this world of intense global competition is not more techniques but a way to structure a whole new product realization system differently and better than any competitor.

PRODUCTIVITY MEASUREMENT

Productivity

Productivity is a common measure of how well a country, industry, or business unit is using its resources (or factors of production). Since operations and supply chain management focuses on making the best use of the resources available to a firm, productivity measurement is fundamental to understanding operations-related performance. In this section, we define various measures of productivity. Throughout the rest of the book, many other performance measures will be defined as they relate to the material.

In its broadest sense, productivity is defined as

$$\text{Productivity} = \frac{\text{Outputs}}{\text{Inputs}}$$

To increase productivity, we want to make this ratio of outputs to inputs as large as practical.

Productivity is what we call a *relative measure*. In other words, to be meaningful, it needs to be compared with something else. For example, what can we learn from the fact that we operate a restaurant and that its productivity last week was 8.4 customers per labor hour? Nothing!

Productivity comparisons can be made in two ways. First, a company can compare itself with similar operations within its industry, or it can use industry data when such data are available (e.g., comparing productivity among the different stores in a franchise). Another approach is to measure productivity over time within the same operation. Here we would compare our productivity in one time period with that in the next.

As Exhibit 2.5 shows, productivity may be expressed as partial measures, multifactor measures, or total measures. If we are concerned with the ratio of output to a single input, we have a *partial productivity measure*. If we want to look at the ratio of output to a group of inputs (but not all inputs), we have a *multifactor productivity measure*. If we want to express the ratio of all outputs to all inputs, we can use a *total factor measure of productivity* to describe the productivity of an entire organization or even a nation.

A numerical example of productivity appears in Exhibit 2.5. The data reflect quantitative measures of input and output associated with the production of a certain product. Notice that for the multifactor and partial measures, it is not necessary to use total output as the numerator. Often it is desirable to create measures that represent productivity as it relates to some particular output of interest. For example, as in Exhibit 2.5, total units might be the output of interest to a production control manager, whereas total output may be of key interest to the plant manager. This process of aggregation and disaggregation of productivity measures provides a means of shifting the level of the analysis to suit a variety of productivity measurement and improvement needs.

Examples of Productivity Measures

exhibit 2.5

Partial measure	$\dfrac{\text{Output}}{\text{Labor}}$ or $\dfrac{\text{Output}}{\text{Capital}}$ or $\dfrac{\text{Output}}{\text{Materials}}$ or $\dfrac{\text{Output}}{\text{Energy}}$
Multifactor measure	$\dfrac{\text{Output}}{\text{Labor} + \text{Capital} + \text{Energy}}$ or $\dfrac{\text{Output}}{\text{Labor} + \text{Capital} + \text{Materials}}$
Total measure	$\dfrac{\text{Output}}{\text{Inputs}}$ or $\dfrac{\text{Goods and services produced}}{\text{All resources used}}$

INPUT AND OUTPUT PRODUCTION DATA ($)		PRODUCTIVITY MEASURE EXAMPLES
OUTPUT		Total measure
1. Finished units	$10,000	$\dfrac{\text{Total output}}{\text{Total input}} = \dfrac{13,500}{15,193} = 0.89$
2. Work in process	2,500	
3. Dividends	1,000	Multifactor measures:
4. Bonds		
5. Other income		$\dfrac{\text{Total output}}{\text{Human} + \text{Material}} = \dfrac{13,500}{3,153} = 4.28$
Total output	$13,500	
		$\dfrac{\text{Finished units}}{\text{Human} + \text{Material}} = \dfrac{10,000}{3,153} = 3.17$
INPUT		Partial measures:
1. Human	$ 3,000	
2. Material	153	
3. Capital	10,000	$\dfrac{\text{Total output}}{\text{Energy}} = \dfrac{13,500}{540} = 25$
4. Energy	540	
5. Other expenses	1,500	$\dfrac{\text{Finished units}}{\text{Energy}} = \dfrac{10,000}{540} = 18.52$
Total input	$ 15,193	

**Excel:
Productivity Measures**

exhibit 2.6   Partial Measures of Productivity

BUSINESS	PRODUCTIVITY MEASURE
Restaurant	Customers (meals) per labor hour
Retail store	Sales per square foot
Chicken farm	Lb. of meat per lb. of feed
Utility plant	Kilowatts per ton of coal
Paper mill	Tons of paper per cord of wood

Exhibit 2.5 shows all units in dollars. Often, however, management can better understand how the company is performing when units other than dollars are used. In these cases, only partial measures of productivity can be used, as we cannot combine dissimilar units such as labor hours and pounds of material. Examples of some commonly used partial measures of productivity are presented in Exhibit 2.6. Such partial measures of productivity give managers information in familiar units, allowing them to easily relate these measures to the actual operations.

HOW DOES WALL STREET EVALUATE OPERATIONS PERFORMANCE

Comparing firms from an operations view is important to investors since the relative cost of providing a good or service is essential to high earnings growth. When you think about it, earnings growth is largely a function of the firm's profitability, and profit can be increased through higher sales and/or reduced cost. Highly efficient firms usually shine when demand drops during recession periods since they often can continue to make a profit due to their low-cost structure. These operations-savvy firms may even see a recession as an opportunity to gain market share as their less-efficient competitors struggle to remain in business.

Take a look at the automobile industry, where efficiency has been such an important factor. Exhibit 2.7 shows a comparison of some of the major companies. These ratios reflect late 2008 performance, prior to the restructuring of General Motors and Chrysler in 2009. As you can see, Toyota dominates the group. Toyota's net income per employee is five times greater than that of Ford and Chrysler, truly an amazing accomplishment. Toyota also shines in receivables turnover, inventory turnover, and asset turnover. Ford and General Motors have worked hard at implementing the inventory management philosophy that was pioneered by Toyota in Japan. True efficiency goes beyond inventory management and requires an integrated product development, sales, manufacturing, and supply system. Toyota is very mature in its approach to these activities, and that clearly shows on its bottom line.

Each summer, *USA Today* publishes annual reports of productivity gains by the largest U.S. firms. Productivity has been on the rise for the past few years, which is very good for the economy. Productivity often increases in times of recession; as workers are fired, those remaining are expected to do more. Increases also come from technological advances. Think of what the tractor did for farm productivity.

In the evaluation of the largest productivity winners and losers, it is important to look for unusual explanations. For example, energy companies have had big productivity gains due almost exclusively to higher oil prices, which boosted the companies' revenue without forcing them to add employees. Pharmaceutical companies such as Merck and Pfizer have not done well recently. Their productivity plunges were due primarily to one-time events, Merck because it spun off a company and Pfizer because it bought a company. Such one-time quirks create a lot of noise for anybody who wants to know how well companies are run. It is best to examine multiyear productivity patterns.

Efficiency Measures Used by Wall Street

exhibit 2.7

A COMPARISON OF AUTOMOBILE COMPANIES

MANAGEMENT EFFICIENCY MEASURE	TOYOTA	FORD	GENERAL MOTORS	CHRYSLER	INDUSTRY
Income per employee	$40,000	$8,000	$10,000	$8,000	$15,000
Revenue per employee	$663,000	$535,000	$597,000	$510,000	$568,000
Receivables turnover	4.0	1.5	1.0	2.2	2.1
Inventory turnover	12.0	11.5	11.7	5.9	11.0
Asset turnover	0.8	0.6	0.4	0.8	0.8

SUMMARY

In this chapter we have stressed the importance of the link between operations and supply chain management and the competitive success of the firm. The topics in this book include those that all managers should be familiar with. The operations and supply activities of the firm need to strategically support the competitive priorities of the firm. IKEA's entire integrated process, including the design of products, design of the packaging, manufacturing, distribution, and retail outlets, is carefully wired toward delivering functionally innovative products at the lowest cost possible.

In this chapter we show how the overall strategy of the firm can be tied to operations and supply chain strategy. Important concepts are the operational competitive dimensions, order winners and qualifiers, and strategic fit. The ideas apply to virtually any business and are critical to the firm's ability to sustain a competitive advantage. For a firm to remain competitive, all of the operational activities must buttress the firm's strategy. Wall Street analysts are constantly monitoring how efficient companies are from an operations view. Companies that are strong operationally are able to generate more profit for each dollar of sales, thus making them attractive investments.

KEY TERMS

Triple bottom line A business strategy that includes social, economic, and environmental criteria.

Operations and supply chain strategy Setting broad policies and plans for using the resources of a firm to best support the firm's long-term competitive strategy.

Straddling Occurs when a firm seeks to match what a competitor is doing by adding new features, services, or technologies to existing activities. This often creates problems if certain trade-offs need to be made.

Order winner A dimension that differentiates the products or services of one firm from those of another.

Order qualifier A dimension used to screen a product or service as a candidate for purchase.

Activity-system maps A diagram that shows how a company's strategy is delivered through a set of supporting activities.

Core capabilities Skills that differentiate a manufacturing or service firm from its competitors.

Productivity A measure of how well resources are used.

SOLVED PROBLEM

A furniture manufacturing company has provided the following data. Compare the labor, raw materials and supplies, and total productivity of 2009 and 2010.

		2009	2010
Output:	Sales value of production	$22,000	$35,000
Input:	Labor	10,000	15,000
	Raw materials and supplies	8,000	12,500
	Capital equipment depreciation	700	1,200
	Other	2,200	4,800

Solution

	2009	2010
Partial productivities		
Labor	2.20	2.33
Raw materials and supplies	2.75	2.80
Total productivity	1.05	1.04

REVIEW AND DISCUSSION QUESTIONS

1 Can a factory be fast, dependable, and flexible; produce high-quality products; and still provide poor service from a customer's perspective?

2 Why should a service organization worry about being world-class if it does not compete outside its own national border? What impact does the Internet have on this?

3 What are the major priorities associated with operations strategy? How has their relationship to one another changed over the years?

4 For each priority in question 3, describe the unique characteristics of the market niche with which it is most compatible.

5 Find examples where companies have used features related to environmental sustainability to "win" new customers.

6 A few years ago, the dollar showed relative weakness with respect to foreign currencies such as the yen, euro, and pound. This stimulated exports. Why would long-term reliance on a lower-valued dollar be at best a short-term solution to the competitiveness problem?

7 In your opinion, do business schools have competitive priorities?

8 Why does the "proper" operations strategy keep changing for companies that are world-class competitors?

9 What is meant by the expressions *order winners* and *order qualifiers*? What was the order winner(s) for your last major purchase of a product or service?

10 What do we mean when we say productivity is a "relative" measure?

PROBLEMS*

1 As operations manager, you are concerned about being able to meet sales requirements in the coming months. You have just been given the following production report.

	JAN	FEB	MAR	APR
Units produced	2,300	1,800	2,800	3,000
Hours per machine	325	200	400	320
Number of machines	3	5	4	4

Find the average monthly productivity (units per hour).

*Special thanks to Bill Ruck of Arizona State University for the problems in this section.

2   Sailmaster makes high-performance sails for competitive windsurfers. Below is information about the inputs and outputs for one model, the Windy 2000.

Units sold	1,217
Sale price each	$1,700
Total labor hours	46,672
Wage rate	$12/hour
Total materials	$60,000
Total energy	$4,000

Calculate the productivity in **sales revenue/labor expense.**

3   Acme Corporation received the data below for its rodent cage production unit. Find the **total** productivity.

OUTPUT	INPUT	
50,000 cages	Production time	620 labor hours
Sales price: $3.50 per unit	Wages	$7.50 per hour
	Raw materials (total cost)	$30,000
	Component parts (total cost)	$15,350

4   Two types of cars (Deluxe and Limited) were produced by a car manufacturer. Quantities sold, price per unit, and labor hours follow. What is the labor productivity for each car? Explain the problem(s) associated with the labor productivity.

	QUANTITY	$/UNIT
Deluxe car	4,000 units sold	$8,000/car
Limited car	6,000 units sold	$9,500/car
Labor, Deluxe	20,000 hours	$12/hour
Labor, Limited	30,000 hours	$14/hour

5   A U.S. manufacturing company operating a subsidiary in an LDC (less developed country) shows the following results:

	U.S.	LDC
Sales (units)	100,000	20,000
Labor (hours)	20,000	15,000
Raw materials (currency)	$20,000	FC 20,000
Capital equipment (hours)	60,000	5,000

a. Calculate partial labor and capital productivity figures for the parent and subsidiary. Do the results seem misleading?

b. Compute the multifactor productivity figures for labor and capital together. Are the results better?

c. Calculate raw material productivity figures (units/$ where $1 = FC 10). Explain why these figures might be greater in the subsidiary.

6   Various financial data for 2009 and 2010 follow. Calculate the total productivity measure and the partial measures for labor, capital, and raw materials for this company for both years. What do these measures tell you about this company?

		2009	2010
Output:	Sales	$200,000	$220,000
Input:	Labor	30,000	40,000
	Raw materials	35,000	45,000
	Energy	5,000	6,000
	Capital	50,000	50,000
	Other	2,000	3,000

7   An electronics company makes communications devices for military contracts. The company just completed two contracts. The navy contract was for 2,300 devices and took 25 workers two weeks (40 hours per week) to complete. The army contract was for 5,500 devices that were produced by 35 workers in three weeks. On which contract were the workers more productive?

8   A retail store had sales of $45,000 in April and $56,000 in May. The store employs eight full-time workers who work a 40-hour week. In April the store also had seven part-time workers at 10 hours per week, and in May the store had nine part-timers at 15 hours per week (assume four weeks in each month). Using sales dollars as the measure of output, what is the percentage change in productivity from April to May?

9   A parcel delivery company delivered 103,000 packages in 2009, when its average employment was 84 drivers. In 2010 the firm handled 112,000 deliveries with 96 drivers. What was the percentage change in productivity from 2009 to 2010?

10 A fast-food restaurant serves hamburgers, cheeseburgers, and chicken sandwiches. The restaurant counts a cheeseburger as equivalent to 1.25 hamburgers and chicken sandwiches as 0.8 hamburger. Current employment is five full-time employees who work a 40-hour week. If the restaurant sold 700 hamburgers, 900 cheeseburgers, and 500 chicken sandwiches in one week, what is its productivity? What would its productivity have been if it had sold the same number of sandwiches (2,100) but the mix was 700 of each type?

CASE: THE TAO OF TIMBUK2*

"Timbuk2 is more than a bag. It's more than a brand. Timbuk2 is a bond. To its owner, a Timbuk2 bag is a dependable, everyday companion. We see fierce, emotional attachments form between Timbuk2 customers and their bags all the time. A well-worn Timbuk2 bag has a certain patina—the stains and scars of everyday urban adventures. Many Timbuk2 bags are worn daily for a decade, or more, accompanying the owner through all sorts of defining life events. True to our legend of 'indestructibility,' it's not uncommon for a Timbuk2 bag to outlive jobs, personal relationships, even pets. This is the Tao of Timbuk2."

What makes Timbuk2 so unique? Visit their Web site at **www.timbuk2.com** and see for yourself. Each bag is custom designed by the customer on their Web site. After the customer selects the basic bag configuration and size, colors for each of the various panels are presented; various lines, logos, pockets, and straps are selected so that the bag is tailored to the exact specifications of the customer. A quick click of the mouse and the bag is delivered directly to the customer in only two days. How do they do this?

This San Francisco–based company is known for producing high-quality custom and classic messenger bags direct to customer order. They have a team of approximately 25 hardworking cutters and sewers in their San Francisco plant. Over the years, they have fine-tuned their production line to make it as efficient as possible while producing the highest-quality messenger bags available.

The local manufacturing is focused on the custom messenger bag. For these bags, orders are taken over the Internet. The customers are given many configuration, size, color, pocket, and strap options. The bag is tailored to the exact specifications of the

customer on the Timbuk2 assembly line in San Francisco and sent via overnight delivery directly to the customer.

Recently, Timbuk2 has begun making some of its new products in China, which is a concern to some of its long-standing customers. The company argues that it has designed its new products to provide the best possible features, quality, and value at reasonable prices and stresses that these new products are designed in San Francisco. Timbuk2 argues that the new bags are much more complex to build and require substantially more labor and a variety of very expensive machines to produce. They argue that the San Francisco factory labor cost alone would make the retail price absurdly high. After researching a dozen factories in China, Timbuk2 found one that it thinks is up to the task of producing these new bags. Much as in San Francisco, the China factory employs a team of hardworking craftspeople who earn good wages and an honest living. Timbuk2 visits the China factory every four to eight weeks to ensure superior quality standards and working conditions.

On the Timbuk2 Web site, the company argues they are the same hardworking group of bag fanatics designing and making great bags, and supporting our local community and increasingly competitive global market. The company reports that demand is still strong for the custom messenger bags made in San Francisco and that the new laptop bags sourced from China are receiving rave reviews. The additional business is allowing them to hire more people in all departments at the San Francisco headquarters—creating even more jobs locally.

QUESTIONS

1 Consider the two categories of products that Timbuk2 makes and sells. For the custom messenger bag, what are the key competitive dimensions that are driving sales? Are their competitive priorities different for the new laptop bags sourced in China?

2 Compare the assembly line in China to that in San Francisco along the following dimensions: (1) volume or rate of production, (2) required skill of the workers, (3) level of automation, and (4) amount of raw materials and finished goods inventory.

3 Draw two diagrams, one depicting the supply chain for those products sourced in China and the other depicting the bags produced in San Francisco. Show all the major steps, including raw material, manufacturing, finished goods, distribution inventory, and transportation. Other than manufacturing cost, what other costs should Timbuk2 consider when making the sourcing decision?

*SPECIAL THANKS TO KYLE CALTANI OF INDIANA UNIVERSITY FOR THIS CASE.

SUPER QUIZ

1 A strategy that is designed to meet current needs without compromising the ability of future generations to meet their needs.

2 The three criteria included in a triple bottom line.

3 It is probably most difficult to compete on this major competitive dimension.

4 Name the seven operations and supply competitive dimensions.

5 This occurs when a company seeks to match what a competitor is doing while maintaining its existing competitive position.

6 A criterion that differentiates the products or services of one firm from those of another.

7 A screening criterion that permits a firm's products to be considered as possible candidates for purchase.

8 A diagram showing the activities that support a company's strategy.

9 A measure calculated by taking the ratio of output to input.

1. Sustainable 2. Social, economic, environmental 3. Cost 4. Cost, quality, delivery speed, delivery reliability, coping with changes in demand, flexibility and new-product introduction speed, other product-specific criteria 5. Straddling 6. Order winner 7. Order qualifier 8. Activity-system map 9. Productivity

SELECTED BIBLIOGRAPHY

Blanchard, David. *Supply Chain Management Best Practices*. New York: John Wiley & Sons, 2006.

Hayes, Robert; Gary Pisano; David Upton; and Steven Wheelwright. *Operations, Strategy, and Technology: Pursuing the Competitive Edge*. New York: John Wiley & Sons, 2004.

Hill, T. J. *Manufacturing Strategy—Text and Cases*. Burr Ridge; IL: Irwin/McGraw-Hill, 2000.

Slack, N., and M. Lewis. *Operations Strategy*. Harlow, England, and New York: Prentice Hall, 2002.

FOOTNOTE

1 J. Elkington, "Toward the Sustainable Corporation: Win-Win-Win Business Strategies for Sustainable Development," *California Management Review* 36, no. 2 (1994), pp. 90–100.

PROJECTS

chapter 10

NATIONAL AERONAUTICS AND SPACE ADMINISTRATION'S CONSTELLATION PROGRAM MAY LAND MEN ON THE MOON BY 2020

It has been over 40 years since United States astronaut Neil Armstrong set foot on the Moon on July 20, 1969. Today the United States Space Exploration Policy calls "... *for a sustained and affordable exploration program to explore the solar system, including a return to the Moon by the end of the next decade, to establish a human presence there, and to open the path to other destinations including Mars.*"

After reading this chapter you will:

1. Explain what project management is and why it is important.

2. Identify the different ways projects can be structured.

3. Describe how projects are organized into major subprojects.

4. Understand what a project milestone is.

5. Determine the "critical path" for a project.

6. Demonstrate how to "crash," or reduce the length of, a project.

NASA's exploration activity is now in a period of transition, as the Agency works to complete the International Space Station and retire the Shuttle fleet by 2010, while developing the next generation of spacecraft to support human space flight.

To complete the goal of returning to the Moon, NASA has initiated the Constellation Program to accomplish the feat. The Constellation Program is developing and testing a set of space exploration systems that include the Orion crew exploration vehicle, the Ares I launch vehicle that is intended to propel Orion to low Earth orbit, and the Ares V, which is intended to carry a lunar lander to low Earth orbit to dock with Orion and deliver the crew and cargo to the Moon.

The implementation schedule shows the timeline for each of the major projects within the program. The Orion, Ares I, and Ares V projects

Source: NASA 2010 Budget request. http://www.nasa.gov.

Implementation Schedule

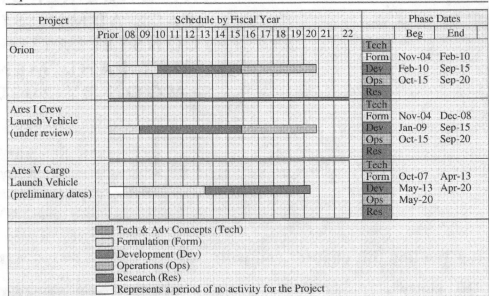

are each divided into major phases starting with Technology and Advanced concepts, Formulation, Development and Operations. NASA uses the techniques described in this chapter to organize the Constellation Program and to manage the projects within the program. It will be exciting to track this nearly trillion dollar program where man will once again have the opportunity to explore our galaxy for real.

> *"The high-impact project is the gem . . . the fundamental nugget . . . the fundamental atomic particle from which the new white collar world will be constructed and/or reconstructed. Projects should be, well WOW!"*
>
> —Tom Peters

Although most of the material in this chapter focuses on the technical aspects of project management (structuring project networks and calculating the critical path), as we see in the opening vignette, the management aspects are certainly equally important. Success in project management is very much an activity that requires careful control of critical resources. We spend much of the time in this book focused on the management of nonhuman resources such as machines and material; for projects, however, the key resource is often our employees' time. Human resources are often the most expensive and those people involved in the projects critical to the success of the firm are often the most valuable managers, consultants, and engineers.

At the highest levels in an organization, management often involves juggling a portfolio of projects. There are many different types of projects ranging from the development of totally new products, revisions to old products, new marketing plans, and a vast array of projects for better serving customers and reducing costs.

Most companies deal with projects individually—pushing each through the pipeline as quickly and cost-effectively as possible. Many of these same companies are very good at applying the techniques described in this chapter in a manner where the myriad of tasks are executed flawlessly, but the projects just do not deliver the expected results. Worse, what often happens is the projects consuming the most resources have the least connection to the firm's strategy.

The vital big-picture decision is what mix of projects is best for the organization. A firm should have the right mix of projects that best support a company's strategy. Projects should be selected from the following types: derivative (incremental changes such as new product

Types of Development Projects

exhibit 10.1

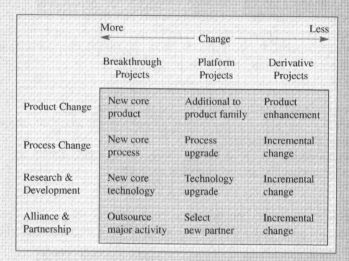

	Breakthrough Projects	Platform Projects	Derivative Projects
	More ←——— Change ———→ *Less*		
Product Change	New core product	Additional to product family	Product enhancement
Process Change	New core process	Process upgrade	Incremental change
Research & Development	New core technology	Technology upgrade	Incremental change
Alliance & Partnership	Outsource major activity	Select new partner	Incremental change

packaging or no-frills versions), breakthrough (major changes that create entirely new markets), platform (fundamental improvements to existing products). Projects can be categorized in four major areas: product change, process change, research and development, and alliance and partnership (see Exhibit 10.1).

In this chapter we only scratch the surface in our introduction to the topic of project management. Professional project managers are individuals skilled at not only the technical aspects of calculating such things as early start and early finish time but, just as important, the people skills related to motivation. In addition, the ability to resolve conflicts as key decision points occur in the project is a critical skill. Without a doubt, leading successful projects is the best way to prove your promotability to the people who make promotion decisions. Virtually all project work is teamwork and leading a project involves leading a team. Your success at leading a project will spread quickly through the individuals on the team. As organizations flatten (through reengineering, downsizing, outsourcing), more will depend on projects and project leaders to get work done, work that previously was handled within departments.

WHAT IS PROJECT MANAGEMENT?

A project may be defined as a series of related jobs usually directed toward some major output and requiring a significant period of time to perform. Project management can be defined as planning, directing, and controlling resources (people, equipment, material) to meet the technical, cost, and time constraints of the project.

Project

Project management

Although projects are often thought to be one-time occurrences, the fact is that many projects can be repeated or transferred to other settings or products. The result will be another project output. A contractor building houses or a firm producing low-volume products such as supercomputers, locomotives, or linear accelerators can effectively consider these as projects.

STRUCTURING PROJECTS

Before the project starts, senior management must decide which of three organizational structures will be used to tie the project to the parent firm: pure project, functional project, or matrix project. We next discuss the strengths and weaknesses of the three main forms.

PURE PROJECT

Tom Peters predicts that most of the world's work will be "brainwork," done in semipermanent networks of small project-oriented teams, each one an autonomous, entrepreneurial center of opportunity, where the necessity for speed and flexibility dooms the hierarchical management structures we and our ancestors grew up with. Thus, out of the three basic project organizational structures, Peters favors the pure project (nicknamed *skunkworks*), where a self-contained team works full time on the project.

Pure project

ADVANTAGES

- The project manager has full authority over the project.
- Team members report to one boss. They do not have to worry about dividing loyalty with a functional-area manager.
- Lines of communication are shortened. Decisions are made quickly.
- Team pride, motivation, and commitment are high.

DISADVANTAGES

- Duplication of resources. Equipment and people are not shared across projects.
- Organizational goals and policies are ignored, as team members are often both physically and psychologically removed from headquarters.
- The organization falls behind in its knowledge of new technology due to weakened functional divisions.
- Because team members have no functional area home, they worry about life-after-project, and project termination is delayed.

FUNCTIONAL PROJECT

Functional project

At the other end of the project organization spectrum is the functional project, housing the project within a functional division.

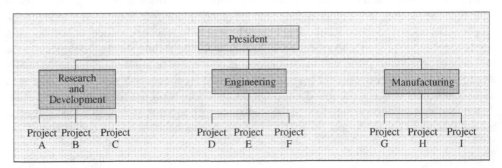

ADVANTAGES

- A team member can work on several projects.
- Technical expertise is maintained within the functional area even if individuals leave the project or organization.
- The functional area is a home after the project is completed. Functional specialists can advance vertically.
- A critical mass of specialized functional-area experts creates synergystic solutions to a project's technical problems.

DISADVANTAGES

- Aspects of the project that are not directly related to the functional area get short-changed.
- Motivation of team members is often weak.
- Needs of the client are secondary and are responded to slowly.

MATRIX PROJECT

Matrix project

The classic specialized organizational form, "the matrix project," attempts to blend properties of functional and pure project structures. Each project utilizes people from different functional areas. The project manager (PM) decides what tasks and when they will be

THE WORLD'S BIGGEST CONSTRUCTION PROJECTS

Think redoing your kitchen is a headache? Imagine supervising one of these megaprojects.

SOUTH-TO-NORTH WATER TRANSFER PROJECT, CHINA

Who's building it: the Chinese government.
Budget: $62 billion (445 billion yuan).
Estimated completion date: 2050.
What it takes: 400,000 relocated citizens and a very thirsty northern China. Economic development in the North China Plain is booming, but its water supplies are falling short, far short. Desperate farming communities are digging wells as deep as 600 feet to find clean water, but the Chinese government has much more digging in mind. Drawing on an unimplemented proposal from Mao himself, the Communist Party has decided to divert water from the Yangtze—a southern river known for its rising tides—to the dry rivers of the north. If it is completed, 12 trillion gallons of water will flow northward yearly through three man-made channels whose combined construction is expected to displace almost 400,000 people. Construction is well under way for the east and central canals, but environmental concerns have kept the western route at the planning stage. The project's $62 billion price tag also makes the South-to-North project by far the most expensive construction project ever in China. But having finished the Three Gorges Dam—a $25 billion project that has forced the relocation of more than 1 million people—China is no stranger to pricey megaprojects.

PANAMA CANAL EXPANSION

Who's building it: the Panamanian government.
Budget: $5.2 billion.
Estimated completion date: 2014.
What it takes: 123 million cubic meters of excavated material and 3,000 ships that just don't fit. Once a marvel of engineering, today's Panama Canal is too narrow to fit 92 percent of the world's shipping fleet through its passage. More than a quarter of the goods that are transported through its locks are carried on Panamax-size vessels—ships that are the maximum size that can fit through the canal. But in a project that broke ground—or canal bed—in the fall of 2007, the Panama Canal will soon be equipped with the world's biggest locks, capable of handling most shipping vessels that are over Panamax size. Also, by adding a wider, deeper, and longer third lock lane to the existing two, the project will more than double the canal's current effective capacity of 15,000 transits per year.

CRYSTAL ISLAND, MOSCOW

Who's building it: Shalva Chigirinsky, oil and real estate mogul.
Budget: $4 billion (98 billion rubles).
Estimated completion date: 2014.
What it takes: 27 million square feet of floor space in the middle of the Moscow River and an eye for the extreme. In a city booming with petro-wealth projects, Crystal Island—designed to be the largest building in the world—is sure to grab most of the attention. Planned as a "city in microcosm," this tentlike structure of steel and glass will, if completed, stand at almost 1,500 feet and house 900 apartments, 3,000 hotel rooms, shopping spaces, offices, an international school for 500 students, a major sports complex, an IMAX theater, and a system of solar panels, wind turbines, and naturally insulating winter gardens designed for energy efficiency. Throw in a few onion domes, and Crystal Island could replace Moscow altogether. Filling one of the few large-scale sites left near the city's center, Crystal Island will sit on the Nagatinskaya, a large peninsula that juts into the Moscow River, less than 5 miles from the Kremlin.

SOURCE: http://www.foreignpolicy.com/

performed, but the functional managers control which people and technologies are used. If the matrix form is chosen, different projects (rows of the matrix) borrow resources from functional areas (columns). Senior management must then decide whether a weak, balanced, or strong form of a matrix is to be used. This establishes whether project managers have little, equal, or more authority than the functional managers with whom they negotiate for resources.

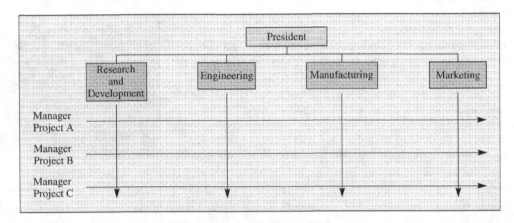

ADVANTAGES
- Communication between functional divisions is enhanced.
- A project manager is held responsible for successful completion of the project.
- Duplication of resources is minimized.
- Team members have a functional "home" after project completion, so they are less worried about life-after-project than if they were a pure project organization.
- Policies of the parent organization are followed. This increases support for the project.

DISADVANTAGES
- There are two bosses. Often the functional manager will be listened to before the project manager. After all, who can promote you or give you a raise?
- It is doomed to failure unless the PM has strong negotiating skills.
- Suboptimization is a danger, as PMs hoard resources for their own project, thus harming other projects.

Note that regardless of which of the three major organizational forms is used, the project manager is the primary contact point with the customer. Communication and flexibility are greatly enhanced because one person is responsible for successful completion of the project.

WORK BREAKDOWN STRUCTURE

A project starts out as a *statement of work* (SOW). The SOW may be a written description of the objectives to be achieved, with a brief statement of the work to be done and a proposed schedule specifying the start and completion dates. It also could contain performance measures in terms of budget and completion steps (milestones) and the written reports to be supplied.

A *task* is a further subdivision of a project. It is usually not longer than several months in duration and is performed by one group or organization. A *subtask* may be used if needed to further subdivide the project into more meaningful pieces.

A *work package* is a group of activities combined to be assignable to a single organizational unit. It still falls into the format of all project management; the package provides a description of what is to be done, when it is to be started and completed, the budget, measures of performance,

and specific events to be reached at points in time. These specific events are called project
milestones. Typical milestones might be the completion of the design, the production of a prototype, the completed testing of the prototype, and the approval of a pilot run.

The work breakdown structure (WBS) defines the hierarchy of project tasks, subtasks,
and work packages. Completion of one or more work packages results in the completion of a
subtask; completion of one or more subtasks results in the completion of a task; and finally,
the completion of all tasks is required to complete the project. A representation of this structure is shown in Exhibit 10.2.

Exhibit 10.3 shows the WBS for an optical scanner project. The WBS is important in
organizing a project because it breaks the project down into manageable pieces. The number

An Example of a Work Breakdown Structure   **exhibit 10.2**

Work Breakdown Structure, Large Optical Scanner Design   **exhibit 10.3**

Level					
1	2	3	4		
x				1	Optical simulator design
	x			1.1	Optical design
		x		1.1.1	Telescope design/fab
		x		1.1.2	Telescope/simulator optical interface
		x		1.1.3	Simulator zoom system design
		x		1.1.4	Ancillary simulator optical component specification
	x			1.2	System performance analysis
		x		1.2.1	Overall system firmware and software control
			x	1.2.1.1	Logic flow diagram generation and analysis
			x	1.2.1.2	Basic control algorithm design
		x		1.2.2	Far beam analyzer
		x		1.2.3	System inter- and intra-alignment method design
		x		1.2.4	Data recording and reduction requirements
	x			1.3	System integration
	x			1.4	Cost analysis
		x		1.4.1	Cost/system schedule analysis
		x		1.4.2	Cost/system performance analysis
	x			1.5	Management
		x		1.5.1	System design/engineering management
		x		1.5.2	Program management
	x			1.6	Long lead item procurement
		x		1.6.1	Large optics
		x		1.6.2	Target components
		x		1.6.3	Detectors

of levels will vary depending on the project. How much detail or how many levels to use depends on the following:

- The level at which a single individual or organization can be assigned responsibility and accountability for accomplishing the work package.
- The level at which budget and cost data will be collected during the project.

There is not a single correct WBS for any project, and two different project teams might develop different WBSs for the same project. Some experts have referred to project management as an art rather than a science, because there are so many different ways that a project can be approached. Finding the correct way to organize a project depends on experience with the particular task.

Activities

Activities are defined within the context of the work breakdown structure and are pieces of work that consume time. Activities do not necessarily require the expenditure of effort by people, although they often do. For example, waiting for paint to dry may be an activity in a project. Activities are identified as part of the WBS. From our sample project in Exhibit 10.3, activities would include telescope design and fabrication (1.1.1), telescope/simulator optical interface (1.1.2), and data recording (1.2.4). Activities need to be defined in such a way that when they are all completed, the project is done.

PROJECT CONTROL CHARTS

The U.S. Department of Defense (one of the earliest large users of project management) has published a variety of helpful standard forms. Many are used directly or have been modified by firms engaged in project management. Computer programs are available to quickly generate the charts described in this section. Charts are useful because their visual presentation is easily understood. Exhibit 10.4 shows a sample of the available charts.

Gantt chart

Exhibit 10.4A is a sample Gantt chart, sometimes referred to as a *bar chart,* showing both the amount of time involved and the sequence in which activities can be performed. The chart is named after Henry L. Gantt, who won a presidential citation for his application of this type of chart to shipbuilding during World War I. In the example in Exhibit 10.4A, "long lead procurement" and "manufacturing schedules" are independent activities and can occur simultaneously. All other activities must be done in the sequence from top to bottom. Exhibit 10.4B graphs the amounts of money spent on labor, material, and overhead. Its value is its clarity in identifying sources and amounts of cost.

Exhibit 10.4C shows the percentage of the project's labor hours that comes from the various areas of manufacturing, finance, and so on. These labor hours are related to the proportion of the project's total labor cost. For example, manufacturing is responsible for 50 percent of the project's labor hours, but this 50 percent has been allocated just 40 percent of the total labor dollars charged.

The top half of Exhibit 10.4D shows the degree of completion of these projects. The dashed vertical line signifies today. Project 1, therefore, is already late because it still has work to be done. Project 2 is not being worked on temporarily, so there is a space before the projected work. Project 3 continues to be worked on without interruption. The bottom of Exhibit 10.4D compares actual total costs and projected costs. As we see, two cost overruns occurred, and the current cumulative costs are over projected cumulative costs.

Exhibit 10.4E is a milestone chart. The three milestones mark specific points in the project where checks can be made to see if the project is on time and where it should be. The best place to locate milestones is at the completion of a major activity. In this exhibit, the major activities completed were "purchase order release," "invoices received," and "material received."

Other standard reports can be used for a more detailed presentation comparing cost to progress (such as cost schedule status report—CSSR) or reports providing the basis for partial payment (such as the earned value report, which we discuss next).

Sample of Graphic Project Reports

exhibit 10.4

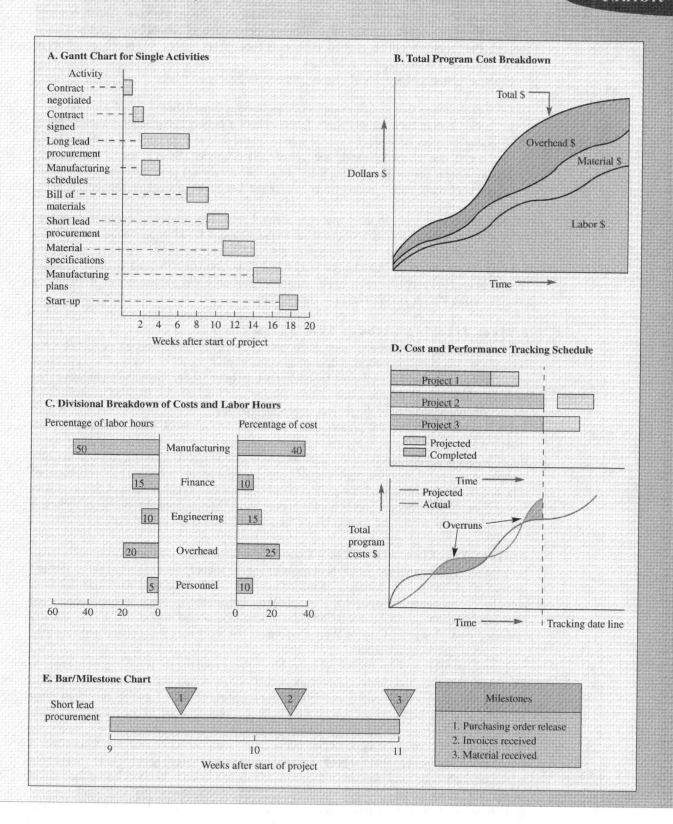

A. Gantt Chart for Single Activities

Activity
- Contract negotiated
- Contract signed
- Long lead procurement
- Manufacturing schedules
- Bill of materials
- Short lead procurement
- Material specifications
- Manufacturing plans
- Start-up

2 4 6 8 10 12 14 16 18 20

Weeks after start of project

B. Total Program Cost Breakdown

Dollars $

Total $
Overhead $
Material $
Labor $

Time

C. Divisional Breakdown of Costs and Labor Hours

Percentage of labor hours   Percentage of cost

	Percentage of labor hours		Percentage of cost
Manufacturing	50		40
Finance	15		10
Engineering	10		15
Overhead	20		25
Personnel	5		10

60 40 20 0   0 20 40

D. Cost and Performance Tracking Schedule

Project 1
Project 2
Project 3

Projected
Completed

Time

Projected
Actual

Total program costs $

Overruns

Time   Tracking date line

E. Bar/Milestone Chart

Short lead procurement

1   2   3

9   10   11

Weeks after start of project

Milestones
1. Purchasing order release
2. Invoices received
3. Material received

EARNED VALUE MANAGEMENT (EVM)

EVM is a technique for measuring project progress in an objective manner. EVM has the ability to combine measurements of scope, schedule, and cost in a project. When properly applied, EVM provides a method for evaluating the relative success of a project at a point in time. The measures can be applied to projects focused on either "revenue generation" or "cost" depending on the type of project.

Essential features of any EVM implementation include

1. a project plan that identifies the activities to be accomplished,
2. a valuation of each activity work. In the case of a project that generates revenue this is called the planned value (PV) of the activity. In the case where a project is evaluated based on cost, this is called the budgeted cost of work scheduled (BCWS) for the activity, and
3. predefined "earning or costing rules" (also called metrics) to quantify the accomplishment of work, called earned value (EV) or budgeted cost of work performed (BCWP).

The terminology used in the features is general since the valuations could be based on either a value measure (revenue or profit) or a cost measure. EVM implementations for large or complex projects include many more features, such as indicators and forecasts of cost performance (over budget or under budget) and schedule performance (behind schedule or ahead of schedule). However, the most basic requirement of an EVM system is that it quantifies progress using PV (or BCWS) and EV (or BCWP).

Project Tracking without EVM   It is helpful to see an example of project tracking that does not include earned value performance management. Consider a project that has been planned in detail, including a time-phased spend plan for all elements of work. This is a case where the project is evaluated based on cost. Exhibit 10.5A shows the cumulative cost budget for this project as a function of time (the orange line, labeled BCWS). It also shows the cumulative actual cost of the project (green line) through week 8. To those unfamiliar with EVM, it might appear that this project was over budget through week 4 and then under budget from week 6 through week 8. However, what is missing from this chart is any understanding of how much work has been accomplished during the project. If the project was actually completed at week 8, then the project would actually be well under budget and well ahead of schedule. If, on the other hand, the project is only 10 percent complete at week 8, the project is significantly over budget and behind schedule. A method is needed to measure technical performance objectively and quantitatively, and that is what EVM accomplishes.

Project Tracking with EVM   Consider the same project, except this time the project plan includes predefined methods of quantifying the accomplishment of work. At the end of each week, the project manager identifies every detailed element of work that has been completed, and sums the Budgeted Cost of Work Performed for each of these completed elements by estimating the percent complete of the activity and multiplying by the activity budgeted cost. Budgeted Cost of Work Performed (BCWP) may be accumulated monthly, weekly, or as progress is made.

Exhibit 10.5B shows the BCWP curve (in blue) along with the BCWS curve from chart A. The chart indicates that technical performance (i.e., progress) started more rapidly than planned, but slowed significantly and fell behind schedule at week 7 and 8. This chart illustrates the schedule performance aspect of EVM. It is complementary to critical path schedule management (described in the next section).

Exhibit 10.5C shows the same BCWP curve (blue) with the actual cost data from Chart A (in green). It can be seen that the project was actually under budget, relative to the amount of work accomplished, since the start of the project. This is a much better conclusion than might be derived from Chart A.

Exhibit 10.5D shows all three curves together—which is a typical EVM line chart. The best way to read these three-line charts is to identify the BCWS curve first, then compare it to BCWP (for schedule performance) and AC (for cost performance). It can be seen from this illustration that a true understanding of cost performance and schedule performance *relies first on measuring technical performance objectively*. This is the *foundational principle* of EVM.

Earned Value Management Charts

exhibit 10.5

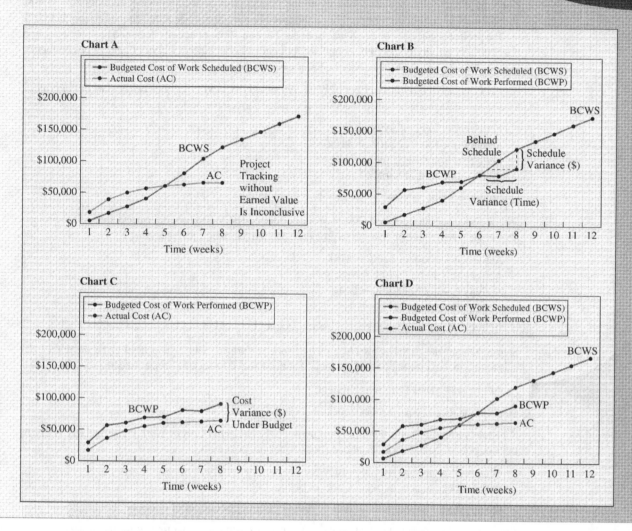

Chart A
- Budgeted Cost of Work Scheduled (BCWS)
- Actual Cost (AC)

BCWS

AC

Project Tracking without Earned Value Is Inconclusive

Time (weeks)

Chart B
- Budgeted Cost of Work Scheduled (BCWS)
- Budgeted Cost of Work Performed (BCWP)

BCWS

Behind Schedule

Schedule Variance ($)

BCWP

Schedule Variance (Time)

Time (weeks)

Chart C
- Budgeted Cost of Work Performed (BCWP)
- Actual Cost (AC)

BCWP

AC

Cost Variance ($) Under Budget

Time (weeks)

Chart D
- Budgeted Cost of Work Scheduled (BCWS)
- Budgeted Cost of Work Performed (BCWP)
- Actual Cost (AC)

BCWS

BCWP

AC

Time (weeks)

EXAMPLE 10.1: Earned Value Management

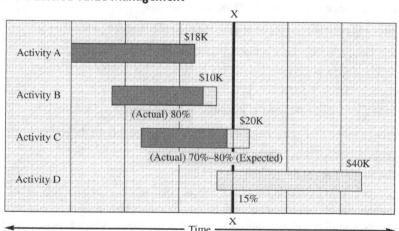

Step by Step

The figure above illustrates how to determine the Budgeted Cost of Work Scheduled by summing the dollar values (in $1,000s of the work scheduled for accomplishment at the end of period X. The Budgeted Cost of Work Performed is determined by summing the earned value for the work actually accomplished, shown in red shading.

SOLUTION

From the diagram the budgeted cost of all the project work is the following: Activity A − $18K, B − $10K, C − $20K, D − $40K. This is the cost of each activity when they are 100% completed.

The project is currently at day X and from the diagram 100% of activity A should be completed, and it is; 100% of activity B should be completed, but only 80% is; 80% of activity C should be completed, but only 70% is; and 15% of activity D, but it has not started.

Step 1: Calculate the Budgeted Cost of Work Scheduled (BCWS) given the current state of the project. This is the value or cost of the project that is expected, given the project is at time X:

Activity A – 100% of $18K = $18K
Activity B – 100% of $10K = $10K
Activity C – 80% of $20K = $16K
Activity D – 15% of $40K = $6K

BCWS = $18K + $10K + $16K + $6K = $50K

Step 2: Calculate the Budgeted Cost of Work Performed (BCWP) given the current state of the project. This is the actual value or cost of the project to date, given the project is at time X:

Activity A – 100% of $18K = $18K
Activity B – 80% of $10K = $8K
Activity C – 70% of $20K = $14K
Activity D – 0% of $40K = $0

BCWP = $18K + $8K + $14K + $0K = $40K

Step 3: Obtain the Actual Cost (AC) of the work performed. This would need to be obtained from accounting records for the project. Assume that the actual cost for this project to date is $45K.

AC = $45K (Data from Acct. System)

Step 4: Calculate key performance measures for the project:

Schedule Variance: This is the difference between the Budgeted Cost of Work Performed (BCWP) and the Budgeted Cost of Work Scheduled (BCWS) for the project:

Schedule Variance = BCWP − BCWS
Schedule Variance = $40K − $50K = 2$10K

Greater than 0 is generally good as it implies the project is ahead of schedule.

Schedule Performance Index: This is the ratio of the BCWP versus the BCWS for the project:

Schedule Performance Index = BCWP/BCWS
Schedule Performance Index = $40K/$50K = 0.8

Greater than 1 is generally good as it implies the project is ahead of schedule.

Cost Variance: This is the difference between BCWP and the Actual Cost (AC):

Cost Variance = BCWP − AC
Cost Variance = $40K − $45K = −$5K

Greater than zero is generally good as it implies under budget.

Cost Performance Index: This is the ratio of the BCWP versus the AC for the project to date:

Cost Performance Index = BCWP/AC
Cost Performance Index = $40K/$45K = 0.89

< 1 means the cost of completing the work is higher than planned, which is bad;
= 1 means the cost of completing the work is right on plan, which is good;
> 1 means the cost of completing the work is lower than planned, which is usually good.

That means the project is spending about $1.13 for every $1.00 of budgeted work accomplished. This is not very good as the project is over budget and tasks are not being completed on time or on budget. A Schedule Performance Index and a Cost Performance Index greater than one are desirable. ●

NETWORK-PLANNING MODELS

The two best-known network-planning models were developed in the 1950s. The Critical Path Method (CPM) was developed for scheduling maintenance shutdowns at chemical processing plants owned by Du Pont. Since maintenance projects are performed often in this industry, reasonably accurate time estimates for activities are available. CPM is based on the assumptions that project activity times can be estimated accurately and that they do not vary. The Program Evaluation and Review Technique (PERT) was developed for the U.S. Navy's Polaris missile project. This was a massive project involving over 3,000 contractors. Because most of the activities had never been done before, PERT was developed to handle uncertain time estimates. As years passed, features that distinguished CPM from PERT have diminished, so in our treatment here we just use the term CPM.

NEW ZEALAND'S TE APITI WIND FARM PROJECT CONSTRUCTED THE LARGEST WIND FARM IN THE SOUTHERN HEMISPHERE, WITHIN ONE YEAR FROM COMMISSION TO COMPLETION, ON-TIME AND WITHIN BUDGET. EMPLOYING EFFECTIVE PROJECT MANAGEMENT AND USING THE CORRECT TOOLS AND TECHNIQUES, THE MERIDIAN ENERGY COMPANY PROVIDED A VIABLE OPTION FOR RENEWABLE ENERGY IN NEW ZEALAND, AND ACTS AS BENCHMARK FOR LATER WIND FARM PROJECTS.

In a sense, the CPM techniques illustrated here owe their development to the widely used predecessor, the Gantt chart. Although the Gantt chart is able to relate activities to time in a usable fashion for small projects, the interrelationship of activities, when displayed in this form, becomes extremely difficult to visualize and to work with for projects that include more than 25 activities. Also, the Gantt chart provides no direct procedure for determining more than 25 activities, nor does the Gantt chart provide any direct procedure for determining the critical path, which is of great practical value to identify.

The critical path of activities in a project is the sequence of activities that form the longest chain in terms of their time to complete. If any one of the activities in the critical path is delayed, then the entire project is delayed. It is possible and it often happens that there are multiple paths of the same length through the network so there are multiple critical paths. Determining scheduling information about each activity in the project is the major goal of CPM techniques. The techniques calculate when an activity must start and end, together with whether the activity is part of the critical path.

Critical path

CRITICAL PATH METHOD (CPM)

Here is a procedure for scheduling a project. In this case, a single time estimate is used because we are assuming that the activity times are known. A very simple project will be scheduled to demonstrate the basic approach.

Consider that you have a group assignment that requires a decision on whether you should invest in a company. Your instructor has suggested that you perform the analysis in the following four steps:

A Select a company.

B Obtain the company's annual report and perform a ratio analysis.

C Collect technical stock price data and construct charts.

D Individually review the data and make a team decision on whether to buy the stock.

Your group of four people decides that the project can be divided into four activities as suggested by the instructor. You decide that all the team members should be involved in selecting the company and that it should take one week to complete this activity. You will meet at the end of the week to decide what company the group will consider. During this meeting you will divide your group: two people will be responsible for the annual report and ratio analysis, and the other two will collect the technical data and construct the charts. Your group expects to take two weeks to get the annual report and perform the ratio analysis, and a week to collect the stock price data and generate the charts. You agree that the two groups can work independently. Finally, you agree to meet as a team to make the purchase decision. Before you meet, you want to allow one week for each team member to review all the data.

This is a simple project, but it will serve to demonstrate the approach. The following are the appropriate steps.

1. **Identify each activity to be done in the project and estimate how long it will take to complete each activity.**   This is simple, given the information from your instructor. We identify the activities as follows: A(1), B(2), C(1), D(1). The number is the expected duration of the activity.

2. **Determine the required sequence of activities and construct a network reflecting the precedence relationships.**   An easy way to do this is to first identify the **immediate predecessors** associated with an activity. The immediate predecessors are the activities that need to be completed immediately before an activity. Activity A needs to be completed before activities B and C can start. B and C need to be completed before D can start. The following table reflects what we know so far:

ACTIVITY	DESIGNATION	IMMEDIATE PREDECESSORS	TIME (WEEKS)
Select company	A	None	1
Obtain annual report and perform ratio analysis	B	A	2
Collect stock price data and perform technical analysis	C	A	1
Review data and make a decision	D	B and C	1

Here is a diagram that depicts these precedence relationships:

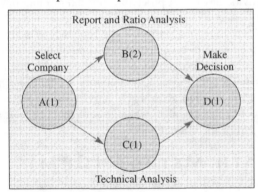

3. **Determine the critical path.**   Consider each sequence of activities that runs from the beginning to the end of the project. For our simple project there are two paths: A–B–D and A–C–D. The critical path is the path where the sum of the activity times is the longest. A–B–D has a duration of four weeks and A–C–D, a duration of three weeks. The critical path, therefore, is A–B–D. If any activity along the critical path is delayed, then the entire project will be delayed.

4. **Determine the early start/finish and late start/finish schedule.**   To schedule the project, find when each activity needs to start and when it needs to finish. For some activities in a project there may be some leeway in when an activity can start and finish. This is called the slack time in an activity. For each activity in the project, we calculate

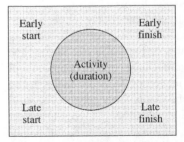

four points in time: the early start, early finish, late start, and late finish times. The early start and early finish are the earliest times that the activity can start and be finished. Similarly, the late start and late finish are the latest times the activities can start and finish. The difference between the late start time and early start time is the slack time. To help keep all of this straight, we place these numbers in special places around the nodes that represent each activity in our network diagram, as shown here.

Immediate predecessors

Slack time

To calculate numbers, start from the beginning of the network and work to the end, calculating the early start and early finish numbers. Start counting with the current period, designated as period 0. Activity A has an early start of 0 and an early finish of 1. Activity B's early start is A's early finish, or 1. Similarly, C's early start is 1. The early finish for B is 3, and the early finish for C is 2. Now consider activity D. D cannot start until both B and C are done. Because B cannot be done until 3, D cannot start until that time. The early start for D, therefore, is 3, and the early finish is 4. Our diagram now looks like this.

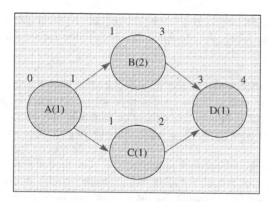

To calculate the late finish and late start times, start from the end of the network and work toward the front. Consider activity D. The earliest that it can be done is at time 4; and if we do not want to delay the completion of the project, the late finish needs to be set to 4. With a duration of 1, the latest that D can start is 3. Now consider activity C. C must be done by time 3 so that D can start, so C's late finish time is 3 and its late start time is 2. Notice the difference between the early and late start and finish times: This activity has one week of slack time. Activity B must be done by time 3 so that D can start, so its late finish time is 3 and late start time is 1. There is no slack in B. Finally, activity A must be done so that B and C can start. Because B must start earlier than C, and A must get done in time for B to start, the late finish time for A is 1. Finally, the late start time for A is 0. Notice there is no slack in activities A, B, and D. The final network looks like this. (Hopefully the stock your investment team has chosen is a winner!)

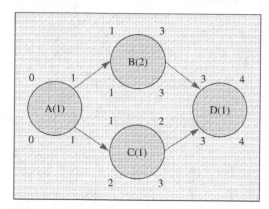

EXAMPLE 10.2: Critical Path Method

Many firms that have tried to enter the notebook computer market have failed. Suppose your firm believes that there is a big demand in this market because existing products have not been designed correctly. They are too heavy, too large, or too small to have standard-size keyboards. Your intended computer will be small enough to carry inside a jacket pocket if need be. The ideal size will be no larger than 5 inches × 9½ inches × 1 inch with a folding keyboard. It should weigh no more than 15 ounces and have an LCD display, a micro disk drive, and a wireless connection. This should appeal to traveling businesspeople, but it could have a much wider market, including students. It should be priced in the $175–$200 range.

Excel: Project Management

Step by Step

The project, then, is to design, develop, and produce a prototype of this small computer. In the rapidly changing computer industry, it is crucial to hit the market with a product of this sort in less than a year. Therefore, the project team has been allowed approximately eight months (35 weeks) to produce the prototype.

SOLUTION

The first charge of the project team is to develop a project network chart and determine if the prototype computer can be completed within the 35-week target. Let's follow the steps in the development of the network.

1. **Activity identification.** The project team decides that the following activities are the major components of the project: design of the computer, prototype construction, prototype testing, methods specification (summarized in a report), evaluation studies of automatic assembly equipment, an assembly equipment study report, and a final report summarizing all aspects of the design, equipment, and methods.

2. **Activity sequencing and network construction.** On the basis of discussion with staff, the project manager develops the precedence table and sequence network shown in Exhibit 10.6. When constructing a network, take care to ensure that the activities are in the proper order and that the logic of their relationships is maintained. For example, it would be illogical to have a situation where Event A precedes Event B, B precedes C, and C precedes A.

3. **Determine the critical path.** The critical path is the longest sequence of connected activities through the network and is defined as the path with zero slack time. This network has four different paths: A–C–F–G, A–C–E–G, A–B–D–F–G, and A–B–D–E–G. The lengths of these paths are 38, 35, 38, and 35 weeks. Note that this project has two different critical paths; this might indicate that this would be a fairly difficult project to manage. Calculating the early start and late start schedules gives additional insight into how difficult this project might be to complete on time. ●

exhibit 10.6   CPM Network for Computer Design Project

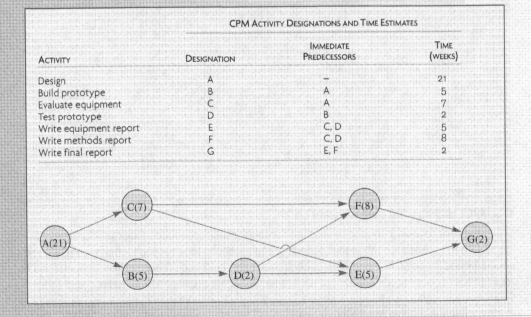

CPM ACTIVITY DESIGNATIONS AND TIME ESTIMATES			
ACTIVITY	DESIGNATION	IMMEDIATE PREDECESSORS	TIME (WEEKS)
Design	A	–	21
Build prototype	B	A	5
Evaluate equipment	C	A	7
Test prototype	D	B	2
Write equipment report	E	C, D	5
Write methods report	F	C, D	8
Write final report	G	E, F	2

CPM Network for Computer Design Project

exhibit 10.7

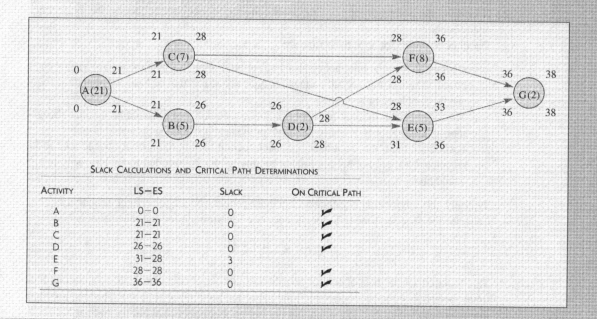

SLACK CALCULATIONS AND CRITICAL PATH DETERMINATIONS

ACTIVITY	LS−ES	SLACK	ON CRITICAL PATH
A	0−0	0	✔
B	21−21	0	✔
C	21−21	0	✔
D	26−26	0	✔
E	31−28	3	
F	28−28	0	✔
G	36−36	0	✔

Early Start and Late Start Schedules   An *early start schedule* is one that lists all of the activities by their early start times. For activities not on the critical path, there is slack time between the completion of each activity and the start of the next activity. The early start schedule completes the project and all its activities as soon as possible.

Early start schedule

A *late start schedule* lists the activities to start as late as possible without delaying the completion date of the project. One motivation for using a late start schedule is that savings are realized by postponing purchases of materials, the use of labor, and other costs until necessary. These calculations are shown in Exhibit 10.7. From this we see that the only activity that has slack is activity E. This certainly would be a fairly difficult project to complete on time.

Late start schedule

CPM WITH THREE ACTIVITY TIME ESTIMATES

If a single estimate of the time required to complete an activity is not reliable, the best procedure is to use three time estimates. These three times not only allow us to estimate the activity time but also let us obtain a probability estimate for completion time for the entire network. Briefly, the procedure is as follows: The estimated activity time is calculated using a weighted average of a minimum, maximum, and most likely time estimate. The expected completion time of the network is computed using the procedure described above. Using estimates of variability for the activities on the critical path, the probability of completing the project by particular times can be estimated. (Note that the probability calculations are a distinguishing feature of the classic PERT approach.)

EXAMPLE 10.3: Three Time Estimates

We use the same information as in Example 10.2 with the exception that activities have three time estimates.

Step by Step

SOLUTION

1. Identify each activity to be done in the project.
2. Determine the sequence of activities and construct a network reflecting the precedence relationships.
3. The three estimates for an activity time are

   a = Optimistic time: the minimum reasonable period of time in which the activity can be completed. (There is only a small probability, typically assumed to be 1 percent, that the activity can be completed in less time.)

   m = Most likely time: the best guess of the time required. Since m would be the time thought most likely to appear, it is also the mode of the beta distribution discussed in step 4.

   b = Pessimistic time: the maximum reasonable period of time the activity would take to be completed. (There is only a small probability, typically assumed to be 1 percent, that it would take longer.)

   Typically, this information is gathered from those people who are to perform the activity.

4. Calculate the expected time (ET) for each activity. The formula for this calculation is

$$\text{ET} = \frac{a + 4m + b}{6} \qquad [10.1]$$

   This is based on the beta statistical distribution and weights the most likely time (m) four times more than either the optimistic time (a) or the pessimistic time (b). The beta distribution is extremely flexible. It can take on the variety of forms that typically arise; it has finite end points (which limit the possible activity times to the area between a and b); and, in the simplified version, it permits straightforward computation of the activity mean and standard deviation.

5. Determine the critical path. Using the expected times, a critical path is calculated in the same way as the single time case.

6. Calculate the variances (σ^2) of the activity times. Specifically, this is the variance, σ^2, associated with each ET and is computed as follows:

$$\sigma^2 = \left(\frac{b - a}{6}\right)^2 \qquad [10.2]$$

   As you can see, the variance is the square of one-sixth the difference between the two extreme time estimates. Of course, the greater this difference, the larger the variance.

7. Determine the probability of completing the project on a given date, based on the application of the standard normal distribution. A valuable feature of using three time estimates is that it enables the analyst to assess the effect of uncertainty on project completion time. (If you are not familiar with this type of analysis, see the box titled "Probability Analysis.") The mechanics of deriving this probability are as follows:

   a. Sum the variance values associated with each activity on the critical path.

   b. Substitute this figure, along with the project due date and the project expected completion time, into the Z transformation formula. This formula is

$$Z = \frac{D - T_E}{\sqrt{\Sigma \sigma_{cp}^2}} \qquad [10.3]$$

   where

$$D = \text{Desired completion date for the project}$$

$$T_E = \text{Expected completion time for the project}$$

$$\Sigma \sigma_{cp}^2 = \text{Sum of the variances along the critical path}$$

   c. Calculate the value of Z, which is the number of standard deviations (of a standard normal distribution) that the project due date is from the expected completion time.

   d. Using the value of Z, find the probability of meeting the project due date (using a table of normal probabilities such as Appendix G). The *expected completion time* is the starting time plus the sum of the activity times on the critical path.

Activity Expected Times and Variances

exhibit 10.8

ACTIVITY	ACTIVITY DESIGNATION	TIME ESTIMATES a	m	b	EXPECTED TIMES (ET) $\dfrac{a + 4m + b}{6}$	ACTIVITY VARIANCES (σ^2) $\left(\dfrac{b-a}{6}\right)^2$
Design	A	10	22	28	21	9
Build prototype	B	4	4	10	5	1
Evaluate equipment	C	4	6	14	7	$2\frac{7}{9}$
Test prototype	D	1	2	3	2	$\frac{1}{9}$
Write report	E	1	5	9	5	$1\frac{7}{9}$
Write methods report	F	7	8	9	8	$\frac{1}{9}$
Write final report	G	2	2	2	2	0

Excel: Project Management

Following the steps just outlined, we developed Exhibit 10.8 showing expected times and variances. The project network was created the same as we did previously. The only difference is that the activity times are weighted averages. We determine the critical path as before, using these values as if they were single numbers. The difference between the single time estimate and the three times (optimistic, most likely, and pessimistic) is in computing probabilities of completion. Exhibit 10.9 shows the network and critical path.

PROBABILITY ANALYSIS

The three-time-estimate approach introduces the ability to consider the probability that a project will be completed within a particular amount of time. The assumption needed to make this probability estimate is that the activity duration times are independent random variables. If this is true, the central limit theorem can be used to find the mean and the variance of the sequence of activities that form the critical path. The central limit theorem says that the sum of a group of independent, identically distributed random variables approaches a normal distribution as the number of random variables increases. In the case of project management problems, the random variables are the actual times for the activities in the project. (Recall that the time for each activity is assumed to be independent of other activities, and to follow a beta statistical distribution.) For this the expected time to complete the critical path activities is the sum of the activity times.

Likewise, because of the assumption of activity time independence, the sum of the variances of the activities along the critical path is the variance of the expected time to complete the path. Recall that the standard deviation is equal to the square root of the variance.

To determine the actual probability of completing the critical path activities within a certain amount of time, we need to find where on our probability distribution the time falls. Appendix G shows the areas of the cumulative standard normal distribution for different values of Z. Z measures the number of standard deviations either to the right or to the left of zero in the distribution. The values correspond to the cumulative probability associated with each value of Z. For example, the first value in the table, −4.00, has a $G(z)$ equal to .00003. This means that the probability associated with a Z value of −4.0 is only .003 percent. Similarly, a Z value of 1.50 has a $G(z)$ equal to .93319 or 93.319 percent. The Z values are calculated using equation (10.3) given in Step 7b of the "Three Time Estimates" example solution. These cumulative probabilities also can be obtained by using the NORMSDIST (Z) function built into Microsoft Excel.

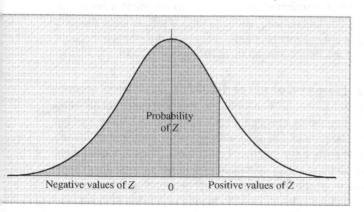

exhibit 10.9   Computer Design Project with Three Time Estimates

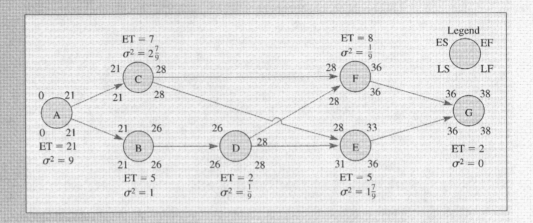

Because there are two critical paths in the network, we must decide which variances to use in arriving at the probability of meeting the project due date. A conservative approach dictates using the path with the largest total variance to focus management's attention on the activities most likely to exhibit broad variations. On this basis, the variances associated with activities A, C, F, and G would be used to find the probability of completion. Thus $\Sigma\sigma_{cp}^2 = 9 + 2\frac{7}{9} + \frac{1}{9} + 0 = 11.89$. Suppose management asks for the probability of completing the project in 35 weeks. D, then, is 35. The expected completion time was found to be 38. Substituting into the Z equation and solving, we obtain

$$Z = \frac{D - T_E}{\sqrt{\Sigma\,\sigma_{cp}^2}} = \frac{35 - 38}{\sqrt{11.89}} = -0.87$$

Looking at Appendix G, we see that a Z value of -0.87 yields a probability of 0.1922, which means that the project manager has only about a 19 percent chance of completing the project in 35 weeks. Note that this probability is really the probability of completing the critical path A–C–F–G. Because there is another critical path and other paths that might become critical, the probability of completing the project in 35 weeks is actually less than 0.19. ●

TIME–COST MODELS AND PROJECT CRASHING

In practice, project managers are as much concerned with the cost to complete a project as with the time to complete the project. For this reason, time–cost models have been devised. These models—extensions of the basic critical path method—attempt to develop a minimum-cost schedule for an entire project and to control expenditures during the project.

Time–cost models

Minimum-Cost Scheduling (Time–Cost Trade-Off)

The basic assumption in minimum-cost scheduling, also known as "Crashing," is that there is a relationship between activity completion time and the cost of a project. Crashing refers to the compression or shortening of the time to complete the project. On one hand, it costs money to expedite an activity; on the other, it costs money to sustain (or lengthen) the project. The costs associated with expediting activities are termed *activity direct costs* and add to the project direct cost. Some may be worker-related, such as overtime work, hiring more workers, and transferring workers from other jobs; others are resource-related, such as buying or leasing additional or more efficient equipment and drawing on additional support facilities.

Example of Time–Cost Trade-Off Procedure

exhibit 10.10

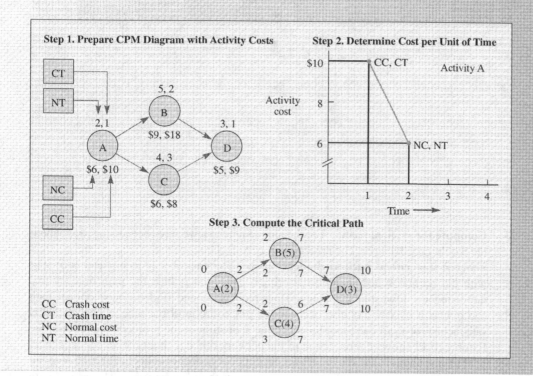

Excel: Project Management

The costs associated with sustaining the project are termed *project indirect costs:* overhead, facilities, and resource opportunity costs, and, under certain contractual situations, penalty costs or lost incentive payments. Because *activity direct costs and project indirect costs* are opposing costs dependent on time, the scheduling problem is essentially one of finding the project duration that minimizes their sum, or in other words, finding the optimum point in a time–cost trade-off.

The procedure for project crashing consists of the following five steps. It is explained by using the simple four-activity network shown in Exhibit 10.10. Assume that the indirect costs remain constant for eight days and then increase at the rate of $5 per day.

1. **Prepare a CPM-type network diagram.** For each activity this diagram should list
   a. Normal cost (NC): the lowest expected activity costs. (These are the lesser of the cost figures shown under each node in Exhibit 10.10.)
   b. Normal time (NT): the time associated with each normal cost.
   c. Crash time (CT): the shortest possible activity time.
   d. Crash cost (CC): the cost associated with each crash time.
2. **Determine the cost per unit of time (assume days) to expedite each activity.** The relationship between activity time and cost may be shown graphically by plotting CC and CT coordinates and connecting them to the NC and NT coordinates by a concave, convex, or straight line—or some other form, depending on the actual cost structure of activity performance, as in Exhibit 10.10. For activity A, we assume a linear relationship between time and cost. This assumption is common in practice and helps us derive the cost per day to expedite because this value may be found directly by taking the slope of the line using the formula Slope = (CC − NC) ÷ (NT − CT). (When the assumption of linearity cannot be made, the cost of expediting must be determined graphically for each day the activity may be shortened.)

   The calculations needed to obtain the cost of expediting the remaining activities are shown in Exhibit 10.11.

exhibit 10.11   Calculation of Cost per Day to Expedite Each Activity

ACTIVITY	CC − NC	NT − CT	$\dfrac{CC - NC}{NT - CT}$	COST PER DAY TO EXPEDITE	NUMBER OF DAYS ACTIVITY MAY BE SHORTENED
A	$10 − $6	2 − 1	$\dfrac{\$10 - \$6}{2 - 1}$	$4	1
B	$18 − $9	5 − 2	$\dfrac{\$18 - \$9}{5 - 2}$	$3	3
C	$8 − $6	4 − 3	$\dfrac{\$8 - \$6}{4 - 3}$	$2	1
D	$9 − $5	3 − 1	$\dfrac{\$9 - \$5}{3 - 1}$	$2	2

3. **Compute the critical path.** For the simple network we have been using, this schedule would take 10 days. The critical path is A–B–D.

4. **Shorten the critical path at the least cost.** The easiest way to proceed is to start with the normal schedule, find the critical path, and reduce the path time by one day using the lowest-cost activity. Then recompute and find the new critical path and reduce it by one day also. Repeat this procedure until the time of completion is satisfactory, or until there can be no further reduction in the project completion time. Exhibit 10.12 shows the reduction of the network one day at a time.

Working though Exhibit 10.12 might initially seem difficult. In the first line, all activities are at their normal time and costs are at their lowest value. The critical path is A–B–D, cost for completing the project is $26, and the project completion time is 10 days.

The goal in line two is to reduce the project completion time by one day. We know it is necessary to reduce the time for one or more of the activities on the critical path. In the second column we note that activity A can be reduced one day (from two to one day), activity B can be reduced three days (from five to two days), and activity D can be reduced two days (from three to one day). The next column tracks the cost to

exhibit 10.12   Reducing the Project Completion Time One Day at a Time

CURRENT CRITICAL PATH(S)	REMAINING NUMBER OF DAYS ACTIVITY MAY BE SHORTENED	COST PER DAY TO EXPEDITE EACH ACTIVITY	LEAST-COST ACTIVITY TO EXPEDITE	TOTAL COST OF ALL ACTIVITIES IN NETWORK	PROJECT COMPLETION TIME
ABD	All activity times and costs are normal.			$26	10
ABD	A−1, B−3, D−2	A−4, B−3, D−2	D	28	9
ABD	A−1, B−3, D−1	A−4, B−3, D−2	D	30	8
ABD	A−1, B−3	A−4, B−3	B	33	7
ABD ACD	A−1, B−2, C−1	A−4, B−3, C−2	A*	37	6
ABD ACD	B−2, C−1	B−3, C−2	B&C†	42	5
ABD ACD	B−1	B−3	B‡	45	5

*To reduce the critical path by one day, reduce either A alone or B and C together at the same time (either B or C by itself just modifies the critical path without shortening it).

†B&C must be crashed together to reduce the path by one day.

‡Crashing activity B does not reduce the length of the project, so this additional cost would not be incurred.

reduce each of the activities by a single day. For example, for activity A, it normally costs $6 to complete in two days. It could be completed in one day at a cost of $10, a $4 increase. So we indicate the cost to expedite activity A by one day is $4. For activity B, it normally costs $9 to complete in five days. It could be completed in two days at a cost of $18. Our cost to reduce B by three days is $9, or $3 per day. For C, it normally costs $5 to complete in three days. It could be completed in one day at a cost of $9; a two-day reduction would cost $4 ($2 per day). The least expensive alternative for a one-day reduction in time is to expedite activity D at a cost of $2. Total cost for the network goes up to $28 and the project completion time is reduced to nine days.

Our next iteration starts in line three, where the goal is to reduce the project completion time to eight days. The nine-day critical path is A–B–D. We could shorten activity A by one day, B by three days, and D by one day (note D has already been reduced from three to two days). Cost to reduce each activity by one day is the same as in line two. Again, the least expensive activity to reduce is D. Reducing activity D from two to one day results in the total cost for all activities in the network going up to $30 and the project completion time coming down to eight days.

Line four is similar to line three, but now only A and B are on the critical path and can be reduced. B is reduced, which takes our cost up $3 to $33 and reduces the project completion time to seven days.

In line five (actually our fifth iteration in solving the problem), activities A, B, C, and D are all critical. D cannot be reduced, so our only options are activities A, B, and C. Note that B and C are in parallel, so it does not help to reduce B without reducing C. Our options are to reduce A alone at a cost of $4 or B and C together at a cost of $5 ($3 for B and $2 for C), so we reduce A in this iteration.

In line six, we take the B and C option that was considered in line five. Finally, in line seven, our only option is to reduce activity B. Since B and C are in parallel and we cannot reduce C, there is no value in reducing B alone. We can reduce the project completion time no further.

5. **Plot project direct, indirect, and total-cost curves and find the minimum-cost schedule.** Exhibit 10.13 shows the indirect cost plotted as a constant $10 per day for up to eight days and increasing $5 per day thereafter. The direct costs are plotted from Exhibit 10.12, and the total project cost is shown as the total of the two costs.

Summing the values for direct and indirect costs for each day yields the project total cost curve. As you can see, this curve is at its minimum with an eight-day schedule, which costs $40 ($30 direct + $10 indirect).

Plot of Costs and Minimum-Cost Schedule

exhibit 10.13

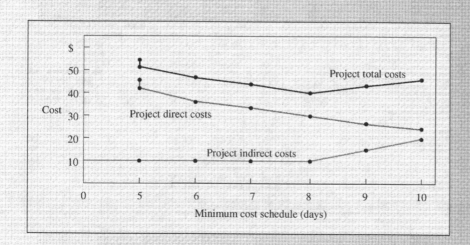

MANAGING RESOURCES

In addition to scheduling each task, we must assign resources. Modern software quickly highlights overallocations—situations in which allocations exceed resources.

To resolve overallocations manually, you can either add resources or reschedule. Moving a task within its slack can free up resources.

Mid- to high-level project management information systems (PMIS) software can resolve overallocations through a "leveling" feature. Several rules of thumb can be used. You can specify that low-priority tasks should be delayed until higher-priority ones are complete, or that the project should end before or after the original deadline.

PROJECT MANAGEMENT INFORMATION SYSTEMS

Interest in the techniques and concepts of project management has exploded in the past 10 years. This has resulted in a parallel increase in project management software offerings. Now there are over 100 companies offering project management software. For the most up-to-date information about software available, check out the Web site of the Project Management Institute (www.pmi.org). Two of the leading companies are Microsoft, with Microsoft Project, and Primavera, with Primavera Project Planner. The following is a brief review of these two programs:

The Microsoft Project program comes with an excellent online tutorial, which is one reason for its overwhelming popularity with project managers tracking midsized projects. This package is compatible with the Microsoft Office Suite, which opens all the communications and Internet integration capability that Microsoft offers. The program includes features for scheduling, allocating, and leveling resources, as well as controlling costs and producing presentation-quality graphics and reports.

Finally, for managing very large projects or programs having several projects, Primavera Project Planner is often the choice. Primavera was the first major vendor of this type of software and has possibly the most sophisticated capability.

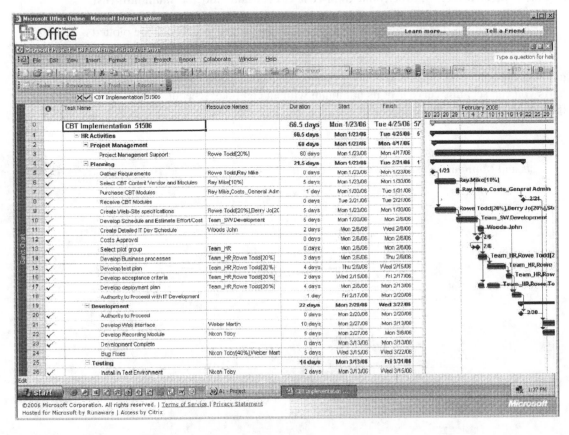

TRACKING PROGRESS

The real action starts after the project gets under way. Actual progress will differ from your original, or baseline, planned progress. Software can hold several different baseline plans, so you can compare monthly snapshots.

A *tracking Gantt chart* superimposes the current schedule onto a baseline plan so deviations are easily noticed. If you prefer, a spreadsheet view of the same information could be output. Deviations between planned start/finish and newly scheduled start/finish also appear, and a "slipping filter" can be applied to highlight or output only those tasks that are scheduled to finish at a later date than the planned baseline.

Management by exception also can be applied to find deviations between budgeted costs and actual costs. (See the box titled "Project Management Information Systems.")

SUMMARY

This chapter provides a description of the basics of managing projects. The chapter first describes how the people involved with a project are organized from a management viewpoint. The scope of the project will help define the organization. This organization spans the use of a dedicated team to a largely undedicated matrix structure. Next, the chapter considers how project activities are organized into subprojects by using the work breakdown structure. Following this, the technical details of calculating the shortest time it should take to complete a project are covered. Finally, the chapter considers how projects can be shortened through the use of "crashing" concepts.

KEY TERMS

Project A series of related jobs usually directed toward some major output and requiring a significant period of time to perform.

Project management Planning, directing, and controlling resources (people, equipment, material) to meet the technical, cost, and time constraints of a project.

Pure project A structure for organizing a project where a self-contained team works full time on the project.

Functional project A structure where team members are assigned from the functional units of the organization. The team members remain a part of their functional units and typically are not dedicated to the project.

Matrix project A structure that blends the functional and pure project structures. Each project uses people from different functional areas. A dedicated project manager decides what tasks need to be performed and when, but the functional managers control which people to use.

Project milestone A specific event in a project.

Work breakdown structure The hierarchy of project tasks, subtasks, and work packages.

Activities Pieces of work within a project that consume time. The completion of all the activities of a project marks the end of the project.

Gantt chart Shows in a graphic manner the amount of time involved and the sequence in which activities can be performed. Often referred to as a *bar chart*.

Earned value management Technique that combines measures of scope, schedule, and cost for evaluating project progress.

Critical path The sequence of activities in a project that forms the longest chain in terms of their time to complete. This path contains zero slack time. It is possible for there to be multiple critical paths in a project. Techniques used to find the critical path are called CPM or Critical Path Method techniques.

Immediate predecessor Activity that needs to be completed immediately before another activity.

Slack time The time that an activity can be delayed; the difference between the late and early start times of an activity.

Early start schedule A project schedule that lists all activities by their early start times.

Late start schedule A project schedule that lists all activities by their late start times. This schedule may create savings by postponing purchases of material and other costs associated with the project.

Time–cost models Extension of the critical path models that considers the trade-off between the time required to complete an activity and cost. This is often referred to as "crashing" the project.

FORMULA REVIEW

Expected Time

$$ET = \frac{a + 4m + b}{6} \qquad [10.1]$$

Variance (σ^2) of the activity times

$$\sigma^2 = \left(\frac{b - a}{6}\right)^2 \qquad [10.2]$$

Z transformation formula

$$Z = \frac{D - T_E}{\sqrt{\Sigma\sigma^2_{cp}}} \qquad [10.3]$$

SOLVED PROBLEMS

SOLVED PROBLEM 1

You have been asked to calculate the Cost Performance Index for a project using Earned Value Management techniques. It is currently day 20 of the project and the following summarizes the current status of the project:

Activity	Expected Cost	Activity Duration	Expected Start Date	Expected Completion Date	Expected % Complete	Actual % Complete	Actual Cost to Date
Startup	$100,000	10 days	0	10	100%	100%	$105,000
Construction	$325,000	14 days	8	22	12/14 = 85.7%	90%	$280,000
Finishing	$50,000	12 days	18	30	2/12 = 16.7%	25%	$2,500

Calculate the Schedule Variance, Schedule Performance Index, and the Cost Performance Index for the project.

Solution

Step 1: Calculate budgeted cost of the work scheduled to date:

Startup is 100% complete and we are beyond the expected completion date, so budgeted cost is $100,000 for this activity.

Would expect Construction to be 85.7% complete and cost $278,200 to date.
Would expect Finishing to be 16.7% complete at a cost of $8,333 to date.

Budgeted cost of work scheduled = $100,000 + 278,200 + 8,333 = $386,533

Step 2: Calculate the budgeted cost of the work performed to date:

Startup is 100% complete, so budgeted cost is $100,000.
Construction is actually only 90% complete, so budget cost for this much of the activity is (325,000 $\times$ .9) = $292,500.

Finishing is now 25% complete, so budgeted cost is (50,000 × .25) = $12,500.

Budgeted cost of work performed = 100,000 + 292,500 + 12,500 = $405,000

Step 3: Actual cost of the project to date is 105,000 + 280,000 + 2,500 = $387,500.

Step 4: Calculate performance measures:

Schedule variance = $405,000 − $386,533 = $18,467
Schedule Performance Index = $405,000/$386,533 = 1.047
Cost Performance Index = $405,000/$387,500 = 1.045

The project looks good since it is both ahead of schedule and ahead of budgeted cost.

SOLVED PROBLEM 2

A project has been defined to contain the following list of activities, along with their required times for completion:

ACTIVITY	TIME (DAYS)	IMMEDIATE PREDECESSORS
A	1	—
B	4	A
C	3	A
D	7	A
E	6	B
F	2	C, D
G	7	E, F
H	9	D
I	4	G, H

**Excel:
PM_Solved
Problems**

a. Draw the critical path diagram.
b. Show the early start, early finish, late start, and late finish times.
c. Show the critical path.
d. What would happen if activity F was revised to take four days instead of two?

Solution

The answers to *a*, *b*, and *c* are shown in the following diagram.

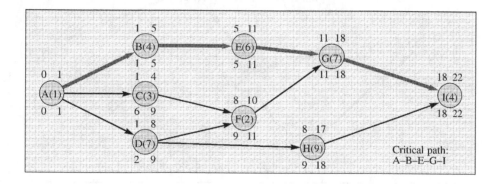

d. New critical path: A–D–F–G–I. Time of completion is 23 days.

SOLVED PROBLEM 3

A project has been defined to contain the following activities, along with their time estimates for completion:

**Excel:
PM_Solved
Problems**

ACTIVITY	TIME ESTIMATES (WK)			IMMEDIATE PREDECESSOR
	a	m	b	
A	1	4	7	—
B	2	6	7	A
C	3	4	6	A, D
D	6	12	14	A
E	3	6	12	D
F	6	8	16	B, C
G	1	5	6	E, F

a. Calculate the expected time and the variance for each activity.
b. Draw the critical path diagram.
c. Show the early start, early finish times and late start, late finish times.
d. Show the critical path.
e. What is the probability that the project can be completed in 34 weeks?

Solution

a.

ACTIVITY	EXPECTED TIME $\dfrac{a + 4m + b}{6}$	ACTIVITY VARIANCE $\left(\dfrac{b - a}{6}\right)^2$
A	4.00	1
B	5.50	$\frac{25}{36}$
C	4.17	$\frac{1}{4}$
D	11.33	$1\frac{7}{9}$
E	6.50	$2\frac{1}{4}$
F	9.00	$2\frac{7}{9}$
G	4.50	$\frac{25}{36}$

b.

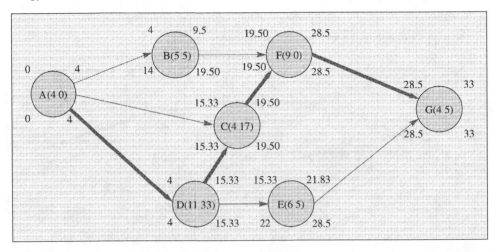

c. Shown on diagram.
d. Shown on diagram.

e. $Z = \dfrac{D - T_E}{\sqrt{\Sigma\sigma^2_{cp}}} = -\dfrac{34 - 33}{\sqrt{1 + 1\frac{7}{9} + \frac{1}{4} + 2\frac{7}{9} + \frac{25}{36}}} = \dfrac{1}{2.5495} = .3922$

Look up that value in Appendix G and we see that there is about a 65 percent chance of completing the project by that date.

SOLVED PROBLEM 4

Here are the precedence requirements, normal and crash activity times, and normal and crash costs for a construction project:

		REQUIRED TIME (WEEKS)		COST	
ACTIVITY	PRECEDING ACTIVITIES	NORMAL	CRASH	NORMAL	CRASH
A	—	4	2	$10,000	$11,000
B	A	3	2	6,000	9,000
C	A	2	1	4,000	6,000
D	B	5	3	14,000	18,000
E	B, C	1	1	9,000	9,000
F	C	3	2	7,000	8,000
G	E, F	4	2	13,000	25,000
H	D, E	4	1	11,000	18,000
I	H, G	6	5	20,000	29,000

a. What are the critical path and the estimated completion time?

b. To shorten the project by three weeks, which tasks would be shortened and what would the final total project cost be?

Solution

The construction project network is shown below:

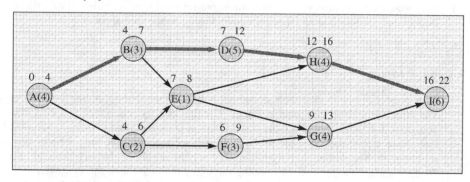

a. Critical path A–B–D–H–I.
  Normal completion time is 22 weeks.

b.

ACTIVITY	CRASH COST	NORMAL COST	NORMAL TIME	CRASH TIME	COST PER WEEK	WEEKS
A	$11,000	$10,000	4	2	$ 500	2
B	9,000	6,000	3	2	3,000	1
C	6,000	4,000	2	1	2,000	1
D	18,000	14,000	5	3	2,000	2
E	9,000	9,000	1	1		0
F	8,000	7,000	3	2	1,000	1
G	25,000	13,000	4	2	6,000	2
H	18,000	11,000	4	1	2,333	3
I	29,000	20,000	6	5	9,000	1

(1) 1st week: CP = A–B–D–H–I. Cheapest is A at $500. Critical path stays the same.

(2) 2nd week: A is still the cheapest at $500. Critical path stays the same.

(3) 3rd week: Because A is no longer available, the choices are B (at $3,000), D (at $2,000), H (at $2,333), or I (at $9,000). Therefore, choose D at $2,000.

Total project cost shortened three weeks is

A	$ 11,000
B	6,000
C	4,000
D	16,000
E	9,000
F	7,000
G	13,000
H	11,000
I	20,000
	$ 97,000

REVIEW AND DISCUSSION QUESTIONS

1   What was the most complex project that you have been involved in? Give examples of the following as they pertain to the project: the work breakdown structure, tasks, subtasks, and work package. Were you on the critical path? Did it have a good project manager?

2   What are some reasons project scheduling is not done well?

3   Discuss the graphic presentations in Exhibit 10.4. Are there any other graphic outputs you would like to see if you were project manager?

4   Which characteristics must a project have for critical path scheduling to be applicable? What types of projects have been subjected to critical path analysis?

5   What are the underlying assumptions of minimum-cost scheduling? Are they equally realistic?

6   "Project control should always focus on the critical path." Comment.

7   Why would subcontractors for a government project want their activities on the critical path? Under what conditions would they try to avoid being on the critical path?

PROBLEMS

1   Your project to obtain charitable donations is now 30 days into a planned 40-day project. The project is divided into three activities. The first activity is designed to solicit individual donations. It is scheduled to run the first 25 days of the project and to bring in $25,000. Even though we are 30 days into the project, we still see that we have only 90% of this activity complete. The second activity relates to company donations and is scheduled to run for 30 days starting on day 5 and extending through day 35. We estimate that even though we should have (25/30) 83% of this activity complete, it is actually only 50% complete. This part of the project was scheduled to bring in $150,000 in donations. The final activity is for matching funds. This activity is scheduled to run the last 10 days of the project and has not started. It is scheduled to bring in an additional $50,000. So far $175,000 has actually been brought in on the project.

Calculate the schedule variance, schedule performance index, and cost (actually value in this case) performance index. How is the project going? Hint: Note that this problem is different since revenue rather than cost is the relevant measure. Use care in how the measures are interpreted.

2   A project to build a new bridge seems to be going very well since the project is well ahead of schedule and costs seem to be running very low. A major milestone has been reached where the first two activities have been totally completed and the third activity is 60% complete. The planners were only expecting to be 50% through the third activity at this time. The first activity involves prepping the site for the bridge. It was expected that this would cost $1,420,000 and it was done for only $1,300,000. The second activity was the pouring of concrete for the bridge. This was expected to cost $10,500,000 but was actually done for

$9,000,000. The third and final activity is the actual construction of the bridge superstructure. This was expected to cost a total of $8,500,000. To date they have spent $5,000,000 on the superstructure.

Calculate the schedule variance, schedule performance index, and the cost index for the project to date. How is the project going?

3 The following activities are part of a project to be scheduled using CPM:

ACTIVITY	IMMEDIATE PREDECESSOR	TIME (WEEKS)
A	——	6
B	A	3
C	A	7
D	C	2
E	B, D	4
F	D	3
G	E, F	7

a. Draw the network.
b. What is the critical path?
c. How many weeks will it take to complete the project?
d. How much slack does activity B have?

4 Schedule the following activities using CPM:

ACTIVITY	IMMEDIATE PREDECESSOR	TIME (WEEKS)
A	——	1
B	A	4
C	A	3
D	B	2
E	C, D	5
F	D	2
G	F	2
H	E, G	3

a. Draw the network.
b. What is the critical path?
c. How many weeks will it take to complete the project?
d. Which activities have slack, and how much?

5 The R&D department is planning to bid on a large project for the development of a new communication system for commercial planes. The accompanying table shows the activities, times, and sequences required:

ACTIVITY	IMMEDIATE PREDECESSOR	TIME (WEEKS)
A	—	3
B	A	2
C	A	4
D	A	4
E	B	6
F	C, D	6
G	D, F	2
H	D	3
I	E, G, H	3

a. Draw the network diagram.
b. What is the critical path?
c. Suppose you want to shorten the completion time as much as possible, and you have the option of shortening any or all of B, C, D, and G each one week. Which would you shorten?
d. What is the new critical path and earliest completion time?

6   The following represents a project that should be scheduled using CPM:

		TIMES (DAYS)		
ACTIVITY	IMMEDIATE PREDECESSORS	a	m	b
A	—	1	3	5
B	—	1	2	3
C	A	1	2	3
D	A	2	3	4
E	B	3	4	11
F	C, D	3	4	5
G	D, E	1	4	6
H	F, G	2	4	5

a. Draw the network.
b. What is the critical path?
c. What is the expected project completion time?
d. What is the probability of completing this project within 16 days?

7   There is an 82% chance the project below can be completed in *X* weeks or less. What is *X*?

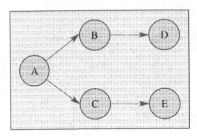

ACTIVITY	MOST OPTIMISTIC	MOST LIKELY	MOST PESSIMISTIC
A	2	5	11
B	3	3	3
C	1	3	5
D	6	8	10
E	4	7	10

8   The following table represents a plan for a project:

		TIMES (DAYS)		
JOB NO.	PREDECESSOR JOB(S)	a	m	b
1	—	2	3	4
2	1	1	2	3
3	1	4	5	12
4	1	3	4	11
5	2	1	3	5
6	3	1	2	3
7	4	1	8	9
8	5, 6	2	4	6
9	8	2	4	12
10	7	3	4	5
11	9, 10	5	7	8

a. Construct the appropriate network diagram.
b. Indicate the critical path.
c. What is the expected completion time for the project?
d. You can accomplish any one of the following at an additional cost of $1,500:
   (1) Reduce job 5 by two days.
   (2) Reduce job 3 by two days.
   (3) Reduce job 7 by two days.
   If you will save $1,000 for each day that the earliest completion time is reduced, which action, if any, would you choose?
e. What is the probability that the project will take more than 30 days to complete?

9   A construction project is broken down into the following 10 activities:

ACTIVITY	IMMEDIATE PREDECESSOR	TIME (WEEKS)
1	—	4
2	1	2
3	1	4
4	1	3
5	2, 3	5
6	3	6
7	4	2
8	5	3
9	6, 7	5
10	8, 9	7

a. Draw the network diagram.

b. Find the critical path.

c. If activities 1 and 10 cannot be shortened, but activities 2 through 9 can be shortened to a minimum of one week each at a cost of $10,000 per week, which activities would you shorten to cut the project by four weeks?

10   Here is a CPM network with activity times in weeks:

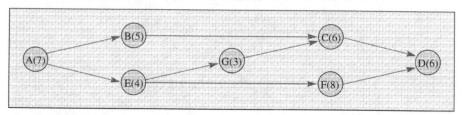

a. Determine the critical path.

b. How many weeks will the project take to complete?

c. Suppose F could be shortened by two weeks and B by one week. How would this affect the completion date?

11   Here is a network with the activity times shown in days:

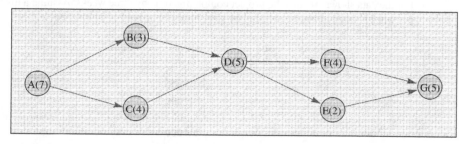

a. Find the critical path.

b. The following table shows the normal times and the crash times, along with the associated costs for each activity.

ACTIVITY	NORMAL TIME	CRASH TIME	NORMAL COST	CRASH COST
A	7	6	$7,000	$ 8,000
B	3	2	5,000	7,000
C	4	3	9,000	10,200
D	5	4	3,000	4,500
E	2	1	2,000	3,000
F	4	2	4,000	7,000
G	5	4	5,000	8,000

If the project is to be shortened by four days, show which activities, in order of reduction, would be shortened and the resulting cost.

12 The home office billing department of a chain of department stores prepares monthly inventory reports for use by the stores' purchasing agents. Given the following information, use the critical path method to determine:

a. How long the total process will take.

b. Which jobs can be delayed without delaying the early start of any subsequent activity.

	JOB AND DESCRIPTION	IMMEDIATE PREDECESSORS	TIME (HOURS)
a	Start	—	0
b	Get computer printouts of customer purchases	a	10
c	Get stock records for the month	a	20
d	Reconcile purchase printouts and stock records	b, c	30
e	Total stock records by department	b, c	20
f	Determine reorder quantities for coming period	e	40
g	Prepare stock reports for purchasing agents	d, f	20
h	Finish	g	0

13 For the network shown:

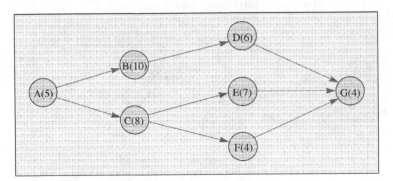

a. Determine the critical path and the early completion time in weeks for the project.

b. For the data shown, reduce the project completion time by three weeks. Assume a linear cost per week shortened, and show, step by step, how you arrived at your schedule.

ACTIVITY	NORMAL TIME	NORMAL COST	CRASH TIME	CRASH COST
A	5	$ 7,000	3	$13,000
B	10	12,000	7	18,000
C	8	5,000	7	7,000
D	6	4,000	5	5,000
E	7	3,000	6	6,000
F	4	6,000	3	7,000
G	4	7,000	3	9,000

14 The following CPM network has estimates of the normal time in weeks listed for the activities:

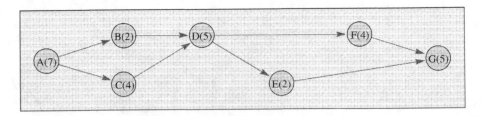

a. Identify the critical path.

b. What is the length of time to complete the project?

c. Which activities have slack, and how much?

d. Here is a table of normal and crash times and costs. Which activities would you shorten to cut two weeks from the schedule in a rational fashion? What would be the incremental cost? Is the critical path changed?

ACTIVITY	NORMAL TIME	CRASH TIME	NORMAL COST	CRASH COST
A	7	6	$7,000	$ 8,000
B	2	1	5,000	7,000
C	4	3	9,000	10,200
D	5	4	3,000	4,500
E	2	1	2,000	3,000
F	4	2	4,000	7,000
G	5	4	5,000	8,000

15 Bragg's Bakery is building a new automated bakery in downtown Sandusky. Here are the activities that need to be completed to get the new bakery built and the equipment installed.

ACTIVITY	PREDECESSOR	NORMAL TIME (WEEKS)	CRASH TIME (WEEKS)	EXPEDITING COST/WEEK
A	—	9	6	$3,000
B	A	8	5	$3,500
C	A	15	10	$4,000
D	B, C	5	3	$2,000
E	C	10	6	$2,500
F	D, E	2	1	$5,000

a. Draw the project diagram.

b. What is the normal project length?

c. What is the project length if all activities are crashed to their minimum?

d. Bragg's loses $3,500 in profit per week for every week the bakery is not completed. How many weeks will the project take if we are willing to pay crashing cost as long as it is less than $3,500?

ADVANCED PROBLEM

16 Assume the network and data that follow:

ACTIVITY	NORMAL TIME (WEEKS)	NORMAL COST	CRASH TIME (WEEKS)	CRASH COST	IMMEDIATE PREDECESSORS
A	2	$50	1	$70	—
B	4	80	2	160	A
C	8	70	4	110	A
D	6	60	5	80	A
E	7	100	6	130	B
F	4	40	3	100	D
G	5	100	4	150	C, E, F

a. Construct the network diagram.

b. Indicate the critical path when normal activity times are used.

c. Compute the minimum total direct cost for each project duration based on the cost associated with each activity. Consider durations of 13, 14, 15, 16, 17, and 18 weeks.

d. If the indirect costs for each project duration are $400 (18 weeks), $350 (17 weeks), $300 (16 weeks), $250 (15 weeks), $200 (14 weeks), and $150 (13 weeks), what is the total project cost for each duration? Indicate the minimum total project cost duration.

CASE: CELL PHONE DESIGN PROJECT

You work for Motorola in its global cell phone group. You have been made project manager for the design of a new cell phone model. Your supervisors have already scoped the project so you have a list showing the work breakdown structure and this includes major project activities. You must plan the project schedule and calculate project duration and project costs. Your boss wants the schedule and costs on his desk tomorrow morning!

You have been given the information in Exhibit 10.14. It includes all the activities required in the project and the duration of each activity. Also, dependencies between the activities have been identified. Remember that the preceding activity must be fully completed before work on the following activity can be started.

Your project is divided into five major tasks. Task P involves developing specifications for the new cell phone. Here decisions related to such things as battery life, size of the phone, and features need to be determined. These details are based on how a customer uses the cell phone. These user specifications are redefined in

terms that have meaning to the subcontractors that will actually make the new cell phone in Task S, supplier specifications. These involve engineering details for how the product will perform. The individual components that make up the product are the focus of Task D. Task I brings all the components together and a working prototype is built and tested. Finally in Task V, vendors are selected and contracts are negotiated.

1 Draw a project network that includes all the activities.
2 Calculate the start and finish times for each activity and determine the minimum number of weeks for completing the project. Find the critical set of activities for the project.
3 Identify slack in the activities not on the project critical path.
4 Your boss would like you to suggest changes that could be made to the project that would significantly shorten it. What would you suggest?

exhibit 10.14   Work Breakdown Structure and Activities for the Cell Phone Design Project

**Excel:
Cell_Phone
Design**

MAJOR PROJECT TASKS/ACTIVITIES	ACTIVITY IDENTIFICATION	DEPENDENCY	DURATION (WEEKS)
Product specifications (P)			
Overall product specifications	P1	—	4
Hardware specifications	P2	P1	5
Software specifications	P3	P1	5
Market research	P4	P2, P3	2
Supplier specifications (S)			
Hardware	S1	P2	5
Software	S2	P3	6
Market research	S3	P4	1
Product design (D)			
Circuits	D1	S1, D7	8
Battery	D2	S1	1
Display	D3	S1	2
Outer cover	D4	S3	4
User interface	D5	S2	4
Camera	D6	S1, S2, S3	1
Functionality	D7	D5, D6	4
Product integration (I)			
Hardware	I1	D1, D2, D3, D4, D6	3
Software	I2	D7	5
Prototype testing	I3	I1, I2	5
Subcontracting (V)			
Vendor selection	V1	D7	10
Contract negotiation	V2	I3, V1	2

CASE: THE CAMPUS WEDDING (A)

On March 31 of last year, Mary Jackson burst into the family living room and announced that she and Larry Adams (her college boyfriend) were going to be married. After recovering from the shock, her mother hugged her and asked, "When?" The following conversation resulted:

Mary: April 22.

Mother: What!

Father: The Adams–Jackson wedding will be the social hit of the year. Why so soon?

Mary: Because on April 22 the cherry blossoms on campus are always in full bloom! The wedding pictures will be beautiful.

Mother: But honey, we can't possibly finish all the things that need to be done by then. Remember all the details that were involved in your sister's wedding? Even if we start tomorrow, it takes a day to reserve the church and reception hall, and they need at least 17 days' notice. That has to be done before we can start decorating the church, which takes three days. An extra $100 contribution on Sunday would probably cut that 17-day notice to 10 days, though.

Father: Ugh!

Mary: I want Jane Summers to be my maid of honor.

Father: But she's in the Peace Corps, in Guatemala, isn't she? It would take her 10 days to get ready and drive up here.

Mary: But we could fly her up in two days, and it would cost only $500. She would have to be here in time to have her dress fitted.

Father: Ugh!

Mother: And catering! It takes two days to choose the cake and table decorations, and Jack's Catering wants at least 10 days' notice prior to the rehearsal dinner (the night before the wedding).

Mary: Can I wear your wedding dress, Mom?

Mother: Well, we'd have to replace some lace, but you could wear it, yes. We could order the lace from New York when we order the material for the bridesmaids' dresses. It takes eight days to order and receive the material. The pattern needs to be chosen first, and that would take three days.

Father: We could get the material here in five days if we paid an extra $25 to airfreight it.

Mary: I want Mrs. Watson to work on the dresses.

Father: But she charges $120 a day!

Mother: If we did all the sewing, we could finish the dresses in 11 days. If Mrs. Watson helped, we could cut that down to six days, at a cost of $120 for each day less than 11 days.

Mary: I don't want anyone but her.

Mother: It would take another two days to do the final fitting. It normally takes two days to clean and press the dresses, but that new cleaner downtown could do them in one day if we pay the $30 charge for express service.

Father: Everything should be completed by rehearsal night, and that's only 21 days from now. I bet that will be a busy day.

Mother: We've forgotten something. The invitations.

Father: We should order the invitations from Bob's Printing Shop, and that usually takes 12 days. I'll bet he would do it in five days if we slipped him an extra $35.

Mother: It would take us three days to choose the invitation style before we could order them, and we want the envelopes printed with our return address.

Mary: Oh! That will be elegant.

Mother: The invitations should go out at least 10 days before the wedding. If we let them go any later, some of the relatives would get theirs too late to come, and that would make them mad. I'll bet that if we didn't get them out until eight days before the wedding, Aunt Ethel couldn't make it, and she would reduce her wedding gift by $200.

Father: Ugh!

Mother: We'll have to take them to the post office to mail them, and that takes a day. Addressing would take four days unless we hired some part-time help, and we can't start until the printer is finished. If we hired someone, we could probably save two days by spending $25 for each day saved.

Mary: We need to get gifts to give to the bridesmaids at the rehearsal dinner. I can spend a day and do that.

Mother: Before we can even start to write out those invitations, we need a guest list. Heavens, that will take four days to get in order, and only I can understand our address file.

Mary: Oh, Mother, I'm so excited. We can start each of the relatives on a different job.

Mother: Honey, I don't see how we can do it. Why, we've got to choose the invitations and patterns and reserve the church and . . .

Father: Why don't you just take $1,500 and elope. Your sister's wedding cost me $1,200, and she didn't have to fly people up from Guatemala, hire extra people, use airfreight, or anything like that.

QUESTIONS

1 Given the activities and precedence relationships described in the (A) case, develop a network diagram for the wedding plans.
2 Identify the paths. Which are critical?
3 What is the minimum-cost plan that meets the April 22 date?

CASE: THE CAMPUS WEDDING (B)

Several complications arose during the course of trying to meet the deadline of April 21 for the Adams–Jackson wedding rehearsal. Because Mary Jackson was adamant about having the wedding on April 22 (as was Larry Adams, because he wanted her to be happy), the implications of each of these complications had to be assessed.

1   On April 1 the chairman of the Vestry Committee at the church was left unimpressed by the added donation and said he wouldn't reduce the notice period from 17 to 10 days.

2   A call to Guatemala revealed that the potential bridesmaid had several commitments and could not possibly leave the country until April 10.

3   Mother came down with the four-day flu just as she started on the guest list.

4   The lace and dress materials were lost in transit. Notice of the loss was delivered to the Jackson home early on April 10.

5   There was a small fire at the caterer's shop on April 8. It was estimated that the shop would be closed two or three days for repairs.

Mary Jackson's father, in particular, was concerned about expenses and kept offering $1,500 to Mary and Larry for them to elope.

QUESTION

1   Given your answers to the (A) case, describe the effects on the wedding plans of each incident noted in the (B) case.

SOURCE: ADAPTED FROM A CASE ORIGINALLY WRITTEN BY PROFESSOR D. C. WHYBANK, UNIVERSITY OF NORTH CAROLINA, CHAPEL HILL, NORTH CAROLINA.

SUPER QUIZ

1   A project structured where a self-contained team works full time on the project.

2   Specific events that upon completion mark important progress toward completing a project.

3   This defines the hierarchy of project tasks, subtasks, and work packages.

4   Pieces of work in a project that consume time to complete.

5   A chart that shows both the time and sequence for completing the activities in a project.

6   Activities that in sequence form the longest chain in a project.

7   The difference between the late and early start time for an activity.

8   When activities are scheduled with probabilistic task times.

9   The procedure used to reduce project completion time by trading off time versus cost.

10   A key assumption related to the resources needed to complete activities when using the critical path method.

1. Pure project or skunkworks 2. Milestones 3. Work breakdown structure 4. Activities 5. Gantt chart 6. Critical path(s) 7. Slack 8. The Program Evaluation and Review Technique (PERT) 9. Crashing 10. Resources are always available

SELECTED BIBLIOGRAPHY

Gray, C. *Agile Project Management: How to Succeed in the Face of Changing Project Requirements*. New York: American Management Association, 2004.

Gray, C. F., and E. W. Larson. *Project Management: The Managerial Process*. New York: Irwin/McGraw-Hill, 2002.

Kerzner, H. *Project Management: A Systems Approach to Planning, Scheduling, and Controlling*. 8th ed. New York: Wiley, 2002.

Lewis, James P. *The Project Manager's Desk Reference*. New York: McGraw-Hill Professional Publishing, 1999.

SIX-SIGMA QUALITY

chapter 9

General Electric (GE) has been a major promoter of Six Sigma for more than 10 years. Jack Welch, the legendary and now retired CEO, declared that "the big myth is that Six Sigma is about quality control and statistics. It is that—but it's much more. Ultimately, it drives leadership to be better by providing tools to think through tough issues. At Six Sigma's core is an idea that can turn a company inside out, focusing the organization outward on the customer." GE's commitment to quality centers on Six Sigma. Six Sigma is defined on the GE Web site as follows:

First, What is Six Sigma? First, what it is not. It is not a secret society, a slogan or a cliché. Six Sigma is a highly disciplined process that helps us focus on developing and delivering

After reading this chapter you will:

1. Understand total quality management.
2. Describe how quality is measured and be aware of the different dimensions of quality.
3. Explain the define, measure, analyze, improve, and control (DMAIC) quality improvement process.
4. Understand what ISO certification means.

near-perfect products and services. Why "Sigma"? The word is a statistical term that measures how far a given process deviates from perfection. The central idea behind Six Sigma is that if you can measure how many "defects" you have in a process, you can systematically figure out how to eliminate them and get as close to "zero defects" as possible. To achieve Six Sigma Quality, a process must produce no more than 3.4 defects per million opportunities. An "opportunity" is defined as a chance for noncon-formance, or not meeting the required specifications. This means we need to be nearly flawless in executing our key processes.

At its core, Six Sigma revolves around a few key concepts.

Critical to Quality:	Attributes most important to the customer
Defect:	Failing to deliver what the customer wants
Process Capability:	What your process can deliver
Variation:	What the customer sees and feels

Stable Operations:	Ensuring consistent, predictable processes to improve what the customer sees and feels
Design for Six Sigma:	Designing to meet customer needs and process capability

In this chapter, we first review the general subject of total quality management and the quality movement. We then develop the basic features and concepts of the Six-Sigma approach to TQM. We then describe the Shingo system, which takes a unique approach to quality by focusing on preventing mistakes. This is followed by a review of ISO 9000 and 14000 standards for quality certification used by many companies throughout the world. Finally, we provide the major steps of external benchmarking for quality improvement.

TOTAL QUALITY MANAGEMENT

Total quality management

Total quality management may be defined as "managing the entire organization so that it excels on all dimensions of products and services that are important to the customer." It has two fundamental operational goals:

1. Careful design of the product or service.
2. Ensuring that the organization's systems can consistently produce the design.

Global

These two goals can only be achieved if the entire organization is oriented toward them—hence the term *total* quality management. TQM became a national concern in the United States in the 1980s primarily as a response to Japanese quality superiority in manufacturing automobiles and other durable goods such as room air conditioners. A widely cited study of Japanese and U.S. air-conditioning manufacturers showed that the best-quality American products had *higher* average defect rates than those of the poorest Japanese manufacturers.[1]

THE MALCOLM BALDRIGE NATIONAL QUALITY AWARD

The Award is given to organizations that have demonstrated outstanding quality in their products and processes. Three Awards may be given annually in each of these categories: manufacturing, service, small business, education, health care, and nonprofit.

Applicants for the Award must submit an application of 50 pages or less that details the processes and results of their activities under seven major categories: Leadership; Strategic Planning; Customer and Market Focus; Measurement, Analysis and Knowledge Management; Workforce Focus; Process Management; and Results. The applications are scored on total points out of 1,000 by the Baldrige Board of Examiners and Judges. High-scoring applications are selected for site visits and Award recipients are selected from this group. The president of the United States traditionally presents the Awards at a special ceremony in Washington, DC. A major benefit to all applicants is the feedback report prepared by Examiners that is based on their processes and practices. Many states have used the Baldrige criteria as the basis of their quality programs. A report, *Building on Baldrige: American Quality for the*

21st Century, by the private Council on Competitiveness, said, "More than any other program, the Baldrige Quality Award is responsible for making quality a national priority and disseminating best practices across the United States."

So severe was the quality shortfall in the United States that improving it throughout industry became a national priority, with the Department of Commerce establishing the Malcolm Baldrige National Quality Award in 1987 to help companies review and structure their quality programs. Also gaining major attention at this time was the requirement that suppliers demonstrate that they are measuring and documenting their quality practices according to specified criteria, called ISO standards, if they wished to compete for international contracts. We will have more to say about this later.

Malcolm Baldrige National Quality Award

The philosophical leaders of the quality movement, notably Philip Crosby, W. Edwards Deming, and Joseph M. Juran—the so-called Quality Gurus—had slightly different definitions of what quality is and how to achieve it (see Exhibit 9.1), but they all had the same general message: To achieve outstanding quality requires quality leadership from senior management, a customer focus, total involvement of the workforce, and continuous improvement based upon rigorous analysis of processes. Later in the chapter, we will discuss how these precepts are applied in the latest approach to TQM—Six Sigma. We will now turn to some fundamental concepts that underlie any quality effort: quality specifications and quality costs.

The Quality Gurus Compared

exhibit 9.1

	CROSBY	DEMING	JURAN
Definition of quality	Conformance to requirements	A predictable degree of uniformity and dependability at low cost and suited to the market	Fitness for use (satisfies customer's needs)
Degree of senior management responsibility	Responsible for quality	Responsible for 94% of quality problems	Less than 20% of quality problems are due to workers
Performance standard/ motivation	Zero defects	Quality has many "scales"; use statistics to measure performance in all areas; critical of zero defects	Avoid campaigns to do perfect work
General approach	Prevention, not inspection	Reduce variability by continuous improvement; cease mass inspection	General management approach to quality, especially human elements
Structure	14 steps to quality improvement	14 points for management	10 steps to quality improvement
Statistical process control (SPC)	Rejects statistically acceptable levels of quality (wants 100% perfect quality)	Statistical methods of quality control must be used	Recommends SPC but warns that it can lead to tool-driven approach
Improvement basis	A process, not a program; improvement goals	Continuous to reduce variation; eliminate goals without methods	Project-by-project team approach; set goals
Teamwork	Quality improvement teams; quality councils	Employee participation in decision making; break down barriers between departments	Team and quality circle approach
Costs of quality	Cost of nonconformance; quality is free	No optimum; continuous improvement	Quality is not free; there is not an optimum
Purchasing and goods received	State requirements; supplier is extension of business; most faults due to purchasers themselves	Inspection too late; sampling allows defects to enter system; statistical evidence and control charts required	Problems are complex; carry out formal surveys
Vendor rating	Yes; quality audits useless	No, critical of most systems	Yes, but help supplier improve

QUALITY SPECIFICATION AND QUALITY COSTS

Fundamental to any quality program is the determination of quality specifications and the costs of achieving (or *not* achieving) those specifications.

DEVELOPING QUALITY SPECIFICATIONS

Design quality

The quality specifications of a product or service derive from decisions and actions made relative to the quality of its design and the quality of its conformance to that design. Design quality refers to the inherent value of the product in the marketplace and is thus a strategic decision for the firm. The dimensions of quality are listed in Exhibit 9.2. These dimensions refer to features of the product or service that relate directly to design issues. A firm designs a product or service to address the need of a particular market.

A firm designs a product or service with certain performance characteristics and features based on what the intended market expects. Materials and manufacturing process attributes can greatly impact the reliability and durability of a product. Here the company attempts to design a product or service that can be produced or delivered at reasonable cost. The serviceability of the product may have a great impact on the cost of the product or service to the customer after the initial purchase is made. It also may impact the warranty and repair cost to the firm. Aesthetics may greatly impact the desirability of the product or service, in particular consumer products. Especially when a brand name is involved, the design often represents the next generation of an ongoing stream of products or services. Consistency in the relative performance of the product compared to the state of the art, for example, may have a great impact on how the quality of the product is perceived. This may be very important to the long-run success of the product or service.

Conformance quality

Conformance quality refers to the degree to which the product or service design specifications are met. The activities involved in achieving conformance are of a tactical, day-to-day nature. It should be evident that a product or service can have high design quality but low conformance quality, and vice versa.

Quality at the source

Quality at the source is frequently discussed in the context of conformance quality. This means that the person who does the work takes responsibility for making sure that his or her output meets specifications. Where a product is involved, achieving the quality specifications is typically the responsibility of manufacturing management; in a service firm, it is usually the responsibility of the branch operations management. Exhibit 9.3 shows two examples of the dimensions of quality. One is a laser printer that meets the pages-per-minute and print density standards; the second is a checking account transaction in a bank.

Dimensions of quality

Both quality of design and quality of conformance should provide products that meet the customer's objectives for those products. This is often termed the product's *fitness for use,* and it entails identifying the dimensions of the product (or service) that the customer wants (that is, the voice of the customer) and developing a quality control program to ensure that these dimensions are met.

| exhibit 9.2 | The Dimensions of Design Quality |

DIMENSION	MEANING
Performance	Primary product or service characteristics
Features	Added touches, bells and whistles, secondary characteristics
Reliability/durability	Consistency of performance over time, probability of failing, useful life
Serviceability	Ease of repair
Aesthetics	Sensory characteristics (sound, feel, look, and so on)
Perceived quality	Past performance and reputation

Examples of Dimensions of Quality

exhibit 9.3

DIMENSION	MEASURES	
	PRODUCT EXAMPLE: LASER PRINTER	SERVICE EXAMPLE: CHECKING ACCOUNT AT A BANK
Performance	Pages per minute Print density	Time to process customer requests
Features	Multiple paper trays Color capability	Automatic bill paying
Reliability/durability	Mean time between failures Estimated time to obsolescence Expected life of major components	Variability of time to process requests Keeping pace with industry trends
Serviceability	Availability of authorized repair centers Number of copies per print cartridge Modular design	Online reports Ease of getting updated information
Aesthetics	Control button layout Case style Courtesy of dealer	Appearance of bank lobby Courtesy of teller
Perceived quality	Brand name recognition Rating in *Consumer Reports*	Endorsed by community leaders

COST OF QUALITY

Although few can quarrel with the notion of prevention, management often needs hard numbers to determine how much prevention activities will cost. This issue was recognized by Joseph Juran, who wrote about it in 1951 in his *Quality Control Handbook*. Today, cost of quality (COQ) analyses are common in industry and constitute one of the primary functions of QC departments.

Cost of quality

There are a number of definitions and interpretations of the term *cost of quality*. From the purist's point of view, it means all of the costs attributable to the production of quality that is not 100 percent perfect. A less stringent definition considers only those costs that are the difference between what can be expected from excellent performance and the current costs that exist.

How significant is the cost of quality? It has been estimated at between 15 and 20 percent of every sales dollar—the cost of reworking, scrapping, repeated service, inspections, tests, warranties, and other quality-related items. Philip Crosby states that the correct cost for a well-run quality management program should be under 2.5 percent.[2]

Three basic assumptions justify an analysis of the costs of quality: (1) failures are caused, (2) prevention is cheaper, and (3) performance can be measured.

The costs of quality are generally classified into four types:

1. **Appraisal costs.** Costs of the inspection, testing, and other tasks to ensure that the product or process is acceptable.
2. **Prevention costs.** The sum of all the costs to prevent defects such as the costs to identify the cause of the defect, to implement corrective action to eliminate the cause, to train personnel, to redesign the product or system, and to purchase new equipment or make modifications.

A GOODYEAR ASSOCIATE INSPECTS A RADIAL TIRE AT THE SAO PAULO, BRAZIL, FACTORY. GOODYEAR PRACTICES BOTH VISUAL AND INTERNAL INSPECTIONS OF TIRES, EVEN PULLING SOME TIRES FROM THE PRODUCTION LINE TO BE X-RAYED.

exhibit 9.4

Quality Cost Report

	CURRENT MONTH'S COST	PERCENTAGE OF TOTAL
Prevention costs		
Quality training	$ 2,000	1.3%
Reliability consulting	10,000	6.5
Pilot production runs	5,000	3.3
Systems development	8,000	5.2
Total prevention	25,000	16.3
Appraisal costs		
Materials inspection	6,000	3.9
Supplies inspection	3,000	2.0
Reliability testing	5,000	3.3
Laboratory testing	25,000	16.3
Total appraisal	39,000	25.5
Internal failure costs		
Scrap	15,000	9.8
Repair	18,000	11.8
Rework	12,000	7.8
Downtime	6,000	3.9
Total internal failure	51,000	33.3
External failure costs		
Warranty costs	14,000	9.2
Out-of-warranty repairs and replacement	6,000	3.9
Customer complaints	3,000	2.0
Product liability	10,000	6.5
Transportation losses	5,000	3.3
Total external failure	38,000	24.9
Total quality costs	$153,000	100.0

3. **Internal failure costs.** Costs for defects incurred within the system: scrap, rework, repair.
4. **External failure costs.** Costs for defects that pass through the system: customer warranty replacements, loss of customers or goodwill, handling complaints, and product repair.

Exhibit 9.4 illustrates the type of report that might be submitted to show the various costs by categories. Prevention is the most important influence. A rule of thumb says that for every dollar you spend in prevention, you can save $10 in failure and appraisal costs.

Often increases in productivity occur as a by-product of efforts to reduce the cost of quality. A bank, for example, set out to improve quality and reduce the cost of quality and found that it had also boosted productivity. The bank developed this productivity measure for the loan processing area: the number of tickets processed divided by the resources required (labor cost, computer time, ticket forms). Before the quality improvement program, the productivity index was 0.2660 [2,080/($11.23 × 640 hours + $0.05 × 2,600 forms + $500 for systems costs)]. After the quality improvement project was completed, labor time fell to 546 hours and the number of forms rose to 2,100, for a change in the index to 0.3088, an increase in productivity of 16 percent.

Service

FUNCTIONS OF THE QC DEPARTMENT

Although the focus of this chapter is on corporatewide quality programs, it is useful to comment on the functions of QC departments.

The typical manufacturing QC department has a variety of functions to perform. These include testing designs for their reliability in the lab and the field; gathering performance data on products in the field and resolving quality problems in the field; planning and budgeting the QC program in the plant; and, finally, designing and overseeing quality control systems and inspection procedures, and actually carrying out inspection activities requiring special

J. D. POWER AND ASSOCIATES INITIAL QUALITY STUDY OF NEW CARS

The J. D. Power and Associates Initial Quality Study℠ serves as the industry benchmark for new-vehicle quality measured at 90 days of ownership. The study is used extensively by manufacturers worldwide to help them design and build higher quality vehicles and by consumers to help them in their purchase decisions. Initial quality has been shown over the years to be a good predictor of long-term durability, which can significantly impact consumer purchase decisions. The study captures problems experienced by owners in two distinct categories: 1) design-related problems and 2) defects and malfunctions.

1 Exterior
   a Design-related problems: front or sliding doors with handles that are difficult to operate.
   b Defects/Malfunctions: front or sliding doors that are difficult to open or close, excessive wind noise, or paint imperfections—including chips or scratches at delivery.

2 The Driving Experience
   a Design-related problem: too much play or looseness in the steering system, excessive brake dust, or foot pedals that are too close together.
   b Defects/Malfunctions: brakes that pull noticeably, are noisy, or emit excessive brake dust.

3 Features/Controls/Displays
   a Design-related problems: problems with the remote keyless entry system, door locks, or cruise control

systems that are difficult to use. Controls that are awkwardly located.
   b Defects/Malfunctions: problems with remote keyless entry systems, door locks, or cruise control systems that are not working properly.

4 Audio/Entertainment/Navigation
   a Design-related problems: audio and entertainment systems with controls that are difficult to use or awkwardly located, or hands-free communication systems that don't recognize commands.
   b Defects/Malfunctions: CD players with loading problems or radios with poor/no reception on AM/FM stations.

5 Seats
   a Design-related problems: forward/backward seat adjustments or memory seat controls that are difficult to understand or use.
   b Defects/Malfunctions: forward/backward seat adjustment or memory seats that are broken or not working properly.

6 Heat, Ventilation and Air Conditioning
   a Design-related problems: a vehicle heater that doesn't get hot fast enough or windows that fog up too often.
   b Defects/Malfunctions: a fan/blower with excessive noise or vents that emit air with a moldy or stale smell.

7 Interior
   a Design-related problems: a glove box or center console that is difficult to use.
   b Defects/Malfunctions: instrument panel or dash lights that are not working or a glove box or center console that is broken or damaged.

8 Engine/Transmission
   a Design-related problems: an engine that loses power when the AC is on or a manual transmission that is hard to operate.
   b Defects/Malfunctions: an engine that runs and then dies/stalls or an automatic transmission that shifts at the wrong time.

SOURCE: DIRECT COMMUNICATION WITH J. D. POWER AND ASSOCIATES.

technical knowledge to accomplish. The tools of the QC department fall under the heading of statistical quality control (SQC) and consist of two main sections: acceptance sampling and process control. These topics are covered in Chapter 9A.

SIX-SIGMA QUALITY

Six Sigma refers to the philosophy and methods companies such as General Electric and   Six Sigma
Motorola use to eliminate defects in their products and processes. A defect is simply any component that does not fall within the customer's specification limits. Each step or activity in a company represents an opportunity for defects to occur, and Six-Sigma programs seek to

reduce the variation in the processes that lead to these defects. Indeed, Six-Sigma advocates see variation as the enemy of quality, and much of the theory underlying Six Sigma is devoted to dealing with this problem. A process that is in Six-Sigma control will produce no more than two defects out of every billion units. Often, this is stated as four defects per million units, which is true if the process is only running somewhere within one sigma of the target specification.

One of the benefits of Six-Sigma thinking is that it allows managers to readily describe the performance of a process in terms of its variability and to compare different processes using a common metric. This metric is defects per million opportunities (DPMO). This calculation requires three pieces of data:

1. **Unit.**   The item produced or being serviced.
2. **Defect.**   Any item or event that does not meet the customer's requirements.
3. **Opportunity.**   A chance for a defect to occur.

A straightforward calculation is made using the following formula:

$$DPMO = \frac{\text{Number of defects}}{\text{Number of opportunities for error per unit} \times \text{Number of units}} \times 1,000,000$$

EXAMPLE 9.1

The customers of a mortgage bank expect to have their mortgage applications processed within 10 days of filing. This would be called a *critical customer requirement*, or CCR, in Six-Sigma terms. Suppose all defects are counted (loans in a monthly sample taking more than 10 days to process) and it is determined that there are 150 loans in the 1,000 applications processed last month that don't meet this customer requirement. Thus, the DPMO = $150/1,000 \times 1,000,000$, or 150,000 loans out of every million processed that fail to meet a CCR. Put differently, it means that only 850,000 loans out of a million are approved within time expectations. Statistically, 15 percent of the loans are defective and 85 percent are correct. This is a case where all the loans processed in less than 10 days meet our criteria. Often there are upper and lower customer requirements rather than just a single upper requirement as we have here. ●

There are two aspects to Six-Sigma programs: the methodology side and the people side. We will take these up in order.

SIX-SIGMA METHODOLOGY

While Six Sigma's methods include many of the statistical tools that were employed in other quality movements, here they are employed in a systematic project-oriented fashion through the define, measure, analyze, improve, and control (DMAIC) cycle. The DMAIC cycle is a more detailed version of the Deming PDCA cycle, which consists of four steps—plan, do, check, and act—that underly continuous improvement. (Continuous improvement, also called kaizen, seeks continual improvement of machinery, materials, labor utilization, and production methods through applications of suggestions and ideas of company teams.) Like Six Sigma, it also emphasizes the scientific method, particularly hypothesis testing about the relationship between process inputs (X's) and outputs (Y's) using design of experiments (DOE) methods. The availability of modern statistical software has reduced the drudgery of analyzing and displaying data and is now part of the Six-Sigma tool kit. The overarching focus of the methodology, however, is understanding and achieving what the customer wants, since that is seen as the key to profitability of a production process. In fact, to get across this point, some use the DMAIC as an acronym for "Dumb Managers Always Ignore Customers."

The standard approach to Six-Sigma projects is the DMAIC methodology developed by General Electric, described below:[3]

1. Define (D)
   • Identify customers and their priorities.
   • Identify a project suitable for Six-Sigma efforts based on business objectives as well as customer needs and feedback.
   • Identify CTQs (critical-to-quality characteristics) that the customer considers to have the most impact on quality.

DPMO

Service

Step by Step

DMAIC
PDCA cycle
Continuous improvement
kaizen

2. Measure (M)
   - Determine how to measure the process and how it is performing.
   - Identify the key internal processes that influence CTQs and measure the defects currently generated relative to those processes.
3. Analyze (A)
   - Determine the most likely causes of defects.
   - Understand why defects are generated by identifying the key variables that are most likely to create process variation.
4. Improve (I)
   - Identify means to remove the causes of defects.
   - Confirm the key variables and quantify their effects on the CTQs.
   - Identify the maximum acceptance ranges of the key variables and a system for measuring deviations of the variables.
   - Modify the process to stay within an acceptable range.
5. Control (C)
   - Determine how to maintain the improvements.
   - Put tools in place to ensure that the key variables remain within the maximum acceptance ranges under the modified process.

ANALYTICAL TOOLS FOR SIX SIGMA AND CONTINUOUS IMPROVEMENT

The analytical tools of Six Sigma have been used for many years in traditional quality improvement programs. What makes their application to Six Sigma unique is the integration of these tools in a corporatewide management system. The tools common to all quality efforts, including Six Sigma, are flowcharts, run charts, Pareto charts, histograms, checksheets, cause-and-effect diagrams, and control charts. Examples of these, along with an opportunity flow diagram, are shown in Exhibit 9.5 arranged according to DMAIC categories where they commonly appear.

Flowcharts.   There are many types of flow charts. The one shown in Exhibit 9.5 depicts the process steps as part of a SIPOC (supplier, input, process, output, customer) analysis. SIPOC in essence is a formalized input-output model, used in the define stage of a project.

Run charts.   They depict trends in data over time, and thereby help to understand the magnitude of a problem at the define stage. Typically, they plot the median of a process.

Pareto charts.   These charts help to break down a problem into the relative contributions of its components. They are based on the common empirical finding that a large percentage of problems are due to a small percentage of causes. In the example, 80 percent of customer complaints are due to late deliveries, which are 20 percent of the causes listed.

Checksheets.   These are basic forms that help standardize data collection. They are used to create histograms such as shown on the Pareto chart.

Cause-and-effect diagrams.   Also called *fishbone diagrams,* they show hypothesized relationships between potential causes and the problem under study. Once the C&E diagram is constructed, the analysis would proceed to find out which of the potential causes were in fact contributing to the problem.

Opportunity flow diagram.   This is used to separate value-added from non-value-added steps in a process.

Control charts.   These are time-sequenced charts showing plotted values of a statistic, including a centerline average and one or more control limits. It is used here to assure that changes introduced are in statistical control. See Chapter 9A for a discussion of the various types and uses of charts for process control.

Other tools that have seen extensive use in Six-Sigma projects are failure mode and effect analysis (FMEA) and design of experiments (DOE).

Failure mode and effect analysis.   This is a structured approach to identify, estimate, prioritize, and evaluate risk of possible failures at each stage of a process. It begins with

exhibit 9.5   Analytical Tools for Six Sigma and Continuous Improvement

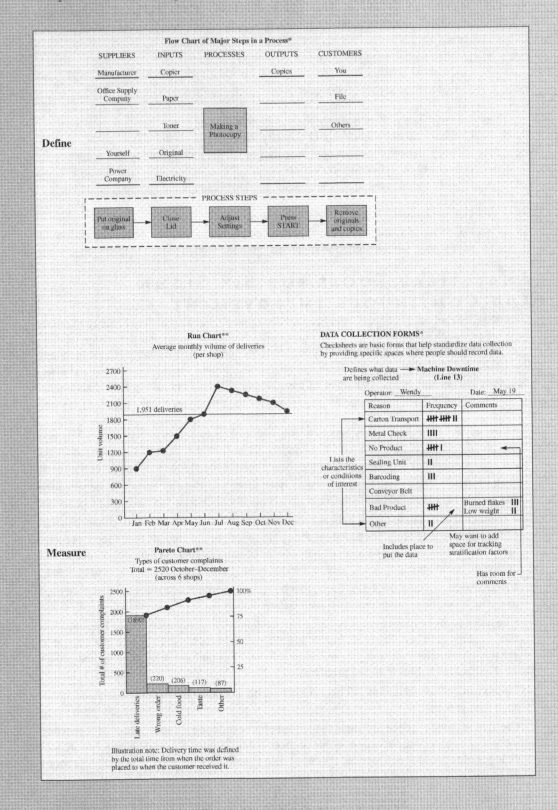

*SOURCE: RATH & STRONG, RATH & STRONG'S SIX SIGMA POCKET GUIDE, 2001.
**SOURCE: RAYTHEON SIX SIGMA; THE MEMORY JOGGER™II, 2001.

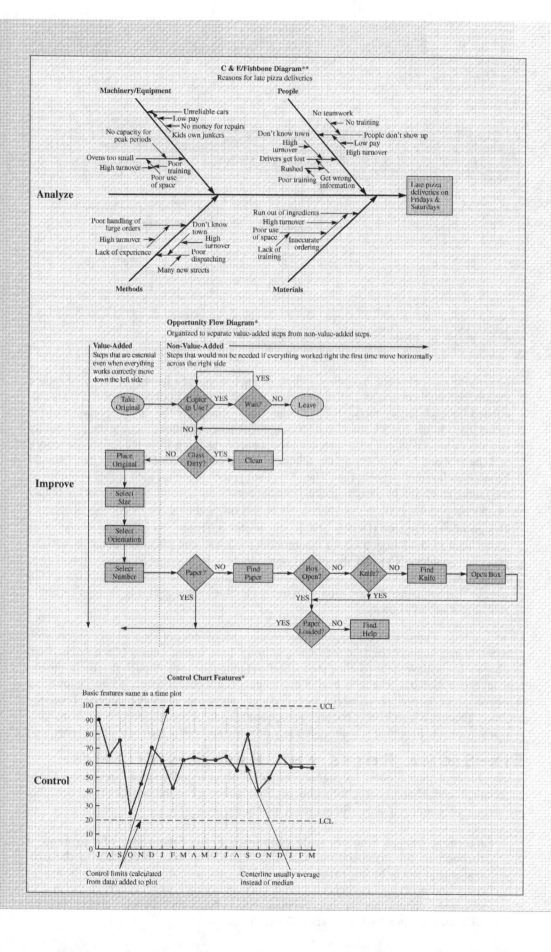

Analyze

C & E/Fishbone Diagram**
Reasons for late pizza deliveries

Machinery/Equipment

People

Methods

Materials

Improve

Opportunity Flow Diagram*
Organized to separate value-added steps from non-value-added steps.

Value-Added
Steps that are essential even when everything works correctly move down the left side

Non-Value-Added
Steps that would not be needed if everything worked right the first time move horizontally across the right side

Control

Control Chart Features*

Basic features same as a time plot

exhibit 9.6   FMEA Form

**FMEA Analysis**															

FMEA Analysis

Project: _____   Date: _____ (original)

Team: _____   _____ (revised)

Item or Process Step	Potential Failure Mode	Potential Effects of Failure	Severity	Potential Cause(s)	Occurrence	Current Controls	Detection	RPN	Recommended Action	Responsibility and Target Date	"After" → Action Taken	Severity	Occurrence	Detection	RPN
Total Risk Priority Number:									"After" Risk Priority Number:						

SOURCE: RATH & STRONG, *RATH & STRONG'S SIX SIGMA POCKET GUIDE*. 2001, P. 31.

identifying each element, assembly, or part of the process and listing the potential failure modes, potential causes, and effects of each failure. A risk priority number (RPN) is calculated for each failure mode. It is an index used to measure the rank importance of the items listed in the FMEA chart. See Exhibit 9.6. These conditions include the probability that the failure takes place (occurrence), the damage resulting from the failure (severity), and the probability of detecting the failure in-house (detection). High RPN items should be targeted for improvement first. The FMEA suggests a recommended action to eliminate the failure condition by assigning a responsible person or department to resolve the failure by redesigning the system, design, or process and recalculating the RPN.

Design of experiments (DOE).   DOE, sometimes referred to as *multivariate testing,* is a statistical methodology used for determining the cause-and-effect relationship between process variables (X's) and the output variable (Y). In contrast to standard statistical tests, which require changing each individual variable to determine the most influential one, DOE permits experimentation with many variables simultaneously through carefully selecting a subset of them.

Lean Six Sigma   Lean Six Sigma combines the implementation and quality control tools of Six Sigma with materials management concepts of *lean manufacturing*. Lean manufacturing (discussed in detail in Chapter 13) achieves high-volume production and minimal waste through the use of just-in-time inventory methods. The term *lean* in this context is a focus on reducing cost by lowering raw material, work-in-process, and finished goods inventory to an absolute minimum. Lowering inventory requires a high level of quality as processes need to be predictable since extra inventory is not available. Reducing variability is a key driver in successful lean Six-Sigma programs.

SIX-SIGMA ROLES AND RESPONSIBILITIES

Successful implementation of Six Sigma is based on using sound personnel practices as well as technical methodologies. The following is a brief summary of the personnel practices that are commonly employed in Six-Sigma implementation.

1. *Executive leaders,* **who are truly committed to Six Sigma and who promote it throughout the organization, and** *champions,* **who take ownership of the processes that are to be improved.**   Champions are drawn from the ranks of the executives, and managers are expected to identify appropriate metrics early in the project and make certain that the improvement efforts focus on business results. (See the Breakthrough box "What Makes a Good Champion?")

BREAKTHROUGH

WHAT MAKES A GOOD CHAMPION?

At a manufacturing company implementing Six Sigma, a designated champion regularly met with his black belts. At one report-out meeting, a black belt informed him that she needed to purchase and install a table for sorting defects off-line. It would cost about $17,000, but it would provide an alternative to shutting down the entire line, which would cost far more. The controller told her to go through the normal requisition process and she'd have her table in about four months. That delay would have killed the project

right then and there: to submit the project to "business as usual" would have shown little real commitment to supporting Six Sigma. So the champion asked for the data that backed up her request, analyzed it, agreed with it, and then got immediate executive sign-off on securing a table the following week.

This is the stuff of a good champion: removing barriers and sending a clear signal that he and upper management are aligned and committed to Six Sigma. The champion does whatever it takes to support the black belts.

SOURCE: GREG BRUE, *SIX SIGMA FOR MANAGERS* (NEW YORK: McGRAW-HILL, 2002), P. 84.

2. **Corporatewide training in Six-Sigma concepts and tools.** GE spent over a billion dollars training its professional workforce in the concepts. Now, virtually every professional in the organization is qualified in Six-Sigma techniques. To convey the need to vigorously attack problems, professionals are given martial arts titles reflecting their skills and roles: black belts, who coach or actually lead a Six-Sigma improvement team; master black belts, who receive in-depth training on statistical tools and process improvement (they perform many of the same functions as black belts but for a larger number of teams); and green belts, who are employees who have received enough Six-Sigma training to participate in a team or, in some companies, to work individually on a small-scale project directly related to their own job. Different companies use these "belts" in different combinations with sponsors and champions to guide teams.

   Black belts
   Master black belts

   Green belts

3. **Setting of stretch objectives for improvement.**
4. **Continuous reinforcement and rewards.** At GE, before any savings from a project are declared, the black belt in charge must provide proof that the problems are fixed permanently.

THE SHINGO SYSTEM: FAIL-SAFE DESIGN

The Shingo system developed in parallel and in many ways in conflict with the statistically based approach to quality control. This system—or, to be more precise, philosophy of production management—is named after the codeveloper of the Toyota just-in-time system, Shigeo Shingo. Two aspects of the Shingo system in particular have received great attention. One is how to accomplish drastic cuts in equipment setup times by *single-minute exchange of die* (SMED) procedures. The other, the focus of this section, is the use of source inspection and the poka-yoke system to achieve zero defects.

Shingo has argued that SQC methods do not prevent defects. Although they provide information to tell us probabilistically when a defect will occur, they are after the fact. The way to prevent defects from coming out at the end of a process is to introduce controls within the process. Central to Shingo's approach is the difference between errors and defects. Defects arise because people make errors. Even though errors are inevitable, defects can be prevented if feedback leading to corrective action takes place immediately after the errors are made. Such feedback and action require inspection, which should be done on 100 percent of the items produced. This inspection can be one of three types: successive check, self-check, and source inspection. *Successive check* inspection is performed by the next person in the process or by an objective evaluator such as a group leader. Information on defects is immediate feedback for the worker who produced the

exhibit 9.7   Poka-Yoke Example (Placing labels on parts coming down a conveyor)

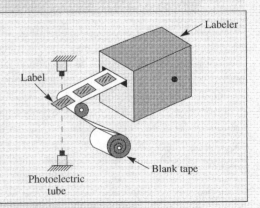

Before Improvement

The operation depended on the worker's vigilance.

After Improvement

Device to ensure attachment of labels

The tape fed out by the labeler turns sharply so that the labels detach and project out from the tape. This is detected by a photoelectric tube and, if the label is not removed and applied to the product within the tact time of 20 seconds, a buzzer sounds and the conveyor stops.

Effect: Label application failures were eliminated.
Cost: ¥15,000 ($145)

---

product, who then makes the repair. *Self-check* is done by the individual worker and is appropriate by itself on all but items that require sensory judgment (such as existence or severity of scratches, or correct matching of shades of paint). These require successive checks. *Source inspection* is also performed by the individual worker, except instead of checking for defects, the worker checks for the errors that will cause defects. This prevents the defects from ever occurring and, hence, requiring rework. All three types of inspection rely on controls consisting of fail-safe procedures or devices (called poka-yoke). Poka-yoke includes such things as checklists or special tooling that (1) prevents the worker from making an error that leads to a defect before starting a process or (2) gives rapid feedback of abnormalities in the process to the worker in time to correct them.

Fail-safe procedures
Poka-yoke

There are a wide variety of poka-yokes, ranging from kitting parts from a bin (to ensure that the right number of parts are used in assembly) to sophisticated detection and electronic signaling devices. An example taken from the writings of Shingo is shown in Exhibit 9.7.

There is a good deal more to say about the work of Shingo. Blasting industry's preoccupation with control charts, Shingo states they are nothing but a mirror reflecting current conditions. When a chemical plant QC manager proudly stated that it had 200 charts in a plant of 150 people, Shingo asked him if "they had a control chart for control charts."[4]

ISO 9000 AND ISO 14000

Global

ISO 9000

ISO 9000 and ISO 14000 are international standards for quality management and assurance. The standards are designed to help companies document that they are maintaining an efficient quality system. The standards were originally published in 1987 by the International Organization for Standardization (ISO), a specialized international agency recognized by affiliates in more than 160 countries. ISO 9000 has become an international reference for quality management requirements in business-to-business dealing, and ISO 14000 is primarily concerned with environmental management.

The idea behind the standards is that defects can be prevented through the planning and application of *best practices* at every stage of business—from design through manufacturing and then installation and servicing. These standards focus on identifying criteria by which any organization, regardless of whether it is manufacturing or service oriented, can ensure that product leaving its facility meets the requirements of its customers. These standards ask a company first to document and implement its systems for quality management and then to verify, by means of an audit conducted by an independent accredited third party, the compliance of those systems with the requirements of the standards.

The ISO 9000 standards are based on eight quality management principles that are defined in the ISO 9000:2000 document. These principles focus on business processes related to the following areas in the firm: (1) customer focus, (2) leadership, (3) involvement of people, (4) process approach, (5) system approach to management, (6) continual improvement, (7) factual approach to decision making, and (8) mutually beneficial supplier relationships. The ISO documents provide detailed requirements for meeting the standards and describe standard tools that are used for improving quality in the firm. These documents are intended to be generic and applicable to any organization producing products or services.

The ISO 14000 family of standards on environmental management addresses the need to be environmentally responsible. The standards define a three-pronged approach for dealing with environmental challenges. The first is the definition of more than 350 international standards for monitoring the quality of air, water, and soil. For many countries, these standards serve as the technical basis for environmental regulation. The second part of ISO 14000 is a strategic approach defining the requirements of an environmental management system that can be implemented using the monitoring tools. Finally, the environmental standard encourages the inclusion of environment aspects in product design and encourages the development of profitable environment-friendly products and services.

In addition to the generic ISO 9000 and ISO 14000 standards, many other specific standards have been defined. The following are some examples:

- QS-9000 is a quality management system developed by DaimlerChrysler, Ford, and General Motors for suppliers of production parts, materials, and services to the automotive industry.
- ISO/TS 16949, developed by the International Automotive Task Force, aligns existing American, German, French, and Italian automotive quality standards within the global automotive industry.
- ISO 14001 environmental standards are applied by automobile suppliers as a requirement from Ford and General Motors.
- ANSI/ASQ Z1.4-2003 provides methods for collecting, analyzing, and interpreting data for inspection by attributes, while Z1.9-2003 relates to inspection by variables.
- TL 9000 defines the telecommunications quality system requirements for the design, development, production, delivery, installation, and maintenance of products and services in the telecommunications industry.

The ISO standards provide accepted global guidelines for quality. Although certification is not required, many companies have found it is essential to be competitive in the global markets. Consider the situation where you need to purchase parts for your firm and several suppliers offer similar parts at similar prices. Assume that one of these firms has been ISO 9000–certified and the others have not. From whom would you purchase? There is no doubt that the ISO 9000–certified company would have the inside track in your decision making. Why? Because ISO 9000 specifies the way the supplier firm operates as well as its quality standards, delivery times, service levels, and so on.

Supply Chain

There are three forms of certification:

1. First party: A firm audits itself against ISO 9000 standards.
2. Second party: A customer audits its supplier.
3. Third party: A "qualified" national or international standards or certifying agency serves as an auditor.

The best certification of a firm is through a third party. Once passed by the third-party audit, a firm is certified and may be registered and recorded as having achieved ISO 9000 status and it becomes a part of a registry of certified companies. This third-party certification also has legal advantages in the European Community. For example, a manufacturer is liable for injury to a user of the product.

The firm, however, can free itself from any liability by showing that it has used the appropriate standards in its production process and carefully selected its suppliers as part of its purchasing requirements. For this reason, there is strong motivation to choose ISO 9000–certified suppliers.

EXTERNAL BENCHMARKING FOR QUALITY IMPROVEMENT

External benchmarking

Global

The quality improvement approaches described so far are more or less inward looking. They seek to make improvements by analyzing in detail the current practices of the company itself. External benchmarking, however, goes outside the organization to examine what industry competitors and excellent performers outside of the industry are doing. Benchmarking typically involves the following steps:

Identify processes needing improvement.   Identify a firm that is the world leader in performing the process. For many processes, this may be a company that is not in the same industry. Examples would be Procter & Gamble using L.L Bean as the benchmark in evaluating its order entry system, or ICL (a large British computer maker) benchmarking Marks and Spencer (a large U.K. clothing retailer) to improve its distribution system. A McKinsey study cited a firm that measured pit stops on a motor racing circuit as a benchmark for worker changes on its assembly line.[5] *Contact the managers of that company and make a personal visit to interview managers and workers.* Many companies select a team of workers from that process as part of the team of visitors.

Analyze data.   This entails looking at gaps between what your company is doing and what the benchmarking company is doing. There are two aspects of the study: one is comparing the actual processes; the other is comparing the performance of these processes according to a set of measures. The processes are often described using flowcharts and subjective evaluations of how workers relate to the process. In some cases, companies permit videotaping, although there is a tendency now for benchmarked companies to keep things under wraps for fear of giving away process secrets.

SUMMARY

How to achieve TQM is no secret any more. The challenge is to make certain that a quality program really does have a customer focus and is sufficiently agile to be able to make improvements quickly without losing sight of the real-time needs of the business. The quality system must be analyzed for its own quality. There is also a need for sustaining a quality culture over the long haul. Some companies (which will remain nameless) that gained a great reputation for quality in the 1980s and 90s simply ran out of gas in their quality efforts—their managers just couldn't sustain the level of enthusiasm necessary for quality to remain a top priority goal. As Tom Peters said, "Most Quality programs fail for one of two reasons: they have system without passion, or passion without system."[6]

KEY TERMS

Total quality management (TQM) Managing the entire organization so that it excels on all dimensions of products and services that are important to the customer.

Malcolm Baldrige National Quality Award An award established by the U.S. Department of Commerce and given annually to companies that excel in quality.

Design quality The inherent value of the product in the marketplace.

Conformance quality The degree to which the product or service design specifications are met.

Quality at the source The person who does the work is responsible for ensuring that specifications are met.

Dimensions of quality Criteria by which quality is measured.

Cost of quality Expenditures related to achieving product or service quality such as the costs of prevention, appraisal, internal failure, and external failure.

Six Sigma A statistical term to describe the quality goal of no more than four defects out of every million units. Also refers to a quality improvement philosophy and program.

DPMO (defects per million opportunities) A metric used to describe the variability of a process.

DMAIC An acronym for the **D**efine, **M**easure, **A**nalyze, **I**mprove, and **C**ontrol improvement methodology followed by companies engaging in Six-Sigma programs.

PDCA cycle Also called the "Deming cycle or wheel"; refers to the plan–do–check–act cycle of continuous improvement.

Continuous improvement The philosophy of continually seeking improvements in processes through the use of team efforts.

Kaizen Japanese term for continuous improvement.

Lean Six Sigma Combines the implementation and quality control tools of Six Sigma with the materials management concept of lean manufacturing with a focus on reducing cost by lowering inventory to an absolute minimum.

Black belts, master black belts, green belts Terms used to describe different levels of personal skills and responsibilities in Six-Sigma programs.

Fail-safe or poka-yoke procedures Simple practices that prevent errors or provide feedback in time for the worker to correct errors.

ISO 9000 Formal standards used for quality certification, developed by the International Organization for Standardization.

External benchmarking Looking outside the company to examine what excellent performers inside and outside the company's industry are doing in the way of quality.

REVIEW AND DISCUSSION QUESTIONS

1   Is the goal of Six Sigma realistic for services such as Blockbuster Video stores?
2   "If line employees are required to work on quality improvement activities, their productivity will suffer." Discuss.
3   "You don't inspect quality into a product; you have to build it in." Discuss the implications of this statement.
4   "Before you build quality in, you must think it in." How do the implications of this statement differ from those in question 3?
5   Business writer Tom Peters has suggested that in making process changes, we should "Try it, test it, and get on with it." How does this square with the DMAIC/continuous improvement philosophy?
6   Shingo told a story of a poka-yoke he developed to make sure that the operators avoided the mistake of putting fewer than the required four springs in a push-button device. The existing method involved assemblers taking individual springs from a box containing several hundred and then placing two of them behind an ON button and two more behind an OFF button. What was the poka-yoke Shingo created?
7   A typical word processing package is loaded with poka-yokes. List three. Are there any others you wish the packages had?

PROBLEMS

1   A manager states that his process is really working well. Out of 1,500 parts, 1,477 were produced free of a particular defect and passed inspection. Based upon Six-Sigma theory, how would you rate this performance, other things being equal?
2   Professor Chase is frustrated by his inability to make a good cup of coffee in the morning. Show how you would use a fishbone diagram to analyze the process he uses to make a cup of his evil brew.
3   Use the benchmarking process and as many DMAIC/CI analytical tools as you can to show how you can improve your performance in your weakest course in school.
4   Prepare a SIPOC flowchart (Exhibit 9.5) of the major steps in the process of boarding a commercial flight. Start the process with the passenger arriving curbside at your local airport.
5   Prepare an opportunity flow diagram for the same process of boarding a commercial flight.
6   The following table lists all costs of quality incurred by Sam's Surf Shop last year. What was Sam's appraisal cost for quality last year?

Annual inspection costs	$ 155,000
Annual cost of scrap materials	$ 286,000
Annual rework cost	$ 34,679
Annual cost of quality training	$ 456,000
Annual warranty cost	$1,546,000
Annual testing cost	$ 543,000

7 Below is a table of data collected over a six-month period in a local grocery store. Construct a Pareto analysis of the data and determine the percentage of total complaints represented by the two most common categories.

All Other	71
Checker	59
General	58
Service Level	55
Policy/Procedures	40
Price Marking	45
Product Quality	87
Product Request	105
Checkout Queue	33
Stock Condition	170

8 A common problem that many drivers encounter is a car that will not start. Create a fishbone diagram to assist in the diagnosis of the potential causes of this problem.

INTERNET ENRICHMENT EXERCISES

1 Visit the Baldrige Award Web site and see who won this year. What quality ideas did the winner demonstrate? What did the winner do that was particularly creative?
2 Visit the Six-Sigma Web site to see how companies are applying the concept.

CASE: HANK KOLB, DIRECTOR OF QUALITY ASSURANCE

Hank Kolb was whistling as he walked toward his office, still feeling a bit like a stranger since he had been hired four weeks before as director of quality assurance. All that week he had been away from the plant at a seminar given for quality managers of manufacturing plants by the corporate training department. He was now looking forward to digging into the quality problems at this industrial products plant employing 1,200 people.

Kolb poked his head into Mark Hamler's office, his immediate subordinate as the quality control manager, and asked him how things had gone during the past week. Hamler's muted smile and an "Oh, fine," stopped Kolb in his tracks. He didn't know Hamler very well and was unsure about pursuing this reply any further. Kolb was still uncertain of how to start building a relationship with him since Hamler had been passed over for the promotion to Kolb's job; Hamler's evaluation form had stated "superb technical knowledge; managerial skills lacking." Kolb decided to inquire a little further and asked Hamler what had happened; he replied, "Oh, just another typical quality snafu. We had a little problem on the Greasex line last week [a specialized degreasing solvent packed in a spray can for the high-technology sector]. A little high pressure was found in some cans on the second shift, but a supervisor vented them so that we could ship them out. We met our delivery schedule!" Because Kolb was still relatively unfamiliar with the plant and its products, he asked Hamler to elaborate; painfully, Hamler continued:

We've been having some trouble with the new filling equipment and some of the cans were pressurized beyond the upper specification limit.

The production rate is still 50 percent of standard, about 14 cases per shift, and we caught it halfway into the shift. Mac Evans [the inspector for that line] picked it up, tagged the cases "hold," and went on about his duties.

When he returned at the end of the shift to write up the rejects, Wayne Simmons, first-line supervisor, was by a pallet of finished goods finishing sealing up a carton of the rejected Greasex; the reject "hold" tags had been removed. He told Mac that he had heard about the high pressure from another inspector at coffee break, had come back, taken off the tags, individually turned the cans upside down and vented every one of them in the eight rejected cartons. He told Mac that production planning was really pushing for the stuff and they couldn't delay by having it sent through the rework area. He told Mac that he would get on the operator to run the equipment right next time. Mac didn't write it up but came in about three days ago to tell me about it. Oh, it happens every once in a while and I told him to make sure to check with maintenance to make sure the filling machine was adjusted; and I saw Wayne in the hall and told him that he ought to send the stuff through rework next time.

Kolb was a bit dumbfounded at this and didn't say much—he didn't know if this was a big deal or not. When he got to his office, he thought again what Morganthal, general manager, had said when he had hired him. He warned Kolb about the "lack of quality attitude" in the plant and said that Kolb "should try and do something about this." Morganthal further emphasized the quality problems in the plant: "We have to improve our quality; it's costing us a lot of money, I'm sure of it, but I can't prove it! Hank, you have my full support in this matter; you're in charge of these quality problems. This downward quality–productivity–turnover spiral has to end!"

The incident had happened a week before; the goods were probably out in the customers' hands by now, and everyone had forgotten about it (or wanted to). There seemed to be more pressing problems than this for Kolb to spend his time on, but this continued to nag him. He felt that the quality department was being treated as a joke, and he also felt that this was a personal slap from manufacturing. He didn't want to start a war with the production people, but what could he do? Kolb was troubled enough to cancel his appointments and spend the morning talking to a few people. After a long and very tactful morning, he learned the following information:

1 **From personnel.** The operator for the filling equipment had just been transferred from shipping two weeks ago. He had no formal training in this job but was being trained by Wayne, on the job, to run the equipment. When Mac had tested the high-pressure cans, the operator was nowhere to be found and had only learned of the rejected material from Wayne after the shift was over.

2 **From plant maintenance.** This particular piece of automated filling equipment had been purchased two years ago for use on another product. It had been switched to the Greasex line six months ago and maintenance completed 12 work orders during the last month for repairs or adjustments on it. The equipment had been adapted by plant maintenance for handling the lower viscosity of Greasex, which it had not originally been designed for. This included designing a special filling head. There was no scheduled preventive maintenance for this equipment and the parts for the sensitive filling head, replaced three times in the last six months, had to be made at a nearby machine shop. Nonstandard downtime was 15 percent of actual running time.

3 **From purchasing.** The plastic nozzle heads for the Greasex can, designed by a vendor for this new product on a rush order, were often found to have slight burrs on the inside rim, and this caused some trouble in fitting the top to the can. An increase in application pressure at the filling head by maintenance adjustment had solved the burr application problem or had at least forced the nozzle heads on despite burrs. Purchasing agents said that they were going to talk to the sales representative of the nozzle head supplier about this the next time he came in.

4 **From product design and packaging.** The can, designed especially for Greasex, had been contoured to allow better gripping by the user. This change, instigated by marketing research, set Greasex apart from the appearance of its competitors and was seen as significant by the designers. There had been no test of the effects of the contoured can on filling speed or filling hydrodynamics from a high-pressured filling head. Kolb had a hunch that the new design was acting as a venturi (carrier creating suction) when being filled, but the packaging designer thought that was unlikely.

5 **From the manufacturing manager.** He had heard about the problem; in fact, Simmons had made a joke about it, bragging about how he beat his production quota to the other foremen and shift supervisors. The manufacturing manager thought Simmons was one of the "best foremen we have . . . he always got his production out." His promotion papers were actually on the manufacturing manager's desk when Kolb dropped by. Simmons was being strongly considered for promotion to shift supervisor. The manufacturing manager, under pressure from Morganthal for cost improvements and reduced delivery times, sympathized with Kolb but said that the rework area would have vented with their pressure gauges what Wayne had done by hand. "But I'll speak with Wayne about the incident," he said.

6 **From marketing.** The introduction of Greasex had been rushed to market to beat competitors, and a major promotional advertising campaign was under way to increase consumer awareness. A deluge of orders was swamping the order-taking department and putting Greasex high on the back-order list. Production had to turn the stuff out; even being a little off spec was tolerable because "it would be better to have it on the shelf than not there at all. Who cares if the label is a little crooked or the stuff comes out with a little too much pressure? We need market share now in that high-tech segment."

What bothered Kolb most was the safety issue of the high pressure in the cans. He had no way of knowing how much of a hazard the high pressure was or if Simmons had vented them enough to effectively reduce the hazard. The data from the can manufacturer, which Hamler had showed him, indicated that the high pressure found by the inspector was not in the danger area. But, again, the inspector had used only a sample testing procedure to reject the eight cases. Even if he could morally accept that there was no product safety hazard, could Kolb make sure that this would never happen again?

Skipping lunch, Kolb sat in his office and thought about the morning's events. The past week's seminar had talked about the role of quality, productivity and quality, creating a new attitude, and the quality challenge; but where had they told him what to do when this happened? He had left a very good job to come here because he thought the company was serious about the importance of quality, and he wanted a challenge. Kolb had demanded and received a salary equal to the manufacturing, marketing, and R&D directors, and he was one of the direct reports to the general manager. Yet he still didn't know exactly what he should or shouldn't do, or even what he could or couldn't do under these circumstances.

QUESTIONS

1 What are the causes of the quality problems on the Greasex line? Display your answer on a fishbone diagram.

2 What general steps should Hank follow in setting up a continuous improvement program for the company? What problems will he have to overcome to make it work?

SOURCE: COPYRIGHT 1981 BY PRESIDENT AND FELLOWS OF HARVARD COLLEGE, HARVARD BUSINESS SCHOOL. CASE 681.083. THIS CASE WAS PREPARED BY FRANK S. LEONARD AS THE BASIS FOR CLASS DISCUSSION RATHER THAN TO ILLUSTRATE EITHER EFFECTIVE OR INEFFECTIVE HANDLING OF AN ADMINISTRATIVE SITUATION. REPRINTED BY PERMISSION OF THE HARVARD BUSINESS SCHOOL.

CASE: APPRECIATIVE INQUIRY—A DIFFERENT KIND OF FISHBONE

The standard cause-and-effect, or fishbone, diagram approach focuses on identifying the root cause of a problem. Finding this cause then becomes an input into developing a solution. On the other hand, improvements aren't always about finding out what went wrong; rather, they may be about identifying what was done right. This is what the AI approach is designed to do. The way it works is

exhibit 9.8   Identifying Excellence Drivers (the Hows of Excellence)

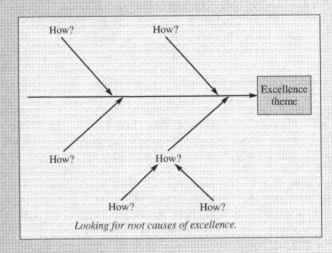

Looking for root causes of excellence.

exhibit 9.9   Root Causes of Excellence

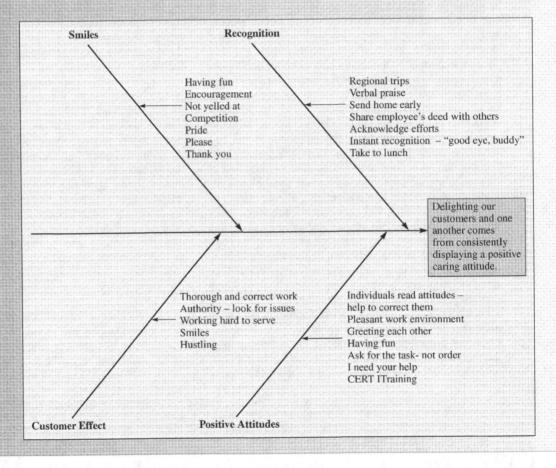

it solicits success stories from employees about how, for example, they delighted their customers. These are then put on the head of the fishbone diagram as the theme for study. (See Exhibit 9.8.) The approach then gathers the causes of success, which are entered on the fishbone as the "hows" of success. One of the particular benefits of this is that it builds on the unique capabilities of the company rather than copying approaches taken by others.

This approach has been used successfully by Direct Discount Tires executive Steve Fornier Jr., who says, "AI is a simple tool that we can use to find out what and why things are done the way they are done. It gives our employees a chance to think for themselves, find solutions, and execute at higher levels rather than being recipients of a 'do this' 'do that' kind of speech. Because they are figuring out answers for themselves, it drives the entrepreneurial spirit, promotes innovation, and eventually creates new leaders and new best practices from the front line that will continue to keep us 'The Best.' Without this new innovation, we risk becoming stagnated." (The fishbone diagram for Direct Discount Tires is shown in Exhibit 9.9.)

QUESTIONS

1   From a worker's perspective, what do you see as the major benefit of appreciative inquiry compared to standard cause-and-effect analysis?
2   As an interesting exercise, think about your favorite instructor. Develop an appreciative inquiry fishbone diagram that identifies why you feel this instructor is so outstanding.

SOURCE: WILLIAM YOUNGDAHL AND CAREN SIEHL, LECTURE NOTES, AMERICAN GRADUATE SCHOOL OF INTERNATIONAL MANAGEMENT, 2006.

SUPER QUIZ

1   This refers to the inherent value of the product in the marketplace and is a strategic decision for the firm.
2   Relates to how well a product or services meets design specifications.
3   Relates to how the customer views quality dimensions of a product or service.

4   The series of international quality standards.
5   What is the enemy of good quality?
6   A Six-Sigma process that is running at the center of its control limits would expect this defect rate.
7   The standard quality improvement methodology developed by General Electric.

1. Design quality 2. Conformance quality 3. Fitness for use 4. ISO 9000 5. Variation 6. 2 parts per billion units 7. DMAIC cycle

SELECTED BIBLIOGRAPHY

Bemowski, K., and B. Stratton, eds. *101 Good Ideas: How to Improve Just About Any Process.* Washington, DC: American Society for Quality, 1999.

Blakeslee, J. A., Jr. "Implementing the Six Sigma Solution." *Quality Progress,* July 1999, pp. 77–85.

Brue, G. *Six Sigma for Managers.* New York: McGraw-Hill, 2002.

Chowdhury, S. *Design for Six Sigma.* Chicago: Dearborn Trade Publishing, 2002.

Chowdhury, S., and K. Zimmer. *QS-9000 Pioneers—Registered Companies Share Their Strategies for Success.* Burr Ridge, IL: Richard D. Irwin, 1996.

Crosby, P. B. *Quality Is Free.* New York: McGraw-Hill, 1979 (reissue 1992).

———. *Quality Is Still Free.* New York: McGraw-Hill, 1996.

Deming, W. E. *Quality, Productivity and Competitive Position.* Cambridge, MA: MIT Center for Advanced Engineering Study, 1982.

Eckes, G. *Six Sigma Revolution: How General Electric and Others Turned Process into Profits.* New York: John Wiley & Sons, 2001.

Evans, J. R., and W. M. Lindsay. *The Management and Control of Quality.* Cincinnati: South-Western/Thomson Learning, 2002.

Feigenbaum, A. V. *Total Quality Control.* New York: McGraw-Hill, 1991.

Gitlow, H.; A. Oppenheim; and R. Oppenheim. *Quality Management: Tools and Methods for Improvement.* 2nd ed. New York: Irwin/McGraw-Hill, 1995.

Juran, J. M. *Quality Control Handbook.* 3rd ed. New York: McGraw-Hill, 1979.

Juran, J. M., and F. M. Gryna. *Quality Planning and Analysis.* 2nd ed. New York: McGraw-Hill, 1980.

Pande, P. S.; R. P. Neuman; and R. R. Cavanagh. *The Six Sigma Way.* New York: McGraw-Hill, 2000.

———. *The Six Sigma Way Team Fieldbook.* New York: McGraw-Hill, 2002.

Robinson, A. *Modern Approaches to Manufacturing Improvement: The Shingo System.* Cambridge, MA: Productivity Press, 1990.

Shingo, S. *Zero Quality Control: Source Inspection and the Poka-Yoke System.* Stamford, CT: Productivity Press, 1986.

Taormina, T. *Virtual Leadership and the ISO 9000 Imperative.* Englewood Cliffs, NJ: Prentice Hall, 1996.

Welch, J. *Jack: Straight from the Gut.* New York: Warner Business Books, 2001.

FOOTNOTES

1   D. A. Garvin, *Managing Quality* (New York: Free Press, 1988).
2   P. B. Crosby, *Quality Is Free* (New York: New American Library, 1979), p. 15.
3   S. Walleck, D. O'Halloran, and C. Leader, "Benchmarking World-Class Performance," *McKinsey Quarterly,* no. 1 (1991), p. 7.
4   A. Robinson, *Modern Approaches to Manufacturing Improvement: The Shingo System* (Cambridge, MA: Productivity Press, 1990), p. 234.
5   Walleck, O'Halloran, and Leader, "Benchmarking World-Class Performance," p. 7.
6   T. Peters, *Thriving on Chaos* (New York: Knopf, 1987), p. 74.

chapter 9A

PROCESS CAPABILITY AND SPC

BRIEFING OUTLINE

After reading this chapter you will:

1. Explain what statistical quality control is.
2. Calculate the capability of a process.
3. Understand how processes are monitored with control charts.
4. Recognize acceptance sampling concepts.

This chapter on statistical process control (SPC) covers the quantitative aspects of quality management. In general, SPC is a number of different techniques designed to evaluate quality from a conformance view. That is, how well are we doing at meeting the specifications that have been set during the design of the parts or services that we are providing? Managing quality performance using SPC techniques usually involves periodic sampling of a process and analysis of these data using statistically derived performance criteria.

As you will see, SPC can be applied to both manufacturing and service processes. Here are some examples of the types of situations where SPC can be applied:

- How many paint defects are there in the finish of a car? Have we improved our painting process by installing a new sprayer?
- How long does it take to execute market orders in our Web-based trading system? Has the installation of a new server improved the service? Does the performance of the system vary over the trading day?
- How well are we able to maintain the dimensional tolerance on our three-inch ball bearing assembly? Given the variability of our process for making this ball bearing, how many defects would we expect to produce per million bearings that we make?
- How long do customers wait to be served from our drive-through window during the busy lunch period?

Service

Processes that provide goods and services usually exhibit some variation in their output. This variation can be caused by many factors, some that we can control and others that are inherent in the process. Variation caused by factors that can be clearly identified and possibly even managed is called assignable variation. For example, variation caused by workers not being equally trained or by improper machine adjustment is assignable variation. Variation that is inherent in the process is called common variation. Common variation is often referred to as *random variation* and may be the result of the type of equipment used to complete a process, for example.

Assignable variation

Common variation

As the title of this chapter implies, this material requires an understanding of very basic statistics. Recall from your study of statistics involving numbers that are normally distributed the definition of the mean and standard deviation. The mean ($\overline{X}$) is just the average value of a set of numbers. Mathematically this is

$$\overline{X} = \sum_{i=1}^{N} x_i / N \qquad \text{[9A.1]}$$

where:

x_i = Observed value

N = Total number of observed values

The standard deviation is

$$\sigma = \sqrt{\frac{\sum_{i=1}^{N}(x_i - \overline{X})^2}{N}}$$ [9A.2]

In monitoring a process using SPC, samples of the process output would be taken and sample statistics calculated. The distribution associated with the samples should exhibit the same kind of variability as the actual distribution of the process, although the actual variance of the sampling distribution would be less. This is good because it allows the quick detection of changes in the actual distribution of the process. The purpose of sampling is to find when the process has changed in some nonrandom way, so that the reason for the change can be quickly determined.

In SPC terminology, *sigma* is often used to refer to the sample standard deviation. As you will see in the examples, sigma is calculated in a few different ways, depending on the underlying theoretical distribution (i.e., a normal distribution or a Poisson distribution).

VARIATION AROUND US

It is generally accepted that as variation is reduced, quality is improved. Sometimes that knowledge is intuitive. If a train is always on time, schedules can be planned more precisely. If clothing sizes are consistent, time can be saved by ordering from a catalog. But rarely are such things thought about in terms of the value of low variability. With engineers, the knowledge is better defined. Pistons must fit cylinders, doors must fit openings, electrical components must be compatible, and boxes of cereal must have the right amount of raisins—otherwise quality will be unacceptable and customers will be dissatisfied.

However, engineers also know that it is impossible to have zero variability. For this reason, designers establish specifications that define not only the target value of something but also acceptable limits about the target. For example, if the aim value of a dimension is 10 inches, the design specifications might then be 10.00 inches ± 0.02 inch. This would tell the manufacturing department that, while it should aim for exactly 10 inches, anything between 9.98 and 10.02 inches is OK. These design limits are often referred to as the upper and lower specification limits or the upper and lower tolerance limits.

Upper and lower specification or tolerance limits

A traditional way of interpreting such a specification is that any part that falls within the allowed range is equally good, whereas any part falling outside the range is totally bad. This is illustrated in Exhibit 9A.1A. (Note that the cost is zero over the entire specification range, and then there is a quantum leap in cost once the limit is violated.)

Genichi Taguchi, a noted quality expert from Japan, has pointed out that the traditional view illustrated in Exhibit 9A.1A is nonsense for two reasons:

1. From the customer's view, there is often practically no difference between a product just inside specifications and a product just outside. Conversely, there is a far greater difference in the quality of a product that is the target and the quality of one that is near a limit.
2. As customers get more demanding, there is pressure to reduce variability. However, Exhibit 9A.1A does not reflect this logic.

Taguchi suggests that a more correct picture of the loss is shown in Exhibit 9A.1B. Notice that, in this graph, the cost is represented by a smooth curve. There are dozens of illustrations of this notion: the meshing of gears in a transmission, the speed of photographic film, the temperature in a workplace or department store. In nearly anything that can be measured, the customer sees not a sharp line, but a gradation of acceptability away from the "Aim" specification. Customers see the loss function as Exhibit 9A.1B rather than Exhibit 9A.1A.

Of course, if products are consistently scrapped when they are outside specifications, the loss curve flattens out in most cases at a value equivalent to scrap cost in the ranges outside

Views of the Cost of Variability

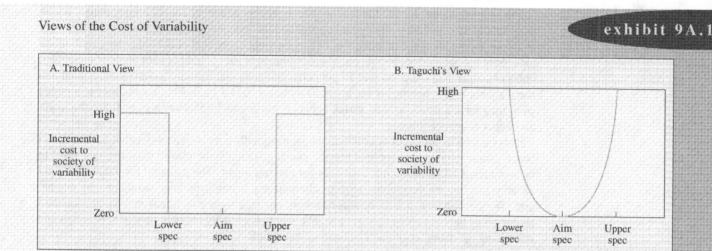

specifications. This is because such products, theoretically at least, will never be sold so there is no external cost to society. However, in many practical situations, either the process is capable of producing a very high percentage of product within specifications and 100 percent checking is not done, or if the process is not capable of producing within specifications, 100 percent checking is done and out-of-spec products can be reworked to bring them within specs. In any of these situations, the parabolic loss function is usually a reasonable assumption.

In the next two sections, we discuss two concepts—process capability and control charts. Process capability relates to how good the process is at making parts when it is running properly. Control charts are used to continuously check that the process is running properly.

PROCESS CAPABILITY

Taguchi argues that being within tolerance is not a yes/no decision, but rather a continuous function. The Motorola quality experts, on the other hand, argue that the process used to produce a good or deliver a service should be so good that the probability of generating a defect should be very, very low. Motorola made process capability and product design famous by adopting Six-Sigma limits. When we design a part, we specify that certain dimensions should be within the upper and lower specification limits.

As a simple example, assume that we are designing a bearing for a rotating shaft—say an axle for the wheel of a car. Both the bearing and the axle are subject to many variables—for example, the width of the bearing, the size of the rollers, the size of the axle, the length of the axle, how it is supported, and so on. The designer specifies tolerances for each of these variables to ensure that the parts will fit properly. Suppose that initially a design is selected and the diameter of the bearing is set at 1.250 inches ± 0.005 inch. This means that acceptable parts may have a diameter that varies between 1.245 and 1.255 inches (which are the lower and upper tolerance limits).

Next, consider the process in which the bearing will be made. Consider that we can select many different processes for making the bearing. Usually there are trade-offs that need to be considered when designing a process for making a part. The process, for example, might be very fast but not very consistent, or alternatively it might be very slow but very consistent. The consistency of a process for making our bearing can be measured by the standard deviation of the diameter measurement. We can run a test by making, say, 100 bearings and measuring the diameter of each bearing in the sample.

Let's say that, after running our test, we find that the average or mean diameter is 1.250 inches. Another way to say this is that the process is "centered" right in the middle of the upper and lower specification limits. In reality, it may be very difficult to have a perfectly centered process like our example. Let's say that the diameter values have a standard deviation or sigma equal to 0.002 inch. What this means is that our process does not make each bearing exactly the same size.

As we will see later in this chapter, normally we monitor a process using control charts such that if the process starts making bearings that are more than three standard deviations (±0.006 inch) above or below 1.250 inches, we stop the process. This means that we will produce parts that vary between 1.244 [this is $1.250 - (3 \times .002)$] and 1.256 [this is $1.250 + (3 \times .002)$] inches. The 1.244 and 1.256 are referred to as the upper and lower process limits. Be careful and do not get confused with the terminology here. The "process" limits relate to how consistent our process is for making the bearing. Our goal in managing the process is to keep it within plus or minus three standard deviations of the process mean. The "specification" limits are related to the design of the part. Recall that, from a design view, acceptable parts have a diameter between 1.245 and 1.255 inches (which are the lower and upper specification limits).

As we can see, our process limits are slightly greater than the specification limits given to us by the designer. This is not good because we will produce some parts that do not meet specifications. Companies with Six-Sigma processes insist that a process making a part be capable of operating so that the design specification limits are six standard deviations away from the process mean. For our bearing process, how small would the process standard deviation need to be for it to be Six-Sigma capable? Recall that our design specification was 1.250 inches plus or minus 0.005 inch. When you think about it, that 0.005 inch must relate to the variation in the process. By dividing 0.005 inch by 6, which equals 0.00083, we can determine our process standard deviation for a Six-Sigma process. So for our process to be Six-Sigma capable, the mean diameter produced by the process would need to be exactly 1.250 inches and the process standard deviation would need to be less than or equal to 0.00083 inch.

We can imagine that some of you are really confused at this point with the whole idea of Six Sigma. Why doesn't our company, for example, just check the diameter of each bearing and throw out the ones with a diameter less than 1.245 or greater than 1.255? This could certainly be done, and for many, many parts 100 percent testing is done. The problem is for a company that is making thousands of parts each hour, testing each critical dimension of each part made can be very expensive. For our bearing, there could easily be 10 or more additional critical dimensions in addition to the diameter. These would all need to be checked. Using a 100 percent testing approach, the company would spend more time testing than it takes to actually make the part! This is why a company uses small samples to periodically check that the process is in statistical control. We discuss exactly how this statistical sampling works later in the chapter.

We say that a process is *capable* when the mean and standard deviation of the process are operating such that the upper and lower control limits are acceptable relative to the upper and lower specification limits. Consider diagram A in Exhibit 9A.2. This represents the distribution of the bearing diameter dimension in our original process. The average or mean

Process Capability

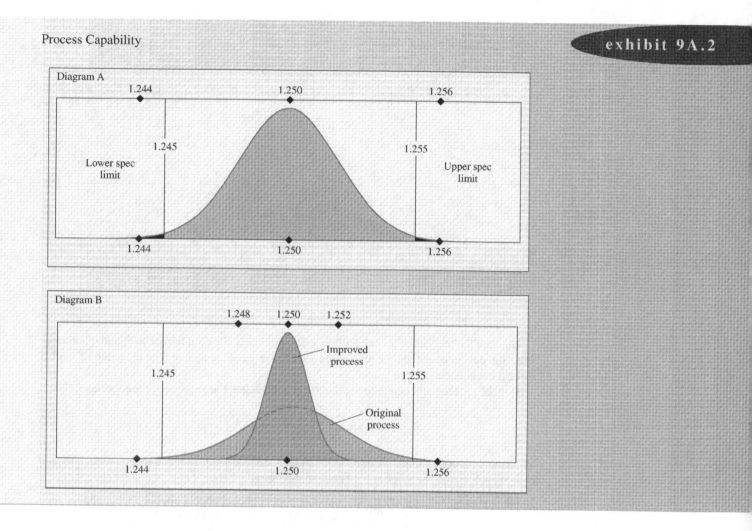

value is 1.250 and the lower and upper design specifications are 1.245 and 1.255, respectively. Process control limits are plus and minus three standard deviations (1.244 and 1.256). Notice that there is a probability (the red areas) of producing defective parts.

If we can improve our process by reducing the standard deviation associated with the bearing diameter, the probability can be reduced. Diagram B in Exhibit 9A.2 shows a new process where the standard deviation has been reduced to 0.00083 (the orange area). Even though we cannot see it in the diagram, there is some probability that a defect could be produced by this new process, but that probability is very, very small.

Suppose that the central value or mean of the process shifts away from the mean. Exhibit 9A.3 shows the mean shifted one standard deviation closer to the upper specification limit. This, of course, causes a slightly higher number of expected defects, but we can see that this is still very, very good. We use the *capability index* to measure how well our process is capable of producing relative to the design tolerances. We describe how to calculate this index in the next section.

CAPABILITY INDEX (C_{pk})

The capability index (C_{pk}) shows how well the parts being produced fit into the range specified by the design limits. If the design limits are larger than the three sigma allowed in the process, then the mean of the process can be allowed to drift off-center before readjustment, and a high percentage of good parts will still be produced.

Referring to Exhibits 9A.2 and 9A.3, the capability index (C_{pk}) is the position of the mean and tails of the process relative to design specifications. The more off-center, the greater the chance to produce defective parts.

Capability index (C_{pk})

Excel: SPC

exhibit 9A.3   Process Capability with a Shift in the Process Mean

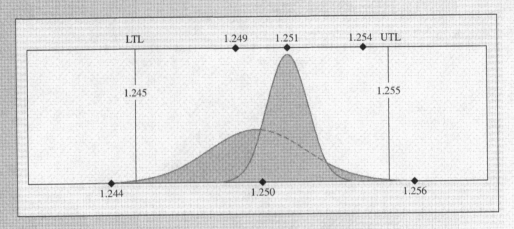

Because the process mean can shift in either direction, the direction of shift and its distance from the design specification set the limit on the process capability. The direction of shift is toward the smaller number.

Formally stated, the capability index (C_{pk}) is calculated as the smaller number as follows:

$$C_{pk} = \min\left[\frac{\overline{X} - \text{LTL}}{3\sigma} \quad \text{or} \quad \frac{\text{UTL} - \overline{X}}{3\sigma}\right] \qquad [\text{9A.3}]$$

Working with our example in Exhibit 9A.3, let's assume our process is centered at 1.251 and $\sigma = 0.00083$ (σ is the symbol for standard deviation).

$$C_{pk} = \min\left[\frac{1.251 - 1.245}{3(.00083)} \quad \text{or} \quad \frac{1.255 - 1.251}{3(.00083)}\right]$$

$$= \min\left[\frac{.006}{.00249} \quad \text{or} \quad \frac{.004}{.00249}\right]$$

$$C_{pk} = \min[2.4 \quad \text{or} \quad 1.6]$$

$C_{pk} = 1.6$, which is the smaller number.

This tells us that the process mean has shifted to the right similar to Exhibit 9A.3, but parts are still well within design limits.

At times it is useful to calculate the actual probability of producing a defect. Assuming that the process is producing with a consistent standard deviation, this is a fairly straightforward calculation, particularly when we have access to a spreadsheet. The approach to use is to calculate the probability of producing a part outside the lower and upper design limits given the mean and standard deviation of the process.

Working with our example, where the process is not centered, with a mean of 1.251 inches, $\sigma = .00083$, LTL = 1.245, and UTL = 1.255, we first need to calculate the Z score associated with the upper and lower tolerance (specification) limits. Recall from your study of statistics that the Z score is the standard deviation either to the right or to the left of zero in a probability distribution.

$$Z_{\text{LTL}} = \frac{\text{LTL} - \overline{X}}{\sigma} \qquad Z_{\text{UTL}} = \frac{\text{UTL} - \overline{X}}{\sigma}$$

For our example,

$$Z_{\text{LTL}} = \frac{1.245 - 1.251}{.00083} = -7.2289 \qquad Z_{\text{UTL}} = \frac{1.255 - 1.251}{.00083} = 4.8193$$

An easy way to get the probabilities associated with these Z values is to use the NORMSDIST function built into Excel (you also can use the table in Appendix G). The format for this function is NORMSDIST(Z), where Z is the Z value calculated above. Excel returns the following values. (We have found that you might get slightly different results from those given here, depending on the version of Excel you are using.)

$$\text{NORMSDIST}(-7.2289) = 2.43461E\text{-}13 \quad \text{and} \quad \text{NORMSDIST}(4.8193) = .99999928$$

Interpreting this information requires understanding exactly what the NORMSDIST function is providing. NORMSDIST is giving the cumulative probability to the left of the given Z value. Since $Z = -7.2289$ is the number of standard deviations associated with the lower specification limit, the fraction of parts that will be produced lower than this is 2.43461E-13. This number is in scientific notation, and that E-13 at the end means we need to move the decimal over 13 places to get the real fraction defective. So the fraction defective is .00000000000024361, which is a very small number! Similarly, we see that approximately .99999928 of our parts will be below our upper specification limit. What we are really interested in is the fraction that will be above this limit since these are the defective parts. This fraction defective above the upper spec is $1 - .99999928 = .00000082$ of our parts.

Adding these two fraction defective numbers together we get .00000082000024361. We can interpret this to mean that we only expect about .82 part per million to be defective. Clearly, this is a great process. You will discover as you work the problems at the end of the chapter that this is not always the case.

EXAMPLE 9A.1

The quality assurance manager is assessing the capability of a process that puts pressurized grease in an aerosol can. The design specifications call for an average of 60 pounds per square inch (psi) of pressure in each can with an upper tolerance limit of 65 psi and a lower tolerance limit of 55 psi. A sample is taken from production and it is found that the cans average 61 psi with a standard deviation of 2 psi. What is the capability of the process? What is the probability of producing a defect?

Step by Step

SOLUTION

Step 1—Interpret the data from the problem

$$\text{LTL} = 55 \quad \text{UTL} = 65 \quad \overline{X} = 61 \quad \sigma = 2$$

Step 2—Calculate the C_{pk}

$$C_{pk} = \min\left[\frac{\overline{X} - \text{LTL}}{3\sigma}, \frac{\text{UTL} - \overline{X}}{3\sigma}\right]$$

$$C_{pk} = \min\left[\frac{61 - 55}{3(2)}, \frac{65 - 61}{3(2)}\right]$$

$$C_{pk} = \min[1, .6667] = .6667$$

Step 3—Calculate the probability of producing a defect
Probability of a can with less than 55 psi

$$Z = \frac{X - \overline{X}}{\sigma} = \frac{55 - 61}{2} = -3$$

$$\text{NORMSDIST}(-3) = .001349898$$

Probability of a can with more than 65 psi

$$Z = \frac{X - \overline{X}}{\sigma} = \frac{65 - 61}{2} = 2$$

$$1 - \text{NORMSDIST}(2) = 1 - .977249868 = .022750132$$

Probability of a can less than 55 psi or more than 65 psi

$$\text{Probability} = .001349898 + .022750132 = .024100030$$

Or approximately 2.4 percent of the cans will be defective. ●

The following table is a quick reference for the fraction of defective units for various design limits (expressed in standard deviations). This table assumes that the standard deviation is constant and that the process is centered exactly between the design limits.

Design Limits	Defective Parts	Fraction Defective
$\pm 1\sigma$	317 per thousand	.3173
$\pm 2\sigma$	45 per thousand	.0455
$\pm 3\sigma$	2.7 per thousand	.0027
$\pm 4\sigma$	63 per million	.000063
$\pm 5\sigma$	574 per billion	.000000574
$\pm 6\sigma$	2 per billion	.000000002

Motorola's design limit of six sigma with a shift of the process off the mean by 1.5σ ($C_{pk} = 1.5$) gives 3.4 defects per million. If the mean is exactly in the center ($C_{pk} = 2$), then 2 defects per *billion* are expected, as the table above shows.

PROCESS CONTROL PROCEDURES

Statistical process control (SPC)

Attributes

Process control is concerned with monitoring quality *while the product or service is being produced.* Typical objectives of process control plans are to provide timely information on whether currently produced items are meeting design specifications and to detect shifts in the process that signal that future products may not meet specifications. Statistical process control (SPC) involves testing a random sample of output from a process to determine whether the process is producing items within a preselected range.

The examples given so far have all been based on quality characteristics (or *variables*) that are measurable, such as the diameter or weight of a part. Attributes are quality characteristics that are classified as either conforming or not conforming to specification. Goods or services may be observed to be either good or bad, or functioning or malfunctioning. For example, a lawnmower either runs or it doesn't; it attains a certain level of torque and horsepower or it doesn't. This type of measurement is known as sampling by attributes. Alternatively, a lawnmower's torque and horsepower can be measured as an amount of deviation from a set standard. This type of measurement is known as sampling by variables. The following section describes some standard approaches to controlling processes: first an approach useful for attribute measures and then an approach for variable measures. Both of these techniques result in the construction of control charts. Exhibit 9A.4 shows some examples of how control charts can be analyzed to understand how a process is operating.

PROCESS CONTROL WITH ATTRIBUTE MEASUREMENTS: USING *p* CHARTS

Measurement by attributes means taking samples and using a single decision—the item is good or it is bad. Because it is a yes or no decision, we can use simple statistics to create a *p* chart with an upper control limit (UCL) and a lower control limit (LCL). We can draw these control limits on a graph and then plot the fraction defective of each individual sample tested. The process is assumed to be working correctly when the samples, which are taken periodically during the day, continue to stay between the control limits.

Control Chart Evidence for Investigation

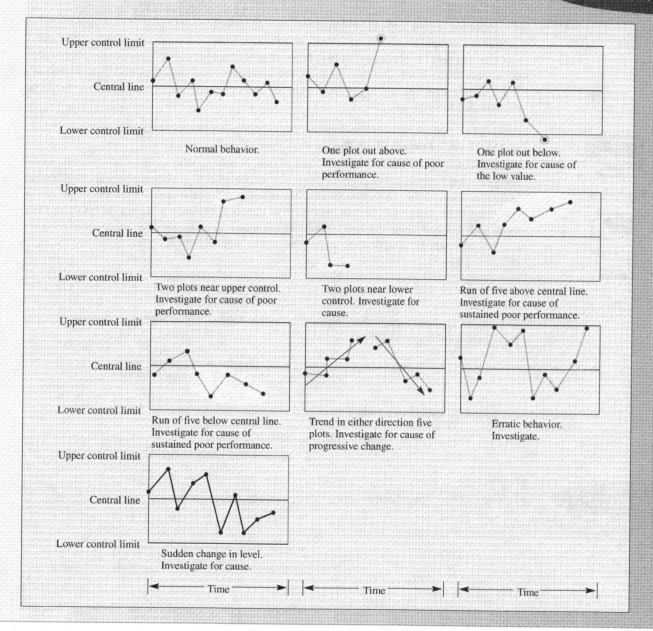

$$\bar{p} = \frac{\text{Total number of defects from all samples}}{\text{Number of samples} \times \text{Sample size}} \qquad \text{[9A.4]}$$

$$s_p = \sqrt{\frac{\bar{p}(1 - \bar{p})}{n}} \qquad \text{[9A.5]}$$

$$\text{UCL} = \bar{p} + zs_p \qquad \text{[9A.6]}$$

$$\text{LCL} = \bar{p} - zs_p \qquad \text{[9A.7]}$$

where $\bar{p}$ is the fraction defective, s_p is the standard deviation, n is the sample size, and z is the number of standard deviations for a specific confidence. Typically, $z = 3$ (99.7 percent confidence) or $z = 2.58$ (99 percent confidence) is used.

Size of the Sample   The size of the sample must be large enough to allow counting of the attribute. For example, if we know that a machine produces 1 percent defects, then a sample size of five would seldom capture a defect. A rule of thumb when setting up a *p* chart is to make the sample large enough to expect to count the attribute twice in each sample. So an appropriate sample size if the defect rate were approximately 1 percent would be 200 units.

One final note: In the calculations shown in equations 9A.4–9A.7, the assumption is that the sample size is fixed. The calculation of the standard deviation depends on this assumption. If the sample size varies, the standard deviation and upper and lower control limits should be recalculated for each sample.

Step by Step

Service

EXAMPLE 9A.2: Control Chart Design

An insurance company wants to design a control chart to monitor whether insurance claim forms are being completed correctly. The company intends to use the chart to see if improvements in the design of the form are effective. To start the process, the company collected data on the number of incorrectly completed claim forms over the past 10 days. The insurance company processes thousands of these forms each day, and due to the high cost of inspecting each form, only a small representative sample was collected each day. The data and analysis are shown in Exhibit 9A.5.

SOLUTION

To construct the control chart, first calculate the overall fraction defective from all samples. This sets the centerline for the control chart.

$$\bar{p} = \frac{\text{Total number of defects from all samples}}{\text{Number of samples} \times \text{Sample size}} = \frac{91}{3000} = 0.03033$$

Next, calculate the sample standard deviation:

$$s_p = \sqrt{\frac{\bar{p}(1 - \bar{p})}{n}} = \sqrt{\frac{0.03033(1 - 0.03033)}{300}} = 0.00990$$

exhibit 9A.5   Insurance Company Claim Form

SAMPLE	NUMBER INSPECTED	NUMBER OF FORMS COMPLETED INCORRECTLY	FRACTION DEFECTIVE
1	300	10	0.03333
2	300	8	0.02667
3	300	9	0.03000
4	300	13	0.04333
5	300	7	0.02333
6	300	7	0.02333
7	300	6	0.02000
8	300	11	0.03667
9	300	12	0.04000
10	300	8	0.02667
Totals	3000	91	0.03033
Sample standard deviation			0.00990

Finally, calculate the upper and lower control limits. A *z*-value of 3 gives 99.7 percent confidence that the process is within these limits.

$$\text{UCL} = \bar{p} + 3s_p = 0.03033 + 3(0.00990) = 0.06003$$

$$\text{LCL} = \bar{p} - 3s_p = 0.03033 - 3(0.00990) = 0.00063$$

The calculations in Exhibit 9A.5, including the control chart, are included in the spreadsheet SPC. ●

Excel: SPC

PROCESS CONTROL WITH ATTRIBUTE MEASUREMENTS: USING c CHARTS

In the case of the *p* chart, the item was either good or bad. There are times when the product or service can have more than one defect. For example, a board sold at a lumber yard may have multiple knotholes and, depending on the quality grade, may or may not be defective. To monitor the number of defects per unit, the *c* chart is appropriate.

The underlying distribution for the *c* chart is the Poisson, which is based on the assumption that defects occur randomly on each unit. If *c* is the number of defects for a particular unit, then $\bar{c}$ is the average number of defects per unit, and the standard deviation is $\sqrt{\bar{c}}$. For the purposes of our control chart we use the normal approximation to the Poisson distribution and construct the chart using the following control limits.

$$\bar{c} = \text{Average number of defects per unit} \qquad [9A.8]$$

$$s_p = \sqrt{\bar{c}} \qquad [9A.9]$$

$$\text{UCL} = \bar{c} + z\sqrt{\bar{c}} \qquad [9A.10]$$

$$\text{LCL} = \bar{c} - z\sqrt{\bar{c}} \quad \text{or} \quad 0 \text{ if less than } 0 \qquad [9A.11]$$

Just as with the *p* chart, typically *z* = 3 (99.7 percent confidence) or *z* = 2.58 (99 percent confidence) is used.

Example 9A.3

The owners of a lumber yard want to design a control chart to monitor the quality of 2 × 4 boards that come from their supplier. For their medium-quality boards they expect an average of four knotholes per 8 foot board. Design a control chart for use by the person receiving the boards using three-sigma (standard deviation) limits.

Step by Step

SOLUTION

For this problem, $\bar{c} = 4$, $s_p = \sqrt{\bar{c}} = 2$

$$\text{UCL} = \bar{c} + z\sqrt{\bar{c}} = 4 + 3(2) = 10$$

$$\text{LCL} = \bar{c} - z\sqrt{\bar{c}} = 4 - 3(2) = -2 \rightarrow 0 \qquad ●$$

PROCESS CONTROL WITH VARIABLE MEASUREMENTS: USING $\overline{X}$ AND R CHARTS

$\overline{X}$ and *R* (range) charts are widely used in statistical process control.

In attribute sampling, we determine whether something is good or bad, fits or doesn't fit—it is a go/no-go situation. In variables sampling, however, we measure the actual weight, volume, number of inches, or other variable measurements, and we develop control charts to determine the acceptability or rejection of the process based on those measurements.

Variables

A FOREMAN AND TEAM COACH EXAMINE PROCESS CONTROL CHARTS AT THE FORD FIESTA ASSEMBLY LINE IN COLOGNE-NIEHL, GERMANY.

For example, in attribute sampling, we might decide that if something is over 10 pounds we will reject it and under 10 pounds we will accept it. In variable sampling, we measure a sample and may record weights of 9.8 pounds or 10.2 pounds. These values are used to create or modify control charts and to see whether they fall within the acceptable limits.

The four main issues to address in creating a control chart are the size of the samples, number of samples, frequency of samples, and control limits.

Size of Samples   For industrial applications in process control involving the measurement of variables, it is preferable to keep the sample size small. There are two main reasons. First, the sample needs to be taken within a reasonable length of time; otherwise, the process might change while the samples are taken. Second, the larger the sample, the more it costs to take.

Sample sizes of four or five units seem to be the preferred numbers. The *means* of samples of this size have an approximately normal distribution, no matter what the distribution of the parent population looks like. Sample sizes greater than five give narrower control limits and thus more sensitivity. For detecting finer variations of a process, it may be necessary, in fact, to use larger sample sizes. However, when sample sizes exceed 15 or so, using $\bar{X}$ charts with standard deviation σ would be better than using $\bar{X}$ charts with the range R as in Example 9A.4.

Number of Samples   Once the chart has been set up, each sample taken can be compared to the chart and a decision can be made about whether the process is acceptable. To set up the charts, however, prudence and statistics suggest that 25 or so samples be taken.

Frequency of Samples   How often to take a sample is a trade-off between the cost of sampling (along with the cost of the unit if it is destroyed as part of the test) and the benefit of adjusting the system. Usually, it is best to start off with frequent sampling of a process and taper off as confidence in the process builds. For example, one might start with a sample of five units every half hour and end up feeling that one sample per day is adequate.

Control Limits   Standard practice in statistical process control for variables is to set control limits three standard deviations above the mean and three standard deviations below. This means that 99.7 percent of the sample means are expected to fall within these control limits (that is, within a 99.7 percent confidence interval). Thus, if one sample mean falls outside this obviously wide band, we have strong evidence that the process is out of control.

HOW TO CONSTRUCT $\overline{X}$ AND R CHARTS

If the standard deviation of the process distribution is known, the $\overline{X}$ chart may be defined:

$$\text{UCL}_{\overline{X}} = \overline{\overline{X}} + zs_{\overline{X}} \qquad \text{and} \qquad \text{LCL}_{\overline{X}} = \overline{\overline{X}} - zs_{\overline{X}} \qquad \text{[9A.12]}$$

where

$S_{\overline{X}} = s/\sqrt{n} =$ Standard deviation of sample means

$s =$ Standard deviation of the process distribution

$n =$ Sample size

$\overline{\overline{X}} =$ Average of sample means or a target value set for the process

$z =$ Number of standard deviations for a specific confidence level (typically, $z = 3$)

An $\overline{X}$ chart is simply a plot of the means of the sample s that were taken from a process. $\overline{\overline{X}}$ is the average of the means.

In practice, the standard deviation of the process is not known. For this reason, an approach that uses actual sample data is commonly used. This practical approach is described in the next section.

An R chart is a plot of the range within each sample. The range is the difference between the highest and the lowest numbers in that sample. R values provide an easily calculated measure of variation used like a standard deviation. An $\overline{R}$ chart is the average of the range of each sample. More specifically defined, these are

$$\overline{X} = \frac{\sum_{i=1}^{n} X_i}{n} \qquad \text{[Same as 9A.1]}$$

where

$\overline{X} =$ Mean of the sample

$i =$ Item number

$n =$ Total number of items in the sample

$$\overline{\overline{X}} = \frac{\sum_{j=1}^{m} \overline{X}_j}{m} \qquad \text{[9A.13]}$$

where

$\overline{\overline{X}} =$ The average of the means of the samples

$j =$ Sample number

$m =$ Total number of samples

$$\overline{R} = \frac{\sum_{j=1}^{m} R_j}{m} \qquad \text{[9A.14]}$$

where

$R_j =$ Difference between the highest and lowest measurement in the sample

$\overline{R} =$ Average of the measurement differences R for all samples

E. L. Grant and R. Leavenworth computed a table (Exhibit 9A.6) that allows us to easily compute the upper and lower control limits for both the $\overline{X}$ chart and the R chart.[1] These are defined as

$$\text{Upper control limit for } \overline{X} = \overline{\overline{X}} + A_2\overline{R} \qquad \text{[9A.15]}$$

exhibit 9A.6   Factor for Determining from $\overline{R}$ the Three-Sigma Control Limits for $\overline{X}$ and R Charts

NUMBER OF OBSERVATIONS IN SUBGROUP n	FACTOR FOR $\overline{X}$ CHART A_2	FACTORS FOR R CHART	
		LOWER CONTROL LIMIT D_3	UPPER CONTROL LIMIT D_4
2	1.88	0	3.27
3	1.02	0	2.57
4	0.73	0	2.28
5	0.58	0	2.11
6	0.48	0	2.00
7	0.42	0.08	1.92
8	0.37	0.14	1.86
9	0.34	0.18	1.82
10	0.31	0.22	1.78
11	0.29	0.26	1.74
12	0.27	0.28	1.72
13	0.25	0.31	1.69
14	0.24	0.33	1.67
15	0.22	0.35	1.65
16	0.21	0.36	1.64
17	0.20	0.38	1.62
18	0.19	0.39	1.61
19	0.19	0.40	1.60
20	0.18	0.41	1.59

Upper control limit for $\overline{X} = \text{UCL}_{\overline{X}} = \overline{\overline{X}} + A_2\overline{R}$

Lower control limit for $\overline{X} = \text{LCL}_{\overline{X}} = \overline{\overline{X}} - A_2\overline{R}$

Upper control limit for $R = \text{UCL}_R = D_4\overline{R}$

Lower control limit for $R = \text{LCL}_R = D_3\overline{R}$

Note: All factors are based on the normal distribution.

Excel: SPC

Step by Step

$$\text{Lower control limit for } \overline{X} = \overline{\overline{X}} - A_2\overline{R} \qquad [9\text{A.16}]$$

$$\text{Upper control limit for } R = D_4\overline{R} \qquad [9\text{A.17}]$$

$$\text{Lower control limit for } R = D_3\overline{R} \qquad [9\text{A.18}]$$

EXAMPLE 9A.4: $\overline{X}$ and R Charts

We would like to create $\overline{X}$ and R charts for a process. Exhibit 9A.7 shows measurements for all 25 samples. The last two columns show the average of the sample $\overline{X}$ and the range R.

Values for A_2, D_3, and D_4 were obtained from Exhibit 9A.6.

$$\text{Upper control limit for } \overline{X} = \overline{\overline{X}} + A_2\overline{R} = 10.21 + 0.58(0.60) = 10.56$$

$$\text{Lower control limit for } \overline{X} = \overline{\overline{X}} - A_2\overline{R} = 10.21 - 0.58(0.60) = 9.86$$

$$\text{Upper control limit for } R = D_4\overline{R} = 2.11(0.60) = 1.27$$

$$\text{Lower control limit for } R = D_3\overline{R} = 0(0.60) = 0$$

Measurements in Samples of Five from a Process

SAMPLE NUMBER	EACH UNIT IN SAMPLE					AVERAGE $\bar{X}$	RANGE R
1	10.60	10.40	10.30	9.90	10.20	10.28	.70
2	9.98	10.25	10.05	10.23	10.33	10.17	.35
3	9.85	9.90	10.20	10.25	10.15	10.07	.40
4	10.20	10.10	10.30	9.90	9.95	10.09	.40
5	10.30	10.20	10.24	10.50	10.30	10.31	.30
6	10.10	10.30	10.20	10.30	9.90	10.16	.40
7	9.98	9.90	10.20	10.40	10.10	10.12	.50
8	10.10	10.30	10.40	10.24	10.30	10.27	.30
9	10.30	10.20	10.60	10.50	10.10	10.34	.50
10	10.30	10.40	10.50	10.10	10.20	10.30	.40
11	9.90	9.50	10.20	10.30	10.35	10.05	.85
12	10.10	10.36	10.50	9.80	9.95	10.14	.70
13	10.20	10.50	10.70	10.10	9.90	10.28	.80
14	10.20	10.60	10.50	10.30	10.40	10.40	.40
15	10.54	10.30	10.40	10.55	10.00	10.36	.55
16	10.20	10.60	10.15	10.00	10.50	10.29	.60
17	10.20	10.40	10.60	10.80	10.10	10.42	.70
18	9.90	9.50	9.90	10.50	10.00	9.96	1.00
19	10.60	10.30	10.50	9.90	9.80	10.22	.80
20	10.60	10.40	10.30	10.40	10.20	10.38	.40
21	9.90	9.60	10.50	10.10	10.60	10.14	1.00
22	9.95	10.20	10.50	10.30	10.20	10.23	.55
23	10.20	9.50	9.60	9.80	10.30	9.88	.80
24	10.30	10.60	10.30	9.90	9.80	10.18	.80
25	9.90	10.30	10.60	9.90	10.10	10.16	.70

$$\bar{\bar{X}} = 10.21$$

$$\bar{R} = 0.60$$

Excel: SPC

$\bar{X}$ Chart and R Chart

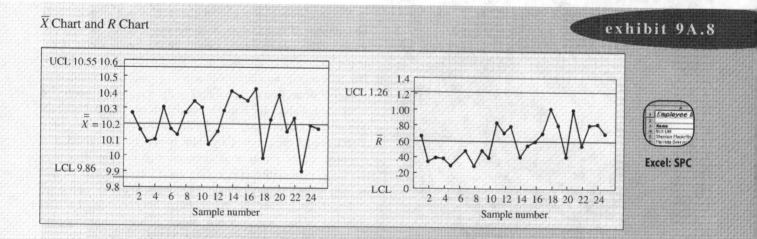

Excel: SPC

SOLUTION

Exhibit 9A.8 shows the $\bar{X}$ chart and R chart with a plot of all the sample means and ranges of the samples. All the points are well within the control limits, although sample 23 is close to the $\bar{X}$ lower control limit. ●

ACCEPTANCE SAMPLING

DESIGN OF A SINGLE SAMPLING PLAN FOR ATTRIBUTES

Acceptance sampling is performed on goods that already exist to determine what percentage of products conform to specifications. These products may be items received from another company and evaluated by the receiving department, or they may be components that have passed through a processing step and are evaluated by company personnel either in production or later in the warehousing function. Whether inspection should be done at all is addressed in the following example.

Acceptance sampling is executed through a sampling plan. In this section, we illustrate the planning procedures for a single sampling plan—that is, a plan in which the quality is determined from the evaluation of one sample. (Other plans may be developed using two or more samples. See J. M. Juran and F. M. Gryna's *Quality Planning and Analysis* for a discussion of these plans.)

Step by Step

Excel: SPC

EXAMPLE 9A.5: Costs to Justify Inspection

Total (100 percent) inspection is justified when the cost of a loss incurred by not inspecting is greater than the cost of inspection. For example, suppose a faulty item results in a $10 loss and the average percentage defective of items in the lot is 3 percent.

SOLUTION

If the average percentage of defective items in a lot is 3 percent, the expected cost of faulty items is $0.03 \times \$10$, or $0.30 each. Therefore, if the cost of inspecting each item is less than $0.30, the economic decision is to perform 100 percent inspection. Not all defective items will be removed, however, because inspectors will pass some bad items and reject some good ones.

The purpose of a sampling plan is to test the lot to either (1) find its quality or (2) ensure that the quality is what it is supposed to be. Thus, if a quality control supervisor already knows the quality (such as the 0.03 given in the example), he or she does not sample for defects. Either all of them must be inspected to remove the defects or none of them should be inspected, and the rejects pass into the process. The choice simply depends on the cost to inspect and the cost incurred by passing a reject. ●

A single sampling plan is defined by n and c, where n is the number of units in the sample and c is the acceptance number. The size of n may vary from one up to all the items in the lot (usually denoted as N) from which it is drawn. The acceptance number c denotes the maximum number of defective items that can be found in the sample before the lot is rejected. Values for n and c are determined by the interaction of four factors (AQL, α, LTPD, and β) that quantify the objectives of the product's producer and its consumer. The objective of the producer is to ensure that the sampling plan has a low probability of rejecting good lots. Lots are defined as high quality if they contain no more than a specified level of defectives, termed the *acceptable quality level (AQL)*.[2] The objective of the consumer is to ensure that the sampling plan has a low probability of accepting bad lots. Lots are defined as low quality if the percentage of defectives is greater than a specified amount, termed *lot tolerance percent defective (LTPD)*. The probability associated with rejecting a high-quality lot is denoted by the Greek letter alpha (α) and is termed the *producer's risk*. The probability associated with

Excerpt from a Sampling Plan Table for $\alpha = 0.05$, $\beta = 0.10$

c	LTPD ÷ AQL	$n \cdot$ AQL	c	LTPD ÷ AQL	$n \cdot$ AQL
0	44.890	0.052	5	3.549	2.613
1	10.946	0.355	6	3.206	3.286
2	6.509	0.818	7	2.957	3.981
3	4.890	1.366	8	2.768	4.695
4	4.057	1.970	9	2.618	5.426

accepting a low-quality lot is denoted by the letter beta (β) and is termed the *consumer's risk*. The selection of particular values for AQL, α, LTPD, and β is an economic decision based on a cost trade-off or, more typically, on company policy or contractual requirements.

There is a humorous story supposedly about Hewlett-Packard during its first dealings with Japanese vendors, who place great emphasis on high-quality production. HP had insisted on 2 percent AQL in a purchase of 100 cables. During the purchase agreement, some heated discussion took place wherein the Japanese vendor did not want this AQL specification; HP insisted that they would not budge from the 2 percent AQL. The Japanese vendor finally agreed. Later, when the box arrived, there were two packages inside. One contained 100 good cables. The other package had 2 cables with a note stating: "We have sent you 100 good cables. Since you insisted on 2 percent AQL, we have enclosed 2 defective cables in this package, though we do not understand why you want them."

The following example, using an excerpt from a standard acceptance sampling table, illustrates how the four parameters—AQL, α, LTPD, and β—are used in developing a sampling plan.

EXAMPLE 9A.6: Values of *n* and *c*

Hi-Tech Industries manufactures Z-Band radar scanners used to detect speed traps. The printed circuit boards in the scanners are purchased from an outside vendor. The vendor produces the boards to an AQL of 2 percent defectives and is willing to run a 5 percent risk (α) of having lots of this level or fewer defectives rejected. Hi-Tech considers lots of 8 percent or more defectives (LTPD) unacceptable and wants to ensure that it will accept such poor-quality lots no more than 10 percent of the time (β). A large shipment has just been delivered. What values of *n* and *c* should be selected to determine the quality of this lot?

Step by Step

SOLUTION

The parameters of the problem are AQL = 0.02, $\alpha = 0.05$, LTPD = 0.08, and $\beta = 0.10$. We can use Exhibit 9A.9 to find *c* and *n*.

First, divide LTPD by AQL ($0.08 \div 0.02 = 4$). Then, find the ratio in column 2 that is equal to or just greater than that amount (4). This value is 4.057, which is associated with $c = 4$.

Finally, find the value in column 3 that is in the same row as $c = 4$ and divide that quantity by AQL to obtain *n* ($1.970 \div 0.02 = 98.5$).

The appropriate sampling plan is $c = 4$, $n = 99$. ●

OPERATING CHARACTERISTIC CURVES

While a sampling plan such as the one just described meets our requirements for the extreme values of good and bad quality, we cannot readily determine how well the plan discriminates between good and bad lots at intermediate values. For this reason, sampling plans are generally displayed graphically through the use of operating characteristic (OC) curves. These curves, which are unique for each combination of *n* and *c*, simply illustrate the probability of accepting lots with varying percentages of defectives. The procedure we have followed in

Operating Characteristic Curve for AQL = 0.02, α = 0.05, LTPD = 0.08, β = 0.10

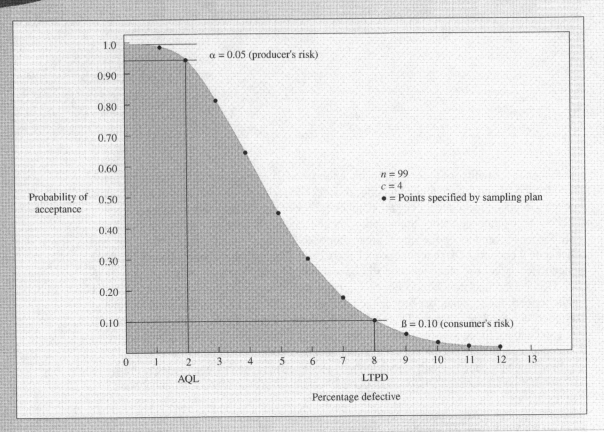

developing the plan, in fact, specifies two points on an OC curve: one point defined by AQL and $1 - \alpha$ and the other point defined by LTPD and β. Curves for common values of n and c can be computed or obtained from available tables.[3]

Shaping the OC Curve   A sampling plan discriminating perfectly between good and bad lots has an infinite slope (vertical) at the selected value of AQL. In Exhibit 9A.10, any percentage defective to the left of 2 percent would always be accepted, and those to the right, always rejected. However, such a curve is possible only with complete inspection of all units and thus is not a possibility with a true sampling plan.

An OC curve should be steep in the region of most interest (between the AQL and the LTPD), which is accomplished by varying n and c. If c remains constant, increasing the sample size n causes the OC curve to be more vertical. While holding n constant, decreasing c (the maximum number of defective units) also makes the slope more vertical, moving closer to the origin.

The Effects of Lot Size   The size of the lot that the sample is taken from has relatively little effect on the quality of protection. Consider, for example, that samples—all of the same size of 20 units—are taken from different lots ranging from a lot size of 200 units to a lot size of infinity. If each lot is known to have 5 percent defectives, the probability of accepting the lot based on the sample of 20 units ranges from about 0.34 to about 0.36. This means that as long as the lot size is several times the sample size, it makes little difference how large the lot is. It seems a bit difficult to accept, but statistically (on the average in the long run) whether we have a carload or box full, we'll get about the same answer. It just seems that a carload should have a larger sample size. Of course, this assumes that the lot is randomly chosen and that defects are randomly spread through the lot.

SUMMARY

Statistical quality control is a vital topic. Quality has become so important that statistical quality procedures are *expected* to be part of successful firms. Sampling plans and statistical process control are taken as given with the emphasis shifting to broader aspects (such as eliminating dockside acceptance sampling because of reliable supplier quality, and employee empowerment transforming much of the process control). World-class manufacturing companies expect people to understand the basic concepts of the material presented in this chapter.

KEY TERMS

Assignable variation Deviation in the output of a process that can be clearly identified and managed.

Common variation Deviation in the output of a process that is random and inherent in the process itself.

Upper and lower specification or tolerance limits The range of values in a measure associated with a process that are allowable given the intended use of the product or service.

Capability index (C_{pk}) The ratio of the range of values produced by a process divided by the range of values allowed by the design specification.

Statistical process control (SPC) Techniques for testing a random sample of output from a process to determine whether the process is producing items within a prescribed range.

Attributes Quality characteristics that are classified as either conforming or not conforming to specification.

Variables Quality characteristics that are measured in actual weight, volume, inches, centimeters, or other measure.

FORMULA REVIEW

Mean or average

$$\bar{X} = \sum_{i=1}^{N} x_i / N \qquad \text{[9A.1]}$$

Standard deviation

$$\sigma = \sqrt{\frac{\sum_{i=1}^{N}(x_i - \bar{X})^2}{N}} \qquad \text{[9A.2]}$$

Capability index

$$C_{pk} = \min\left[\frac{\bar{X} - \text{LTL}}{3\sigma}, \quad \frac{\text{UTL} - \bar{X}}{3\sigma}\right] \qquad \text{[9A.3]}$$

Process control charts using attribute measurements

$$\bar{p} = \frac{\text{Total number of defects from all samples}}{\text{Number of samples} \times \text{Sample size}} \qquad \text{[9A.4]}$$

$$s_p = \sqrt{\frac{\bar{p}(1 - \bar{p})}{n}} \qquad \text{[9A.5]}$$

$$\text{UCL} = \bar{p} + z s_p \qquad \text{[9A.6]}$$

$$\text{LCL} = \bar{p} - z s_p \qquad \text{[9A.7]}$$

Process control c charts

$$\bar{c} = \text{Average number of defects per unit} \qquad \text{[9A.8]}$$

$$s_p = \sqrt{\bar{c}} \qquad \text{[9A.9]}$$

$$\text{UCL} = \bar{c} + z\sqrt{\bar{c}} \qquad \text{[9A.10]}$$

$$\text{LCL} = \bar{c} - z\sqrt{\bar{c}} \quad \text{or} \quad 0 \text{ if less than } 0 \qquad \text{[9A.11]}$$

Process control $\overline{X}$ and R charts

$$\text{UCL}_{\overline{x}} = \overline{\overline{X}} + zs_{\overline{x}} \quad \text{and} \quad \text{LCL}_{\overline{x}} = \overline{\overline{X}} - zs_{\overline{x}} \qquad [9A.12]$$

$$\overline{\overline{X}} = \frac{\sum_{j=1}^{m} X_j}{m} \qquad [9A.13]$$

$$\overline{R} = \frac{\sum_{j=1}^{m} R_j}{m} \qquad [9A.14]$$

Upper control limit for $\overline{X} = \overline{\overline{X}} + A_2\overline{R}$ [9A.15]

Lower control limit for $\overline{X} = \overline{\overline{X}} - A_2\overline{R}$ [9A.16]

Upper control limit for $R = D_4\overline{R}$ [9A.17]

Lower control limit for $R = D_3\overline{R}$ [9A.18]

SOLVED PROBLEMS

SOLVED PROBLEM 1

Excel: SPC

Completed forms from a particular department of an insurance company were sampled daily to check the performance quality of that department. To establish a tentative norm for the department, one sample of 100 units was collected each day for 15 days, with these results:

Sample	Sample Size	Number of Forms with Errors	Sample	Sample Size	Number of Forms with Errors
1	100	4	9	100	4
2	100	3	10	100	2
3	100	5	11	100	7
4	100	0	12	100	2
5	100	2	13	100	1
6	100	8	14	100	3
7	100	1	15	100	1
8	100	3			

a. Develop a p chart using a 95 percent confidence interval ($1.96s_p$).
b. Plot the 15 samples collected.
c. What comments can you make about the process?

Solution

a. $\overline{p} = \dfrac{46}{15(100)} = 0.0307$

$$s_p = \sqrt{\frac{\overline{p}(1 - \overline{p})}{n}} = \sqrt{\frac{0.0307(1 - 0.0307)}{100}} = \sqrt{0.0003} = 0.017$$

$\text{UCL} = \overline{p} + 1.96s_p = 0.031 + 1.96(0.017) = 0.064$

$\text{LCL} = \overline{p} - 1.96s_p = 0.031 - 1.96(0.017) = -0.00232 \text{ or zero}$

b. The defectives are plotted below.

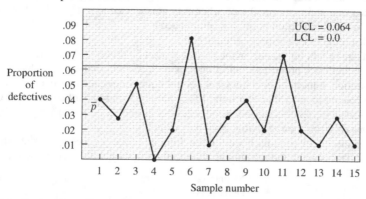

c. Of the 15 samples, 2 were out of the control limits. Because the control limits were established as 95 percent, or 1 out of 20, we would say that the process is out of control. It needs to be examined to find the cause of such widespread variation.

SOLVED PROBLEM 2

Management is trying to decide whether Part A, which is produced with a consistent 3 percent defective rate, should be inspected. If it is not inspected, the 3 percent defectives will go through a product assembly phase and have to be replaced later. If all Part A's are inspected, one-third of the defectives will be found, thus raising the quality to 2 percent defectives.

a. Should the inspection be done if the cost of inspecting is $0.01 per unit and the cost of replacing a defective in the final assembly is $4.00?

b. Suppose the cost of inspecting is $0.05 per unit rather than $0.01. Would this change your answer in *a*?

Solution

Should Part A be inspected?

0.03 defective with no inspection.

0.02 defective with inspection.

a. This problem can be solved simply by looking at the opportunity for 1 percent improvement.

Benefit = 0.01($4.00) = $0.04

Cost of inspection = $0.01

Therefore, inspect and save $0.03 per unit.

b. A cost of $0.05 per unit to inspect would be $0.01 greater than the savings, so inspection should not be performed.

REVIEW AND DISCUSSION QUESTIONS

1   The capability index allows for some drifting of the process mean. Discuss what this means in terms of product quality output.

2   Discuss the purposes of and differences between *p* charts, *c* charts and $\overline{X}$ and *R* charts.

3   In an agreement between a supplier and a customer, the supplier must ensure that all parts are within tolerance before shipment to the customer. What is the effect on the cost of quality to the customer?

4   In the situation described in Question 3, what would be the effect on the cost of quality to the supplier?

5   Discuss the trade-off between achieving a zero AQL (acceptable quality level) and a positive AQL (such as an AQL of 2 percent).

PROBLEMS

1   A company currently using an inspection process in its material receiving department is trying to install an overall cost reduction program. One possible reduction is the elimination of one inspection position. This position tests material that has a defective content on the average of 0.04. By inspecting all items, the inspector is able to remove all defects. The inspector can inspect 50 units per hour. The hourly rate including fringe benefits for this position is $9. If

the inspection position is eliminated, defects will go into product assembly and will have to be replaced later at a cost of $10 each when they are detected in final product testing.

a. Should this inspection position be eliminated?

b. What is the cost to inspect each unit?

c. Is there benefit (or loss) from the current inspection process? How much?

2 A metal fabricator produces connecting rods with an outer diameter that has a 1 ± 0.01 inch specification. A machine operator takes several sample measurements over time and determines the sample mean outer diameter to be 1.002 inches with a standard deviation of 0.003 inch.

a. Calculate the process capability index for this example.

b. What does this figure tell you about the process?

3 Ten samples of 15 parts each were taken from an ongoing process to establish a p chart for control. The samples and the number of defectives in each are shown in the following table:

SAMPLE	n	NUMBER OF DEFECTS IN SAMPLE	SAMPLE	n	NUMBER OF DEFECTS IN SAMPLE
1	15	3	6	15	2
2	15	1	7	15	0
3	15	0	8	15	3
4	15	0	9	15	1
5	15	0	10	15	0

a. Develop a p chart for 95 percent confidence (1.96 standard deviations).

b. Based on the plotted data points, what comments can you make?

4 Output from a process contains 0.02 defective unit. Defective units that go undetected into final assemblies cost $25 each to replace. An inspection process, which would detect and remove all defectives, can be established to test these units. However, the inspector, who can test 20 units per hour, is paid $8 per hour, including fringe benefits. Should an inspection station be established to test all units?

a. What is the cost to inspect each unit?

b. What is the benefit (or loss) from the inspection process?

5 There is a 3 percent error rate at a specific point in a production process. If an inspector is placed at this point, all the errors can be detected and eliminated. However, the inspector is paid $8 per hour and can inspect units in the process at the rate of 30 per hour.

If no inspector is used and defects are allowed to pass this point, there is a cost of $10 per unit to correct the defect later on.

Should an inspector be hired?

6 Resistors for electronic circuits are manufactured on a high-speed automated machine. The machine is set up to produce a large run of resistors of 1,000 ohms each.

To set up the machine and to create a control chart to be used throughout the run, 15 samples were taken with four resistors in each sample. The complete list of samples and their measured values are as follows:

SAMPLE NUMBER	READINGS (IN OHMS)			
1	1010	991	985	986
2	995	996	1009	994
3	990	1003	1015	1008
4	1015	1020	1009	998
5	1013	1019	1005	993
6	994	1001	994	1005
7	989	992	982	1020
8	1001	986	996	996
9	1006	989	1005	1007
10	992	1007	1006	979
11	996	1006	997	989
12	1019	996	991	1011
13	981	991	989	1003
14	999	993	988	984
15	1013	1002	1005	992

Develop an $\overline{X}$ chart and an R chart and plot the values. From the charts, what comments can you make about the process? (Use three-sigma control limits as in Exhibit 9A.6.)

7   In the past, Alpha Corporation has not performed incoming quality control inspections but has taken the word of its vendors. However, Alpha has been having some unsatisfactory experience recently with the quality of purchased items and wants to set up sampling plans for the receiving department to use.

For a particular component, X, Alpha has a lot tolerance percentage defective of 10 percent. Zenon Corporation, from which Alpha purchases this component, has an acceptable quality level in its production facility of 3 percent for component X. Alpha has a consumer's risk of 10 percent, and Zenon has a producer's risk of 5 percent.

a. When a shipment of Product X is received from Zenon Corporation, what sample size should the receiving department test?

b. What is the allowable number of defects in order to accept the shipment?

8   You are the newly appointed assistant administrator at a local hospital and your first project is to investigate the quality of the patient meals put out by the food-service department. You conducted a 10-day survey by submitting a simple questionnaire to the 400 patients with each meal, asking that they simply check off that the meal was either satisfactory or unsatisfactory. For simplicity in this problem, assume that the response was 1,000 returned questionnaires from the 1,200 meals each day. The results are as follows:

	NUMBER OF UNSATISFACTORY MEALS	SAMPLE SIZE
December 1	74	1,000
December 2	42	1,000
December 3	64	1,000
December 4	80	1,000
December 5	40	1,000
December 6	50	1,000
December 7	65	1,000
December 8	70	1,000
December 9	40	1,000
December 10	75	1,000
	600	10,000

a. Construct a *p* chart based on the questionnaire results, using a confidence interval of 95.5 percent, which is two standard deviations.

b. What comments can you make about the results of the survey?

9   Large-scale integrated (LSI) circuit chips are made in one department of an electronics firm. These chips are incorporated into analog devices that are then encased in epoxy. The yield is not particularly good for LSI manufacture, so the AQL specified by that department is 0.15 while the LTPD acceptable by the assembly department is 0.40.

a. Develop a sampling plan.

b. Explain what the sampling plan means; that is, how would you tell someone to do the test?

10   The state and local police departments are trying to analyze crime rates so they can shift their patrols from decreasing-rate areas to areas where rates are increasing. The city and county have been geographically segmented into areas containing 5,000 residences. The police recognize that not all crimes and offenses are reported: people do not want to become involved, consider the offenses too small to report, are too embarrassed to make a police report, or do not take the time, among other reasons. Every month, because of this, the police are contacting by phone a random sample of 1,000 of the 5,000 residences for data on crime. (Respondents are guaranteed anonymity.) Here are the data collected for the past 12 months for one area:

MONTH	CRIME INCIDENCE	SAMPLE SIZE	CRIME RATE
January	7	1,000	0.007
February	9	1,000	0.009
March	7	1,000	0.007
April	7	1,000	0.007

(continued)

MONTH	CRIME INCIDENCE	SAMPLE SIZE	CRIME RATE
May	7	1,000	0.007
June	9	1,000	0.009
July	7	1,000	0.007
August	10	1,000	0.010
September	8	1,000	0.008
October	11	1,000	0.011
November	10	1,000	0.010
December	8	1,000	0.008

Construct a p chart for 95 percent confidence (1.96) and plot each of the months. If the next three months show crime incidences in this area as

$$January = 10 \text{ (out of 1,000 sampled)}$$

$$February = 12 \text{ (out of 1,000 sampled)}$$

$$March = 11 \text{ (out of 1,000 sampled)}$$

what comments can you make regarding the crime rate?

11 Some citizens complained to city council members that there should be equal protection under the law against the occurrence of crimes. The citizens argued that this equal protection should be interpreted as indicating that high-crime areas should have more police protection than low-crime areas. Therefore, police patrols and other methods for preventing crime (such as street lighting or cleaning up abandoned areas and buildings) should be used proportionately to crime occurrence.

In a fashion similar to Problem 10, the city has been broken down into 20 geographic areas, each containing 5,000 residences. The 1,000 sampled from each area showed the following incidence of crime during the past month:

AREA	NUMBER OF CRIMES	SAMPLE SIZE	CRIME RATE
1	14	1,000	0.014
2	3	1,000	0.003
3	19	1,000	0.019
4	18	1,000	0.018
5	14	1,000	0.014
6	28	1,000	0.028
7	10	1,000	0.010
8	18	1,000	0.018
9	12	1,000	0.012
10	3	1,000	0.003
11	20	1,000	0.020
12	15	1,000	0.015
13	12	1,000	0.012
14	14	1,000	0.014
15	10	1,000	0.010
16	30	1,000	0.030
17	4	1,000	0.004
18	20	1,000	0.020
19	6	1,000	0.006
20	30	1,000	0.030
	300		

Suggest a reallocation of crime protection effort, if indicated, based on a p chart analysis. To be reasonably certain in your recommendation, select a 95 percent confidence level (that is, $Z = 1.96$).

12 The following table contains the measurements of the key length dimension from a fuel injector. These samples of size five were taken at one-hour intervals.

| | OBSERVATIONS | | | | |
SAMPLE NUMBER	1	2	3	4	5
1	0.486	0.499	0.493	0.511	0.481
2	0.499	0.506	0.516	0.494	0.529
3	0.496	0.500	0.515	0.488	0.521
4	0.495	0.506	0.483	0.487	0.489
5	0.472	0.502	0.526	0.469	0.481
6	0.473	0.495	0.507	0.493	0.506
7	0.495	0.512	0.490	0.471	0.504
8	0.525	0.501	0.498	0.474	0.485
9	0.497	0.501	0.517	0.506	0.516
10	0.495	0.505	0.516	0.511	0.497
11	0.495	0.482	0.468	0.492	0.492
12	0.483	0.459	0.526	0.506	0.522
13	0.521	0.512	0.493	0.525	0.510
14	0.487	0.521	0.507	0.501	0.500
15	0.493	0.516	0.499	0.511	0.513
16	0.473	0.506	0.479	0.480	0.523
17	0.477	0.485	0.513	0.484	0.496
18	0.515	0.493	0.493	0.485	0.475
19	0.511	0.536	0.486	0.497	0.491
20	0.509	0.490	0.470	0.504	0.512

Construct a three-sigma $\overline{X}$ chart and R chart (use Exhibit 9A.6) for the length of the fuel injector. What can you say about this process?

13 C-Spec, Inc., is attempting to determine whether an existing machine is capable of milling an engine part that has a key specification of 4 ± 0.003 inches. After a trial run on this machine, C-Spec has determined that the machine has a sample mean of 4.001 inches with a standard deviation of 0.002 inch.

a. Calculate the C_{pk} for this machine.

b. Should C-Spec use this machine to produce this part? Why?

14 The manager of an assembly line took five samples, each with six observations, under ideal conditions to develop control limits for an X-bar chart. The mean and range of each sample is shown in the table below:

SAMPLE NUMBER	SAMPLE MEAN	SAMPLE RANGE
1	2.18	0.33
2	2.12	0.38
3	1.86	0.40
4	1.98	0.38
5	2.02	0.35

What would be the 3 standard deviation lower control limit?

15 Interpret the following control chart and determine what action, if any, is appropriate.

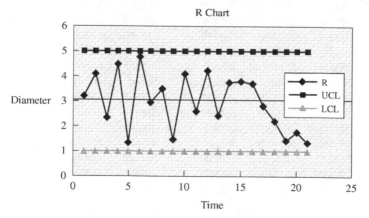

16 Below are the X-bar and R values for five samples. If the lower control limit for the X-bar chart is 8.34, what is the sample size?

SAMPLE	$\overline{X}$ BAR	R
1	8.51	0.44
2	8.37	0.58
3	8.42	0.66
4	8.61	0.47
5	8.54	0.60

ADVANCED PROBLEM

17 Design specifications require that a key dimension on a product measure 100 ± 10 units. A process being considered for producing this product has a standard deviation of four units.
   a. What can you say (quantitatively) regarding the process capability?
   b. Suppose the process average shifts to 92. Calculate the new process capability.
   c. What can you say about the process after the shift? Approximately what percentage of the items produced will be defective?

CASE: HOT SHOT PLASTICS COMPANY

Plastic keychains are being produced in a company named Hot Shot Plastics. The plastic material is first molded and then trimmed to the required shape. The curetimes (which is the time for the plastic to cool) during the molding process affect the edge quality of the keychains produced. The aim is to achieve statistical control of the curetimes using $\overline{X}$ and R charts.

Curetime data of 25 samples, each of size four, have been taken when the process is assumed to be in control. These are shown below (note: the spreadsheet "Hot Shot Plastics.xls" has these data).

SAMPLE NO.	OBSERVATIONS				MEAN	RANGE
1	27.34667	27.50085	29.94412	28.21249	28.25103	2.59745
2	27.79695	26.15006	31.21295	31.33272	29.12317	5.18266
3	33.53255	29.32971	29.70460	31.05300	30.90497	4.20284
4	37.98409	32.26942	31.91741	29.44279	32.90343	8.54130
5	33.82722	30.32543	28.38117	33.70124	31.55877	5.44605
6	29.68356	29.56677	27.23077	34.00417	30.12132	6.77340
7	32.62640	26.32030	32.07892	36.17198	31.79940	9.85168
8	30.29575	30.52868	24.43315	26.85241	28.02750	6.09553
9	28.43856	30.48251	32.43083	30.76162	30.52838	3.99227
10	28.27790	33.94916	30.47406	28.87447	30.39390	5.67126
11	26.91885	27.66133	31.46936	29.66928	28.92971	4.55051
12	28.46547	28.29937	28.99441	31.14511	29.22609	2.84574
13	32.42677	26.10410	29.47718	37.20079	31.30221	11.09669
14	28.84273	30.51801	32.23614	30.47104	30.51698	3.39341
15	30.75136	32.99922	28.08452	26.19981	29.50873	6.79941
16	31.25754	24.29473	35.46477	28.41126	29.85708	11.17004
17	31.24921	28.57954	35.00865	31.23591	31.51833	6.42911
18	31.41554	35.80049	33.60909	27.82131	32.16161	7.97918
19	32.20230	32.02005	32.71018	29.37620	31.57718	3.33398
20	26.91603	29.77775	33.92696	33.78366	31.10110	7.01093
21	35.05322	32.93284	31.51641	27.73615	31.80966	7.31707
22	32.12483	29.32853	30.99709	31.39641	30.96172	2.79630
23	30.09172	32.43938	27.84725	30.70726	30.27140	4.59213
24	30.04835	27.23709	22.01801	28.69624	26.99992	8.03034
25	29.30273	30.83735	30.82735	31.90733	30.71869	2.60460
				Means	30.40289	5.932155

QUESTIONS

1 Prepare $\bar{X}$ and R charts using these data using the method described in the chapter.
2 Analyze the chart and comment on whether the process appears to be in control and stable.
3 Twelve additional samples of curetime data from the molding process were collected from an actual production run.

The data from these new samples are shown below. Update your control charts and compare the results with the previous data. The $\bar{X}$ and R charts are drawn with the new data using the same control limits established before. Comment on what the new charts show.

SAMPLE No.	OBSERVATIONS				MEAN	RANGE
1	31.65830	29.78330	31.87910	33.91250	31.80830	4.12920
2	34.46430	25.18480	37.76689	39.21143	34.15686	14.02663
3	41.34268	39.54590	29.55710	32.57350	35.75480	11.78558
4	29.47310	25.37840	25.04380	24.00350	25.97470	5.46960
5	25.46710	34.85160	30.19150	31.62220	30.53310	9.38450
6	46.25184	34.71356	41.41277	44.63319	41.75284	11.53828
7	35.44750	38.83289	33.08860	31.63490	34.75097	7.19799
8	34.55143	33.86330	35.18869	42.31515	36.47964	8.45185
9	43.43549	37.36371	38.85718	39.25132	39.72693	6.07178
10	37.05298	42.47056	35.90282	38.21905	38.41135	6.56774
11	38.57292	39.06772	32.22090	33.20200	35.76589	6.84682
12	27.03050	33.63970	26.63060	42.79176	32.52314	16.16116

SUPER QUIZ

1 Variation that can be clearly identified and possibly managed.
2 Variation inherent in the process itself.
3 If a process has a capability index of 1 and is running normally (centered between the design limits), what percentage of the units would one expect to be defective?
4 An alternative to viewing an item as simply good or bad due to its falling in or out of the tolerance range.
5 Quality characteristics that are classified as either conforming or not conforming to specification.
6 Quality characteristics that are actually measured, such as the weight of an item.
7 A quality chart suitable for when an item is either good or bad.
8 A quality chart suitable for when a number of blemishes are expected on each unit, such as a spool of yarn.
9 Useful for checking quality when we periodically purchase large quantities of an item and it would be very costly to check each unit individually.
10 A chart that depicts the manufacturer's and consumer's risk associated with a sampling plan.

1. Assignable variation 2. Common variation 3. Design limits are at $\pm 3\sigma$ or 2.7 defects per thousand
4. Taguchi loss function 5. Attributes 6. Variables 7. p-chart 8. c-chart 9. Acceptance sampling
10. Operating characteristic curve

SELECTED BIBLIOGRAPHY

Evans, J. R., and W. M. Lindsay. *Managing for Quality and Performance Excellence.* 7th ed. Mason, OH: South-Western College Publications, 2007.

Juran, J. M., and F. M. Gryna. *Quality Planning and Analysis.* 2nd ed. New York: McGraw-Hill, 1980.

Rath & Strong. *Rath & Strong's Six Sigma Pocket Guide.* Rath & Strong, Inc., 2000.

Small, B. B. (with committee). *Statistical Quality Control Handbook.* Western Electric Co., Inc., 1956.

Zimmerman, S. M., and M. L. Icenogel. *Statistical Quality Control; Using Excel.* 2nd ed. Milwaukee, WI: ASQ Quality Press, 2002.

FOOTNOTES

1 E. L. Grant and R. S. Leavenworth, *Statistical Quality Control* (New York: McGraw-Hill, 1996).

2 There is some controversy surrounding AQLs. This is based on the argument that specifying some acceptable percentage of defectives is inconsistent with the philosophical goal of zero defects. In practice, even in the best QC companies, there is an acceptable quality level. The difference is that it may be stated in parts per million rather than in parts per hundred. This is the case in Motorola's Six-Sigma quality standard, which holds that no more than 3.4 defects per million parts are acceptable.

3 See, for example, H. F. Dodge and H. G. Romig, *Sampling Inspection Tables—Single and Double Sampling* (New York: John Wiley & Sons, 1959); and *Military Standard Sampling Procedures and Tables for Inspection by Attributes* (MIL-STD-105D) (Washington, DC: U.S. Government Printing Office, 1983).

chapter 16

SALES AND OPERATIONS PLANNING

Let's eavesdrop on an executive staff meeting at the Acme Widget Company. The participants are not happy campers.

President:	This shortage situation is terrible. When will we ever get our act together? Whenever business gets good, we run out of product and our customer service is lousy.
VP Operations:	I'll tell you when. When we start to get some decent forecasts from the Sales Department . . .

After reading the chapter you will:

1. Understand what sales and operations planning is and how it coordinates manufacturing, logistics, service, and marketing plans.
2. Construct aggregate plans that employ different strategies for meeting demand.
3. Describe what yield management is and why it is an important strategy for leveling demand.

VP Sales (interrupting):	Wait a minute. We forecasted this upturn.
VP Operations:	. . . in time to do something about it. Yeah, we got the revised forecast—four days after the start of the month. By then it was too late.
VP Sales:	I could have told you months ago. All you had to do was ask.

SOURCE: ADAPTED FROM THOMAS F. WALLACE, *SALES AND OPERATIONS PLANNING: THE HOW-TO HANDBOOK* (CINCINNATI, OH: T. F. WALLACE & CO., 2000), P. 3. COPYRIGHT © 2000 THOMAS WALLACE. USED WITH PERMISSION.

VP Finance: I'd like to be in on those conversations. We've been burned more than once by building inventories for a business upturn that doesn't happen. Then we get stuck with tons of inventory and run out of cash.

And the beat goes on. Back orders, dissatisfied customers, high inventories, late shipments, finger-pointing, cash-flow problems, demand and supply out of balance, missing the business plan. This is the norm in many companies.

It does not, however, have to be that way. Today many companies are using a business process called sales and operations planning (S&OP) to help avoid such problems. To learn what it is, and how to make it work, read on.

Aggregate operations plan

In this chapter, we focus on the aggregate operations plan, which translates annual and quarterly business plans into broad labor and output plans for the intermediate term (3 to 18 months). The objective of the aggregate operations plan is to minimize the cost of resources required to meet demand over that period.

WHAT IS SALES AND OPERATIONS PLANNING?

Sales and operations planning is a process that helps firms provide better customer service, lower inventory, shorten customer lead times, stabilize production rates, and give top management a handle on the business. The process is designed to coordinate activities in the field with the manufacturing and service functions that are required to meet demand over time. Depending on the situation, activities in the field may include the supply of warehouse distribution centers, retail sales outlets, or direct sales channels. The process is designed to help a company get demand and supply in balance and keep them in balance over time. The process requires teamwork among sales, distribution and logistics, operations, finance, and product development.

The sales and operations planning process consists of a series of meetings, finishing with a high-level meeting where key intermediate-term decisions are made. The end goal is an agreement between various departments on the best course of action to achieve the optimal balance between supply and demand. The idea is to put the operational plan in line with the business plan.

This balance must occur at an aggregate level and also at the detailed individual product level. By *aggregate* we mean at the level of major groups of products. Over time, we need to ensure that we have enough total capacity. Since demand is often quite dynamic, it is important that we monitor our expected needs 3 to 18 months or further in the future. When planning this far into the future, it is difficult to know exactly how many of a particular product we will need, but we should be able to know how a larger group of similar products should sell. The term *aggregate* refers to this group of products. Given that we have enough aggregate capacity, our individual product schedulers, working within aggregate capacity constraints, can handle the daily and weekly launching of individual product orders to meet short-term demand.

OVERVIEW OF SALES AND OPERATIONS PLANNING ACTIVITIES

Sales and operations planning

Exhibit 16.1 positions sales and operations planning relative to other major operations planning activities. The term sales and operations planning was coined by companies to refer to the process that helps firms keep demand and supply in balance. In operations management this process traditionally was called *aggregate planning*. The new terminology is meant to capture the importance of cross-functional work. Typically, this activity requires an integrated effort with cooperation from sales, distribution and logistics, operations, finance, and product development.

Within sales and operations planning, marketing develops a sales plan that extends through the next 3 to 18 months. This sales plan typically is stated in units of aggregate product

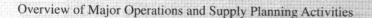

Overview of Major Operations and Supply Planning Activities

exhibit 16.1

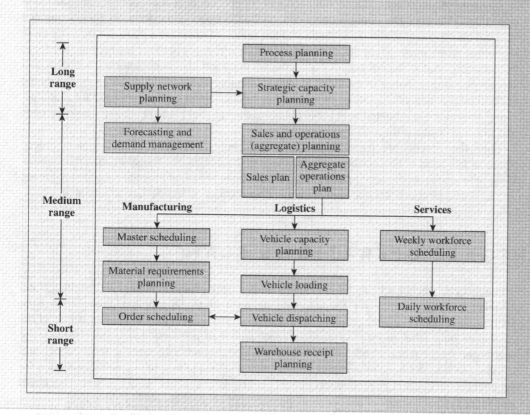

groups and often is tied into sales incentive programs and other marketing activities. The operations side develops an operations plan as an output of the process, which is discussed in depth in this chapter. By focusing on aggregate product and sales volumes, the marketing and operations functions are able to develop plans for the way demand will be met. This is a particularly difficult task when demand changes significantly changes over time as a result of market trends or other factors.

Aggregation on the supply side is done by product families, and on the demand side it is done by groups of customers. Individual product production schedules and matching customer orders can be handled more readily as a result of the sales and operations planning process. Typically, sales and operations planning occurs on a monthly cycle. Sales and operations planning links a company's strategic plans and business plan to its detailed operations and supply processes. These detailed processes include manufacturing, logistics, and service activities, as shown in Exhibit 16.1.

In Exhibit 16.1 the time dimension is shown as long, intermediate, and short range. Long-range planning generally is done annually, focusing on a horizon greater than one year. Intermediate-range planning usually covers a period from 3 to 18 months, with time increments that are weekly, monthly, or sometimes quarterly. Short-range planning covers a period from one day to six months, with daily or weekly time increments.

Long-range planning activities are done in two major areas. The first is the design of the manufacturing and service processes that produce the products of the firm, and the second is the design of the logistics activities that deliver products to the customer. Process planning deals with determining the specific technologies and procedures required to produce a product or service. Strategic capacity planning deals with determining the long-term capabilities (such as size and scope) of the production systems. Similarly, from a logistics point of view, supply network planning determines how the product will be distributed to the customer on the outbound side, with decisions relating to the location of warehouses and the types of transportation systems to

Long-range planning
Intermediate-range planning
Short-range planning

Supply Chain

be used. On the inbound side, supply network planning involves decisions relating to outsourcing production, selection of parts and component suppliers, and related decisions.

Intermediate-term activities include forecasting and demand management and sales and operations planning. The determination of expected demand is the focus of forecasting and demand management. From these data, detailed sales and operations plans for meeting these requirements are made. The sales plans are inputs to sales force activities, which are the focus of marketing books. The operations plan provides input into the manufacturing, logistics, and service planning activities of the firm. Master scheduling and material requirements planning are designed to generate detailed schedules that indicate when parts are needed for manufacturing activities. Coordinated with these plans are the logistics plans needed to move the parts and finished products through the supply chain.

Short-term details are focused mostly on scheduling production and shipment orders. These orders need to be coordinated with the actual vehicles that transport material through the supply chain. On the service side, short-term scheduling of employees is needed to ensure that adequate customer service is provided and fair worker schedules are maintained.

Service

THE AGGREGATE OPERATIONS PLAN

The aggregate operations plan is concerned with setting production rates by product group or other broad categories for the intermediate term (3 to 18 months). Note again from Exhibit 16.1 that the aggregate plan precedes the master schedule. *The main purpose of the aggregate plan is to specify the optimal combination of production rate, workforce level, and inventory on hand.* Production rate refers to the number of units completed per unit of time (such as per hour or per day). Workforce level is the number of workers needed for production (production = production rate × workforce level). Inventory on hand is unused inventory carried over from the previous period.

Production rate
Workforce level
Inventory on hand

Here is a formal statement of the aggregate planning problem: Given the demand forecast F_t for each period t in the planning horizon that extends over T periods, determine the production level P_t, inventory level I_t, and workforce level W_t for periods $t = 1, 2, \ldots, T$ that minimize the relevant costs over the planning horizon.

The form of the aggregate plan varies from company to company. In some firms, it is a formalized report containing planning objectives and the planning premises on which it is based. In other companies, particularly smaller ones, the owner may make simple calculations of workforce needs that reflect a general staffing strategy.

The process by which the plan itself is derived also varies. One common approach is to derive it from the corporate annual plan, as shown in Exhibit 16.1. A typical corporate plan contains a section on manufacturing that specifies how many units in each major product line need to be produced over the next 12 months to meet the sales forecast. The planner takes this information and attempts to determine how best to meet these requirements with available resources. Alternatively, some organizations combine output requirements into equivalent units and use this as the basis for the aggregate plan. For example, a division of General Motors may be asked to produce a certain number of cars of all types at a particular facility. The production planner would then take the average labor hours required for all models as a basis for the overall aggregate plan. Refinements to this plan, specifically model types to be produced, would be reflected in shorter-term production plans.

Another approach is to develop the aggregate plan by simulating various master production schedules and calculating corresponding capacity requirements to see if adequate labor and equipment exist at each work center. If capacity is inadequate, additional requirements for overtime, subcontracting, extra workers, and so forth are specified for each product line and combined into a rough-cut plan. This plan is then modified by cut-and-try or mathematical methods to derive a final and (one hopes) lower-cost plan.

PRODUCTION PLANNING ENVIRONMENT

Exhibit 16.2 illustrates the internal and external factors that constitute the production planning environment. In general, the external environment is outside the production planner's

Required Inputs to the Production Planning Systems

exhibit 16.2

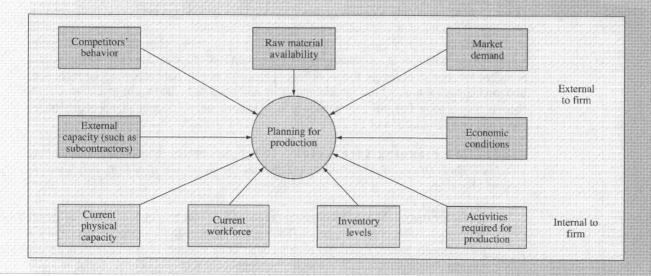

direct control, but in some firms, demand for the product can be managed. Through close cooperation between marketing and operations, promotional activities and price cutting can be used to build demand during slow periods. Conversely, when demand is strong, promotional activities can be curtailed and prices raised to maximize the revenues from those products or services that the firm has the capacity to provide. The current practices in managing demand will be discussed later in the section titled "Yield Management."

Complementary products may work for firms facing cyclical demand fluctuations. For instance, lawnmower manufacturers will have strong demand for spring and summer, but weak demand during fall and winter. Demands on the production system can be smoothed out by producing a complementary product with high demand during fall and winter, and low demand during spring and summer (for instance, snowmobiles, snowblowers, or leafblowers). With services, cycles are more often measured in hours than months. Restaurants with strong demand during lunch and dinner will often add a breakfast menu to increase demand during the morning hours.

But even so, there are limits to how much demand can be controlled. Ultimately, the production planner must live with the sales projections and orders promised by the marketing function, leaving the internal factors as variables that can be manipulated in deriving a

Service

WATER SKIS AND SNOW SKIS ARE GREAT EXAMPLES OF COMPLEMENTARY PRODUCTS.

production plan. A new approach to facilitate managing these internal factors is termed *accurate response.* This entails refined measurement of historical demand patterns blended with expert judgment to determine when to begin production of particular items. The key element of the approach is clearly identifying those products for which demand is relatively predictable from those for which demand is relatively unpredictable.[1]

The internal factors themselves differ in their controllability. Current physical capacity (plant and equipment) is usually nearly fixed in the short run; union agreements often constrain what can be done in changing the workforce; physical capacity cannot always be increased; and top management may limit the amount of money that can be tied up in inventories. Still, there is always some flexibility in managing these factors, and production planners can implement one or a combination of the production planning strategies discussed here.

Production planning strategies

Production Planning Strategies   There are essentially three production planning strategies. These strategies involve trade-offs among the workforce size, work hours, inventory, and backlogs.

1. **Chase strategy.**   Match the production rate to the order rate by hiring and laying off employees as the order rate varies. The success of this strategy depends on having a pool of easily trained applicants to draw on as order volumes increase. There are obvious motivational impacts. When order backlogs are low, employees may feel compelled to slow down out of fear of being laid off as soon as existing orders are completed.
2. **Stable workforce—variable work hours.**   Vary the output by varying the number of hours worked through flexible work schedules or overtime. By varying the number of work hours, you can match production quantities to orders. This strategy provides workforce continuity and avoids many of the emotional and tangible costs of hiring and firing associated with the chase strategy.
3. **Level strategy.**   Maintain a stable workforce working at a constant output rate. Shortages and surpluses are absorbed by fluctuating inventory levels, order backlogs, and lost sales. Employees benefit from stable work hours at the costs of potentially decreased customer service levels and increased inventory costs. Another concern is the possibility of inventoried products becoming obsolete.

Pure strategy
Mixed strategy

When just one of these variables is used to absorb demand fluctuations, it is termed a pure strategy; two or more used in combination constitute a mixed strategy. As you might suspect, mixed strategies are more widely applied in industry.

Subcontracting   In addition to these strategies, managers also may choose to subcontract some portion of production. This strategy is similar to the chase strategy, but hiring and laying off are translated into subcontracting and not subcontracting. Some level of subcontracting can be desirable to accommodate demand fluctuations. However, unless the relationship with the supplier is particularly strong, a manufacturer can lose some control over schedule and quality.

RELEVANT COSTS

Four costs are relevant to the aggregate production plan. These relate to the production cost itself as well as the cost to hold inventory and to have unfilled orders. More specifically, these are

1. **Basic production costs.**   These are the fixed and variable costs incurred in producing a given product type in a given time period. Included are direct and indirect labor costs and regular as well as overtime compensation.
2. **Costs associated with changes in the production rate.**   Typical costs in this category are those involved in hiring, training, and laying off personnel. Hiring temporary help is a way of avoiding these costs.
3. **Inventory holding costs.**   A major component is the cost of capital tied up in inventory. Other components are storing, insurance, taxes, spoilage, and obsolescence.
4. **Backordering costs.**   Usually these are very hard to measure and include costs of expediting, loss of customer goodwill, and loss of sales revenues resulting from backordering.

IT'S ALL IN THE PLANNING

You're sitting anxiously in the suddenly assembled general manager's staff meeting. Voices are nervously subdued. The rumor mill is in high gear about another initiative-of-the-month about to be loosed among the leery survivors of the last purge. The meeting begins. Amid the tricolor visuals and 3D spreadsheets, the same old message is skeptically received by managers scrambling for politically correct responses in an endless game of shoot the messenger.

This is a familiar scene in corporations around the world. But interestingly, firms such as Finisar Corporation have learned how to manage the process of successfully matching supply and demand. Finisar has developed a new semiconductor laser used in computing, networking, and sensing applications. Forecasting and managing production capacity is a unique challenge for companies with a stream of new and innovative products coming to market. Using a monthly sales and operations planning process, Finisar has been able to improve their short- and long-term forecasting accuracy from 60 percent to

consistently hitting 95 percent or better. The specific steps within their plan focus the executive team on (1) the demand opportunities for current and new products and (2) the constraints on the organization's ability to produce product to meet this demand. The plan, developed in a monthly sales and operations planning executive meeting, ensures that demand is synchronized with supply, so customers get the product they want, when they want it, while inventory and costs are kept to a minimum.

Finisar managers indicated that a critical step was getting the general manager to champion the process. The second step was achieving a complete understanding of required behavior from the team, including committing to a balanced and synchronized demand/supply plan, being accountable for meeting the performance standards, having open and honest communication, not promising what cannot be delivered, and making the decisions needed to address the identified opportunities and constraints.

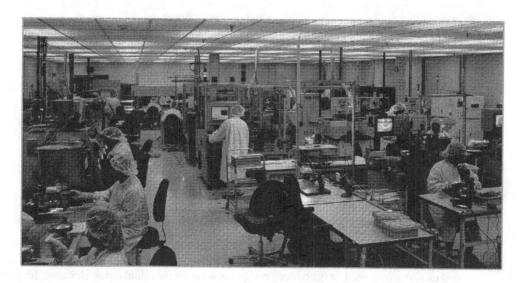

SOURCE: ADAPTED FROM http://www.themanufacturer.com.

Budgets To receive funding, operations managers are generally required to submit annual, and sometimes quarterly, budget requests. The aggregate plan is key to the success of the budgeting process. Recall that the goal of the aggregate plan is to minimize the total production-related costs over the planning horizon by determining the optimal combination of workforce levels and inventory levels. Thus, the aggregate plan provides justification for the requested budget amount. Accurate medium-range planning increases the likelihood of (1) receiving the requested budget and (2) operating within the limits of the budget.

In the next section we provide an example of medium-range planning in a manufacturing setting. This example illustrates the trade-offs associated with different production planning strategies.[2]

AGGREGATE PLANNING TECHNIQUES

Companies commonly use simple cut-and-try charting and graphic methods to develop aggregate plans. A cut-and-try approach involves costing out various production planning alternatives and selecting the one that is best. Elaborate spreadsheets are developed to facilitate the decision process. Sophisticated approaches involving linear programming and simulation are often incorporated into these spreadsheets. In the following, we demonstrate a spreadsheet approach to evaluate four strategies for meeting demand for the JC Company. Later we discuss more sophisticated approaches using linear programming (see Appendix A).

A CUT-AND-TRY EXAMPLE: THE JC COMPANY

Service

A firm with pronounced seasonal variation normally plans production for a full year to capture the extremes in demand during the busiest and slowest months. But we can illustrate the general principles involved with a shorter horizon. Suppose we wish to set up a production plan for the JC Company for the next six months. We are given the following information:

DEMAND AND WORKING DAYS

	JANUARY	FEBRUARY	MARCH	APRIL	MAY	JUNE	TOTALS
Demand forecast	1,800	1,500	1,100	900	1,100	1,600	8,000
Number of working days	22	19	21	21	22	20	125

COSTS

Materials	$100.00/unit
Inventory holding cost	$1.50/unit/month
Marginal cost of stockout	$5.00/unit/month
Marginal cost of subcontracting	$20.00/unit ($120 subcontracting cost less $100 material savings)
Hiring and training cost	$200.00/worker
Layoff cost	$250.00/worker
Labor hours required	5/unit
Straight-time cost (first eight hours each day)	$4.00/hour
Overtime cost (time and a half)	$6.00/hour

INVENTORY

Beginning inventory	400 units
Safety stock	25% of month demand

In solving this problem, we can exclude the material costs. We could have included this $100 cost in all our calculations, but if we assume that a $100 cost is common to each demanded unit, then we need only concern ourselves with the marginal costs. Because the subcontracting cost is $120, our true cost for subcontracting is just $20 because we save the materials.

Note that many costs are expressed in a different form than typically found in the accounting records of a firm. Therefore, do not expect to obtain all these costs directly from such records, but obtain them indirectly from management personnel, who can help interpret the data.

Inventory at the beginning of the first period is 400 units. Because the demand forecast is imperfect, the JC Company has determined that a *safety stock* (buffer inventory) should be established to reduce the likelihood of stockouts. For this example, assume the safety stock should be one-quarter of the demand forecast. (Chapter 17 covers this topic in depth.)

Before investigation of alternative production plans, it is often useful to convert demand forecasts into *production requirements,* which take into account the safety stock estimates. In Exhibit 16.3, note that these requirements implicitly assume that the safety stock is never actually used, so that the ending inventory each month equals the safety stock for that month. For example, the January safety stock of 450 (25 percent of January demand of 1,800) becomes the inventory at the end of January. The production requirement for January is demand plus safety stock minus beginning inventory (1,800 + 450 − 400 = 1,850).

Aggregate Production Planning Requirements

exhibit 16.3

**Excel:
Aggregate
Planning**

	JANUARY	FEBRUARY	MARCH	APRIL	MAY	JUNE
Beginning inventory	400	450	375	275	225	275
Demand forecast	1,800	1,500	1,100	900	1,100	1,600
Safety stock (.25 × Demand forecast)	450	375	275	225	275	400
Production requirement (Demand forecast + Safety stock − Beginning inventory)	1,850	1,425	1,000	850	1,150	1,725
Ending inventory (Beginning inventory + Production requirement − Demand forecast)	450	375	275	225	275	400

Now we must formulate alternative production plans for the JC Company. Using a spreadsheet, we investigate four different plans with the objective of finding the one with the lowest total cost.

Plan 1. Produce to exact monthly production requirements using a regular eight-hour day by varying workforce size.

Plan 2. Produce to meet expected average demand over the next six months by maintaining a constant workforce. This constant number of workers is calculated by finding the average number of workers required each day over the horizon. Take the total production requirements and multiply by the time required for each unit. Then divide by the total time that one person works over the horizon [(8,000 units × 5 hours per unit) ÷ (125 days × 8 hours per day) = 40 workers]. Inventory is allowed to accumulate, with shortages filled from next month's production by backordering. Negative beginning inventory balances indicate that demand is backordered. In some cases, sales may be lost if demand is not met. The lost sales can be shown with a negative ending inventory balance followed by a zero beginning inventory balance in the next period. Notice that in this plan we use our safety stock in January, February, March, and June to meet expected demand.

Plan 3. Produce to meet the minimum expected demand (April) using a constant workforce on regular time. Subcontract to meet additional output requirements. The number of workers is calculated by locating the minimum monthly production requirement and determining how many workers would be needed for that month [(850 units × 5 hours per unit) ÷ (21 days × 8 hours per day) = 25 workers] and subcontracting any monthly difference between requirements and production.

Plan 4. Produce to meet expected demand for all but the first two months using a constant workforce on regular time. Use overtime to meet additional output requirements. The number of workers is more difficult to compute for this plan, but the goal is to finish June with an ending inventory as close as possible to the June safety stock. By trial and error it can be shown that a constant workforce of 38 workers is the closest approximation.

The next step is to calculate the cost of each plan. This requires the series of simple calculations shown in Exhibit 16.4. Note that the headings in each row are different for each plan because each is a different problem requiring its own data and calculations.

The final step is to tabulate and graph each plan and compare their costs. From Exhibit 16.5 we can see that using subcontractors resulted in the lowest cost (Plan 3). Exhibit 16.6 shows the effects of the four plans. This is a cumulative graph illustrating the expected results on the total production requirement.

Note that we have made one other assumption in this example: The plan can start with any number of workers with no hiring or layoff cost. This usually is the case because an aggregate plan draws on existing personnel, and we can start the plan that way. However, in an actual application, the availability of existing personnel transferable from other areas of the firm may change the assumptions.

exhibit 16.4   Costs of Four Production Plans

**Excel:
Aggregate
Planning**

PRODUCTION PLAN 1: EXACT PRODUCTION; VARY WORKFORCE							
	JANUARY	FEBRUARY	MARCH	APRIL	MAY	JUNE	TOTAL
Production requirement (from Exhibit 16.3)	1,850	1,425	1,000	850	1,150	1,725	
Production hours required (Production requirement × 5 hr./unit)	9,250	7,125	5,000	4,250	5,750	8,625	
Working days per month	22	19	21	21	22	20	
Hours per month per worker (Working days × 8 hrs./day)	176	152	168	168	176	160	
Workers required (Production hours required/Hours per month per worker)	53	47	30	25	33	54	
New workers hired (assuming opening workforce equal to first month's requirement of 53 workers)	0	0	0	0	8	21	
Hiring cost (New workers hired × $200)	$0	$0	$0	$0	$1,600	$4,200	$5,800
Workers laid off	0	6	17	5	0	0	
Layoff cost (Workers laid off × $250)	$0	$1,500	$4,250	$1,250	$0	$0	$7,000
Straight-time cost (Production hours required × $4)	$37,000	$28,500	$20,000	$17,000	$23,000	$34,500	$160,000
						Total cost	$172,800

PRODUCTION PLAN 2: CONSTANT WORKFORCE; VARY INVENTORY AND STOCKOUT							
	JANUARY	FEBRUARY	MARCH	APRIL	MAY	JUNE	TOTAL
Beginning inventory	400	8	−276	−32	412	720	
Working days per month	22	19	21	21	22	20	
Production hours available (Working days per month × 8 hr./day × 40 workers)*	7,040	6,080	6,720	6,720	7,040	6,400	
Actual production (Production hours available/5 hr./unit)	1,408	1,216	1,344	1,344	1,408	1,280	
Demand forecast (from Exhibit 16.3)	1,800	1,500	1,100	900	1,100	1,600	
Ending inventory (Beginning inventory + Actual production − Demand forecast)	8	−276	−32	412	720	400	
Shortage cost (Units short × $5)	$0	$1,380	$160	$0	$0	$0	$1,540
Safety stock (from Exhibit 16.3)	450	375	275	225	275	400	
Units excess (Ending inventory − Safety stock) only if positive amount	0	0	0	187	445	0	
Inventory cost (Units excess × $1.50)	$0	$0	$0	$281	$668	$0	$948
Straight-time cost (Production hours available × $4)	$28,160	$24,320	$26,880	$26,880	$28,160	$25,600	$160,000
						Total cost	$162,488

*(SUM OF PRODUCTION REQUIREMENT IN EXHIBIT 16.3 × 5 HR./UNIT)/(SUM OF PRODUCTION HOURS AVAILABLE × 8 HR./DAY) = (8,000 × 5)/(125 × 8) = 40.

Plan 1 is the "S" curve when we chase demand by varying workforce. Plan 2 has the highest average production rate (the line representing cumulative demand has the greatest slope). Using subcontracting in Plan 3 results in it having the lowest production rate. Limits on the amount of overtime available results in Plan 4 being similar to Plan 2.

Each of these four plans focused on one particular cost, and the first three were simple pure strategies. Obviously, there are many other feasible plans, some of which would use a combination of workforce changes, overtime, and subcontracting. The problems at the end of this chapter include examples of such mixed strategies. In practice, the final plan chosen

PRODUCTION PLAN 3: CONSTANT LOW WORKFORCE; SUBCONTRACT

	JANUARY	FEBRUARY	MARCH	APRIL	MAY	JUNE	TOTAL
Production requirement (from Exhibit 16.3)	1,850	1,425	1,000	850	1,150	1,725	
Working days per month	22	19	21	21	22	20	
Production hours available (Working days × 8 hrs./day × 25 workers)*	4,400	3,800	4,200	4,200	4,400	4,000	
Actual production (Production hours available/5 hr. per unit)	880	760	840	840	880	800	
Units subcontracted (Production requirement − Actual production)	970	665	160	10	270	925	
Subcontracting cost (Units subcontracted × $20)	$19,400	$13,300	$3,200	$200	$5,400	$18,500	$60,000
Straight-time cost (Production hours available × $4)	$17,600	$15,200	$16,800	$16,800	$17,600	$16,000	$100,000
						Total cost	$160,000

*MINIMUM PRODUCTION REQUIREMENT. IN THIS EXAMPLE, APRIL IS MINIMUM OF 850 UNITS. NUMBER OF WORKERS REQUIRED FOR APRIL IS $(850 \times 5)/(21 \times 8) = 25$.

PRODUCTION PLAN 4: CONSTANT WORKFORCE; OVERTIME

	JANUARY	FEBRUARY	MARCH	APRIL	MAY	JUNE	TOTAL
Beginning inventory	400	0	0	177	554	792	
Working days per month	22	19	21	21	22	20	
Production hours available (Working days × 8 hr./day × 38 workers)*	6,688	5,776	6,384	6,384	6,688	6,080	
Regular shift production (Production hours available/5 hrs. per unit)	1,338	1,155	1,277	1,277	1,338	1,216	
Demand forecast (from Exhibit 16.3)	1,800	1,500	1,100	900	1,100	1,600	
Units available before overtime (Beginning inventory + Regular shift production − Demand forecast). This number has been rounded to the nearest integer.	−62	−345	177	554	792	408	
Units overtime	62	375	0	0	0	0	
Overtime cost (Units overtime × 5 hr./unit × $6/hr.)	$1,860	$10,350	$0	$0	$0	$0	$12,210
Safety stock (from Exhibit 16.3)	450	375	275	225	275	400	
Units excess (Units available before overtime − Safety stock) only if positive amount	0	0	0	329	517	8	
Inventory cost (Units excessive × $1.50)	$0	$0	$0	$494	$776	$12	$1,281
Straight-time cost (Production hours available × $4)	$26,752	$23,104	$25,536	$25,536	$26,752	$24,320	$152,000
						Total cost	$165,491

*Workers determined by trial and error. See text for explanation.

would come from searching a variety of alternatives and future projections beyond the six-month planning horizon we have used.

Keep in mind that the cut-and-try approach does not guarantee finding the minimum-cost solution. However, spreadsheet programs, such as Microsoft Excel, can perform cut-and-try cost estimates in seconds and have elevated this kind of what-if analysis to a fine art. More sophisticated programs can generate much better solutions without the user having to intercede, as in the cut-and-try method.

exhibit 16.5   Comparison of Four Plans

**Excel:
Aggregate
Planning**

COSTS	PLAN 1: EXACT PRODUCTION; VARY WORKFORCE	PLAN 2: CONSTANT WORKFORCE; VARY INVENTORY AND STOCKOUT	PLAN 3: CONSTANT LOW WORKFORCE; SUBCONTRACT	PLAN 4: CONSTANT WORKFORCE; OVERTIME
Hiring	$ 5,800	$ 0	$ 0	$ 0
Layoff	7,000	0	0	0
Excess inventory	0	948	0	1,281
Shortage	0	1,540	0	0
Subcontract	0	0	60,000	0
Overtime	0	0	0	12,210
Straight time	160,000	160,000	100,000	152,000
	$172,800	$162,488	$160,000	$165,491

exhibit 16.6   Four Plans for Satisfying a Production Requirement over the Number of Production Days Available

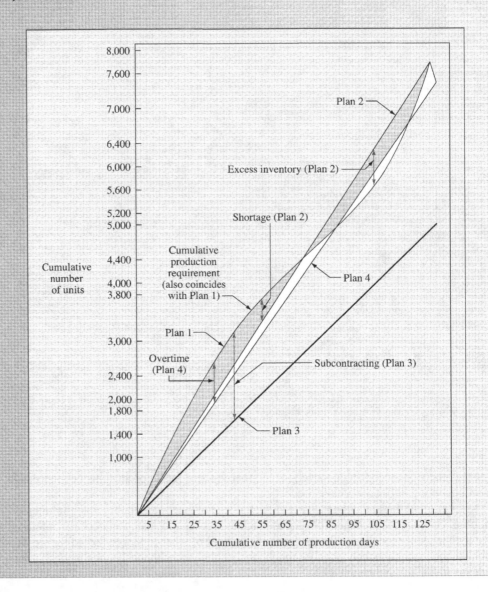

AGGREGATE PLANNING APPLIED TO SERVICES: TUCSON PARKS AND RECREATION DEPARTMENT

Service

Charting and graphic techniques are also useful for aggregate planning in service applications. The following example shows how a city's parks and recreation department could use the alternatives of full-time employees, part-time employees, and subcontracting to meet its commitment to provide a service to the city.

Tucson Parks and Recreation Department has an operation and maintenance budget of $9,760,000. The department is responsible for developing and maintaining open space, all public recreational programs, adult sports leagues, golf courses, tennis courts, pools, and so forth. There are 336 full-time-equivalent employees (FTEs). Of these, 216 are full-time permanent personnel who provide the administration and year-round maintenance to all areas. The remaining 120 FTE positions are staffed with part-timers; about three-quarters of them are used during the summer, and the remaining quarter in the fall, winter, and spring seasons. The three-fourths (or 90 FTE positions) show up as approximately 800 part-time summer jobs: lifeguards, baseball umpires, and instructors in summer programs for children. Eight hundred part-time jobs came from 90 FTEs because many last only for a month or two, while the FTEs are a year long.

Currently, the only parks and recreation work subcontracted amounts to less than $100,000. This is for the golf and tennis pros and for grounds maintenance at the libraries and veterans' cemetery.

Because of the nature of city employment, the probable bad public image, and civil service rules, the option to hire and fire full-time help daily or weekly to meet seasonal demand is out of the question. However, temporary part-time help is authorized and traditional. Also, it is virtually impossible to have regular (full-time) staff for all the summer jobs. During the summer months, the approximately 800 part-time employees are staffing many programs that occur simultaneously, prohibiting level scheduling over a normal 40-hour week. A wider variety of skills are required (such as umpires, coaches, lifeguards, and teachers of ceramics, guitar, karate, belly dancing, and yoga) than can be expected from full-time employees.

Three options are open to the department in its aggregate planning:

1. The present method, which is to maintain a medium-level full-time staff and schedule work during off-seasons (such as rebuilding baseball fields during the winter months) and to use part-time help during peak demands.
2. Maintain a lower level of staff over the year and subcontract all additional work presently done by full-time staff (still using part-time help).
3. Maintain an administrative staff only and subcontract all work, including part-time help. (This would entail contracts to landscaping firms and pool maintenance companies as well as to newly created private firms to employ and supply part-time help.)

The common unit of measure of work across all areas is full-time equivalent jobs or employees. For example, assume in the same week that 30 lifeguards worked 20 hours each, 40 instructors worked 15 hours each, and 35 baseball umpires worked 10 hours each. This is equivalent to $(30 \times 20) + (40 \times 15) + (35 \times 10) = 1,550 \div 40 = 38.75$ FTE positions for that week. Although a considerable amount of workload can be shifted to off-season, most of the work must be done when required.

Full-time employees consist of three groups: (1) the skeleton group of key department personnel coordinating with the city, setting policy, determining budgets, measuring performance, and so forth; (2) the administrative group of supervisory and office personnel who are responsible for or whose jobs are directly linked to the direct-labor workers; and (3) the direct-labor workforce of 116 full-time positions. These workers physically maintain the department's areas of responsibility, such as cleaning up, mowing golf greens and ballfields, trimming trees, and watering grass.

Cost information needed to determine the best alternative strategy is

Full-time direct-labor employees	
Average wage rate	$4.45 per hour
Fringe benefits	17% of wage rate
Administrative costs	20% of wage rate
Part-time employees	
Average wage rate	$4.03 per hour
Fringe benefits	11% of wage rate
Administrative costs	25% of wage rate
Subcontracting all full-time jobs	$1.6 million
Subcontracting all part-time jobs	$1.85 million

June and July are the peak demand seasons in Tucson. Exhibit 16.7 shows the high requirements for June and July personnel. The part-time help reaches 576 FTE positions (although, in actual numbers, this is approximately 800 different employees). After a low fall and winter staffing level, the demand shown as "full-time direct" reaches 130 in March (when grounds are reseeded and fertilized) and then increases to a high of 325 in July. The present method levels this uneven demand over the year to an average of 116 full-time year-round employees by early scheduling of work. As previously mentioned, no attempt is made to hire and lay off full-time workers to meet this uneven demand.

exhibit 16.7

Actual Demand Requirement for Full-Time Direct Employees and Full-Time Equivalent (FTE) Part-Time Employees

Excel: Aggregate Planning

	JAN.	FEB.	MAR.	APR.	MAY	JUNE	JULY	AUG.	SEPT.	OCT.	NOV.	DEC.	TOTAL
Days	22	20	21	22	21	20	21	21	21	23	18	22	252
Full-time employees	66	28	130	90	195	290	325	92	45	32	29	60	
Full-time days*	1,452	560	2,730	1,980	4,095	5,800	6,825	1,932	945	736	522	1,320	28,897
Full-time equivalent part-time employees	41	75	72	68	72	302	576	72	0	68	84	27	
FTE days	902	1,500	1,512	1,496	1,512	6,040	12,096	1,512	0	1,564	1,512	594	30,240

*FULL-TIME DAYS ARE DERIVED BY MULTIPLYING THE NUMBER OF DAYS IN EACH MONTH BY THE NUMBER OF WORKERS.

Monthly Requirement for Full-Time Direct-Labor Employees (Other Than Key Personnel) and Full-Time Equivalent Part-Time Employees

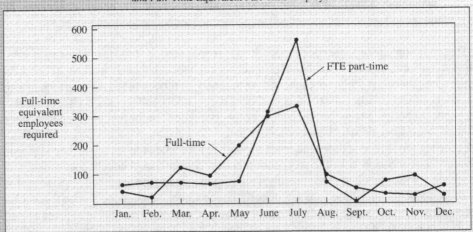

Three Possible Plans for the Parks and Recreation Department

exhibit 16.8

Excel: Aggregate Planning

Alternative 1: Maintain 116 full-time regular direct workers. Schedule work during off-seasons to level workload throughout the year. Continue to use 120 full-time equivalent (FTE) part-time employees to meet high demand periods.

Costs	Days per Year (Exhibit 16.7)	Hours (Employees × Days × 8 Hours)	Wages (Full-Time, $4.45; Part-Time, $4.03)	Fringe Benefits (Full-Time, 17%; Part-Time, 11%)	Administrative Cost (Full-Time, 20%; Part-Time, 25%)
116 full-time regular employees	252	233,856	$1,040,659	$176,912	$208,132
120 part-time employees	252	241,920	974,938	107,243	243,735
Total cost = $2,751,619			$2,015,597	$284,155	$451,867

Alternative 2: Maintain 50 full-time regular direct workers and the present 120 FTE part-time employees. Subcontract jobs releasing 66 full-time regular employees. Subcontract cost, $1,100,000.

Cost	Days per Year (Exhibit 16.7)	Hours (Employees × Days × 8 Hours)	Wages (Full-Time, $4.45; Part-Time, $4.03)	Fringe Benefits (Full-Time, 17%; Part-Time, 11%)	Administrative Cost (Full-Time, 20%; Part-Time, 25%)	Subcontract Cost
50 full-time employees	252	100,800	$ 448,560	$ 76,255	$ 89,712	
120 FTE part-time employees	252	241,920	974,938	107,243	243,735	
Subcontracting cost						$1,100,000
Total cost = $3,040,443			$1,423,498	$183,498	$333,447	$1,100,000

Alternative 3: Subcontract all jobs previously performed by 116 full-time regular employees. Subcontract cost $1,600,000. Subcontract all jobs previously performed by 120 FTE part-time employees. Subcontract cost $1,850,000.

Cost	Subcontract Cost
0 full-time employees	
0 part-time employees	
Subcontract full-time jobs	$1,600,000
Subcontract part-time jobs	1,850,000
Total cost	$3,450,000

Exhibit 16.8 shows the cost calculations for all three alternatives and compares the total costs for each alternative. From this analysis, it appears that the department is already using the lowest-cost alternative (Alternative 1).

LEVEL SCHEDULING

In this chapter we looked at four primary strategies for production planning: vary workforce size to meet demand, work overtime and part-time, vary inventory through excesses and shortages, and subcontract.

A level schedule holds production constant over a period of time. It is something of a combination of the strategies we have mentioned here. For each period, it keeps the workforce constant and inventory low, and depends on demand to pull products through. Level production has a number of advantages, which makes it the backbone of JIT production:

1. The entire system can be planned to minimize inventory and work-in-process.
2. Product modifications are up-to-date because of the low amount of work-in-process.

3. There is a smooth flow throughout the production system.
4. Purchased items from vendors can be delivered when needed and, in fact, often directly to the production line.

Global

Toyota Motor Corporation, for example, creates a yearly production plan that shows the total number of cars to be made and sold. The aggregate production plan creates the system requirements to produce this total number with a level schedule. The secret to success in the Japanese level schedule is *production smoothing*. The aggregate plan is translated into monthly and daily schedules that *sequence* products through the production system. The procedure is essentially this: Two months in advance, the car types and quantities needed are established. This is converted to a detailed plan one month ahead. These quantities are given to subcontractors and vendors so that they can plan on meeting Toyota's needs. The monthly needs of various car types are then translated into daily schedules. For example, if 8,000 units of car type A are needed in one month, along with 6,000 type B, 4,000 type C, and 2,000 type D, and if we assume the line operates 20 days per month, then this would be translated to a daily output of 400, 300, 200, and 100, respectively. Further, this would be sequenced as four units of A, three of B, two of C, and one of D each 9.6 minutes of a two-shift day (960 minutes).

Each worker operates a number of machines, producing a sequence of products. To use this level scheduling technique,

1. Production should be repetitive (assembly-line format).
2. The system must contain excess capacity.
3. Output of the system must be fixed for a period of time (preferably a month).
4. There must be a smooth relationship among purchasing, marketing, and production.
5. The cost of carrying inventory must be high.
6. Equipment costs must be low.
7. The workforce must be multiskilled.

For more about level scheduling, see lean production schedules in Chapter 13. Also see the discussion on mixed-model line balancing in Chapter 6.

YIELD MANAGEMENT

Yield management

Why is it that the guy sitting next to you on the plane paid half the price you paid for your ticket? Why was a hotel room you booked more expensive when you booked it six months in advance than when you checked in without a reservation (or vice versa)? The answers lie in the practice known as yield management. Yield management can be defined as the process of allocating the right type of capacity to the right type of customer at the right price and time to maximize revenue or yield. Yield management can be a powerful approach to making demand more predictable, which is important to aggregate planning.

Service

Yield management has existed as long as there has been limited capacity for serving customers. However, its widespread scientific application began with American Airlines' computerized reservation system (SABRE), introduced in the mid-1980s. The system allowed the airline to change ticket prices on any routes instantaneously as a function of forecast demand. Peoples' Express, a no-frills, low-cost competitor airline, was one of the most famous victims of American's yield management system. Basically, the system enabled hour-by-hour updating on competing routes so that American could match or better prices wherever Peoples' Express was flying. The president of Peoples' Express realized that the game was lost when his mother flew on American to Peoples' hub for a lower price than Peoples' could offer!

From an operational perspective, yield management is most effective when

1. Demand can be segmented by customer.
2. Fixed costs are high and variable costs are low.
3. Inventory is perishable.

4. Product can be sold in advance.
5. Demand is highly variable.

Hotels illustrate these five characteristics well. They offer one set of rates during the week for the business traveler and another set during the weekend for the vacationer. The variable costs associated with a room (such as cleaning) are low in comparison to the cost of adding rooms to the property. Available rooms cannot be transferred from night to night, and blocks of rooms can be sold to conventions or tours. Finally, potential guests may cut short their stay or not show up at all.

Most organizations (such as airlines, rental car agencies, cruise lines, and hotels) manage yield by establishing decision rules for opening or closing rate classes as a function of expected demand and available supply. The methodologies for doing this can be quite sophisticated. A common approach is to forecast demand over the planning horizon and then use marginal analysis to determine the rates that will be charged if demand is forecast as being above or below set control limits around the forecast mean.

OPERATING YIELD MANAGEMENT SYSTEMS

A number of interesting issues arise in managing yield. One is that pricing structures must appear logical to the customer and justify the different prices. Such justification, commonly called *rate fences,* may have either a physical basis (such as a room with a view) or a nonphysical basis (like unrestricted access to the Internet). Pricing also should relate to addressing specific capacity problems. If capacity is sufficient for peak demand, price reductions stimulating off-peak demand should be the focus. If capacity is insufficient, offering deals to customers who arrive during nonpeak periods (or creating alternative service locations) may enhance revenue generation.

A second issue is handling variability in arrival or starting times, duration, and time between customers. This entails employing maximally accurate forecasting methods (the greater the accuracy in forecasting demand, the more likely yield management will succeed); coordinated policies on overbooking, deposits, and no-show or cancellation penalties; and well-designed service processes that are reliable and consistent.

A third issue relates to managing the service process. Some strategies include scheduling additional personnel to meet peak demand; increasing customer self service; creating adjustable capacity; utilizing idle capacity for complementary services; and cross-training employees to create reserves for peak periods.

THE HOTEL WITH FREE INTERNET ACCESS IS AN EXAMPLE OF A NON-PHYSICAL RATE FENCE.

The fourth and perhaps most critical issue is training workers and managers to work in an environment where overbooking and price changes are standard occurrences that directly impact the customer. Companies have developed creative ways of mollifying overbooked customers. A golf course company offers $100 putters to players who have been overbooked at a popular tee time. Airlines, of course, frequently give overbooked passengers free tickets for other flights.

Service

The essence of yield management is the ability to manage demand. Kimes and Chase suggest that two strategic levers can be used to accomplish this goal: pricing and duration control.[3] If these two levers are thought of in matrix form (see Exhibit 16.9) with price being either fixed or variable and duration being either predictable or unpredictable, then firms located in the variable price/predictable duration quadrant have practiced traditional applications of yield management. This type of matrix provides a framework for a firm to identify its position and the necessary actions to manage yield. For example, an action controlling duration would be to convert the service offering from an event of indeterminate time to an offering that is time-based. This improves reservation planning and hence allocation of resources. An example would be having diners reserve a fixed block of time for dining at a restaurant (e.g., 7–8 P.M.) rather than an open-ended table reservation for 7 P.M.

exhibit 16.9   Price/Service Duration Matrix: Positioning of Selected Service Industries

		PRICE	
		FIXED	VARIABLE
DURATION	PREDICTABLE	Movies Stadiums/arenas Convention centers	Hotels Airlines Rental cars Cruise lines
	UNPREDICTABLE	Restaurants Golf courses Internet service providers	Continuing care hospitals

SOURCE: S. KIMES AND R. B. CHASE, "THE STRATEGIC LEVERS OF YIELD MANAGEMENT," *JOURNAL OF SERVICE RESEARCH* 1, NO. 2 (1998), PP. 298–308. COPYRIGHT © 1998 BY SAGE PUBLISHERS. USED BY PERMISSION OF SAGE PUBLICATIONS, INC.

SUMMARY

Sales and operations planning and the aggregate plan translate corporate strategic and capacity plans into broad categories of workforce size, inventory quantity, and production levels.

Demand variations are a fact of life, so the planning system must include sufficient flexibility to cope with such variations. Flexibility can be achieved by developing alternative sources of supply, cross-training workers to handle a wide variety of orders, and engaging in more frequent replanning during high-demand periods.

Decision rules for production planning should be adhered to once they have been selected. However, they should be carefully analyzed prior to implementation by checks such as simulation of historical data to see what really would have happened if the decision rules had operated in the past.

Yield management is an important tool that can be used to shape demand patterns so a firm can operate more efficiently.

KEY TERMS

Aggregate operations plan Translating annual and quarterly business plans into labor and production output plans for the intermediate term. The objective is to minimize the cost of resources required to meet demand.

Sales and operations planning A term that refers to the process that helps companies keep demand and supply in balance. The terminology is meant to capture the importance of cross-functional work.

Long-range planning Activity typically done annually and focusing on a horizon of a year or more.

Intermediate-range planning Activity that usually covers a period from 3 to 18 months with weekly, monthly, or quarterly time increments.

Short-range planning Planning that covers a period less than six months with either daily or weekly increments of time.

Production rate The number of units completed per unit of time.

Workforce level The number of production workers needed each period.

Inventory on hand Unused inventory carried from a previous period.

Production planning strategies Plans that involve trade-offs among workforce size, work hours, inventory, and backlogs.

Pure strategy A plan that uses just one of the options available for meeting demand. Typical options include chasing demand, using a stable workforce with overtime or part-time work, and constant production with shortages and overages absorbed by inventory.

Mixed strategy A plan that combines options available for meeting demand.

Yield management Allocating the right type of capacity to the right type of customer at the right price and time to maximize revenue or yield.

SOLVED PROBLEM

Jason Enterprises (JE) produces video telephones for the home market. Quality is not quite as good as it could be at this point, but the selling price is low and Jason can study market response while spending more time on R&D.

At this stage, however, JE needs to develop an aggregate production plan for the six months from January through June. You have been commissioned to create the plan. The following information should help:

Excel: Aggregate Planning Solved Problem

DEMAND AND WORKING DAYS

	JANUARY	FEBRUARY	MARCH	APRIL	MAY	JUNE	TOTALS
Demand forecast	500	600	650	800	900	800	4,250
Number of working days	22	19	21	21	22	20	125

COSTS

Materials	$100.00/unit
Inventory holding cost	$10.00/unit/month
Marginal cost of stockout	$20.00/unit/month
Marginal cost of subcontracting	$100.00/unit ($200 subcontracting cost less $100 material savings)
Hiring and training cost	$50.00/worker
Layoff cost	$100.00/worker
Labor hours required	4/unit
Straight-time cost (first eight hours each day)	$12.50/hour
Overtime cost (time and a half)	$18.75/hour

INVENTORY

Beginning inventory	200 units
Safety stock required	0% of month demand

What is the cost of each of the following production strategies?

a. Produce exactly to meet demand; vary workforce (assuming opening workforce equal to first month's requirements).

b. Constant workforce; vary inventory and allow shortages only (assuming a starting workforce of 10).

c. Constant workforce of 10; use subcontracting.

Solution

AGGREGATE PRODUCTION PLANNING REQUIREMENTS

	JANUARY	FEBRUARY	MARCH	APRIL	MAY	JUNE	TOTAL
Beginning inventory	200	0	0	0	0	0	
Demand forecast	500	600	650	800	900	800	
Safety stock (0.0 × Demand forecast)	0	0	0	0	0	0	
Production requirement (Demand forecast + Safety stock − Beginning inventory)	300	600	650	800	900	800	
Ending inventory (Beginning inventory + Production requirement − Demand forecast)	0	0	0	0	0	0	

(continued)

PRODUCTION PLAN 1: EXACT PRODUCTION; VARY WORKFORCE

	JANUARY	FEBRUARY	MARCH	APRIL	MAY	JUNE	TOTAL
Production requirement	300	600	650	800	900	800	
Production hours required (Production requirement × 4 hr./unit)	1,200	2,400	2,600	3,200	3,600	3,200	
Working days per month	22	19	21	21	22	20	
Hours per month per worker (Working days × 8 hrs./day)	176	152	168	168	176	160	
Workers required (Production hours required/Hours per month per worker)	7	16	15	19	20	20	
New workers hired (assuming opening workforce equal to first month's requirement of 7 workers)	0	9	0	4	1	0	
Hiring cost (New workers hired × $50)	$0	$450	$0	$200	$50	$0	$700
Workers laid off	0	0	1	0	0	0	
Layoff cost (Workers laid off × $100)	$0	$0	$100	$0	$0	$0	$100
Straight-time cost (Production hours required × $12.50)	$15,000	$30,000	$32,500	$40,000	$45,000	$40,000	$202,500

Total cost $203,300

PRODUCTION PLAN 2: CONSTANT WORKFORCE; VARY INVENTORY AND STOCKOUT

	JANUARY	FEBRUARY	MARCH	APRIL	MAY	JUNE	TOTAL
Beginning inventory	200	140	−80	−310	−690	−1150	
Working days per month	22	19	21	21	22	20	
Production hours available (Working days per month × 8 hr./day × 10 workers)*	1,760	1,520	1,680	1,680	1,760	1,600	
Actual production (Production hours available/4 hr./unit)	440	380	420	420	440	400	
Demand forecast	500	600	650	800	900	800	
Ending inventory (Beginning inventory + Actual production − Demand forecast)	140	−80	−310	−690	−1150	−1550	
Shortage cost (Units short × $20)	$0	$1,600	$6,200	$13,800	$23,000	$31,000	$75,600
Safety stock	0	0	0	0	0	0	
Units excess (Ending inventory − Safety stock; only if positive amount)	140	0	0	0	0	0	
Inventory cost (Units excess × $10)	$1,400	$0	$0	$0	$0	$0	$1,400
Straight-time cost (Production hours available × $12.50)	$22,000	$19,000	$21,000	$21,000	$22,000	$20,000	$125,000

Total cost $202,000

*Assume a constant workforce of 10.

PRODUCTION PLAN 3: CONSTANT WORKFORCE; SUBCONTRACT

	JANUARY	FEBRUARY	MARCH	APRIL	MAY	JUNE	TOTAL
Production requirement	300	460†	650	800	900	800	
Working days per month	22	19	21	21	22	20	
Production hours available (Working days × 8 hrs./ day × 10 workers)*	1,760	1,520	1,680	1,680	1,760	1,600	
Actual production (Production hours available/4 hr. per unit)	440	380	420	420	440	400	
Units subcontracted (Production requirements − Actual production)	0	80	230	380	460	400	
Subcontracting cost (Units subcontracted × $100)	$0	$8,000	$23,000	$38,000	$46,000	$40,000	$155,000
Straight-time cost (Production hours available × $12.50)	$22,000	$19,000	$21,000	$21,000	$22,000	$20,000	$125,000

Total cost $280,000

*Assume a constant workforce of 10.

†600 − 140 units of beginning inventory in February.

SUMMARY

PLAN DESCRIPTION	HIRING	LAYOFF	SUBCONTRACT	STRAIGHT TIME	SHORTAGE	EXCESS INVEN- TORY	TOTAL COST
1. Exact production; vary workforce	$700	$100		$202,500			$203,300
2. Constant workforce; vary inventory and shortages				$125,000	$75,600	$1,400	$202,000
3. Constant workforce; subcontract			$155,000	$125,000			$280,000

REVIEW AND DISCUSSION QUESTIONS

1 What are the major differences between aggregate planning in manufacturing and aggregate planning in services?
2 What are the basic controllable variables of a production planning problem? What are the four major costs?
3 Distinguish between pure and mixed strategies in production planning.
4 Define level scheduling. How does it differ from the pure strategies in production planning?
5 How does forecast accuracy relate, in general, to the practical application of the aggregate planning models discussed in the chapter?
6 In which way does the time horizon chosen for an aggregate plan determine whether it is the best plan for the firm?
7 Review the opening vignette. How does sales and operations planning help resolve product shortage problems?
8 How would you apply yield management concepts to a barbershop? A soft drink vending machine?

PROBLEMS

1 For the solved problem, devise the least costly plan you can. You may choose your starting workforce level.
2 Develop a production plan and calculate the annual cost for a firm whose demand forecast is fall, 10,000; winter, 8,000; spring, 7,000; summer, 12,000. Inventory at the beginning of fall is 500 units. At the beginning of fall you currently have 30 workers, but you plan to hire temporary workers at the beginning of summer and lay them off at the end of the summer. In

addition, you have negotiated with the union an option to use the regular workforce on overtime during winter or spring if overtime is necessary to prevent stockouts at the end of those quarters. Overtime is *not* available during the fall. Relevant costs are: hiring, $100 for each temp; layoff, $200 for each worker laid off; inventory holding, $5 per unit-quarter; backorder, $10 per unit; straight time, $5 per hour; overtime, $8 per hour. Assume that the productivity is 0.5 unit per worker hour, with eight hours per day and 60 days per season.

3   Plan production for a four-month period: February through May. For February and March, you should produce to exact demand forecast. For April and May, you should use overtime and inventory with a stable workforce; *stable* means that the number of workers needed for March will be held constant through May. However, government constraints put a maximum of 5,000 hours of overtime labor per month in April and May (zero overtime in February and March). If demand exceeds supply, then backorders occur. There are 100 workers on January 31. You are given the following demand forecast: February, 80,000; March, 64,000; April, 100,000; May, 40,000. Productivity is four units per worker hour, eight hours per day, 20 days per month. Assume zero inventory on February 1. Costs are hiring, $50 per new worker; layoff, $70 per worker laid off; inventory holding, $10 per unit-month; straight-time labor, $10 per hour; overtime, $15 per hour; backorder, $20 per unit. Find the total cost of this plan.

4   Plan production for the next year. The demand forecast is spring, 20,000; summer, 10,000; fall, 15,000; winter, 18,000. At the beginning of spring you have 70 workers and 1,000 units in inventory. The union contract specifies that you may lay off workers only once a year, at the beginning of summer. Also, you may hire new workers only at the end of summer to begin regular work in the fall. The number of workers laid off at the beginning of summer and the number hired at the end of summer should result in planned production levels for summer and fall that equal the demand forecasts for summer and fall, respectively. If demand exceeds supply, use overtime in spring only, which means that backorders could occur in winter. You are given these costs: hiring, $100 per new worker; layoff, $200 per worker laid off; holding, $20 per unit-quarter; backorder cost, $8 per unit; straight-time labor, $10 per hour; overtime, $15 per hour. Productivity is 0.5 unit per worker hour, eight hours per day, 50 days per quarter. Find the total cost.

5   DAT, Inc., needs to develop an aggregate plan for its product line. Relevant data are

Production time	1 hour per unit	Beginning inventory	500 units
Average labor cost	$10 per hour	Safety stock	One-half month
Workweek	5 days, 8 hours each day	Shortage cost	$20 per unit per month
Days per month	Assume 20 work days per month	Carrying cost	$5 per unit per month

The forecast for next year is

JAN.	FEB.	MAR.	APR.	MAY	JUNE	JULY	AUG.	SEPT.	OCT.	NOV.	DEC.
2,500	3,000	4,000	3,500	3,500	3,000	3,000	4,000	4,000	4,000	3,000	3,000

Management prefers to keep a constant workforce and production level, absorbing variations in demand through inventory excesses and shortages. Demand not met is carried over to the following month.

Develop an aggregate plan that will meet the demand and other conditions of the problem. Do not try to find the optimum; just find a good solution and state the procedure you might use to test for a better solution. Make any necessary assumptions.

6   Old Pueblo Engineering Contractors creates six-month "rolling" schedules, which are recomputed monthly. For competitive reasons (it would need to divulge proprietary design criteria, methods, and so on), Old Pueblo does not subcontract. Therefore, its only options to meet customer requirements are (1) work on regular time; (2) work on overtime, which is limited to 30 percent of regular time; (3) do customers' work early, which would cost an additional $5 per hour per month; and (4) perform customers' work late, which would cost an additional $10 per hour per month penalty, as provided by their contract.

Old Pueblo has 25 engineers on its staff at an hourly rate of $30. The overtime rate is $45. Customers' hourly requirements for the six months from January to June are

JANUARY	FEBRUARY	MARCH	APRIL	MAY	JUNE
5,000	4,000	6,000	6,000	5,000	4,000

Develop an aggregate plan using a spreadsheet. Assume 20 working days in each month.

7   Alan Industries is expanding its product line to include new models: Model A, Model B, and Model C. These are to be produced on the same production equipment, and the objective is to meet the demands for the three products using overtime where necessary. The demand forecast for the next four months, in required hours, is

PRODUCT	APRIL	MAY	JUNE	JULY
Model A	800	600	800	1,200
Model B	600	700	900	1,100
Model C	700	500	700	850

Because the products deteriorate rapidly, there is a high loss in quality and, consequently, a high carryover cost into subsequent periods. Each hour's production carried into future months costs $3 per production hour of Model A, $4 for Model B, and $5 for Model C.

Production can take place during either regular working hours or overtime. Regular time is paid at $4 when working on Model A, $5 for Model B, and $6 for Model C. Overtime premium is 50 percent.

The available production capacity for regular time and overtime is

	APRIL	MAY	JUNE	JULY
Regular time	1,500	1,300	1,800	1,700
Overtime	$700	650	900	850

a. Set up the problem in matrix form and show appropriate costs.
b. Show a feasible solution.

8   Shoney Video Concepts produces a line of videodisc players to be linked to personal computers for video games. With such a computer/video link, the game becomes a very realistic experience. In a simple driving game where the joystick steers the vehicle, for example, rather than seeing computer graphics on the screen, the player is actually viewing a segment of a videodisc shot from a real moving vehicle. Depending on the action of the player (hitting a guard rail, for example), the disc moves virtually instantaneously to that segment and the player becomes part of an actual accident of real vehicles (staged, of course).

Shoney is trying to determine a production plan for the next 12 months. The main criterion for this plan is that the employment level is to be held constant over the period. Shoney is continuing in its R&D efforts to develop new applications and prefers not to cause any adverse feeling with the local workforce. For the same reason, all employees should put in full work-weeks, even if this is not the lowest-cost alternative. The forecast for the next 12 months is

MONTH	FORECAST DEMAND	MONTH	FORECAST DEMAND
January	600	July	200
February	800	August	200
March	900	September	300
April	600	October	700
May	400	November	800
June	300	December	900

Manufacturing cost is $200 per set, equally divided between materials and labor. Inventory storage cost is $5 per month. A shortage of sets results in lost sales and is estimated to cost an overall $20 per unit short.

The inventory on hand at the beginning of the planning period is 200 units. Ten labor hours are required per videodisc player. The workday is eight hours.

Develop an aggregate production schedule for the year using a constant workforce. For simplicity, assume 22 working days each month except July, when the plant closes down for three weeks' vacation (leaving seven working days). Assume that total production capacity is greater than or equal to total demand.

9   Develop a production schedule to produce the exact production requirements by varying the workforce size for the following problem. Use the example in the chapter as a guide (Plan 1).

The monthly forecasts for Product X for January, February, and March are 1,000, 1,500, and 1,200, respectively. Safety stock policy recommends that half of the forecast for that month be defined as safety stock. There are 22 working days in January, 19 in February, and 21 in March. Beginning inventory is 500 units.

Manufacturing cost is $200 per unit, storage cost is $3 per unit per month, standard pay rate is $6 per hour, overtime rate is $9 per hour, cost of stockout is $10 per unit per month, marginal cost of subcontracting is $10 per unit, hiring and training cost is $200 per worker, layoff cost is $300 per worker, and worker productivity is 0.1 unit per hour. Assume that you start off with 50 workers and that they work 8 hours per day.

10 Helter Industries, a company that produces a line of women's bathing suits, hires temporaries to help produce its summer product demand. For the current four-month rolling schedule, there are three temps on staff and 12 full-time employees. The temps can be hired when needed and can be used as needed, whereas the full-time employees must be paid whether they are needed or not. Each full-time employee can produce 205 suits, while each part-time employee can produce 165 suits per month.

Demand for bathing suits for the next four months is as follows:

MAY	JUNE	JULY	AUGUST
3,200	2,800	3,100	3,000

Beginning inventory in May is 403 complete (a complete two-piece includes both top and bottom) bathing suits. Bathing suits cost $40 to produce and carrying cost is 24 percent per year. Develop an aggregate plan using a spreadsheet.

CASE: BRADFORD MANUFACTURING—PLANNING PLANT PRODUCTION

Excel: Bradford Manufacturing

THE SITUATION

You are the operations manager for a manufacturing plant that produces pudding food products. One of your important responsibilities is to prepare an aggregate plan for the plant. This plan is an important input into the annual budget process. The plan provides information on production rates, manufacturing labor requirements, and projected finished goods inventory levels for the next year.

You make those little boxes of pudding mix on packaging lines in your plant. A packaging line has a number of machines that are linked by conveyors. At the start of the line the pudding is mixed; it is then placed in small packets. These packets are inserted into the small pudding boxes, which are collected and placed in cases that hold 48 boxes of pudding. Finally, 160 cases are collected and put on a pallet. The pallets are staged in a shipping area from which they are sent to four distribution centers. Over the years, the technology of the packaging lines has improved so that all the different flavors can be made in relatively small batches with no setup time to switch between flavors. The plant has 15 of these lines, but currently only 10 are being used. Six employees are required to run each line.

The demand for this product fluctuates from month to month. In addition, there is a seasonal component, with peak sales before Thanksgiving, Christmas, and Easter each year. To complicate matters, at the end of the first quarter of each year the marketing group runs a promotion in which special deals are made for large purchases. Business is going well, and the company has been experiencing a general increase in sales.

The plant sends product to four large distribution warehouses strategically located in the United States. Trucks move product daily. The amounts shipped are based on maintaining target inventory levels at the warehouses. These targets are calculated based on anticipated weeks of supply at each warehouse. Current targets are set at two weeks of supply.

In the past, the company has had a policy of producing very close to what it expects sales to be because of limited capacity for storing finished goods. Production capacity has been adequate to support this policy.

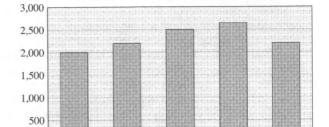

Forecast Demand by Quarter (1,000 Case Units)

A sales forecast for next year has been prepared by the marketing department. The forecast is based on quarterly sales quotas, which are used to set up an incentive program for the salespeople. Sales are mainly to the large U.S. retail grocers. The pudding is shipped to the grocers from the distribution warehouses based on orders taken by the salespeople.

Your immediate task is to prepare an aggregate plan for the coming year. The technical and economic factors that must be considered in this plan are shown next.

TECHNICAL AND ECONOMIC INFORMATION

1 Currently the plant is running 10 lines with no overtime. Each line requires six people to run. For planning purposes, the lines are run for 7.5 hours each normal shift. Employees, though, are paid for eight hours' work. It is possible to run up to two hours of overtime each day, but it must be scheduled for a week at a time, and all the lines must run overtime when it is scheduled. Workers are paid $20.00/hour during a regular shift and $30.00/hour on overtime. The standard production rate for each line is 450 cases/hour.

2 The marketing forecast for demand is as follows: Q1—2,000; Q2—2,200; Q3—2,500; Q4—2,650; and Q1 (next year)—

2,200. These numbers are in 1,000-case units. Each number represents a 13-week forecast.

3 Management has instructed manufacturing to maintain a two-week supply of pudding inventory in the warehouses. The two-week supply should be based on future expected sales. The following are ending inventory target levels for each quarter: Q1—338; Q2—385; Q3—408; Q4—338.

4 Inventory carrying cost is estimated by accounting to be $1.00 per case per year. This means that if a case of pudding is held in inventory for an entire year, the cost to just carry that case in inventory is $1.00. If a case is carried for only one week, the cost is $1.00/52, or $.01923. The cost is proportional to the time carried in inventory. There are 200,000 cases in inventory at the beginning of Q1 (this is 200 cases in the 1,000-case units that the forecast is given in).

5 If a stockout occurs, the item is backordered and shipped at a later date. The cost when a backorder occurs is $2.40 per case due to the loss of goodwill and the high cost of emergency shipping.

6 The human resource group estimates that it costs $5,000 to hire and train a new production employee. It costs $3,000 to lay off a production worker.

QUESTIONS

1 Prepare an aggregate plan for the coming year, assuming that the sales forecast is perfect. Use the spreadsheet "Bradford Manufacturing." In the spreadsheet an area has been designated for your aggregate plan solution. Supply the number of packaging lines to run and the number of overtime hours for each quarter. You will need to set up the cost calculations in the spreadsheet.

You may want to try using the Excel Solver to find a solution. Remember that your final solution needs an integer number of lines and an integer number of overtime hours for each quarter. (Solutions that require 8.9134 lines and 1.256 hours of overtime are not feasible.)

2 Review your solution carefully and be prepared to defend it. Bring a printout of your solution to class.

SUPER QUIZ

1 Term for the process a firm uses to balance supply and demand.

2 In aggregate planning, these are the three general operations–related variables that can be varied.

3 A strategy where the production rate is set to match expected demand.

4 When overtime is used to meet demand and avoid the costs associated with hiring and firing.

5 A strategy that uses inventory and backorders as part of the strategy to meet demand.

6 Sometimes a firm may choose to have all or part of the work done by an outside vendor. This is the term used for the approach.

7 If expected demand during the next four quarters were 150, 125, 100, 75 thousand units and each worker can produce 1,000 units per quarter; how many workers should be used if a level strategy were being employed?

8 Given the data from question 7, how many workers would be needed for a chase strategy?

9 In a service setting, what general operations–related variable is not available compared to a production setting?

10 The practice of allocating capacity and manipulating demand to make it more predictable.

1. Sales and operations planning 2. Production rate, workforce level, inventory 3. Chase 4. Stable workforce—variable work hours 5. Level strategy 6. Subcontracting 7. 113 8. 150, 125, 100, 75 9. Inventory 10. Yield management

SELECTED BIBLIOGRAPHY

Brandimarte, P., and A. Villa (eds.). *Modeling Manufacturing Systems: From Aggregate Planning to Real-Time Control*. New York: Springer, 1999.

Fisher, M. L.; J. H. Hammond; W. R. Obermeyer; and A. Raman. "Making Supply Meet Demand in an Uncertain World." *Harvard Business Review* 72, no. 3 (May–June 1994), pp. 83–93.

Narasimhan, S.; D. W. McLeavey; and P. J. Billington. *Production Planning and Inventory Control*. Englewood Cliffs, NJ: Prentice Hall, 1995.

Silver, E. A.; D. F. Pyke; and R. Peterson. *Inventory Management and Production Planning and Scheduling*. New York: Wiley, 1998.

Vollmann, T. E.; W. L. Berry; D. C. Whybark; and F. R. Jacobs. *Manufacturing Planning and Control for Supply Chain Management*. 5th ed. New York: Irwin/McGraw-Hill, 2004.

Wallace, T. F. *Sales and Operations Planning: The How-To Handbook*. Cincinnati, OH: T. F. Wallace & Company, 2000.

FOOTNOTES

1 M. L. Fisher, J. H. Hammond, W. R. Obermeyer, and A. Raman, "Making Supply Meet Demand in an Uncertain World," *Harvard Business Review* 72, no. 3 (May–June 1994), p. 84.

2 For an interesting application of aggregate planning in nonprofit humanitarian organizations, see C. Sheu and J. G. Wacker, "A Planning and Control Framework for Nonprofit Humanitarian Organizations," *International Journal of Operations and Production Management* 14, no. 4 (1994), pp. 64–77.

3 S. Kimes and R. B. Chase, "The Strategic Levers of Yield Management," *Journal of Service Research* 1, no. 2 (1998), pp. 298–308.

chapter 17

INVENTORY CONTROL

Supply Chain

After reading the chapter you will:

1. Explain the different purposes for keeping inventory.

2. Understand that the type of inventory system logic that is appropriate for an item depends on the type of demand for that item.

3. Calculate the appropriate order size when a one-time purchase must be made.

4. Describe what the economic order quantity is and how to calculate it.

5. Summarize fixed–order quantity and fixed–time period models, including ways to determine safety stock when there is variability in demand.

6. Discuss why inventory turn is directly related to order quantity and safety stock.

Global

DIRECT TO STORE—THE UPS VISION

Logistics visionaries have talked for years about eliminating—or, at least, drastically reducing—the role of inventory in modern supply chains. The most efficient, slack-free supply chains, after all, wouldn't require any inventory buffer, because supply and demand would be in perfect sync. This vision certainly has its appeal: The death of inventory would mean dramatically reduced logistics costs and simplified fulfillment.

There's no need to write a eulogy for inventory just yet. Most companies haven't honed their networks and technolo-

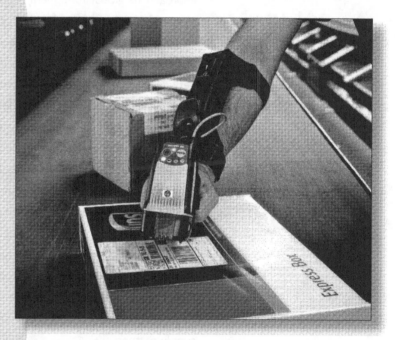

gies well enough to eliminate the need for at least minimal inventory. Logistics managers have to perform a daily, delicate balancing act, balancing

- Transportation costs against fulfillment speed
- Inventory costs against the cost of stock-outs
- Customer satisfaction against cost to serve
- New capabilities against profitability

What's more, two accelerating business trends are making it even harder to synchronize supply chains.

First, global sourcing is forcing supply chains to stretch farther across borders. The goods people consume are increasingly made in some other part of the world, particularly in Asia. This acceleration in global sourcing changes the logistics equation. When goods cross borders, considerations such as fulfillment speed (these are the activities performed once an order is received) and inventory costs get more complicated. Second, powerful retailers and other end customers with clout are starting to push value-added supply chain responsibilities further up the supply chain. More customers are asking manufacturers or third-party logistics providers to label and prepare individual items so the products are ready to go directly to store shelves. With added responsibilities, of course, come added costs. Upstream suppliers are always looking for ways to squeeze more costs out of other areas of the supply chain, such as transportation and distribution.

THE UPS DIRECT APPROACH

A growing number of companies are overcoming these barriers by taking a more direct approach to global fulfillment. This direct-to-store approach—also known as distribution center bypass or direct distribution—keeps inventory moving from manufacturer to end customer by eliminating stops at warehouses along the way. Because companies can shrink the fulfillment cycle and eliminate inventory costs, direct-to-store can offer a good balance between fulfillment speed and logistics costs.

What accounts for the emergence of the direct-to-store model?

Global sourcing and the upstream migration of value-added logistics services are certainly primary drivers. But other pieces of the puzzle have fallen into place in recent years to make direct-to-store shipments feasible.

Internet-enabled electronic links between supply chain partners have allowed better coordination and collaboration among the various supply chain segments. Meanwhile, at the front of the supply chain, increasingly sophisticated point-of-sale systems can capture product demand patterns. This information can then be fed up the supply chain to manufacturers and components suppliers. More accurate sales-forecasting tools take some of the guesswork out of production and reduce the need for large inventory safety stocks. Tracking and tracing tools are also available to follow orders across borders and through the hands of different supply partners.

In short, companies no longer need as much inventory gathering dust in warehouses because they can better synchronize production and distribution with demand. Direct-to-store lets them keep inventory in motion—across borders and around the world.

See United Parcel Service of America (UPS) Supply Chain Solutions for more information about these types of services: www.ups.com.

You should visualize inventory as stacks of money sitting on forklifts, on shelves, and in trucks and planes while in transit. That's what inventory is—money. For many businesses, inventory is the largest asset on the balance sheet at any given time, even though it is often not very liquid. It is a good idea to try to get your inventory down as far as possible.

A few years ago, Heineken, the Netherlands beer company, figured it could save a whole bunch of money on inventory-in-transit if it could just shorten the forecasting lead time. Management expected two things to happen. First, they expected to reduce the need for inventory in the pipeline, therefore cutting down the amount of money devoted to inventory itself. Second, they figured that with a shorter forecasting time, forecasts would be more accurate, reducing emergencies and waste. The Heineken system, called HOPS, cut overall inventory in the system from 16 to 18 weeks to 4 to 6 weeks—a huge

Global

drop in time, and a big gain in cash. Forecasts were more accurate, and there was another benefit, too.

Heineken found that its salespeople were suddenly more productive. That is because they were not dealing with all those calls where they had to check on inventory or solve bad forecasting problems, or change orders that were already in process. Instead, they could concentrate on good customer service and helping distributors do better. It was a "win" all the way around.

The key here involves doing things that decrease your inventory order cycle time and increase the accuracy of your forecast. Look for ways to use automated systems and electronic communication to substitute the rapid movement of electrons for the cumbersome movement of masses of atoms.

The economic benefit from inventory reduction is evident from the following statistics: The average cost of inventory in the United States is 30 to 35 percent of its value. For example, a firm that carries an inventory of $20 million accrues costs of more than $6 million per year mainly through obsolescence, insurance, and last opportunity. If the amount of inventory could be reduced to $10 million, for instance, the firm would save over $3 million, which goes directly to the bottom line. That is, the savings from reduced inventory results in increased profit.

This chapter and Chapter 18 present techniques designed to manage inventory in different supply chain settings. In this chapter, the focus is on settings where the desire is to maintain a stock of inventory that can be delivered to customers on demand. Recall in Chapter 6 the concept of *customer order decoupling point,* which is a point where inventory is positioned to allow processes or entities in the supply chain to operate independently. For example, if a product is stocked at a retailer, the customer pulls the item from the shelf and the manufacturer never sees a customer order. In this case, inventory acts as a buffer to separate the customer from the manufacturing process. Selection of decoupling points is a strategic decision that determines customer lead times and can greatly impact inventory investment. The closer this point is to the customer, the quicker the customer can be served.

Supply Chain

The techniques described in this chapter are suited for managing the inventory at these decoupling points. Typically, there is a trade-off where quicker response to customer demand comes at the expense of greater inventory investment. This is because finished goods inventory is more expensive than raw material inventory. In practice, the idea of a single decoupling point in a supply chain is unrealistic. There may actually be multiple points where buffering takes place.

Good examples of where the models described in this chapter are used include retail stores, grocery stores, wholesale distributors, hospital suppliers, and suppliers of repair parts needed to fix or maintain equipment quickly. Situations in which it is necessary to have the item "in-stock" are ideal candidates for the models described in this chapter. A distinction that needs to be made with the models included in this chapter is whether this is a one-time purchase, for example, for a seasonal item or for use at a special event, or whether the item will be stocked on an ongoing basis.

Service

Exhibit 17.1 depicts different types of supply chain inventories that would exist in a make-to-stock environment, typical of items directed at the consumer. In the upper echelons of the supply chain, which are supply points closer to the customer, stock usually is kept so that an item can be delivered quickly when a customer need occurs. Of course, there are many exceptions, but in general this is the case. The raw materials and manufacturing plant inventory held in the lower echelon potentially can be managed in a special way to take advantage of the planning and synchronization that are needed to efficiently operate this part of the supply chain. In this case, the models in this chapter are most appropriate for the upper echelon inventories (retail and warehouse), and the lower echelon should use the Material Requirements Planning (MRP) technique described in Chapter 18. The applicability of these models could be different for other environments such as when we produce directly to customer order as in the case of an aircraft manufacturer.

Supply Chain

The techniques described here are most appropriate when demand is difficult to predict with great precision. In these models, we characterize demand by using a probability

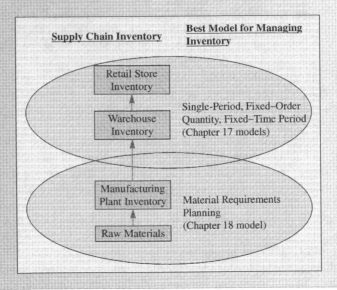

exhibit 17.1   Supply Chain Inventories—Make-to-Stock Environment

distribution and maintain stock so that the risk associated with stock out is managed. For these applications, the following three models are discussed:

1. **The single-period model.** This is used when we are making a one-time purchase of an item. An example might be purchasing T-shirts to sell at a one-time sporting event.
2. **Fixed–order quantity model.** This is used when we want to maintain an item "in-stock," and when we resupply the item, a certain number of units must be ordered each time. Inventory for the item is monitored until it gets down to a level where the risk of stocking out is great enough that we are compelled to order.
3. **Fixed–time period model.** This is similar to the fixed–order quantity model; it is used when the item should be in-stock and ready to use. In this case, rather than monitoring the inventory level and ordering when the level gets down to a critical quantity, the item is ordered at certain intervals of time, for example, every Friday morning. This is often convenient when a group of items is ordered together. An example is the delivery of different types of bread to a grocery store. The bakery supplier may have 10 or more products stocked in a store, and rather than delivering each product individually at different times, it is much more efficient to deliver all 10 together at the same time and on the same schedule.

In this chapter, we want to show not only the mathematics associated with great inventory control but also the "art" of managing inventory. Ensuring accuracy in inventory records is essential to running an efficient inventory control process. Techniques such as ABC analysis and cycle counting are essential to the actual management of the system since they focus attention on the high-value items and ensure the quality of the transactions that affect the tracking of inventory levels.

DEFINITION OF INVENTORY

Inventory

Inventory is the stock of any item or resource used in an organization. An *inventory system* is the set of policies and controls that monitor levels of inventory and determine what levels should be maintained, when stock should be replenished, and how large orders should be.

By convention, *manufacturing inventory* generally refers to items that contribute to or become part of a firm's product output. Manufacturing inventory is typically classified into *raw materials, finished products, component parts, supplies,* and *work-in-process.* In services, *inventory* generally refers to the tangible goods to be sold and the supplies necessary to administer the service.

The basic purpose of inventory analysis in manufacturing and stockkeeping services is to specify (1) when items should be ordered and (2) how large the order should be. Many firms are tending to enter into longer-term relationships with vendors to supply their needs for perhaps the entire year. This changes the "when" and "how many to order" to "when" and "how many to deliver."

PURPOSES OF INVENTORY

All firms (including JIT operations) keep a supply of inventory for the following reasons:

1. **To maintain independence of operations.**   A supply of materials at a work center allows that center flexibility in operations. For example, because there are costs for making each new production setup, this inventory allows management to reduce the number of setups.

    Independence of workstations is desirable on assembly lines as well. The time needed to do identical operations will naturally vary from one unit to the next. Therefore, it is desirable to have a cushion of several parts within the workstation so that shorter performance times can compensate for longer performance times. This way the average output can be fairly stable.

2. **To meet variation in product demand.**   If the demand for the product is known precisely, it may be possible (though not necessarily economical) to produce the product to exactly meet the demand. Usually, however, demand is not completely known, and a safety or buffer stock must be maintained to absorb variation.

3. **To allow flexibility in production scheduling**.   A stock of inventory relieves the pressure on the production system to get the goods out. This causes longer lead times, which permit production planning for smoother flow and lower-cost operation through larger lot-size production. High setup costs, for example, favor producing a larger number of units once the setup has been made.

4. **To provide a safeguard for variation in raw material delivery time.**   When material is ordered from a vendor, delays can occur for a variety of reasons: a normal variation in shipping time, a shortage of material at the vendor's plant causing backlogs, an unexpected strike at the vendor's plant or at one of the shipping companies, a lost order, or a shipment of incorrect or defective material.

5. **To take advantage of economic purchase order size.**   There are costs to place an order: labor, phone calls, typing, postage, and so on. Therefore, the larger each order is, the fewer the orders that need to be written. Also, shipping costs favor larger orders—the larger the shipment, the lower the per-unit cost.

For each of the preceding reasons (especially for items 3, 4, and 5), be aware that inventory is costly and large amounts are generally undesirable. Long cycle times are caused by large amounts of inventory and are undesirable as well.

INVENTORY COSTS

In making any decision that affects inventory size, the following costs must be considered.

1. **Holding (or carrying) costs.**   This broad category includes the costs for storage facilities, handling, insurance, pilferage, breakage, obsolescence, depreciation, taxes,

and the opportunity cost of capital. Obviously, high holding costs tend to favor low inventory levels and frequent replenishment.

2. **Setup (or production change) costs.** To make each different product involves obtaining the necessary materials, arranging specific equipment setups, filling out the required papers, appropriately charging time and materials, and moving out the previous stock of material.

   If there were no costs or loss of time in changing from one product to another, many small lots would be produced. This would reduce inventory levels, with a resulting savings in cost. One challenge today is to try to reduce these setup costs to permit smaller lot sizes. (This is the goal of a JIT system.)

3. **Ordering costs.** These costs refer to the managerial and clerical costs to prepare the purchase or production order. Ordering costs include all the details, such as counting items and calculating order quantities. The costs associated with maintaining the system needed to track orders are also included in ordering costs.

4. **Shortage costs.** When the stock of an item is depleted, an order for that item must either wait until the stock is replenished or be canceled. There is a trade-off between carrying stock to satisfy demand and the costs resulting from stockout. This balance is sometimes difficult to obtain, because it may not be possible to estimate lost profits, the effects of lost customers, or lateness penalties. Frequently, the assumed shortage cost is little more than a guess, although it is usually possible to specify a range of such costs.

Establishing the correct quantity to order from vendors or the size of lots submitted to the firm's production facilities involves a search for the minimum total cost resulting from the combined effects of four individual costs: holding costs, setup costs, ordering costs, and shortage costs. Of course, the timing of these orders is a critical factor that may impact inventory cost.

TOYOTA PRIUSES AND OTHER VEHICLES CLAD IN PROTECTIVE COVERING AWAIT SHIPMENT TO U.S. DEALERS AT THE LONG BEACH, CA, PORT. IN 2008 THE VALUE OF THE COMPANY'S INVENTORY TOTALED ABOUT ¥1.83 TRILLION AND THE COST OF GOODS SOLD WAS ¥21.5 TRILLION. SO TOYOTA'S INVENTORY TURNED OVER ABOUT 11.7 TIMES PER YEAR, OR ROUGHLY 31 DAYS OF INVENTORY ON HAND.

Global

INDEPENDENT VERSUS DEPENDENT DEMAND

In inventory management, it is important to understand the trade-offs involved in using different types of inventory control logic. Exhibit 17.2 is a framework that shows how characteristics of demand, transaction cost, and the risk of obsolete inventory map into different types of systems. The systems in the upper left of the exhibit are described in this chapter, and those in the lower right in Chapter 18.

Transaction cost is dependent on the level of integration and automation incorporated in the system. Manual systems such as simple *two-bin* logic depend on human posting of the transactions to replenish inventory, which is relatively expensive compared to using a computer to automatically detect when an item needs to be ordered. Integration relates to how connected systems are. For example, it is common for orders for material to be automatically transferred to suppliers electronically and for these orders to be automatically captured by the supplier inventory control system. This type of integration greatly reduces transaction cost.

The risk of obsolescence is also an important consideration. If an item is used infrequently or only for a specific purpose, there is considerable risk in using inventory control logic that does not track the specific source of demand for the item. Further, items that are sensitive to technical obsolescence, such as computer memory chips, and processors, need to be managed carefully based on actual need to reduce the risk of getting stuck with inventory that is outdated.

An important characteristic of demand relates to whether demand is derived from an end item or is related to the item itself. We use the terms independent and dependent demand to describe this characteristic. Briefly, the distinction between independent and dependent demand is this. In independent demand, the demands for various items are unrelated to each other. For example, a workstation may produce many parts that are unrelated but meet some external demand requirement. In dependent demand, the need for any one item is a direct result of the need for some other item, usually a higher-level item of which it is part.

In concept, dependent demand is a relatively straightforward computational problem. Needed quantities of a dependent-demand item are simply computed, based on the number needed in each higher-level item in which it is used. For example, if an automobile company plans on producing 500 cars per day, then obviously it will need 2,000 wheels and tires (plus spares). The number of wheels and tires needed is *dependent* on the production levels and

Independent and dependent demand

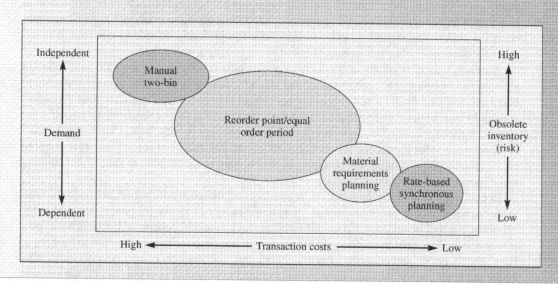

Inventory Control-System Design Matrix: Framework Describing Inventory Control Logic   exhibit 17.2

is not derived separately. The demand for cars, on the other hand, is *independent*—it comes from many sources external to the automobile firm and is not a part of other products; it is unrelated to the demand for other products.

To determine the quantities of independent items that must be produced, firms usually turn to their sales and market research departments. They use a variety of techniques, including customer surveys, forecasting techniques, and economic and sociological trends, as we discussed in Chapter 11 on forecasting. Because independent demand is uncertain, extra units must be carried in inventory. This chapter presents models to determine how many units need to be ordered, and how many extra units should be carried to reduce the risk of stocking out.

INVENTORY SYSTEMS

**Tutorial:
Inventory**

Service

An inventory system provides the organizational structure and the operating policies for maintaining and controlling goods to be stocked. The system is responsible for ordering and receipt of goods: timing the order placement and keeping track of what has been ordered, how much, and from whom. The system also must follow up to answer such questions as, Has the supplier received the order? Has it been shipped? Are the dates correct? Are the procedures established for reordering or returning undesirable merchandise?

This section divides systems into single-period systems and multiple-period systems. The classification is based on whether the decision is just a one-time purchasing decision where the purchase is designed to cover a fixed period of time and the item will not be reordered, or the decision involves an item that will be purchased periodically where inventory should be kept in stock to be used on demand. We begin with a look at the one-time purchasing decision and the single-period inventory model.

A SINGLE-PERIOD INVENTORY MODEL

Certainly, an easy example to think about is the classic single-period "newsperson" problem. For example, consider the problem that the newsperson has in deciding how many newspapers to put in the sales stand outside a hotel lobby each morning. If the person does not put enough papers in the stand, some customers will not be able to purchase a paper and the newsperson will lose the profit associated with these sales. On the other hand, if too many papers are placed in the stand, the newsperson will have paid for papers that were not sold during the day, lowering profit for the day.

Actually, this is a very common type of problem. Consider the person selling T-shirts promoting a championship basketball or football game. This is especially difficult, since the person must wait to learn what teams will be playing. The shirts can then be printed with the proper team logos. Of course, the person must estimate how many people will actually want the shirts. The shirts sold prior to the game can probably be sold at a premium price, whereas those sold after the game will need to be steeply discounted.

A simple way to think about this is to consider how much risk we are willing to take for running out of inventory. Let's consider that the newsperson selling papers in the sales stand had collected data over a few months and had found that on average each Monday 90 papers were sold with a standard deviation of 10 papers (assume that during this time the papers were purposefully overstocked in order not to run out, so the newsperson would know what "real" demand was). With these data, our newsperson could simply state a service rate that is felt to be acceptable. For example, the newsperson might want to be 80 percent sure of not running out of papers each Monday.

Recall from your study of statistics, assuming that the probability distribution associated with the sales of the paper is normal, then if we stocked exactly 90 papers each Monday morning, the risk of stocking out would be 50 percent, since 50 percent of the time we expect demand to be less than 90 papers and 50 percent of the time we expect demand to be greater than 90. To be 80 percent sure of not stocking out, we need to carry a few more papers. From the "cumulative standard normal distribution" table given in Appendix G, we see that we need approximately 0.85 standard deviation of extra papers to be 80 percent sure of not stocking out. A quick way to find the exact number of standard deviations needed for a given probability of stocking out is with the NORMSINV(probability) function in Microsoft Excel (NORMSINV(0.8) = 0.84162). Given our result from Excel, which is more accurate than what we can get from the tables, the number of extra papers would be $0.84162 \times 10 = 8.416$, or 9 papers (there is no way to sell 0.4 paper!).

To make this more useful, it would be good to actually consider the potential profit and loss associated with stocking either too many or too few papers on the stand. Let's say that our newspaper person pays $0.20 for each paper and sells the papers for $0.50. In this case the marginal cost associated with underestimating demand is $0.30, the lost profit. Similarly, the marginal cost of overestimating demand is $0.20, the cost of buying too many papers. The optimal stocking level, using marginal analysis, occurs at the point where the expected benefits derived from carrying the next unit are less than the expected costs for that unit. Keep in mind that the specific benefits and costs depend on the problem.

In symbolic terms, define

$$C_o = \text{Cost per unit of demand overestimated}$$
$$C_u = \text{Cost per unit of demand underestimated}$$

By introducing probabilities, the expected marginal cost equation becomes

$$P(C_o) \leq (1 - P)C_u$$

where P is the probability that the unit will not be sold and $1 - P$ is the probability of it being sold, because one or the other must occur. (The unit is sold or is not sold.)[1]

Then, solving for P, we obtain

$$P \leq \frac{C_u}{C_o + C_u} \qquad [17.1]$$

This equation states that we should continue to increase the size of the order so long as the probability of selling what we order is equal to or less than the ratio $C_u/(C_o + C_u)$.

Returning to our newspaper problem, our cost of overestimating demand (C_o) is $0.20 per paper and the cost of underestimating demand (C_u) is $0.30. The probability therefore is $0.3/(0.2 + 0.3) = 0.6$. Now, we need to find the point on our demand distribution that corresponds to the cumulative probability of 0.6. Using the NORMSINV function to get the number of standard deviations (commonly referred to as the Z-score) of extra newspapers to carry, we get 0.253, which means that we should stock $0.253(10) = 2.53$ or 3 extra papers. The total number of papers for the stand each Monday morning, therefore, should be 93 papers.

This model is very useful and, as we will see in our solved sample problem, can even be used for many service sector problems, such as the number of seats to book on a full airline flight or the number of reservations to book on a full night at a hotel.

EXAMPLE 17.1: Hotel Reservations

A hotel near the university always fills up on the evening before football games. History has shown that when the hotel is fully booked, the number of last-minute cancellations has a mean of 5 and standard deviation of 3. The average room rate is $80. When the hotel is overbooked, policy is to find a room in a nearby hotel and to pay for the room for the customer. This usually costs the hotel approximately $200 since rooms booked on such late notice are expensive. How many rooms should the hotel overbook?

Step by Step

SOLUTION

The cost of underestimating the number of cancellations is $80 and the cost of overestimating cancellations is $200.

$$P \leq \frac{C_u}{C_o + C_u} = \frac{\$80}{\$200 + \$80} = 0.2857$$

Service

Using NORMSINV(.2857) from Excel gives a Z-score of -0.56599. The negative value indicates that we should overbook by a value less than the average of 5. The actual value should be $-0.56599(3) = -1.69797$, or 2 reservations less than 5. The hotel should overbook three reservations on the evening prior to a football game.

Another common method for analyzing this type of problem is with a discrete probability distribution found using actual data and marginal analysis. For our hotel, consider that we have collected data and our distribution of no-shows is as follows:

NUMBER OF NO-SHOWS	PROBABILITY	CUMULATIVE PROBABILITY
0	0.05	0.05
1	0.08	0.13
2	0.10	0.23
3	0.15	0.38
4	0.20	0.58
5	0.15	0.73
6	0.11	0.84
7	0.06	0.90
8	0.05	0.95
9	0.04	0.99
10	0.01	1.00

Using these data, a table showing the impact of overbooking is created. Total expected cost of each overbooking option is then calculated by multiplying each possible outcome by its probability and summing the weighted costs. The best overbooking strategy is the one with minimum cost.

Excel: Inventory Control

		NUMBER OF RESERVATIONS OVERBOOKED										
NO-SHOWS	PROBABILITY	0	1	2	3	4	5	6	7	8	9	10
0	0.05	0	200	400	600	800	1,000	1,200	1,400	1,600	1,800	2,000
1	0.08	80	0	200	400	600	800	1,000	1,200	1,400	1,600	1,800
2	0.1	160	80	0	200	400	600	800	1,000	1,200	1,400	1,600
3	0.15	240	160	80	0	200	400	600	800	1,000	1,200	1,400
4	0.2	320	240	160	80	0	200	400	600	800	1,000	1,200
5	0.15	400	320	240	160	80	0	200	400	600	800	1,000
6	0.11	480	400	320	240	160	80	0	200	400	600	800
7	0.06	560	480	400	320	240	160	80	0	200	400	600
8	0.05	640	560	480	400	320	240	160	80	0	200	400
9	0.04	720	640	560	480	400	320	240	160	80	0	200
10	0.01	800	720	640	560	480	400	320	240	160	80	0
Total cost		337.6	271.6	228	212.4	238.8	321.2	445.6	600.8	772.8	958.8	1,156

From the table, the minimum total cost is when three extra reservations are taken. This approach using discrete probability is useful when valid historic data are available. ●

Single-period inventory models are useful for a wide variety of service and manufacturing applications. Consider the following:

Service

1. **Overbooking of airline flights.**   It is common for customers to cancel flight reservations for a variety of reasons. Here the cost of underestimating the number of cancellations is the revenue lost due to an empty seat on a flight. The cost of overestimating cancellations is the awards, such as free flights or cash payments, that are given to customers unable to board the flight.

2. **Ordering of fashion items.** A problem for a retailer selling fashion items is that often only a single order can be placed for the entire season. This is often caused by long lead times and limited life of the merchandise. The cost of underestimating demand is the lost profit due to sales not made. The cost of overestimating demand is the cost that results when it is discounted.

3. **Any type of one-time order.** Two examples are ordering T-shirts for a sporting event and printing maps that become obsolete after a certain period of time.

MULTIPERIOD INVENTORY SYSTEMS

There are two general types of multiperiod inventory systems: fixed–order quantity models (also called the *economic order quantity,* EOQ, and Q-model) and fixed–time period models (also referred to variously as the *periodic* system, *periodic review* system, *fixed-order interval* system, and P-model). Multiperiod inventory systems are designed to ensure that an item will be available on an ongoing basis throughout the year. Usually the item will be ordered multiple times throughout the year where the logic in the system dictates the actual quantity ordered and the timing of the order.

The basic distinction is that fixed–order quantity models are "event triggered" and fixed–time period models are "time triggered." That is, a fixed–order quantity model initiates an order when the event of reaching a specified reorder level occurs. This event may take place at any time, depending on the demand for the items considered. In contrast, the fixed–time period model is limited to placing orders at the end of a predetermined time period; only the passage of time triggers the model.

To use the fixed–order quantity model (which places an order when the remaining inventory drops to a predetermined order point, R), the inventory remaining must be continually monitored. Thus, the fixed–order quantity model is a *perpetual* system, which requires that every time a withdrawal from inventory or an addition to inventory is made, records must be updated to reflect whether the reorder point has been reached. In a fixed–time period model, counting takes place only at the review period. (We will discuss some variations of systems that combine features of both.)

Some additional differences tend to influence the choice of systems (also see Exhibit 17.3):

- The fixed–time period model has a larger average inventory because it must also protect against stockout during the review period, T; the fixed–order quantity model has no review period.
- The fixed–order quantity model favors more expensive items because average inventory is lower.

Fixed–order quantity models (Q-model)

Fixed–time period models (P-model)

Tutorial: Inventory

Fixed–Order Quantity and Fixed–Time Period Differences   **exhibit 17.3**

FEATURE	Q-MODEL FIXED–ORDER QUANTITY MODEL	P-MODEL FIXED–TIME PERIOD MODEL
Order quantity	Q—constant (the same amount ordered each time)	q—variable (varies each time order is placed)
When to place order	R—when inventory position drops to the reorder level	T—when the review period arrives
Recordkeeping	Each time a withdrawal or addition is made	Counted only at review period
Size of inventory	Less than fixed–time period model	Larger than fixed–order quantity model
Time to maintain	Higher due to perpetual recordkeeping	
Type of items	Higher-priced, critical, or important items	

exhibit 17.4   Comparison for Fixed–Order Quantity and Fixed–Time Period Reordering Inventory Systems

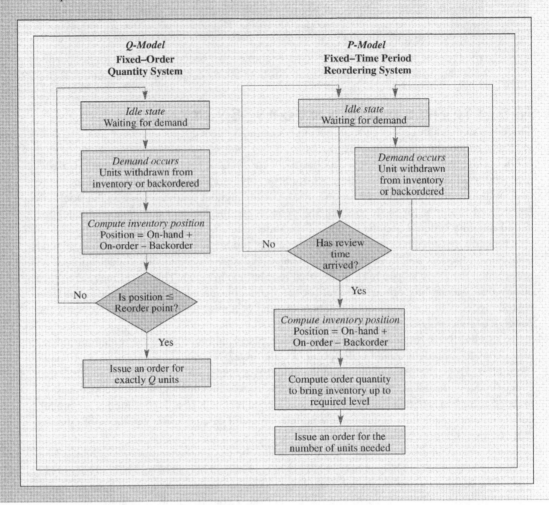

- The fixed–order quantity model is more appropriate for important items such as critical repair parts because there is closer monitoring and therefore quicker response to potential stockout.
- The fixed–order quantity model requires more time to maintain because every addition or withdrawal is logged.

Exhibit 17.4 shows what occurs when each of the two models is put into use and becomes an operating system. As we can see, the fixed–order quantity system focuses on order quantities and reorder points. Procedurally, each time a unit is taken out of stock, the withdrawal is logged and the amount remaining in inventory is immediately compared to the reorder point. If it has dropped to this point, an order for Q items is placed. If it has not, the system remains in an idle state until the next withdrawal.

In the fixed–time period system, a decision to place an order is made after the stock has been counted or reviewed. Whether an order is actually placed depends on the inventory position at that time.

FIXED–ORDER QUANTITY MODELS

Fixed–order quantity models attempt to determine the specific point, R, at which an order will be placed and the size of that order, Q. The order point, R, is always a specified number of units. An order of size Q is placed when the inventory available (currently in stock and on

Basic Fixed–Order Quantity Model

exhibit 17.5

**Excel:
Inventory
Control**

order) reaches the point *R*. Inventory position is defined as the on-hand plus on-order minus backordered quantities. The solution to a fixed–order quantity model may stipulate something like this: When the inventory position drops to 36, place an order for 57 more units.

Inventory position

The simplest models in this category occur when all aspects of the situation are known with certainty. If the annual demand for a product is 1,000 units, it is precisely 1,000—not 1,000 plus or minus 10 percent. The same is true for setup costs and holding costs. Although the assumption of complete certainty is rarely valid, it provides a good basis for our coverage of inventory models.

Exhibit 17.5 and the discussion about deriving the optimal order quantity are based on the following characteristics of the model. These assumptions are unrealistic, but they represent a starting point and allow us to use a simple example.

- Demand for the product is constant and uniform throughout the period.
- Lead time (time from ordering to receipt) is constant.
- Price per unit of product is constant.
- Inventory holding cost is based on average inventory.
- Ordering or setup costs are constant.
- All demands for the product will be satisfied. (No backorders are allowed.)

The "sawtooth effect" relating *Q* and *R* in Exhibit 17.5 shows that when the inventory position drops to point *R*, a reorder is placed. This order is received at the end of time period *L*, which does not vary in this model.

In constructing any inventory model, the first step is to develop a functional relationship between the variables of interest and the measure of effectiveness. In this case, because we are concerned with cost, the following equation pertains:

$$\text{Total annual cost} = \text{Annual purchase cost} + \text{Annual ordering cost} + \text{Annual holding cost}$$

or

$$TC = DC + \frac{D}{Q}S + \frac{Q}{2}H \qquad [17.2]$$

where

TC = Total annual cost

D = Demand (annual)

C = Cost per unit

Q = Quantity to be ordered (the optimal amount is termed the *economic order quantity*— EOQ—or Q_{opt})

S = Setup cost or cost of placing an order

Excel: Inventory Control

exhibit 17.6   Annual Product Costs, Based on Size of the Order

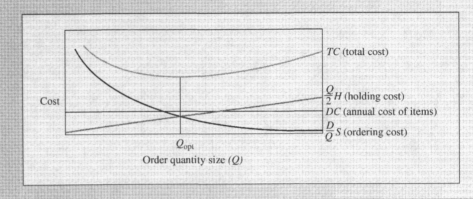

H = Annual holding and storage cost per unit of average inventory (often holding cost is taken as a percentage of the cost of the item, such as $H = iC$, where i is the percent carrying cost)

On the right side of the equation, DC is the annual purchase cost for the units; $(D/Q)S$ is the annual ordering cost (the actual number of orders placed, D/Q, times the cost of each order, S); and $(Q/2)H$ is the annual holding cost (the average inventory, $Q/2$, times the cost per unit for holding and storage, H). These cost relationships are graphed in Exhibit 17.6.

The second step in model development is to find that order quantity Q_{opt} at which total cost is a minimum. In Exhibit 17.5, the total cost is minimal at the point where the slope of the curve is zero. Using calculus, we take the derivative of total cost with respect to Q and set this equal to zero. For the basic model considered here, the calculations are

$$TC = DC + \frac{D}{Q}S + \frac{Q}{2}H$$

$$\frac{dTC}{dQ} = 0 + \left(\frac{-DS}{Q^2}\right) + \frac{H}{2} = 0$$

$$Q_{opt} = \sqrt{\frac{2DS}{H}} \qquad [17.3]$$

Because this simple model assumes constant demand and lead time, neither safety stock nor stockout cost is necessary, and the reorder point, R, is simply

$$R = \bar{d}L \qquad [17.4]$$

where

$\bar{d}$ = Average daily demand (constant)

L = Lead time in days (constant)

Excel: Inventory Control

Step by Step

EXAMPLE 17.2: Economic Order Quantity and Reorder Point

Find the economic order quantity and the reorder point, given

Annual demand (D) = 1,000 units
Average daily demand $(\bar{d})$ = 1,000/365
Ordering cost (S) = \$5 per order
Holding cost (H) = \$1.25 per unit per year
Lead time (L) = 5 days
Cost per unit (C) = \$12.50

What quantity should be ordered?

SOLUTION

The optimal order quantity is

$$Q_{opt} = \sqrt{\frac{2DS}{H}} = \sqrt{\frac{2(1,000)5}{1.25}} = \sqrt{8,000} = 89.4 \text{ units}$$

The reorder point is

$$R = \bar{d}L = \frac{1,000}{365}(5) = 13.7 \text{ units}$$

Rounding to the nearest unit, the inventory policy is as follows: When the inventory position drops to 14, place an order for 89 more.

The total annual cost will be

$$TC = DC + \frac{D}{Q}S + \frac{Q}{2}H$$

$$= 1,000(12.50) + \frac{1,000}{89}(5) + \frac{89}{2}(1.25)$$

$$= \$12,611.81$$

Note that in this example, the purchase cost of the units was not required to determine the order quantity and the reorder point because the cost was constant and unrelated to order size. ●

ESTABLISHING SAFETY STOCK LEVELS

The previous model assumed that demand was constant and known. In the majority of cases, though, demand is not constant but varies from day to day. Safety stock must therefore be maintained to provide some level of protection against stockouts. Safety stock can be defined as the amount of inventory carried in addition to the expected demand. In a normal distribution, this would be the mean. For example, if our average monthly demand is 100 units and we expect next month to be the same, if we carry 120 units, then we have 20 units of safety stock.

Safety stock

Safety stock can be determined based on many different criteria. Frequently a company simply states that a certain number of weeks of supply must be kept in safety stock. It is better, though, to use an approach that captures the variability in demand. For example, an objective may be something like "set the safety stock level so that there will only be a 5 percent chance of stocking out if demand exceeds 300 units." We call this approach to setting safety stock the probability approach.

The Probability Approach Using the probability criterion to determine safety stock is pretty simple. With the models described in this chapter, we assume that the demand over a period of time is normally distributed with a mean and a standard deviation. *Again, remember that this approach considers only the probability of running out of stock, not how many units we are short.* To determine the probability of stocking out over the time period, we can simply plot a normal distribution for the expected demand and note where the amount we have on hand lies on the curve.

Let's take a few simple examples to illustrate this. Say we expect demand to be 100 units over the next month, and we know that the standard deviation is 20 units. If we go into the month with just 100 units, we know that our probability of stocking out is 50 percent. Half of the months we would expect demand to be greater than 100 units; half of the months we would expect it to be less than 100 units. Taking this further, if we ordered a month's worth of inventory of 100 units at a time and received it at the beginning of the month, over the long run we would expect to run out of inventory in six months of the year.

NETFLIX IS THE WORLD'S LARGEST ONLINE MOVIE RENTAL SERVICE, PROVIDING ACCESS TO MORE THAN 100,000 DVD TITLES PLUS A GROWING LIBRARY OF OVER 12,000 MOVIES AVAILABLE FOR INSTANT WATCHING ON PC OR MAC. ON AVERAGE, NETFLIX SHIPS 1.9 MILLION DVDS TO CUSTOMERS EACH DAY FROM 58 DISTRIBUTION CENTERS.

If running out this often was not acceptable, we would want to carry extra inventory to reduce this risk of stocking out. One idea might be to carry an extra 20 units of inventory for the item. In this case, we would still order a month's worth of inventory at a time, but we would schedule delivery to arrive when we still have 20 units remaining in inventory. This would give us that little cushion of safety stock to reduce the probability of stocking out. If the standard deviation associated with our demand was 20 units, we would then be carrying one standard deviation worth of safety stock. Looking at the cumulative standard normal distribution (Appendix G), and moving one standard deviation to the right of the mean, gives a probability of 0.8413. So approximately 84 percent of the time we would not expect to stock out, and 16 percent of the time we would. Now if we order every month, we would expect to stock out approximately two months per year ($0.16 \times 12 = 1.92$). For those using Excel, given a z value, the probability can be obtained with the NORMSDIST function.

Companies using this approach generally set the probability of not stocking out at 95 percent. This means we would carry about 1.64 standard deviations of safety stock, or 33 units ($1.64 \times 20 = 32.8$) for our example. Once again, keep in mind that this does not mean that we would order 33 units extra each month. Rather, it means that we would still order a month's worth each time, but we would schedule the receipt so that we could expect to have 33 units in inventory when the order arrives. In this case, we would expect to stock out approximately 0.6 month per year, or that stockouts would occur in 1 of every 20 months.

FIXED–ORDER QUANTITY MODEL WITH SAFETY STOCK

A fixed–order quantity system perpetually monitors the inventory level and places a new order when stock reaches some level, R. The danger of stockout in this model occurs only during the lead time, between the time an order is placed and the time it is received. As shown in Exhibit 17.7, an order is placed when the inventory position drops to the reorder point, R. During this lead time L, a range of demands is possible. This range is determined either from an analysis of past demand data or from an estimate (if past data are not available).

The amount of safety stock depends on the service level desired, as previously discussed. The quantity to be ordered, Q, is calculated in the usual way considering the demand, shortage cost, ordering cost, holding cost, and so forth. A fixed–order quantity model can be used to compute Q, such as the simple Q_{opt} model previously discussed. The reorder point is then set to cover the expected demand during the lead time plus a safety stock determined by the desired service level. Thus, *the key difference between a fixed–order quantity model where demand is known and one where demand is uncertain is in computing the reorder point. The order quantity is the same in both cases.* The uncertainty element is taken into account in the safety stock.

exhibit 17.7   Fixed–Order Quantity Model

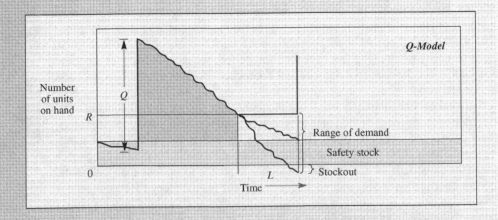

The reorder point is

$$R = \bar{d}L + z\sigma_L \qquad [17.5]$$

where

R = Reorder point in units

$\bar{d}$ = Average daily demand

L = Lead time in days (time between placing an order and receiving the items)

z = Number of standard deviations for a specified service probability

σ_L = Standard deviation of usage during lead time

The term $z\sigma_L$ is the amount of safety stock. Note that if safety stock is positive, the effect is to place a reorder sooner. That is, R without safety stock is simply the average demand during the lead time. If lead time usage was expected to be 20, for example, and safety stock was computed to be 5 units, then the order would be placed sooner, when 25 units remained. The greater the safety stock, the sooner the order is placed.

Computing $\bar{d}$, σ_L, and z Demand during the replenishment lead time is really an estimate or forecast of expected use of inventory from the time an order is placed to when it is received. It may be a single number (for example, if the lead time is a month, the demand may be taken as the previous year's demand divided by 12), or it may be a summation of expected demands over the lead time (such as the sum of daily demands over a 30-day lead time). For the daily demand situation, d can be a forecast demand using any of the models in Chapter 15 on forecasting. For example, if a 30-day period was used to calculate d, then a simple average would be

$$\bar{d} = \frac{\sum_{i=1}^{n} d_i}{n} \qquad [17.6]$$

$$= \frac{\sum_{i=1}^{30} d_i}{30}$$

where n is the number of days.

The standard deviation of the daily demand is

$$\sigma_d = \sqrt{\frac{\sum_{i=1}^{n} (d_i - \bar{d})^2}{n}} \qquad [17.7]$$

$$= \sqrt{\frac{\sum_{i=1}^{30} (d_i - \bar{d})^2}{30}}$$

Because σ_d refers to one day, if lead time extends over several days, we can use the statistical premise that the standard deviation of a series of independent occurrences is equal to the square root of the sum of the variances. That is, in general,

$$\sigma_L = \sqrt{\sigma_1^2 + \sigma_2^2 + \cdots + \sigma_L^2} \qquad [17.8]$$

For example, suppose we computed the standard deviation of demand to be 10 units per day. If our lead time to get an order is five days, the standard deviation for the five-day period, assuming each day can be considered independent, is

$$\sigma_5 = \sqrt{(10)^2 + (10)^2 + (10)^2 + (10)^2 + (10)^2} = 22.36$$

Next we need to find z, the number of standard deviations of safety stock.

Suppose we wanted our probability of not stocking out during the lead time to be 0.95. The z value associated with a 95 percent probability of not stocking out is 1.64 (see Appendix G or use the Excel NORMSINV function). Given this, safety stock is calculated as follows:

$$SS = z\sigma_L \qquad\qquad [17.9]$$
$$= 1.64 \times 22.36$$
$$= 36.67$$

We now compare two examples. The difference between them is that in the first, the variation in demand is stated in terms of standard deviation over the entire lead time, while in the second, it is stated in terms of standard deviation per day.

Step by Step

EXAMPLE 17.3: Reorder Point

Consider an economic order quantity case where annual demand $D = 1{,}000$ units, economic order quantity $Q = 200$ units, the desired probability of not stocking out $P = 0.95$, the standard deviation of demand during lead time $\sigma_L = 25$ units, and lead time $L = 15$ days. Determine the reorder point. Assume that demand is over a 250-workday year.

SOLUTION

In our example, $\bar{d} = \dfrac{1000}{250} = 4$, and lead time is 15 days. We use the equation

$$R = \bar{d}L + z\sigma_L$$
$$= 4(15) + z(25)$$

In this case z is 1.64.

Completing the solution for R, we have

$$R = 4(15) + 1.64(25) = 60 + 41 = 101 \text{ units}$$

This says that when the stock on hand gets down to 101 units, order 200 more. ●

Step by Step

Excel: Inventory Control

EXAMPLE 17.4: Order Quantity and Reorder Point

Daily demand for a certain product is normally distributed with a mean of 60 and standard deviation of 7. The source of supply is reliable and maintains a constant lead time of six days. The cost of placing the order is $10 and annual holding costs are $0.50 per unit. There are no stockout costs, and unfilled orders are filled as soon as the order arrives. Assume sales occur over the entire 365 days of the year. Find the order quantity and reorder point to satisfy a 95 percent probability of not stocking out during the lead time.

SOLUTION

In this problem we need to calculate the order quantity Q as well as the reorder point R.

$$\bar{d} = 60 \qquad\qquad S = \$10$$
$$\sigma_d = 7 \qquad\qquad H = \$0.50$$
$$D = 60(365) \qquad L = 6$$

The optimal order quantity is

$$Q_{opt} = \sqrt{\frac{2DS}{H}} = \sqrt{\frac{2(60)365(10)}{0.50}} = \sqrt{876{,}000} = 936 \text{ units}$$

To compute the reorder point, we need to calculate the amount of product used during the lead time and add this to the safety stock.

The standard deviation of demand during the lead time of six days is calculated from the variance of the individual days. Because each day's demand is independent[2]

$$\sigma_L = \sqrt{\sum_{i=1}^{L} \sigma_d^2} = \sqrt{6(7)^2} = 17.15$$

Once again, z is 1.64.

$$R = \bar{d}L + z\sigma_L = 60(6) + 1.64(17.15) = 388 \text{ units}$$

To summarize the policy derived in this example, an order for 936 units is placed whenever the number of units remaining in inventory drops to 388. ●

FIXED–TIME PERIOD MODELS

In a fixed–time period system, inventory is counted only at particular times, such as every week or every month. Counting inventory and placing orders periodically is desirable in situations such as when vendors make routine visits to customers and take orders for their complete line of products, or when buyers want to combine orders to save transportation costs. Other firms operate on a fixed time period to facilitate planning their inventory count; for example, Distributor X calls every two weeks and employees know that all Distributor X's product must be counted.

Fixed–time period models generate order quantities that vary from period to period, depending on the usage rates. These generally require a higher level of safety stock than a fixed–order quantity system. The fixed–order quantity system assumes continual tracking of inventory on hand, with an order immediately placed when the reorder point is reached. In contrast, the standard fixed–time period models assume that inventory is counted only at the time specified for review. It is possible that some large demand will draw the stock down to zero right after an order is placed. This condition could go unnoticed until the next review period. Then the new order, when placed, still takes time to arrive. Thus, it is possible to be out of stock throughout the entire review period, T, and order lead time, L. Safety stock, therefore, must protect against stockouts during the review period itself as well as during the lead time from order placement to order receipt.

FIXED–TIME PERIOD MODEL WITH SAFETY STOCK

In a fixed–time period system, reorders are placed at the time of review (T), and the safety stock that must be reordered is

$$\text{Safety stock} = z\sigma_{T+L} \qquad [17.10]$$

Exhibit 17.8 shows a fixed–time period system with a review cycle of T and a constant lead time of L. In this case, demand is randomly distributed about a mean d. The quantity to order, q, is

$$
\begin{array}{ccccc}
\begin{array}{c}\text{Order}\\\text{quantity}\end{array} & = & \begin{array}{c}\text{Average demand}\\\text{over the}\\\text{vulnerable period}\end{array} & + \begin{array}{c}\text{Safety}\\\text{stock}\end{array} & - \begin{array}{c}\text{Inventory currently}\\\text{on hand (plus on}\\\text{order, if any)}\end{array} \qquad [17.11]\\
q & = & \bar{d}(T+L) & + z\sigma_{T+L} & - \qquad I
\end{array}
$$

where

q = Quantity to be ordered

T = The number of days between reviews

Tutorials

exhibit 17.8   Fixed–Time Period Inventory Model

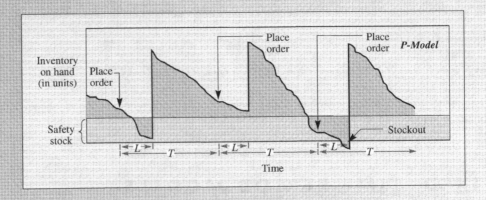

L = Lead time in days (time between placing an order and receiving it)

$\bar{d}$ = Forecast average daily demand

z = Number of standard deviations for a specified service probability

σ_{T+L} = Standard deviation of demand over the review and lead time

I = Current inventory level (includes items on order)

Note: The demand, lead time, review period, and so forth can be any time units such as days, weeks, or years so long as they are consistent throughout the equation.

In this model, demand ($\bar{d}$) can be forecast and revised each review period if desired or the yearly average may be used if appropriate. We assume that demand is normally distributed.

The value of z is dependent on the probability of stocking out and can be found using Appendix G or by using the Excel NORMSINV function.

Step by Step

Excel: Inventory Control

EXAMPLE 17.5: Quantity to Order

Daily demand for a product is 10 units with a standard deviation of 3 units. The review period is 30 days, and lead time is 14 days. Management has set a policy of satisfying 98 percent of demand from items in stock. At the beginning of this review period, there are 150 units in inventory.

How many units should be ordered?

SOLUTION

The quantity to order is

$$q = \bar{d}(T + L) + z\sigma_{T+L} - I$$
$$= 10(30 + 14) + z\sigma_{T+L} - 150$$

Before we can complete the solution, we need to find σ_{T+L} and z. To find σ_{T+L}, we use the notion, as before, that the standard deviation of a sequence of independent random variables equals the square root of the sum of the variances. Therefore, the standard deviation during the period $T + L$ is the square root of the sum of the variances for each day:

$$\sigma_{T+L} = \sqrt{\sum_{i=1}^{T+L} \sigma_d^2} \qquad [17.12]$$

Because each day is independent and σ_d is constant,

$$\sigma_{T+L} = \sqrt{(T + L)\sigma_d^2} = \sqrt{(30 + 14)(3)^2} = 19.90$$

The z value for $P = 0.98$ is 2.05.

The quantity to order, then, is

$$q = \bar{d}(T + L) + z\sigma_{T+L} - I = 10(30 + 14) + 2.05(19.90) - 150 = 331 \text{ units}$$

To ensure a 98 percent probability of not stocking out, order 331 units at this review period. ●

INVENTORY CONTROL AND SUPPLY CHAIN MANAGEMENT

Supply Chain

It is important for managers to realize that how they run items using inventory control logic relates directly to the financial performance of the firm. A key measure that relates to company performance is inventory turn. Recall that inventory turn is calculated as follows:

$$\text{Inventory turn} = \frac{\text{Cost of goods sold}}{\text{Average inventory value}}$$

So what is the relationship between how we manage an item and the inventory turn for that item? Here, let us simplify things and consider just the inventory turn for an individual item or a group of items. First, if we look at the numerator, the cost of goods sold for an individual item relates directly to the expected yearly demand (D) for the item. Given a cost per unit (C) for the item, the cost of goods sold is just D times C. Recall this is the same as what was used in our EOQ equation. Next, consider average inventory value. Recall from EOQ that the average inventory is $Q/2$, which is true if we assume that demand is constant. When we bring uncertainty into the equation, safety stock is needed to manage the risk created by demand variability. The fixed–order quantity model and fixed–time period model both have equations for calculating the safety stock required for a given probability of stocking out. In both models, we assume that when going through an order cycle, half the time we need to use the safety stock and half the time we do not. So on average, we expect the safety stock (SS) to be on hand. Given this, the average inventory is equal to the following:

$$\text{Average inventory value} = (Q/2 + SS)C \qquad [17.13]$$

The inventory turn for an individual item then is

$$\text{Inventory turn} = \frac{DC}{(Q/2 + SS)C} = \frac{D}{Q/2 + SS} \qquad [17.14]$$

EXAMPLE 17.6: Average Inventory Calculation—Fixed–Order Quantity Model

Suppose the following item is being managed using a fixed–order quantity model with safety stock.

Step by Step

Annual demand (D) = 1,000 units
Order quantity (Q) = 300 units
Safety stock (SS) = 40 units

What are the average inventory level and inventory turn for the item?

SOLUTION

$$\text{Average inventory} = Q/2 + SS = 300/2 + 40 = 190 \text{ units}$$

$$\text{Inventory turn} = \frac{D}{Q/2 + SS} = \frac{1,000}{190} = 5.263 \text{ turns per year} \text{ ●}$$

Step by Step

EXAMPLE 17.7: Average Inventory Calculation—Fixed–Time Period Model

Consider the following item that is being managed using a fixed–time period model with safety stock.

Weekly demand (d) = 50 units
Review cycle (T) = 3 weeks
Safety stock (SS) = 30 units

What are the average inventory level and inventory turn for the item?

SOLUTION

Here we need to determine how many units we expect to order each cycle. If we assume that demand is fairly steady, then we would expect to order the number of units that we expect demand to be during the review cycle. This expected demand is equal to dT if we assume that there is no trend or seasonality in the demand pattern.

$$\text{Average inventory} = dT/2 + SS = 50(3)/2 + 30 = 105 \text{ units}$$

$$\text{Inventory turn} = \frac{52d}{dT/2 + SS} = \frac{52(50)}{105} = 24.8 \text{ turns per year}$$

assuming there are 52 weeks in the year.

PRICE-BREAK MODELS

Price-break models deal with the fact that, generally, the selling price of an item varies with the order size. This is a discrete or step change rather than a per-unit change. For example, wood screws may cost $0.02 each for 1 to 99 screws, $1.60 per 100, and $13.50 per 1,000. To determine the optimal quantity of any item to order, we simply solve for the economic order quantity for each price and at the point of price change. But not all of the economic order quantities determined by the formula are feasible. In the wood screw example, the Q_{opt} formula might tell us that the optimal decision at the price of 1.6 cents is to order 75 screws. This would be impossible, however, because 75 screws would cost 2 cents each.

In general, to find the lowest-cost order quantity, we need to calculate the economic order quantity for each possible price and check to see whether the quantity is feasible. It is possible that the economic order quantity that is calculated is either higher or lower than the range to which the price corresponds. Any feasible quantity is a potential candidate order quantity. We also need to calculate the cost at each of the price-break quantities, since we know that price is feasible at these points and the total cost may be lowest at one of these values.

The calculations can be simplified a little if holding cost is based on a percentage of unit price (they will be in all the examples and problems given in this book). In this case, we only need to look at a subset of the price-break quantities. The following two-step procedure can be used:

Step 1.   Sort the prices from lowest to highest and then, beginning with the lowest price, calculate the economic order quantity for each price level until a feasible economic order quantity is found. By feasible, we mean that the price is in the correct corresponding range.

Step 2.   If the first feasible economic order quantity is for the lowest price, this quantity is best and you are finished. Otherwise, calculate the total cost for the first feasible economic order quantity (you did these from lowest to highest price) and also calculate the total cost at each price break lower than the price associated with the first feasible economic order quantity. This is the lowest order quantity at which you can take advantage of the price break. The optimal Q is the one with the lowest cost.

Curves for Three Separate Order Quantity Models in a Three-Price-Break Situation (red line depicts feasible range of purchases)

exhibit 17.9

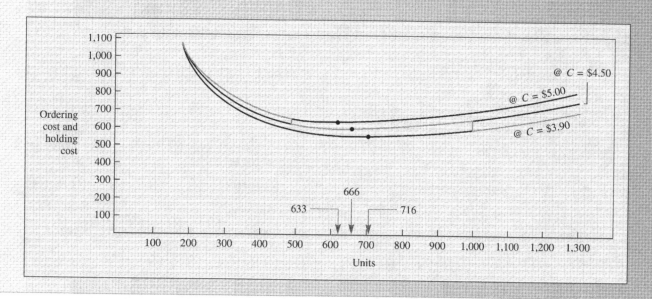

Looking at Exhibit 17.9, we see that order quantities are solved from right to left, or from the lowest unit price to the highest, until a valid Q is obtained. Then the order quantity at each *price break* above this Q is used to find which order quantity has the least cost—the computed Q or the Q at one of the price breaks.

EXAMPLE 17.8: Price Break

Consider the following case, where

Step by Step

D = 10,000 units (annual demand)

S = \$20 to place each order

i = 20 percent of cost (annual carrying cost, storage, interest, obsolescence, etc.)

C = Cost per unit (according to the order size; orders of 0 to 499 units, \$5.00 per unit; 500 to 999, \$4.50 per unit; 1,000 and up, \$3.90 per unit)

What quantity should be ordered?

SOLUTION

The appropriate equations from the basic fixed–order quantity case are

$$TC = DC + \frac{D}{Q}S + \frac{Q}{2}iC$$

and

$$Q = \sqrt{\frac{2DS}{iC}}$$ [17.15]

Solving for the economic order size, we obtain

@ C = \$3.90,	Q = 716	Not feasible
@ C = \$4.50,	Q = 667	Feasible, cost = \$45,600
Check Q = 1,000,	Cost = \$39,590	Optimal solution

In Exhibit 17.10, which displays the cost relationship and order quantity range, note that most of the order quantity–cost relationships lie outside the feasible range and that only a single, continuous

<table>
<tr><td>exhibit 17.10</td><td colspan="5">Relevant Costs in a Three-Price-Break Model</td></tr>
</table>

	$Q = 633$ WHERE $C = \$5$	$Q = 667$ WHERE $C = \$4.50$	$Q = 716$ WHERE $C = \$3.90$	PRICE BREAK 1,000
Holding cost $\left(\frac{Q}{2}iC\right)$		$\frac{667}{2}(0.20)4.50$ $= \$300.15$		$\frac{1,000}{2}(0.20)3.90$ $= \$390$
Ordering cost $\left(\frac{D}{Q}S\right)$	Not feasible	$\frac{10,000(20)}{667}$ $= \$299.85$	Not feasible	$\frac{10,000(20)}{1,000}$ $= \$200$
Holding and ordering cost		$\$600.00$		$\$590$
Item cost (DC)		$10,000(4.50)$		$10,000(3.90)$
Total cost		$\$45,600$		$\$39,590$

range results. This should be readily apparent because, for example, the first order quantity specifies buying 633 units at $5.00 per unit. However, if 633 units are ordered, the price is $4.50, not $5.00. The same holds true for the third order quantity, which specifies an order of 716 units at $3.90 each. This $3.90 price is not available on orders of fewer than 1,000 units.

Exhibit 17.10 itemizes the total costs at the economic order quantities and at the price breaks. The optimal order quantity is shown to be 1,000 units.

One practical consideration in price-break problems is that the price reduction from volume purchases frequently makes it seemingly economical to order amounts larger than the Q_{opt}. Thus, when applying the model, we must be particularly careful to obtain a valid estimate of product obsolescence and warehousing costs.

ABC INVENTORY PLANNING

Maintaining inventory through counting, placing orders, receiving stock, and so on, takes personnel time and costs money. When there are limits on these resources, the logical move is to try to use the available resources to control inventory in the best way. In other words, focus on the most important items in inventory.

In the nineteenth century Vilfredo Pareto, in a study of the distribution of wealth in Milan, found that 20 percent of the people controlled 80 percent of the wealth. This logic of the few having the greatest importance and the many having little importance has been broadened to include many situations and is termed the *Pareto principle*.[3] This is true in our everyday lives (most of our decisions are relatively unimportant, but a few shape our future) and is certainly true in inventory systems (where a few items account for the bulk of our investment).

Any inventory system must specify when an order is to be placed for an item and how many units to order. Most inventory control situations involve so many items that it is not practical to model and give thorough treatment to each item. To get around this problem, the ABC classification scheme divides inventory items into three groupings: high dollar volume (A), moderate dollar volume (B), and low dollar volume (C). Dollar volume is a measure of importance; an item low in cost but high in volume can be more important than a high-cost item with low volume.

ABC CLASSIFICATION

If the annual usage of items in inventory is listed according to dollar volume, generally, the list shows that a small number of items account for a large dollar volume and that a large number of items account for a small dollar volume. Exhibit 17.11A illustrates the relationship.

The ABC approach divides this list into three groupings by value: A items constitute roughly the top 15 percent of the items, B items the next 35 percent, and C items the last 50 percent. From observation, it appears that the list in Exhibit 17.11A can be meaningfully grouped with A including 20 percent (2 of the 10), B including 30 percent, and C including 50 percent. These points show clear delineations between sections. The result of this segmentation is shown in Exhibit 17.11B and plotted in Exhibit 17.11C.

Segmentation may not always occur so neatly. The objective, though, is to try to separate the important from the unimportant. Where the lines actually break depends on the particular inventory under question and on how much personnel time is available. (With more time, a firm could define larger A or B categories.)

The purpose of classifying items into groups is to establish the appropriate degree of control over each item. On a periodic basis, for example, class A items may be more clearly controlled with weekly ordering, B items may be ordered biweekly, and C items may be ordered monthly or bimonthly. Note that the unit cost of items is not related to their classification.

exhibit 17.11

A. Annual Usage of Inventory by Value

ITEM NUMBER	ANNUAL DOLLAR USAGE	PERCENTAGE OF TOTAL VALUE
22	$ 95,000	40.69%
68	75,000	32.13
27	25,000	10.71
03	15,000	6.43
82	13,000	5.57
54	7,500	3.21
36	1,500	0.64
19	800	0.34
23	425	0.18
41	225	0.10
	$233,450	100.0%

B. ABC Grouping of Inventory Items

CLASSIFICATION	ITEM NUMBER	ANNUAL DOLLAR USAGE	PERCENTAGE OF TOTAL
A	22, 68	$170,000	72.9%
B	27, 03, 82	53,000	22.7
C	54, 36, 19, 23, 41	10,450	4.4
		$233,450	100.0%

C. ABC Inventory Classification (inventory value for each group versus the group's portion of the total list)

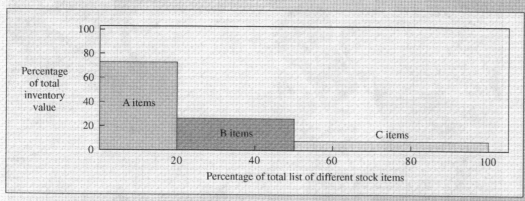

An A item may have a high dollar volume through a combination of either low cost and high usage or high cost and low usage. Similarly, C items may have a low dollar volume because of either low demand or low cost. In an automobile service station, gasoline would be an A item with daily or weekly replenishment; tires, batteries, oil, grease, and transmission fluid may be B items and ordered every two to four weeks; and C items would consist of valve stems, windshield wiper blades, radiator caps, hoses, fan belts, oil and gas additives, car wax, and so forth. C items may be ordered every two or three months or even be allowed to run out before reordering because the penalty for stockout is not serious.

Sometimes an item may be critical to a system if its absence creates a sizable loss. In this case, regardless of the item's classification, sufficiently large stocks should be kept on hand to prevent runout. One way to ensure closer control is to designate this item an A or a B, forcing it into the category even if its dollar volume does not warrant such inclusion.

INVENTORY ACCURACY AND CYCLE COUNTING

Inventory records usually differ from the actual physical count; inventory accuracy refers to how well the two agree. Companies such as Walmart understand the importance of inventory accuracy and expend considerable effort ensuring it. The question is, How much error is acceptable? If the record shows a balance of 683 of part X and an actual count shows 652, is this within reason? Suppose the actual count shows 750, an excess of 67 over the record; is this any better?

Every production system must have agreement, within some specified range, between what the record says is in inventory and what actually is in inventory. There are many reasons why records and inventory may not agree. For example, an open stockroom area allows items to be removed for both legitimate and unauthorized purposes. The legitimate removal may have been done in a hurry and simply not recorded. Sometimes parts are misplaced, turning up months later. Parts are often stored in several locations, but records may be lost or the location recorded incorrectly. Sometimes stock replenishment orders are recorded as received, when in fact they never were. Occasionally, a group of parts is recorded as removed

A SALES CLERK AT TOKYO'S MITSUKOSHI DEPARTMENT STORE READS AN RFID TAG ON JEANS TO CHECK STOCK. MITSUKOSHI AND JAPAN'S ELECTRONIC GIANT FUJITSU PARTNERED TO USE RFID TO IMPROVE STOCK CONTROL AND CUSTOMER SERVICE.

from inventory, but the customer order is canceled and the parts are replaced in inventory without canceling the record. To keep the production system flowing smoothly without parts shortages and efficiently without excess balances, records must be accurate.

How can a firm keep accurate, up-to-date records? Using bar codes and RFID tags is important to minimizing errors caused by inputting wrong numbers in the system. It is also important to keep the storeroom locked. If only storeroom personnel have access, and one of their measures of performance for personnel evaluation and merit increases is record accuracy, there is a strong motivation to comply. Every location of inventory storage, whether in a locked storeroom or on the production floor, should have a recordkeeping mechanism. A second way is to convey the importance of accurate records to all personnel and depend on them to assist in this effort. (This all boils down to this: Put a fence that goes all the way to the ceiling around the storage area so that workers cannot climb over to get parts; put a lock on the gate and give one person the key. Nobody can pull parts without having the transaction authorized and recorded.)

Another way to ensure accuracy is to count inventory frequently and match this against records. A widely used method is called *cycle counting*.

Cycle counting is a physical inventory-taking technique in which inventory is counted frequently rather than once or twice a year. The key to effective cycle counting and, therefore, to accurate records lies in deciding which items are to be counted, when, and by whom.

Cycle counting

Virtually all inventory systems these days are computerized. The computer can be programmed to produce a cycle count notice in the following cases:

1. When the record shows a low or zero balance on hand. (It is easier to count fewer items.)
2. When the record shows a positive balance but a backorder was written (indicating a discrepancy).
3. After some specified level of activity.
4. To signal a review based on the importance of the item (as in the ABC system) such as in the following table:

Annual Dollar Usage	Review Period
$10,000 or more	30 days or less
$3,000–$10,000	45 days or less
$250–$3,000	90 days or less
Less than $250	180 days or less

The easiest time for stock to be counted is when there is no activity in the stockroom or on the production floor. This means on the weekends or during the second or third shift, when the facility is less busy. If this is not possible, more careful logging and separation of items are required to count inventory while production is going on and transactions are occurring.

The counting cycle depends on the available personnel. Some firms schedule regular stockroom personnel to do the counting during lulls in the regular working day. Other companies hire private firms that come in and count inventory. Still other firms use full-time cycle counters who do nothing but count inventory and resolve differences with the records. Although this last method sounds expensive, many firms believe that it is actually less costly than the usual hectic annual inventory count generally performed during the two- or three-week annual vacation shutdown.

The question of how much error is tolerable between physical inventory and records has been much debated. Some firms strive for 100 percent accuracy, whereas others accept 1, 2, or 3 percent error. The accuracy level often recommended by experts is ±0.2 percent for A items, ±1 percent for B items, and ±5 percent for C items. Regardless of the specific accuracy decided on, the important point is that the level be dependable so that safety stocks may be provided as a cushion. Accuracy is important for a smooth production process so that customer orders can be processed as scheduled and not held up because of unavailable parts.

SUMMARY

This chapter introduced the two main classes of demand: (1) independent demand, referring to the external demand for a firm's end product, and (2) dependent demand, usually referring—within the firm—to the demand for items created because of the demand for more complex items of which they are a part. Most industries have items in both classes. In manufacturing, for example, independent demand is common for finished products, service and repair parts, and operating supplies; and dependent demand is common for those parts and materials needed to produce the end product. In wholesale and retail sales of consumer goods, most demand is independent—each item is an end item, with the wholesaler or retailer doing no further assembly or fabrication.

Independent demand, the focus of this chapter, is based on statistics. In the fixed–order quantity and fixed–time period models, the influence of service level was shown on safety stock and reorder point determinations. One special-purpose model—the single-period model—was also presented.

To distinguish among item categories for analysis and control, the ABC method was offered. The importance of inventory accuracy was also noted, and cycle counting was described.

In this chapter, we also pointed out that inventory reduction requires a knowledge of the operating system. It is not simply a case of selecting an inventory model off the shelf and plugging in some numbers. In the first place, a model might not even be appropriate. In the second case, the numbers might be full of errors or even based on erroneous data. Determining order quantities is often referred to as a trade-off problem; that is, trading off holding costs for setup costs. Note that companies really want to reduce both.

The simple fact is that firms have very large investments in inventory, and the cost to carry this inventory runs from 25 to 35 percent of the inventory's worth annually. Therefore, a major goal of most firms today is to reduce inventory.

A caution is in order, though. The formulas in this chapter try to minimize cost. Bear in mind that a firm's objective should be something like "making money"—so be sure that reducing inventory cost does, in fact, support this. Usually, correctly reducing inventory lowers cost, improves quality and performance, and enhances profit.

KEY TERMS

Inventory The stock of any item or resource used in an organization.

Independent demand The demands for various items are unrelated to each other.

Dependent demand The need for any one item is a direct result of the need for some other item, usually an item of which it is a part.

Fixed–order quantity model (or Q-model) An inventory control model where the amount requisitioned is fixed and the actual ordering is triggered by inventory dropping to a specified level of inventory.

Fixed–time period model (or P-model) An inventory control model that specifies inventory is ordered at the end of a predetermined time period. The interval of time between orders is fixed and the order quantity varies.

Inventory position The amount on-hand plus on-order minus back-ordered quantities. In the case where inventory has been allocated for special purposes, the inventory position is reduced by these allocated amounts.

Safety stock The amount of inventory carried in addition to the expected demand.

Cycle counting A physical inventory-taking technique in which inventory is counted on a frequent basis rather than once or twice a year.

FORMULA REVIEW

Single-period model. Cumulative probability of not selling the last unit. Ratio of marginal cost of underestimating demand and marginal cost of overestimating demand.

$$P \leq \frac{C_u}{C_o + C_u}$$

[17.1]

Q-model. Total annual cost for an order *Q*, a per-unit cost *C*, setup cost *S*, and per-unit holding cost *H*.

$$TC = DC + \frac{D}{Q}S + \frac{Q}{2}H \qquad [17.2]$$

Q-model. Optimal (or economic) order quantity.

$$Q_{opt} = \sqrt{\frac{2DS}{H}} \qquad [17.3]$$

Q-model. Reorder point *R* based on average daily demand $\bar{d}$ and lead time *L* in days.

$$R = \bar{d}L \qquad [17.4]$$

Q-model. Reorder point providing a safety stock of $z\sigma_L$.

$$R = \bar{d}L + z\sigma_L \qquad [17.5]$$

Average daily demand over a period of *n* days.

$$\bar{d} = \frac{\sum_{i=1}^{n}d_i}{n} \qquad [17.6]$$

Standard deviation of demand over a period of *n* days.

$$\sigma_d = \sqrt{\frac{\sum_{i=1}^{n}(d_i - \bar{d})^2}{n}} \qquad [17.7]$$

Standard deviation of a series of independent demands.

$$\sigma_L = \sqrt{\sigma_1^2 + \sigma_2^2 + \cdots + \sigma_L^2} \qquad [17.8]$$

Q-model. Safety stock calculation.

$$SS = z\sigma_L \qquad [17.9]$$

P-model. Safety stock calculation.

$$SS = z\sigma_{T+L} \qquad [17.10]$$

P-model. Optimal order quantity in a fixed-period system with a review period of *T* days and lead time of *L* days.

$$q = \bar{d}(T + L) + z\sigma_{T+L} - I \qquad [17.11]$$

P-model. Standard deviation of a series of independent demands over the review period *T* and lead time *L*.

$$\sigma_{T+L} = \sqrt{\sum_{i=1}^{T+L}\sigma_d^2} \qquad [17.12]$$

Average inventory.

$$\text{Average inventory value} = (Q/2 + SS)C \qquad [17.13]$$

Inventory turn.

$$\text{Inventory turn} = \frac{DC}{(Q/2 + SS)C} = \frac{D}{Q/2 + SS} \qquad [17.14]$$

Economic order quantity (with carrying cost percentage).

$$Q = \sqrt{\frac{2DS}{iC}} \qquad [17.15]$$

SOLVED PROBLEMS

SOLVED PROBLEM 1

**Excel:
Inventory
Control**

A product is priced to sell at $100 per unit, and its cost is constant at $70 per unit. Each unsold unit has a salvage value of $20. Demand is expected to range between 35 and 40 units for the period; 35 definitely can be sold and no units over 40 will be sold. The demand probabilities and the associated cumulative probability distribution (P) for this situation are shown below.

NUMBER OF UNITS DEMANDED	PROBABILITY OF THIS DEMAND	CUMULATIVE PROBABILITY
35	0.10	0.10
36	0.15	0.25
37	0.25	0.50
38	0.25	0.75
39	0.15	0.90
40	0.10	1.00

How many units should be ordered?

Solution

The cost of underestimating demand is the loss of profit, or $C_u = \$100 - \$70 = \$30$ per unit. The cost of overestimating demand is the loss incurred when the unit must be sold at salvage value, $C_o = \$70 - \$20 = \$50$.

The optimal probability of not being sold is

$$P \le \frac{C_u}{C_o + C_u} = \frac{30}{50 + 30} = 0.375$$

From the distribution data above, this corresponds to the 37th unit.

The following is a full marginal analysis for the problem. Note that the minimum cost is when 37 units are purchased.

		NUMBER OF UNITS PURCHASED					
UNITS DEMANDED	PROBABILITY	35	36	37	38	39	40
35	0.1	0	50	100	150	200	250
36	0.15	30	0	50	100	150	200
37	0.25	60	30	0	50	100	150
38	0.25	90	60	30	0	50	100
39	0.15	120	90	60	30	0	50
40	0.1	150	120	90	60	30	0
Total cost		75	53	43	53	83	125

SOLVED PROBLEM 2

Items purchased from a vendor cost $20 each, and the forecast for next year's demand is 1,000 units. If it costs $5 every time an order is placed for more units and the storage cost is $4 per unit per year, what quantity should be ordered each time?
a. What is the total ordering cost for a year?
b. What is the total storage cost for a year?

Solution

The quantity to be ordered each time is

$$Q = \sqrt{\frac{2DS}{H}} = \sqrt{\frac{2(1,000)5}{4}} = 50 \text{ units}$$

a. The total ordering cost for a year is

$$\frac{D}{Q}S = \frac{1,000}{50}(\$5) = \$100$$

b. The storage cost for a year is

$$\frac{Q}{2}H = \frac{50}{2}(\$4) = \$100$$

SOLVED PROBLEM 3

Daily demand for a product is 120 units, with a standard deviation of 30 units. The review period is 14 days and the lead time is 7 days. At the time of review, 130 units are in stock. If only a 1 percent risk of stocking out is acceptable, how many units should be ordered?

Solution

$$\sigma_{T+L} = \sqrt{(14 + 7)(30)^2} = \sqrt{18,900} = 137.5$$

$$z = 2.33$$

$$q = \bar{d}(T + L) + z\sigma_{T+L} - I$$

$$= 120(14 + 7) + 2.33(137.5) - 130$$

$$= 2,710 \text{ units}$$

**Excel:
Inventory
Control**

SOLVED PROBLEM 4

A company currently has 200 units of a product on hand that it orders every two weeks when the salesperson visits the premises. Demand for the product averages 20 units per day with a standard deviation of 5 units. Lead time for the product to arrive is seven days. Management has a goal of a 95 percent probability of not stocking out for this product.

The salesperson is due to come in late this afternoon when 180 units are left in stock (assuming that 20 are sold today). How many units should be ordered?

Solution

Given $I = 180$, $T = 14$, $L = 7$, $d = 20$

$$\sigma_{T+L} = \sqrt{21(5)^2} = 23$$

$$z = 1.64$$

$$q = \bar{d}(T + L) + z\sigma_{T+L} - I$$

$$= 20(14 + 7) + 1.64(23) - 180$$

$$q = 278 \text{ units}$$

**Excel:
Inventory
Control**

REVIEW AND DISCUSSION QUESTIONS

1 Distinguish between dependent and independent demand in a McDonald's restaurant, in an integrated manufacturer of personal copiers, and in a pharmaceutical supply house.
2 Distinguish between in-process inventory, safety stock inventory, and seasonal inventory.
3 Discuss the nature of the costs that affect inventory size.
4 Under which conditions would a plant manager elect to use a fixed–order quantity model as opposed to a fixed–time period model? What are the disadvantages of using a fixed–time period ordering system?
5 What two basic questions must be answered by an inventory-control decision rule?
6 Discuss the assumptions that are inherent in production setup cost, ordering cost, and carrying costs. How valid are they?
7 "The nice thing about inventory models is that you can pull one off the shelf and apply it so long as your cost estimates are accurate." Comment.
8 Which type of inventory system would you use in the following situations?
   a. Supplying your kitchen with fresh food.
   b. Obtaining a daily newspaper.
   c. Buying gas for your car.
   To which of these items do you impute the highest stockout cost?
9 Why is it desirable to classify items into groups, as the ABC classification does?

PROBLEMS

1   The local supermarket buys lettuce each day to ensure really fresh produce. Each morning any lettuce that is left from the previous day is sold to a dealer that resells it to farmers who use it to feed their animals. This week the supermarket can buy fresh lettuce for $4.00 a box. The lettuce is sold for $10.00 a box and the dealer that sells old lettuce is willing to pay $1.50 a box. Past history says that tomorrow's demand for lettuce averages 250 boxes with a standard deviation of 34 boxes. How many boxes of lettuce should the supermarket purchase tomorrow?

2   Next week, Super Discount Airlines has a flight from New York to Los Angeles that will be booked to capacity. The airline knows from past history that an average of 25 customers (with a standard deviation of 15) cancel their reservation or do not show for the flight. Revenue from a ticket on the flight is $125. If the flight is overbooked, the airline has a policy of getting the customer on the next available flight and giving the person a free round-trip ticket on a future flight. The cost of this free round-trip ticket averages $250. Super Discount considers the cost of flying the plane from New York to Los Angeles a sunk cost. By how many seats should Super Discount overbook the flight?

3   Ray's Satellite Emporium wishes to determine the best order size for its best-selling satellite dish (model TS111). Ray has estimated the annual demand for this model at 1,000 units. His cost to carry one unit is $100 per year per unit, and he has estimated that each order costs $25 to place. Using the EOQ model, how many should Ray order each time?

4   Dunstreet's Department Store would like to develop an inventory ordering policy of a 95 percent probability of not stocking out. To illustrate your recommended procedure, use as an example the ordering policy for white percale sheets.

   Demand for white percale sheets is 5,000 per year. The store is open 365 days per year. Every two weeks (14 days) inventory is counted and a new order is placed. It takes 10 days for the sheets to be delivered. Standard deviation of demand for the sheets is five per day. There are currently 150 sheets on hand.

   How many sheets should you order?

5   Charlie's Pizza orders all of its pepperoni, olives, anchovies, and mozzarella cheese to be shipped directly from Italy. An American distributor stops by every four weeks to take orders. Because the orders are shipped directly from Italy, they take three weeks to arrive.

   Charlie's Pizza uses an average of 150 pounds of pepperoni each week, with a standard deviation of 30 pounds. Charlie's prides itself on offering only the best-quality ingredients and a high level of service, so it wants to ensure a 98 percent probability of not stocking out on pepperoni.

   Assume that the sales representative just walked in the door and there are currently 500 pounds of pepperoni in the walk-in cooler. How many pounds of pepperoni would you order?

6   Given the following information, formulate an inventory management system. The item is demanded 50 weeks a year.

Item cost	$10.00	Standard deviation of weekly demand	25 per week
Order cost	$250.00		
Annual holding cost (%)	33% of item cost	Lead time	1 week
Annual demand	25,750	Service probability	95%
Average demand	515 per week		

   a. State the order quantity and reorder point.
   b. Determine the annual holding and order costs.
   c. If a price break of $50 per order was offered for purchase quantities of over 2,000, would you take advantage of it? How much would you save annually?

7   Lieutenant Commander Data is planning to make his monthly (every 30 days) trek to Gamma Hydra City to pick up a supply of isolinear chips. The trip will take Data about two days. Before he leaves, he calls in the order to the GHC Supply Store. He uses chips at an average rate of five per day (seven days per week) with a standard deviation of demand of one per day. He needs a 98 percent service probability. If he currently has 35 chips in inventory, how many should he order? What is the most he will ever have to order?

8 Jill's Job Shop buys two parts (Tegdiws and Widgets) for use in its production system from two different suppliers. The parts are needed throughout the entire 52-week year. Tegdiws are used at a relatively constant rate and are ordered whenever the remaining quantity drops to the reorder level. Widgets are ordered from a supplier who stops by every three weeks. Data for both products are as follows:

ITEM	TEGDIW	WIDGET
Annual demand	10,000	5,000
Holding cost (% of item cost)	20%	20%
Setup or order cost	$150.00	$25.00
Lead time	4 weeks	1 week
Safety stock	55 units	5 units
Item cost	$10.00	$2.00

   a. What is the inventory control system for Tegdiws? That is, what is the reorder quantity and what is the reorder point?

   b. What is the inventory control system for Widgets?

9 Demand for an item is 1,000 units per year. Each order placed costs $10; the annual cost to carry items in inventory is $2 each. In what quantities should the item be ordered?

10 The annual demand for a product is 15,600 units. The weekly demand is 300 units with a standard deviation of 90 units. The cost to place an order is $31.20, and the time from ordering to receipt is four weeks. The annual inventory carrying cost is $0.10 per unit. Find the reorder point necessary to provide a 98 percent service probability.

   Suppose the production manager is asked to reduce the safety stock of this item by 50 percent. If she does so, what will the new service probability be?

11 Daily demand for a product is 100 units, with a standard deviation of 25 units. The review period is 10 days and the lead time is 6 days. At the time of review there are 50 units in stock. If 98 percent service probability is desired, how many units should be ordered?

12 Item X is a standard item stocked in a company's inventory of component parts. Each year the firm, on a random basis, uses about 2,000 of item X, which costs $25 each. Storage costs, which include insurance and cost of capital, amount to $5 per unit of average inventory. Every time an order is placed for more item X, it costs $10.

   a. Whenever item X is ordered, what should the order size be?

   b. What is the annual cost for ordering item X?

   c. What is the annual cost for storing item X?

13 Annual demand for a product is 13,000 units; weekly demand is 250 units with a standard deviation of 40 units. The cost of placing an order is $100, and the time from ordering to receipt is four weeks. The annual inventory carrying cost is $0.65 per unit. To provide a 98 percent service probability, what must the reorder point be?

   Suppose the production manager is told to reduce the safety stock of this item by 100 units. If this is done, what will the new service probability be?

14 In the past, Taylor Industries has used a fixed–time period inventory system that involved taking a complete inventory count of all items each month. However, increasing labor costs are forcing Taylor Industries to examine alternative ways to reduce the amount of labor involved in inventory stockrooms, yet without increasing other costs, such as shortage costs. Here is a random sample of 20 of Taylor's items.

ITEM NUMBER	ANNUAL USAGE	ITEM NUMBER	ANNUAL USAGE
1	$ 1,500	11	$13,000
2	12,000	12	600
3	2,200	13	42,000
4	50,000	14	9,900
5	9,600	15	1,200
6	750	16	10,200
7	2,000	17	4,000
8	11,000	18	61,000
9	800	19	3,500
10	15,000	20	2,900

    a. What would you recommend Taylor do to cut back its labor cost? (Illustrate using an ABC plan.)

    b. Item 15 is critical to continued operations. How would you recommend it be classified?

15 Gentle Ben's Bar and Restaurant uses 5,000 quart bottles of an imported wine each year. The effervescent wine costs $3 per bottle and is served only in whole bottles because it loses its bubbles quickly. Ben figures that it costs $10 each time an order is placed, and holding costs are 20 percent of the purchase price. It takes three weeks for an order to arrive. Weekly demand is 100 bottles (closed two weeks per year) with a standard deviation of 30 bottles.

    Ben would like to use an inventory system that minimizes inventory cost and will provide a 95 percent service probability.

    a. What is the economic quantity for Ben to order?

    b. At what inventory level should he place an order?

16 Retailers Warehouse (RW) is an independent supplier of household items to department stores. RW attempts to stock enough items for a 98 percent service probability.

    A stainless steel knife set is one item it stocks. Demand (2,400 sets per year) is relatively stable over the entire year. Whenever new stock is ordered, a buyer must assure that numbers are correct for stock on hand and then phone in a new order. The total cost involved to place an order is about $5. RW figures that holding inventory in stock and paying for interest on borrowed capital, insurance, and so on, adds up to about $4 holding cost per unit per year.

    Analysis of the past data shows that the standard deviation of demand from retailers is about four units per day for a 365-day year. Lead time to get the order is seven days.

    a. What is the economic order quantity?

    b. What is the reorder point?

17 Daily demand for a product is 60 units with a standard deviation of 10 units. The review period is 10 days, and lead time is 2 days. At the time of review there are 100 units in stock. If 98 percent service probability is desired, how many units should be ordered?

18 University Drug Pharmaceuticals orders its antibiotics every two weeks (14 days) when a salesperson visits from one of the pharmaceutical companies. Tetracycline is one of its most prescribed antibiotics, with average daily demand of 2,000 capsules. The standard deviation of daily demand was derived from examining prescriptions filled over the past three months and was found to be 800 capsules. It takes five days for the order to arrive. University Drug would like to satisfy 99 percent of the prescriptions. The salesperson just arrived, and there are currently 25,000 capsules in stock.

    How many capsules should be ordered?

19 Sally's Silk Screening produces specialty T-shirts that are primarily sold at special events. She is trying to decide how many to produce for an upcoming event. During the event itself, which lasts one day, Sally can sell T-shirts for $20 apiece. However, when the event ends, any unsold T-shirts are sold for $4 apiece. It costs Sally $8 to make a specialty T-shirt. Using Sally's estimate of demand that follows, how many T-shirts should she produce for the upcoming event?

DEMAND	PROBABILITY
300	0.05
400	0.10
500	0.40
600	0.30
700	0.10
800	0.05

20 Famous Albert prides himself on being the Cookie King of the West. Small, freshly baked cookies are the specialty of his shop. Famous Albert has asked for help to determine the number of cookies he should make each day. From an analysis of past demand he estimates demand for cookies as

DEMAND	PROBABILITY OF DEMAND
1,800 dozen	0.05
2,000	0.10
2,200	0.20
2,400	0.30
2,600	0.20
2,800	0.10
3,000	0.05

Each dozen sells for $0.69 and costs $0.49, which includes handling and transportation. Cookies that are not sold at the end of the day are reduced to $0.29 and sold the following day as day-old merchandise.

a. Construct a table showing the profits or losses for each possible quantity.

b. What is the optimal number of cookies to make?

c. Solve this problem by using marginal analysis.

21   Sarah's Muffler Shop has one standard muffler that fits a large variety of cars. Sarah wishes to establish a reorder point system to manage inventory of this standard muffler. Use the following information to determine the best order size and the reorder point:

Annual demand	3,500 mufflers	Ordering cost	$50 per order
Standard deviation of daily demand	6 mufflers per working day	Service probability	90%
Item cost	$30 per muffler	Lead time	2 working days
Annual holding cost	25% of item value	Working days	300 per year

22   Alpha Products, Inc., is having a problem trying to control inventory. There is insufficient time to devote to all its items equally. Here is a sample of some items stocked, along with the annual usage of each item expressed in dollar volume.

ITEM	ANNUAL DOLLAR USAGE	ITEM	ANNUAL DOLLAR USAGE
a	$ 7,000	k	$80,000
b	1,000	l	400
c	14,000	m	1,100
d	2,000	n	30,000
e	24,000	o	1,900
f	68,000	p	800
g	17,000	q	90,000
h	900	r	12,000
i	1,700	s	3,000
j	2,300	t	32,000

a. Can you suggest a system for allocating control time?

b. Specify where each item from the list would be placed.

23   After graduation, you decide to go into a partnership in an office supply store that has existed for a number of years. Walking through the store and stockrooms, you find a great discrepancy in service levels. Some spaces and bins for items are completely empty; others have supplies that are covered with dust and have obviously been there a long time. You decide to take on the project of establishing consistent levels of inventory to meet customer demands. Most of your supplies are purchased from just a few distributors that call on your store once every two weeks.

You choose, as your first item for study, computer printer paper. You examine the sales records and purchase orders and find that demand for the past 12 months was 5,000 boxes. Using your calculator you sample some days' demands and estimate that the standard deviation of daily demand is 10 boxes. You also search out these figures:

Cost per box of paper: $11.

Desired service probability: 98 percent.

Store is open every day.

Salesperson visits every two weeks.

Delivery time following visit is three days.

Using your procedure, how many boxes of paper would be ordered if, on the day the salesperson calls, 60 boxes are on hand?

24   A distributor of large appliances needs to determine the order quantities and reorder points for the various products it carries. The following data refer to a specific refrigerator in its product line:

Cost to place an order	$100
Holding cost	20 percent of product cost per year
Cost of refrigerator	$500 each
Annual demand	500 refrigerators
Standard deviation during lead time	10 refrigerators
Lead time	7 days

Consider an even daily demand and a 365-day year.
a. What is the economic order quantity?
b. If the distributor wants a 97 percent service probability, what reorder point, R, should be used?

25   It is your responsibility, as the new head of the automotive section of Nichols Department Store, to ensure that reorder quantities for the various items have been correctly established. You decide to test one item and choose Michelin tires, XW size 185 × 14 BSW. A perpetual inventory system has been used, so you examine this as well as other records and come up with the following data:

Cost per tire	$35 each
Holding cost	20 percent of tire cost per year
Demand	1,000 per year
Ordering cost	$20 per order
Standard deviation of daily demand	3 tires
Delivery lead time	4 days

Because customers generally do not wait for tires but go elsewhere, you decide on a service probability of 98 percent. Assume the demand occurs 365 days per year.
a. Determine the order quantity.
b. Determine the reorder point.

26   UA Hamburger Hamlet (UAHH) places a daily order for its high-volume items (hamburger patties, buns, milk, and so on). UAHH counts its current inventory on hand once per day and phones in its order for delivery 24 hours later. Determine the number of hamburgers UAHH should order for the following conditions:

Average daily demand	600
Standard deviation of demand	100
Desired service probability	99%
Hamburger inventory	800

27   DAT, Inc., produces digital audiotapes to be used in the consumer audio division. DAT lacks sufficient personnel in its inventory supply section to closely control each item stocked, so it has asked you to determine an ABC classification. Here is a sample from the inventory records:

ITEM	AVERAGE MONTHLY DEMAND	PRICE PER UNIT	ITEM	AVERAGE MONTHLY DEMAND	PRICE PER UNIT
1	700	$6.00	6	100	10.00
2	200	4.00	7	3,000	2.00
3	2,000	12.00	8	2,500	1.00
4	1,100	20.00	9	500	10.00
5	4,000	21.00	10	1,000	2.00

Develop an ABC classification for these 10 items.

28 A local service station is open 7 days per week, 365 days per year. Sales of 10W40 grade premium oil average 20 cans per day. Inventory holding costs are $0.50 per can per year. Ordering costs are $10 per order. Lead time is two weeks. Backorders are not practical—the motorist drives away.

   a. Based on these data, choose the appropriate inventory model and calculate the economic order quantity and reorder point. Describe in a sentence how the plan would work. Hint: Assume demand is deterministic.

   b. The boss is concerned about this model because demand really varies. The standard deviation of demand was determined from a data sample to be 6.15 cans per day. The manager wants a 99.5 percent service probability. Determine a new inventory plan based on this information and the data in *a*. Use Q_{opt} from *a*.

29 Dave's Auto Supply custom mixes paint for its customers. The shop performs a weekly inventory count of the main colors that are used for mixing paint. Determine the amount of white paint that should be ordered using the following information:

Average weekly demand	20 gallons
Standard deviation of demand	5 gallons/week
Desired service probability	98%
Current inventory	25 gallons
Lead time	1 week

30 A particular raw material is available to a company at three different prices, depending on the size of the order:

Less than 100 pounds	$20 per pound
100 pounds to 1,000 pounds	$19 per pound
More than 1,000 pounds	$18 per pound

   The cost to place an order is $40. Annual demand is 3,000 units. Holding (or carrying) cost is 25 percent of the material price.

   What is the economic order quantity to buy each time?

31 CU, Incorporated (CUI), produces copper contacts that it uses in switches and relays. CUI needs to determine the order quantity, Q, to meet the annual demand at the lowest cost. The price of copper depends on the quantity ordered. Here are price-break and other data for the problem:

Price of copper	$0.82 per pound up to 2,499 pounds
	$0.81 per pound for orders between 2,500 and 5,000 pounds
	$0.80 per pound for orders greater than 5,000 pounds
Annual demand	50,000 pounds per year
Holding cost	20 percent per unit per year of the price of the copper
Ordering cost	$30

   Which quantity should be ordered?

CASE: HEWLETT-PACKARD—SUPPLYING THE DESKJET PRINTER IN EUROPE

The DeskJet printer was introduced in 1988 and has become one of Hewlett-Packard's (HP's) most successful products. Sales have grown steadily, now reaching a level of over 600,000. Unfortunately, inventory growth has tracked sales growth closely.

HP's distribution centers are filled with pallets of the DeskJet printer. Worse yet, the organization in Europe claims that inventory levels there need to be raised even further to maintain satisfactory product availability.

HP DeskJet Supply Chain

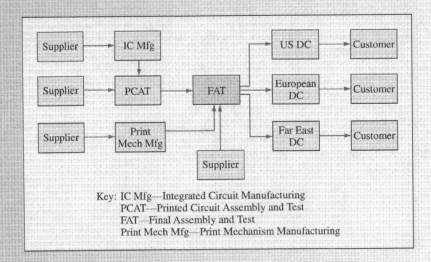

Key: IC Mfg—Integrated Circuit Manufacturing
PCAT—Printed Circuit Assembly and Test
FAT—Final Assembly and Test
Print Mech Mfg—Print Mechanism Manufacturing

THE DESKJET SUPPLY CHAIN

The network of suppliers, manufacturing sites, distribution centers (DCs), dealers, and customers for the DeskJet product make up the DeskJet supply chain (see Exhibit 17.12). HP in Vancouver does manufacturing. There are two key stages in the manufacturing process: (1) printed circuit assembly and test (PCAT) and (2) final assembly and test (FAT). PCAT involves the assembly and testing of electronic components (like integrated circuits, read-only memories, and raw printed circuit boards) to make logic boards used in the printer. FAT involves the assembly of other subassemblies (like motors, cables, keypads, plastic chassis, gears, and the printed circuit assemblies from PCAT) to produce a working printer, as well as the final testing of the printer. The components needed for PCAT and FAT are sourced from other HP divisions as well as from external suppliers worldwide.

Selling the DeskJet in Europe requires customizing the printer to meet the language and power supply requirements of the local countries, a process known as "localization." Specifically, the localization of the DeskJet of different countries involves assembling the appropriate power supply module, which reflects the correct voltage requirements (110 or 220) and power cord plug, and packaging it with the working printer and a manual written in the appropriate language. Currently, the final test is done with the actual power supply module included with the printer. Hence, the finished products of the factory are "localized" versions of the printer destined for all the different countries. For the European Union six different versions are currently produced. These are designated A, AA, AB, AQ, AU, and AY as indicated in the Bills of Materials shown in Exhibit 17.13.

The total factory throughput time through the PCAT and FAT stages is about one week. The transportation time from Vancouver to the European DC is five weeks. The long shipment time to Europe is due to ocean transit and the time to clear customs and duties at port of entry. The plant sends a weekly shipment of printers to the DC in Europe.

Global

Supply
Chain

HP DeskJet Bill of Materials

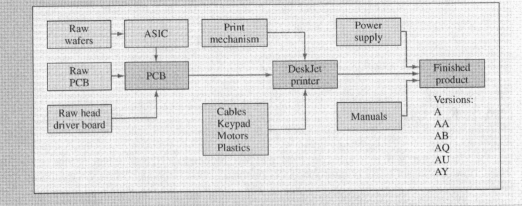

DeskJet Demand Data from Europe

exhibit 17.14

EUROPE OPTIONS	NOV.	DEC.	JAN.	FEB.	MAR.	APR.	MAY	JUN.	JUL.	AUG.	SEP.	OCT.
A	80	—	60	90	21	48	—	9	20	54	84	42
AB	20,572	20,895	19,252	11,052	19,864	20,316	13,336	10,578	6,095	14,496	23,712	9,792
AU	4,564	3,207	7,485	4,908	5,295	90	—	5,004	4,385	5,103	4,302	6,153
AA	400	255	408	645	210	87	432	816	430	630	456	273
AQ	4,008	2,196	4,761	1,953	1,008	2,358	1,676	540	2,310	2,046	1,797	2,961
AY	248	450	378	306	219	204	248	484	164	363	384	234
Total	29,872	27,003	32,344	18,954	26,617	23,103	15,692	17,431	13,405	22,692	30,735	19,455

Excel:
HP Deskjet

The printer industry is highly competitive. Resellers want to carry as little inventory as possible. Consequently there has been increasing pressure for HP as a manufacturer to provide high levels of availability at the DC. In response, management has decided to stock the DCs so that a high level of availability is maintained.

THE INVENTORY SERVICE CRISIS

To limit the amount of inventory throughout the DeskJet supply chain and at the same time provide the high level of service needed has been quite a challenge to Vancouver's management. The manufacturing group has been very successful in reducing the uncertainties caused by delivery to the European DC. Forecasting demand in Europe, though, is a significant problem. It has become common to have product shortages for model demands from some countries, while inventory of other models keeps piling up. In the past, the target inventory levels at the DCs were based on safety stocks that were a result of some judgmental rule of thumb. Specifically, target inventory levels, equal to one-month average sales, were set for each model carried in the DC. Now, however, it seems that the increasing difficulty of getting accurate forecasts means the safety stock rules should be revisited.

HP has put together a team of employees to help implement a scientifically based safety stock system that will be responsive to forecast errors and replenishment lead times. They are to recommend a method for calculating appropriate safety stock levels for the various DeskJet models carried in the European DC. The team has a good sample of demand data that can be used for developing the safety stock methodology (see Exhibit 17.14). HP hopes this new methodology will solve the inventory and service problem.

One issue that continually comes up is the choice of inventory carrying cost to be used in safety stock analyses. Estimates within the company range from 12 percent (HP's cost of debt plus some warehousing expenses) to 60 percent (based on the ROI expected of new product development projects). Management has decided to use 25 percent for this study. Assume that all printers cost an average of approximately $250 each to produce and ship to Europe. Another issue is the choice of safety stock probability for the model. The company has decided to use a probability of 98 percent, a number that marketing feels is appropriate.

THE DISTRIBUTION PROCESS

The DCs have traditionally envisioned their process as a simple, straight-line, standardized process. There are four process stops:

1 Receive (complete) products from various suppliers and stock them.
2 Pick the various products needed to fill a customer order.
3 Shrink-wrap the complete order and label it.
4 Ship the order via the appropriate carrier.

The DeskJet printer fits well into the standard process. In contrast, other products, such as personal computers and monitors, require special processing called "integration," which includes addition of an appropriate keyboard and manual for the destination country. Although this extra processing does not require much extra labor, it is difficult to accommodate in the standard process and disrupts the material flow. There is considerable frustration within DC management regarding the support of assembly processes. In general, DC management stresses the DCs' role as warehouses and the need to continue to do what they are best at—distribution.

Top management, though, feels that integration of the product at the warehouse is extremely valuable because it allows generic products to be sent to the DC with final configuration of the product done just prior to shipment to the customer. Rather than the factory making products specific to a country, generic products could be produced and shipped to Europe. Management is very interested in studying the value of this approach as it could be applied to the DeskJet printers.

QUESTIONS

1 Develop an inventory model for managing the DeskJet printers in Europe assuming that the Vancouver plant continues to produce the six models sold in Europe. Using the data in Exhibit 17.13, apply your model and calculate the expected yearly investment in DeskJet printer inventory in the Europe DC.
2 Compare your results from question 1 to the current policy of carrying one month's average inventory at the DC.

3   Evaluate the idea of supplying generic printers to the Europe DC and integrating the product by packaging the power supply and the instruction manual at the DC just prior to delivery to the European resellers. Focus on the impact on DC inventory investment in this analysis.

4   What is your recommendation to HP?

SUPER QUIZ

1   Model most appropriate for making a one-time purchase of an item.

2   Model most appropriate when inventory is replenished only in fixed intervals of time, for example, on the first Monday of each month.

3   Model most appropriate when a fixed amount must be purchased each time an order is placed.

4   Based on an EOQ-type ordering criterion, what cost must be taken to zero if the desire is to have an order quantity of a single unit?

5   Term used to describe demand that can be accurately calculated to meet the need of a production schedule, for example.

6   Term used to describe demand that is uncertain and needs to be forecast.

7   We are ordering T-shirts for the spring party and are selling them for twice what we paid for them. We expect to sell 100 shirts and the standard deviation associated with our forecast is 10 shirts. How many shirts should we order?

8   We have an item that we stock in our store that has fairly steady demand. Our supplier insists that we buy 1,200 units at a time. The lead time is very short on the item, since the supplier is only a few blocks away and we can pick up another 1,200 units when we run out. How many units do you expect to have in inventory on average?

9   For the item described in question 8, if we expect to sell approximately 15,600 units next year, how many trips will we need to make to the supplier over the year?

10 If we decide to carry 10 units of safety stock for the item described in questions 8 and 9, and we implemented this by going to our supplier when we had 10 units left, how much inventory would you expect to have on average now?

11 We are being evaluated based on the percentage of total demand met in a year (not the probability of stocking out as used in the chapter). Consider an item that we are managing using a fixed-order quantity model with safety stock. We decide to double the order quantity, but leave the reorder point the same. Would you expect the percent of total demand met next year to go up or down? Why?

12 Consider an item that we have 120 units currently in inventory. The average demand for the item is 60 units per week. The lead time for the item is exactly 2 weeks and we carry 16 units for safety stock. What is the probability of running out of the item if we order right now?

13 If we take advantage of a quantity discount, would you expect your average inventory to go up or down? Assume that the probability of stocking out criterion stays the same.

14 This is an inventory auditing technique where inventory levels are checked more frequently than one time a year.

1. Single-period model 2. Fixed–time period model 3. Fixed–order quantity model 4. Setup or ordering cost 5. Dependent demand 6. Independent demand 7. 100 shirts 8. 600 units 9. 13 trips 10. 610 units 11. Go up (we are taking fewer chances of running out) 12. 50 percent 13. Will probably go up if the probability of stocking out stays the same 14. Cycle counting

SELECTED BIBLIOGRAPHY

Brooks, R. B., and L. W. Wilson. *Inventory Record Accuracy: Unleashing the Power of Cycle Counting.* Essex Junction, VT: Oliver Wight, 1993.

Silver, E.; D. Pyke; and R. Peterson. *Decision Systems for Inventory Management and Production Planning and Control.* 3rd ed. New York: Wiley, 1998.

Sipper, D., and R. L. Bulfin Jr. *Production Planning, Control, and Integration.* New York: McGraw-Hill, 1997.

Tersine, R. J. *Principles of Inventory and Materials Management.* 4th ed. New York: North-Holland, 1994.

Vollmann, T. E.; W. L. Berry; D. C. Whybark; and F. R. Jacobs. *Manufacturing Planning and Control Systems for Supply Chain Management.* 5th ed. New York: McGraw-Hill, 2004.

Wild, T. *Best Practices in Inventory Management.* New York: Wiley, 1998.

Zipkin, P. H. *Foundations of Inventory Management.* New York: Irwin/McGraw-Hill, 2000.

FOOTNOTES

1 *P* is actually a cumulative probability because the sale of the *n*th unit depends not only on exactly *n* being demanded but also on the demand for any number greater than *n*.

2 As previously discussed, the standard deviation of a sum of independent variables equals the square root of the sum of the variances.

3 The Pareto principle is also widely applied in quality problems through the use of Pareto charts. (See Chapter 6.)

LINEAR PROGRAMMING USING THE EXCEL SOLVER

The key to profitable operations is making the best use of available resources of people, material, plant and equipment, and money. Today's manager has a powerful mathematical modeling tool available for this purpose with linear programming. In this appendix, we will show how the use of the Microsoft Excel Solver to solve LP problems opens a whole new world to the innovative manager and provides an invaluable addition to the technical skill set for those who seek careers in consulting. In this appendix, we use a product-planning problem to introduce this tool. Here we find the optimal mix of products that have different costs and resource requirements. This problem is certainly relevant to today's competitive market. Extremely successful companies provide a mix of products, from standard to high-end luxury models. All these products compete for the use of limited production and other capacity. Maintaining the proper mix of these products over time can significantly bolster earnings and the return on a firm's assets.

We begin with a quick introduction to linear programming and conditions under which the technique is applicable. Then we solve a simple product-mix problem. Other linear programming applications appear throughout the rest of the book.

INTRODUCTION

Linear programming (LP)

Linear programming (or simply LP) refers to several related mathematical techniques used to allocate limited resources among competing demands in an optimal way. LP is the most widely used of the approaches falling under the general heading of mathematical optimization techniques and has been applied to many operations management problems. The following are typical applications:

Aggregate sales and operations planning: Finding the minimum-cost production schedule. The problem is to develop a three- to six-month plan for meeting expected demand given constraints on expected production capacity and workforce size. Relevant costs considered in the problem include regular and overtime labor rates, hiring and firing, subcontracting, and inventory carrying cost.

Service/manufacturing productivity analysis: Comparing how efficiently different service and manufacturing outlets are using their resources compared to the best-performing unit. This is done using an approach called data envelopment analysis.

Product planning: Finding the optimal product mix where several products have different costs and resource requirements. Examples include finding the optimal blend of chemicals for gasoline, paints, human diets, and animal feeds. Examples of this problem are covered in this chapter.

Product routing: Finding the optimal way to produce a product that must be processed sequentially through several machine centers, with each machine in the center having its own cost and output characteristics.

Vehicle/crew scheduling: Finding the optimal way to use resources such as aircraft, buses, or trucks and their operating crews to provide transportation services to customers and materials to be moved between different locations.

Process control: Minimizing the amount of scrap material generated by cutting steel, leather, or fabric from a roll or sheet of stock material.

Inventory control: Finding the optimal combination of products to stock in a network of warehouses or storage locations.

Distribution scheduling: Finding the optimal shipping schedule for distributing products between factories and warehouses or between warehouses and retailers.

Plant location studies: Finding the optimal location of a new plant by evaluating shipping costs between alternative locations and supply and demand sources.

Material handling: Finding the minimum-cost routings of material-handling devices (such as forklift trucks) between departments in a plant, or hauling materials from a supply yard to work sites by trucks, for example. Each truck might have different capacity and performance capabilities.

Linear programming is gaining wide acceptance in many industries due to the availability of detailed operating information and the interest in optimizing processes to reduce cost. Many software vendors offer optimization options to be used with enterprise resource planning systems. Some firms refer to these as *advanced planning option, synchronized planning,* and *process optimization.*

For linear programming to pertain in a problem situation, five essential conditions must be met. First, there must be *limited resources* (such as a limited number of workers, equipment, finances, and material); otherwise there would be no problem. Second, there must be an *explicit objective* (such as maximize profit or minimize cost). Third, there must be *linearity* (two is twice as much as one; if three hours are needed to make a part, then two parts would take six hours and three parts would take nine hours). Fourth, there must be *homogeneity* (the products produced on a machine are identical, or all the hours available from a worker are equally productive). Fifth, there must be *divisibility:* Normal linear programming assumes products and resources can be subdivided into fractions. If this subdivision is not possible (such as flying half an airplane or hiring one-fourth of a person), a modification of linear programming, called *integer programming,* can be used.

When a single objective is to be maximized (like profit) or minimized (like costs), we can use linear programming. When multiple objectives exist, *goal programming* is used. If a problem is best solved in stages or time frames, *dynamic programming* is employed. Other restrictions on the nature of the problem may require that it be solved by other variations of the technique, such as *nonlinear programming* or *quadratic programming.*

THE LINEAR PROGRAMMING MODEL

Stated formally, the linear programming problem entails an optimizing process in which nonnegative values for a set of decision variables $X_1, X_2, \ldots, X_n$ are selected so as to maximize (or minimize) an objective function in the form

$$\text{Maximize (minimize) } Z = C_1 X_1 + C_2 X_2 + \cdots + C_n X_n$$

subject to resource constraints in the form

$$A_{11} X_1 + A_{12} X_2 + \cdots + A_{1n} X_n \le B_1$$
$$A_{21} X_1 + A_{22} X_2 + \cdots + A_{2n} X_n \le B_2$$
$$\cdot$$
$$\cdot$$
$$\cdot$$
$$A_{m1} X_1 + A_{m2} X_2 + \cdots + A_{mn} X_n \le B_m$$

where C_n, A_{mn}, and B_m are given constants.

**Tutorial:
Intro to Solver**

Step by Step

Depending on the problem, the constraints also may be stated with equal signs ($=$) or greater-than-or-equal-to signs ($\geq$).

EXAMPLE A.1: Puck and Pawn Company

We describe the steps involved in solving a simple linear programming model in the context of a sample problem, that of Puck and Pawn Company, which manufactures hockey sticks and chess sets. Each hockey stick yields an incremental profit of $2, and each chess set, $4. A hockey stick requires 4 hours of processing at machine center A and 2 hours at machine center B. A chess set requires 6 hours at machine center A, 6 hours at machine center B, and 1 hour at machine center C. Machine center A has a maximum of 120 hours of available capacity per day, machine center B has 72 hours, and machine center C has 10 hours.

If the company wishes to maximize profit, how many hockey sticks and chess sets should be produced per day?

SOLUTION

Formulate the problem in mathematical terms. If H is the number of hockey sticks and C is the number of chess sets, to maximize profit the objective function may be stated as

$$\text{Maximize } Z = \$2H + \$4C$$

The maximization will be subject to the following constraints:

$$4H + 6C \leq 120 \quad \text{(machine center A constraint)}$$
$$2H + 6C \leq 72 \quad \text{(machine center B constraint)}$$
$$1C \leq 10 \quad \text{(machine center C constraint)}$$
$$H, C \geq 0 \; \bullet$$

This formulation satisfies the five requirements for standard LP stated in the first section of this appendix:

1. There are limited resources (a finite number of hours available at each machine center).
2. There is an explicit objective function (we know what each variable is worth and what the goal is in solving the problem).
3. The equations are linear (no exponents or cross-products).
4. The resources are homogeneous (everything is in one unit of measure, machine hours).
5. The decision variables are divisible and nonnegative (we can make a fractional part of a hockey stick or chess set; however, if this were deemed undesirable, we would have to use integer programming).

GRAPHICAL LINEAR PROGRAMMING

Graphical linear programming

Though limited in application to problems involving two decision variables (or three variables for three-dimensional graphing), graphical linear programming provides a quick insight into the nature of linear programming. We describe the steps involved in the graphical method in the context of Puck and Pawn Company. The following steps illustrate the graphical approach:

1. **Formulate the problem in mathematical terms.** The equations for the problem are given above.
2. **Plot constraint equations.** The constraint equations are easily plotted by letting one variable equal zero and solving for the axis intercept of the other. (The inequality portions of the restrictions are disregarded for this step.) For the machine center A constraint equation, when $H = 0$, $C = 20$, and when $C = 0$, $H = 30$. For the machine center B constraint equation, when $H = 0$, $C = 12$, and when $C = 0$, $H = 36$. For the machine center C constraint equation, $C = 10$ for all values of H. These lines are graphed in Exhibit A.1.
3. **Determine the area of feasibility.** The direction of inequality signs in each constraint determines the area where a feasible solution is found. In this case, all inequalities

Graph of Hockey Stick and Chess Set Problem

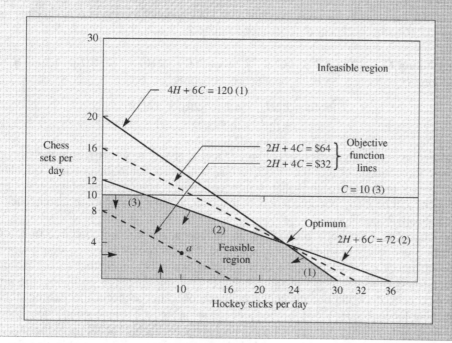

are of the less-than-or-equal-to variety, which means it would be impossible to produce any combination of products that would lie to the right of any constraint line on the graph. The region of feasible solutions is unshaded on the graph and forms a convex polygon. A convex polygon exists when a line drawn between any two points in the polygon stays within the boundaries of that polygon. If this condition of convexity does not exist, the problem is either incorrectly set up or is not amenable to linear programming.

4.   **Plot the objective function.**   The objective function may be plotted by assuming some arbitrary total profit figure and then solving for the axis coordinates, as was done for the constraint equations. Other terms for the objective function when used in this context are the *iso-profit* or *equal contribution line,* because it shows all possible production combinations for any given profit figure. For example, from the dotted line closest to the origin on the graph, we can determine all possible combinations of hockey sticks and chess sets that yield $32 by picking a point on the line and reading the number of each product that can be made at that point. The combination yielding $32 at point *a* would be 10 hockey sticks and three chess sets. This can be verified by substituting $H = 10$ and $C = 3$ in the objective function:

$$\$2(10) + \$4(3) = \$20 + \$12 = \$32$$

H	C	EXPLANATION
0	120/6 = 20	Intersection of Constraint (1) and C axis
120/4 = 30	0	Intersection of Constraint (1) and H axis
0	72/6 = 12	Intersection of Constraint (2) and C axis
72/2 = 36	0	Intersection of Constraint (2) and H axis
0	10	Intersection of Constraint (3) and C axis
0	32/4 = 8	Intersection of $32 iso-profit line (objective function) and C axis
32/2 = 16	0	Intersection of $32 iso-profit line and H axis
0	64/4 = 16	Intersection of $64 iso-profit line and C axis
64/2 = 32	0	Intersection of $64 iso-profit line and H axis

5.   **Find the optimum point.**   It can be shown mathematically that the optimal combination of decision variables is always found at an extreme point (corner point) of the convex polygon. In Exhibit A.1, there are four corner points (excluding the origin), and we

can determine which one is the optimum by either of two approaches. The first approach is to find the values of the various corner solutions algebraically. This entails simultaneously solving the equations of various pairs of intersecting lines and substituting the quantities of the resultant variables in the objective function. For example, the calculations for the intersection of $2H + 6C = 72$ and $C = 10$ are as follows:

Substituting $C = 10$ in $2H + 6C = 72$ gives $2H + 6(10) = 72$, $2H = 12$, or $H = 6$. Substituting $H = 6$ and $C = 10$ in the objective function, we get

$$\text{Profit} = \$2H + \$4C = \$2(6) + \$4(10)$$
$$= \$12 + \$40 = \$52$$

A variation of this approach is to read the H and C quantities directly from the graph and substitute these quantities into the objective function, as shown in the previous calculation. The drawback in this approach is that in problems with a large number of constraint equations, there will be many possible points to evaluate, and the procedure of testing each one mathematically is inefficient.

The second and generally preferred approach entails using the objective function or iso-profit line directly to find the optimum point. The procedure involves simply drawing a straight line *parallel* to any arbitrarily selected initial iso-profit line so the iso-profit line is farthest from the origin of the graph. (In cost minimization problems, the objective would be to draw the line through the point closest to the origin.) In Exhibit A.1, the dashed line labeled $\$2H + \$4C = \$64$ intersects the most extreme point. Note that the initial arbitrarily selected iso-profit line is necessary to display the slope of the objective function for the particular problem.[1] This is important since a different objective function (try Profit $= 3H + 3C$) might indicate that some other point is farthest from the origin. Given that $\$2H + \$4C = \$64$ is optimal, the amount of each variable to produce can be read from the graph: 24 hockey sticks and four chess sets. No other combination of the products yields a greater profit.

LINEAR PROGRAMMING USING MICROSOFT EXCEL

Spreadsheets can be used to solve linear programming problems. Microsoft Excel has an optimization tool called *Solver* that we will demonstrate by solving the hockey stick and chess problem. We invoke the Solver from the Data tab. A dialogue box requests information required by the program. The following example describes how our sample problem can be solved using Excel.

If the Solver option does not appear in your Data tab, click on Excel Options → Add-Ins, select the Solver Add-In, and then click OK. Solver should then be available directly from the Data tab for future use.

In the following example, we work in a step-by-step manner, setting up a spreadsheet and then solving our Puck and Pawn Company problem. Our basic strategy is to first define the problem within the spreadsheet. Following this, we invoke the Solver and feed it required information. Finally, we execute the Solver and interpret results from the reports provided by the program.

Step 1: Define Changing Cells   A convenient starting point is to identify cells to be used for the decision variables in the problem. These are H and C, the number of hockey sticks and the number of chess sets to produce. Excel refers to these cells as changing cells in Solver. Referring to our Excel screen (Exhibit A.2), we have designated B4 as the location for the number of hockey sticks to produce and C4 for the number of chess sets. Note that we have set these cells equal to 2 initially. We could set these cells to anything, but a value other than zero will help verify that our calculations are correct.

Step 2: Calculate Total Profit (or Cost)   This is our objective function and is calculated by multiplying profit associated with each product by the number of units produced. We have placed the profits in cells B5 and C5 ($2 and $4), so the profit is calculated by the following equation: B4*B5 + C4*C5, which is calculated in cell D5. Solver refers to this as the Target Cell, and it corresponds to the objective function for a problem.

Microsoft Excel Screen for Puck and Pawn Company

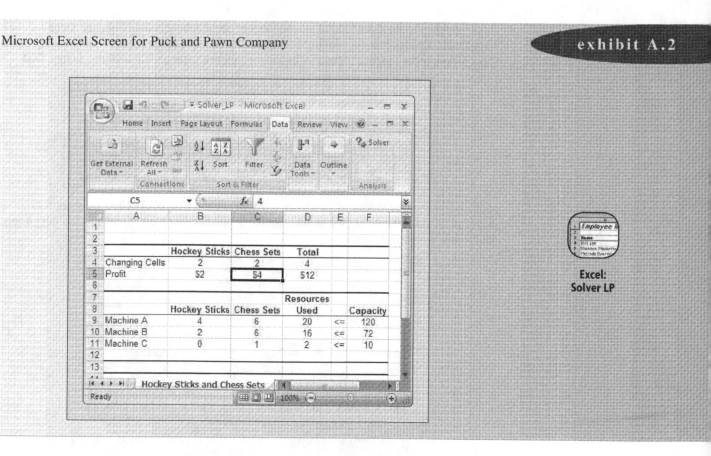

Excel:
Solver LP

Step 3: Set Up Resource Usage   Our resources are machine centers A, B, and C as defined in the original problem. We have set up three rows (9, 10, and 11) in our spreadsheet, one for each resource constraint. For machine center A, 4 hours of processing time are used for each hockey stick produced (cell B9) and 6 hours for each chess set (cell C9). For a particular solution, the total amount of the machine center A resource used is calculated in D9 (B9*B4 + C9*C4). We have indicated in cell E9 that we want this value to be less than the 120-hour capacity of machine center A, which is entered in F9. Resource usage for machine centers B and C is set up in the exact same manner in rows 10 and 11.

Step 4: Set Up Solver   Go to the Data tab and select the Solver option.

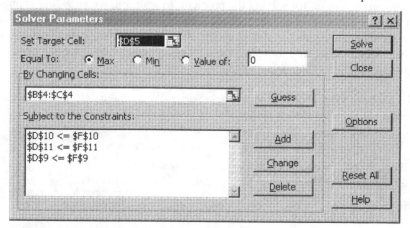

 1.   Set Target Cell: is set to the location where the value that we want to optimize is calculated. This is the profit calculated in D5 in our spreadsheet.
 2.   Equal To: is set to Max since the goal is to maximize profit.
 3.   By Changing Cells: are the cells that Solver can change to maximize profit. Cells B4 through C4 are the changing cells in our problem.

4. Subject to the Constraints: corresponds to our machine center capacity. Here we click on Add and indicate that the total used for a resource is less than or equal to the capacity available. A sample for machine center A follows. Click OK after each constraint is specified.

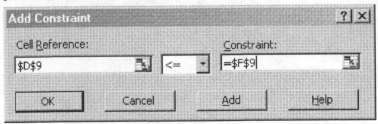

5. Clicking on Options allows us to tell Solver what type of problem we want it to solve and how we want it solved. Solver has numerous options, but we will need to use only a few. The screen is shown below.

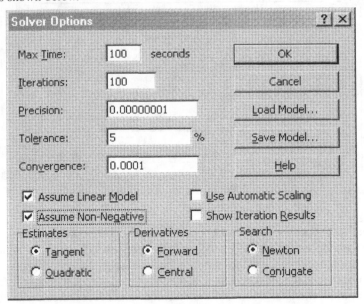

Most of the options relate to how Solver attempts to solve nonlinear problems. These can be very difficult to solve, and optimal solutions difficult to find. Luckily our problem is a linear problem. We know this since our constraints and our objective function are all calculated using linear equations. Click on Assume Linear Model to tell Solver that we want to use the linear programming option for solving the problem. In addition, we know our changing cells (decision variables) must be numbers that are greater than or equal to zero since it makes no sense to make a negative number of hockey sticks or chess sets. We indicate this by selecting Assume Non-Negative as an option. We are now ready to actually solve the problem. Click OK to return to the Solver Parameters box.

Step 5: Solve the Problem   Click Solve. We immediately get a Solver Results acknowledgment like that shown below.

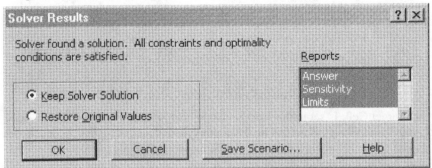

Excel Solver Answer and Sensitivity Reports

Answer Report

TARGET CELL (MAX)

CELL	NAME	ORIGINAL VALUE	FINAL VALUE
$D$5	Profit Total	$12	$64

ADJUSTABLE CELLS

CELL	NAME	ORIGINAL VALUE	FINAL VALUE
$B$4	Changing Cells Hockey Sticks	2	24
$C$4	Changing Cells Chess Sets	2	4

CONSTRAINTS

CELL	NAME	CELL VALUE	FORMULA	STATUS	SLACK
$D$11	Machine C Used	4	$D$11<=$F$11	Not Binding	6
$D$10	Machine B Used	72	$D$10<=$F$10	Binding	0
$D$9	Machine A Used	120	$D$9<=$F$9	Binding	0

Sensitivity Report

ADJUSTABLE CELLS

CELL	NAME	FINAL VALUE	REDUCED COST	OBJECTIVE COEFFICIENT	ALLOWABLE INCREASE	ALLOWABLE DECREASE
$B$4	Changing Cells Hockey Sticks	24	0	2	0.666666667	0.666666667
$C$4	Changing Cells Chess Sets	4	0	4	2	1

CONSTRAINTS

CELL	NAME	FINAL VALUE	SHADOW PRICE	CONSTRAINT R.H. SIDE	ALLOWABLE INCREASE	ALLOWABLE DECREASE
$D$11	Machine C Used	4	0	10	1E+30	6
$D$10	Machine B Used	72	0.333333333	72	18	12
$D$9	Machine A Used	120	0.333333333	120	24	36

Solver acknowledges that a solution was found that appears to be optimal. On the right side of this box are options for three reports: an Answer Report, a Sensitivity Report, and a Limits Report. Click on each report to have Solver provide these. After highlighting the reports, click OK to exit back to the spreadsheet. Three new tabs have been created that correspond to these reports.

The most interesting reports for our problem are the Answer Report and the Sensitivity Report, both of which are shown in Exhibit A.3. The Answer Report shows the final answers for the total profit ($64) and the amounts produced (24 hockey sticks and 4 chess sets). In the constraints section of the Answer Report, the status of each resource is given. All of machine A and machine B are used, and there are six units of slack for machine C.

The Sensitivity Report is divided into two parts. The first part, titled "Adjustable Cells," corresponds to objective function coefficients. The profit per unit for the hockey sticks can be either up or down $0.67 (between $2.67 and $1.33) without having an impact on the solution. Similarly, the profit of the chess sets could be between $6 and $3 without changing the solution. In the case of machine A, the right-hand side could increase to 144 (120 + 24) or decrease to 84 with a resulting $0.33 increase or decrease per unit in the objective function. The right-hand side of machine B can increase to 90 units or decrease to 60 units with the same $0.33 change for each unit in the objective function. For machine C, the right-hand side could increase to infinity (1E+30 is scientific notation for a very large number) or decrease to 4 units with no change in the objective function.

Key Terms

Linear programming (LP) Refers to several related mathematical techniques used to allocate limited resources among competing demands in an optimal way.

Graphical linear programming Provides a quick insight into the nature of linear programming.

Solved Problems

SOLVED PROBLEM 1

A furniture company produces three products: end tables, sofas, and chairs. These products are processed in five departments: the saw lumber, fabric cutting, sanding, staining, and assembly departments. End tables and chairs are produced from raw lumber only, and the sofas require lumber and fabric. Glue and thread are plentiful and represent a relatively insignificant cost that is included in operating expense. The specific requirements for each product are as follows:

Resource or Activity (Quantity Available per Month)	Required per End Table	Required per Sofa	Required per Chair
Lumber (4,350 board feet)	10 board feet @ $10/foot = $100/table	7.5 board feet @ $10/foot = $75	4 board feet @ $10/foot = $40
Fabric (2,500 yards)	None	10 yards @ $17.50/yard = $175	None
Saw lumber (280 hours)	30 minutes	24 minutes	30 minutes
Cut fabric (140 hours)	None	24 minutes	None
Sand (280 hours)	30 minutes	6 minutes	30 minutes
Stain (140 hours)	24 minutes	12 minutes	24 minutes
Assemble (700 hours)	60 minutes	90 minutes	30 minutes

The company's direct labor expenses are $75,000 per month for the 1,540 hours of labor, at $48.70 per hour. Based on current demand, the firm can sell 300 end tables, 180 sofas, and 400 chairs per month. Sales prices are $400 for end tables, $750 for sofas, and $240 for chairs. Assume that labor cost is fixed and the firm does not plan to hire or fire any employees over the next month.

Required:

1   What is the most limiting resource to the furniture company?
2   Determine the product mix needed to maximize profit at the furniture company. What is the optimal number of end tables, sofas, and chairs to produce each month?

Solution

Define X_1 as the number of end tables, X_2 as the number of sofas, and X_3 as the number of chairs to produce each month. Profit is calculated as the revenue for each item minus the cost of materials (lumber and fabric), minus the cost of labor. Since labor is fixed, we subtract this out as a total sum. Mathematically we have $(400 - 100)X_1 + (750 - 75 - 175)X_2 + (240 - 40)X_3 - 75,000$. Profit is calculated as follows:

$$\text{Profit} = 300X_1 + 500X_2 + 200X_3 - 75,000$$

Constraints are the following:

Lumber: $10X_1 + 7.5X_2 + 4X_3 \leq 4,350$
Fabric: $10X_2 \leq 2,500$
Saw: $.5X_1 + .4X_2 + .5X_3 \leq 280$

Cut: $.4X_2 \leq 140$

Sand: $.5X_1 + .1X_2 + .5X_3 \leq 280$

Stain: $.4X_1 + .2X_2 + .4X_3 \leq 140$

Assemble: $1X_1 + 1.5X_2 + .5X_3 \leq 700$

Demand:

    Table: $X_1 \leq 300$

    Sofa: $X_2 \leq 180$

    Chair: $X_3 \leq 400$

Step 1: Define Changing Cells   These are B3, C3, and D3. Note that these cells have been set equal to zero.

		E4		f_x =B4*$B$3+C4*$C$3+D4*$D$3-75000			
	A	B	C	D	E	F	
1	**Furniture Company**						
2		End Tables	Sofas	Chairs	Total	Limit	
3	**Changing cells**	0	0	0			
4	**Profit**	$300	$500	$200	-$75,000		
5							
6	**Lumber**	10	7.5	4	0	4350	
7	**Fabric**	0	10	0	0	2500	
8	**Saw**	0.5	0.4	0.5	0	280	
9	**Cut fabric**	0	0.4	0	0	140	
10	**Sand**	0.5	0.1	0.5	0	280	
11	**Stain**	0.4	0.2	0.4	0	140	
12	**Assemble**	1	1.5	0.5	0	700	
13	**Table Demand**	1			0	300	
14	**Sofa Demand**		1		0	180	
15	**Chair Demand**			1	0	400	
16							

Solved Problem

Ready   NUM

Step 2: Calculate Total Profit   This is E4 (this is equal to B3 times the $300 revenue associated with each end table, plus C3 times the $500 revenue for each sofa, plus D3 times the $200 revenue associated with each chair). Note the $75,000 fixed expense that has been subtracted from revenue to calculate profit.

Step 3: Set Up Resource Usage   In cells E6 through E15, the usage of each resource is calculated by multiplying B3, C3, and D3 by the amount needed for each item and summing the product (for example, E6 = B3*B6 + C3*C6 + D3*D6). The limits on these constraints are entered in cells F6 to F15.

Step 4: Set Up Solver   Go to Tools and select the Solver option.

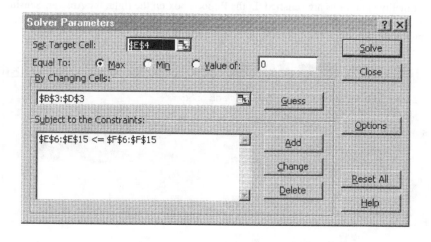

a. Set Target Cell: is set to the location where the value that we want to optimize is calculated. This is the profit calculated in E4 in this spreadsheet.

b. Equal To: is set to Max since the goal is to maximize profit.

c. By Changing Cells: are the cells that Solver can change to maximize profit (cells B3 through D3 in this problem).

d. Subject to the Constraints: is where a constraint set is added; we indicate that the range E6 to E15 must be less than or equal to F6 to F15.

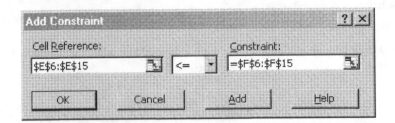

Step 5: Set Options There are many options here, but for our purposes we just need to indicate Assume Linear Model and Assume Non-Negative. Assume Linear Model means all of our formulas are simple linear equations. Assume Non-Negative indicates that changing cells must be greater than or equal to zero. Click OK and we are ready to solve our problem.

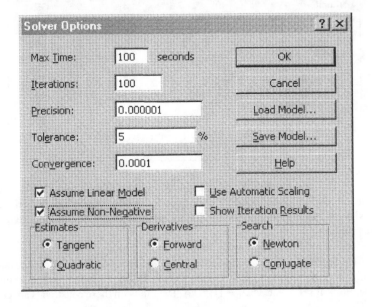

Step 6: Solve the Problem Click Solve. We can see the solution and two special reports by highlighting items on the Solver Results acknowledgment that is displayed after a solution is found. Note that in the following report, Solver indicates that it has found a solution and all constraints and optimality conditions are satisfied. In the Reports box on the right, the Answer, Sensitivity, and Limits options have been highlighted, indicating that we would like to see these items. After highlighting the reports, click OK to exit back to the spreadsheet.

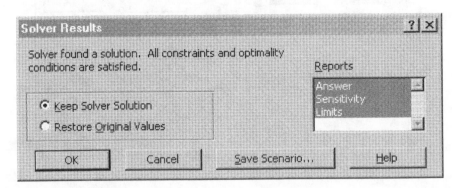

Note that three new tabs have been created: an Answer Report, a Sensitivity Report, and a Limits Report. The Answer Report indicates in the Target Cell section that the profit associated with this solution is $93,000 (we started at −$75,000). From the Target Cell section, we should make 260 end tables, 180 sofas, and no chairs. From the Constraints section, notice that the only constraints limiting profit are the staining capacity and the demand for sofas. We can see this from the column indicating whether a constraint is binding or nonbinding. Nonbinding constraints have slack, as indicated in the last column.

Target Cell (Max)

CELL	NAME	ORIGINAL VALUE	FINAL VALUE
$E$4	Profit Total	−$75,000	$93,000

Adjustable Cells

CELL	NAME	ORIGINAL VALUE	FINAL VALUE
$B$3	Changing cells End Tables	0	260
$C$3	Changing cells Sofas	0	180
$D$3	Changing cells Chairs	0	0

Constraints

CELL	NAME	CELL VALUE	FORMULA	STATUS	SLACK
$E$6	Lumber Total	3950	$E$6<=$F$6	Not Binding	400
$E$7	Fabric Total	1800	$E$7<=$F$7	Not Binding	700
$E$8	Saw Total	202	$E$8<=$F$8	Not Binding	78
$E$9	Cut fabric Total	72	$E$9<=$F$9	Not Binding	68
$E$10	Sand Total	148	$E$10<=$F$10	Not Binding	132
$E$11	Stain Total	140	$E$11<=$F$11	Binding	0
$E$12	Assemble Total	530	$E$12<=$F$12	Not Binding	170
$E$13	Table Demand Total	260	$E$13<=$F$13	Not Binding	40
$E$14	Sofa Demand Total	180	$E$14<=$F$14	Binding	0
$E$15	Chair Demand Total	0	$E$15<=$F$15	Not Binding	400

Of course, we may not be too happy with this solution since we are not meeting all the demand for tables, and it may not be wise to totally discontinue the manufacturing of chairs.

The Sensitivity Report (shown below) gives additional insight into the solution. The Adjustable Cells section of this report shows the final value for each cell and the reduced cost. The reduced cost indicates how much the target cell value would change if a cell that was currently set to zero were brought into the solution. Since the end tables (B3) and sofas (C3) are in the current solution, their reduced cost is zero. For each chair (D3) that we make, our target cell would be reduced $100 (just round these numbers for interpretation purposes). The final three columns in the adjustable cells section of the report are the Objective Coefficient from the original spreadsheet and columns titled Allowable Increase and Allowable Decrease. Allowable Increase and Decrease show by how much the value of the corresponding coefficient could change so there would not be a change in the changing cell values (of course, the target cell value would change). For example, revenue for each end table could be as high as $1,000 ($300 + $700) or as low as $200 ($300 − $100), and we would still want to produce 260 end tables. Keep in mind that these values assume nothing else is changing in the problem. For the allowable increase value for sofas, note the value 1E+30. This is a very large number, essentially infinity, represented in scientific notation.

Adjustable Cells

CELL	NAME	FINAL VALUE	REDUCED COST	OBJECTIVE COEFFICIENT	ALLOWABLE INCREASE	ALLOWABLE DECREASE
$B$3	Changing cells End Tables	260	0	299.9999997	700.0000012	100.0000004
$C$3	Changing cells Sofas	180	0	500.0000005	1E+30	350.0000006
$D$3	Changing cells Chairs	0	−100.0000004	199.9999993	100.0000004	1E+30

Constraints

CELL	NAME	FINAL VALUE	SHADOW PRICE	CONSTRAINT R.H. SIDE	ALLOWABLE INCREASE	ALLOWABLE DECREASE
$E$6	Lumber Total	3950	0	4350	1E+30	400
$E$7	Fabric Total	1800	0	2500	1E+30	700
$E$8	Saw Total	202	0	280	1E+30	78
$E$9	Cut fabric Total	72	0	140	1E+30	68
$E$10	Sand Total	148	0	280	1E+30	132
$E$11	Stain Total	140	749.9999992	140	16	104
$E$12	Assemble Total	530	0	700	1E+30	170
$E$13	Table Demand Total	260	0	300	1E+30	40
$E$14	Sofa Demand Total	180	350.0000006	180	70	80
$E$15	Chair Demand Total	0	0	400	1E+30	400

For the Constraints section of the report, the actual final usage of each resource is given in Final Value. The Shadow Price is the value to our target cell for each unit increase in the resource. If we could increase staining capacity, it would be worth $750 per hour. The Constraint Right-Hand Side is the current limit on the resource. Allowable Increase is the amount the resource could be increased while the shadow price is still valid. Another 16 hours' work of staining capacity could be added with a value of $750 per hour. Similarly, the Allowable Decrease column shows the amount the resource could be reduced without changing the shadow price. There is some valuable information available in this report.

The Limits Report provides additional information about our solution.

CELL	TARGET NAME	VALUE
$E$4	Profit Total	$93,000

CELL	ADJUSTABLE NAME	VALUE	LOWER LIMIT	TARGET RESULT	UPPER LIMIT	TARGET RESULT
$B$3	Changing cells End Tables	260	0	15000	260.0000002	93000
$C$3	Changing cells Sofas	180	0	3000	180	93000
$D$3	Changing cells Chairs	0	0	93000	0	93000

Total profit for the current solution is $93,000. Current value for B3 (end tables) is 260 units. If this were reduced to 0 units, profit would be reduced to $15,000. At an upper limit of 260, profit is $93,000 (the current solution). Similarly, for C3 (sofas), if this were reduced to 0, profit would be reduced to $3,000. At an upper limit of 180, profit is $93,000. For D3 (chairs), if this were reduced to 0, profit is $93,000 (current solution), and in this case the upper limit on chairs is also 0 units.

Acceptable answers to the questions are as follows:

1   *What is the most limiting resource to the furniture company?*
    In terms of our production resources, staining capacity is really hurting profit at this time. We could use another 16 hours of capacity.
2   *Determine the product mix needed to maximize profit at the furniture company.*
    The product mix would be to make 260 end tables, 180 sofas, and no chairs.

Of course, we have only scratched the surface with this solution. We could actually experiment with increasing staining capacity. This would give insight into the next most limiting resource. We also could run scenarios where we are required to produce a minimum number of each product, which is probably a more realistic scenario. This could help us determine how we could possibly reallocate the use of labor in our shop.

SOLVED PROBLEM 2

It is 2:00 on Friday afternoon and Joe Bob, the head chef (grill cook) at Bruce's Diner, is trying to decide the best way to allocate the available raw material to the four Friday night specials. The decision has to be made in the early afternoon because three of the items must be started now (Sloppy Joes, Tacos, and Chili). The table below contains the information on the food in inventory and the amounts required for each item.

FOOD	CHEESE BURGER	SLOPPY JOES	TACO	CHILI	AVAILABLE
Ground Beef (lbs.)	0.3	0.25	0.25	0.4	100 lbs.
Cheese (lbs.)	0.1	0	0.3	0.2	50 lbs.
Beans (lbs.)	0	0	0.2	0.3	50 lbs.
Lettuce (lbs.)	0.1	0	0.2	0	15 lbs.
Tomato (lbs.)	0.1	0.3	0.2	0.2	50 lbs.
Buns	1	1	0	0	80 buns
Taco Shells	0	0	1	0	80 shells

One other fact relevant to Joe Bob's decision is the estimated market demand and selling price.

	CHEESE BURGER	SLOPPY JOES	TACO	CHILI
Demand	75	60	100	55
Selling Price	$2.25	$2.00	$1.75	$2.50

Joe Bob wants to maximize revenue since he has already purchased all the materials that are sitting in the cooler.

Required:

1 What is the best mix of the Friday night specials to maximize Joe Bob's revenue?
2 If a supplier offered to provide a rush order of buns at $1.00 a bun, is it worth the money?

Solution

Define X_1 as the number of Cheese Burgers, X_2 as the number of Sloppy Joes, X_3 as the number of Tacos, and X_4 as the number of bowls of chili made for the Friday night specials.

$$\text{Revenue} = \$2.25\, X_1 + \$2.00\, X_2 + \$1.75\, X_3 + \$2.50\, X_4$$

Constraints are the following:

Ground Beef:	$0.30\, X_1 + 0.25\, X_2 + 0.25\, X_3 + 0.40\, X_4 \leq 100$
Cheese:	$0.10\, X_1 + 0.30\, X_3 + 0.20\, X_4 \leq 50$
Beans:	$0.20\, X_3 + 0.30\, X_4 \leq 50$
Lettuce:	$0.10\, X_1 + 0.20\, X_3 \leq 15$
Tomato:	$0.10\, X_1 + 0.30\, X_2 + 0.20\, X_3 + 0.20\, X_4 \leq 50$
Buns:	$X_1 + X_2 \leq 80$
Taco Shells:	$X_3 \leq 80$

Demand

Cheese Burger	$X_1 \leq 75$
Sloppy Joes	$X_2 \leq 60$
Taco	$X_3 \leq 100$
Chili	$X_4 \leq 55$

Step 1: Define the Changing Cells   These are B3, C3, D3, and E3. Note the values in the changing cell are set to 10 each so the formulas can be checked.

F7		*fx* =SUMPRODUCT($B$3:$E$3,B7:E7)					
	A	B	C	D	E	F	G	H
1								
2		Cheese Burger	Sloppy Joes	Taco	Chili			
3	Changing Cells	10	10	10	10			
4		>=	>=	>=	>=			
5	Demand	75	60	100	55			
6						Total		
7	Revenue	$ 2.25	$ 2.00	$ 1.75	$ 2.50	$ 85.00		
8								
9								
10	Food	Cheese Burger	Sloppy Joes	Taco	Chili	Total		Available
11	Ground Beef (lbs.)	0.3	0.25	0.25	0.4	12.00 <=		100
12	Cheese (lbs.)	0.1	0	0.3	0.2	6.00 <=		50
13	Beans (lbs.)	0	0	0.2	0.3	5.00 <=		50
14	Lettuce (lbs.)	0.1	0	0.2	0	3.00 <=		15
15	Tomato (lbs.)	0.1	0.3	0.2	0.2	8.00 <=		50
16	Buns	1	1	0	0	20.00 <=		80
17	Taco Shells	0	0	1	0	10.00 <=		80
18								

Step 2: Calculate Total Revenue   This is in cell F7 (this is equal to B3 times the $2.25 for each cheese burger, plus C3 times the $2.00 for a Sloppy Joe, plus D3 times the $1.75 for each taco, plus E3 times the $2.50 for each bowl of chili; the SUMPRODUCT function in Excel was used to make this calculation faster). Note that the current value is $85, which is a result of selling 10 of each item.

Step 3: Set Up the Usage of the Food   In cells F11 to F17, the usage of each food is calculated by multiplying the changing cells row times the per item use in the table and then summing the result. The limits on each of these food types are given in H11 through H17.

Step 4: Set Up Solver and Select the Solver Option

a. Set Target Cell: is set to the location where the value that we want to optimize is calculated. The revenue is calculated in F7 in this spreadsheet.
b. Equal to: is set to Max since the goal is to maximize revenue.
c. By Changing Cells: are the cells that tell how many of each special to produce.
d. Subject to the Constraints: is where we add two separate constraints, one for demand and one for the usage of food.

Step 5: Set Options   Click on Options. We will leave all the settings as the default values and only need to make sure of two changes: (1) check the Assume Linear Model option and (2) check the Assume Non-Negative option. These two options make sure that Solver knows that this is a linear programming problem and that all changing cells should be nonnegative. Click OK to return to the Solver Parameters screen.

Step 6: Solve the Problem   Click Solve. We will get a Solver Results box. Make sure it says that it has the following statement: "Solver found a solution. All constraints and optimality conditions are satisfied."

On the right-hand side of the box, there is an option for three reports: Answer, Sensitivity, and Limit. Click on all three reports and then click OK; this will exit you back to the spreadsheet, but you will have three new worksheets in your workbook.

The answer report indicates that the target cell has a final solution of $416.25 and started at $85. From the adjustable cells area we can see that we should make 20 cheese burgers, 60 Sloppy Joes, 65 tacos, and 55 bowls of chili. This answers the first requirement from the problem of what the mix of Friday night specials should be.

Target Cell (Max)

CELL	NAME	ORIGINAL VALUE	FINAL VALUE
$F$7	Revenue Total	$85.00	$416.25

Adjustable Cells

CELL	NAME	ORIGINAL VALUE	FINAL VALUE
$B$3	Changing Cells Cheese Burger	10	20
$C$3	Changing Cells Sloppy Joes	10	60
$D$3	Changing Cells Taco	10	65
$E$3	Changing Cells Chili	10	55

Constraints

CELL	NAME	CELL VALUE	FORMULA	STATUS	SLACK
$F$11	Ground Beef (lbs.) Total	59.25	$F$11<=$H$11	Not Binding	40.75
$F$12	Cheese (lbs.) Total	32.50	$F$12<=$H$12	Not Binding	17.5
$F$13	Beans (lbs.) Total	29.50	$F$13<=$H$13	Not Binding	20.5
$F$14	Lettuce (lbs.) Total	15.00	$F$14<=$H$14	Binding	0
$F$15	Tomato (lbs.) Total	44.00	$F$15<=$H$15	Not Binding	6
$F$16	Buns Total	80.00	$F$16<=$H$16	Binding	0
$F$17	Taco Shells Total	65.00	$F$17<=$H$17	Not Binding	15
$B$3	Changing Cells Cheese Burger	20	$B$3<=$B$5	Not Binding	55
$C$3	Changing Cells Sloppy Joes	60	$C$3<=$C$5	Binding	0
$D$3	Changing Cells Taco	65	$D$3<=$D$5	Not Binding	35
$E$3	Changing Cells Chili	55	$E$3<=$E$5	Binding	0

The second required answer was whether it is worth it to pay a rush supplier $1 a bun for additional buns. The answer report shows us that the buns constraint was binding. This means that if we had more buns, we could make more money. However, the answer report does not tell us whether a rush order of buns at $1 a bun is worthwhile. In order to answer that question, we have to look at the sensitivity report.

Adjustable Cells

CELL	NAME	FINAL VALUE	REDUCED COST	OBJECTIVE COEFFICIENT	ALLOWABLE INCREASE	ALLOWABLE DECREASE
$B$3	Changing Cells Cheese Burger	20	0	2.25	0.625	1.375
$C$3	Changing Cells Sloppy Joes	60	0.625	2	1E+30	0.625
$D$3	Changing Cells Taco	65	0	1.75	2.75	1.25
$E$3	Changing Cells Chili	55	2.5	2.5	1E+30	2.5

Constraints

CELL	NAME	FINAL VALUE	SHADOW PRICE	CONSTRAINT R.H. SIDE	ALLOWABLE INCREASE	ALLOWABLE DECREASE
$F$11	Ground Beef (lbs.) Total	59.25	0.00	100	1E+30	40.75
$F$12	Cheese (lbs.) Total	32.50	0.00	50	1E+30	17.5
$F$13	Beans (lbs.) Total	29.50	0.00	50	1E+30	20.5
$F$14	Lettuce (lbs.) Total	15.00	8.75	15	3	13
$F$15	Tomato (lbs.) Total	44.00	0.00	50	1E+30	6
$F$16	Buns Total	80.00	1.38	80	55	20
$F$17	Taco Shells Total	65.00	0.00	80	1E+30	15

We have highlighted the buns row to answer the question. We can see that buns have a shadow price of $1.38. This shadow price means that each additional bun will generate $1.38 of profit. We also can see that other foods such as ground beef have a shadow price of $0. The items with a shadow price of $0 add nothing to profit since we are currently not using all that we have now. The other important piece of information that we have on the buns is that they are only worth $1.38 up until the next 55 buns and that is why the allowable increase is 55. We also can see that a pound of lettuce is worth $8.75. It might be wise to also look for a rush supplier of lettuce so we can increase our profit on Friday nights.

Acceptable answers to the questions are as follows:

1   *What is the best mix of the Friday night specials to maximize Joe Bob's revenue?*
    20 cheese burgers, 60 Sloppy Joes, 65 tacos, and 55 bowls of chili.
2   *If a supplier offered to provide a rush order of buns at $1.00 a bun, is it worth the money?*
    Yes, each additional bun brings in $1.38, so if they cost us $1, then we will net $0.38 per bun. However, this is true only up to 55 additional buns.

PROBLEMS

1   Solve the following problem with Excel Solver:

$$\text{Maximize } Z = 3X + Y.$$
$$12X + 14Y \le 85$$
$$3X + 2Y \le 18$$
$$Y \le 4$$

2   Solve the following problem with Excel Solver:

$$\text{Minimize } Z = 2A + 4B.$$
$$4A + 6B \ge 120$$
$$2A + 6B \ge 72$$
$$B \ge 10$$

3   A manufacturing firm has discontinued production of a certain unprofitable product line. Considerable excess production capacity was created as a result. Management is considering devoting this excess capacity to one or more of three products: X_1, X_2, and X_3.

Machine hours required per unit are

MACHINE TYPE	PRODUCT		
	X_1	X_2	X_3
Milling machine	8	2	3
Lathe	4	3	0
Grinder	2	0	1

The available time in machine hours per week is

	MACHINE HOURS PER WEEK
Milling machines	800
Lathes	480
Grinders	320

The salespeople estimate they can sell all the units of X_1 and X_2 that can be made. But the sales potential of X_3 is 80 units per week maximum.

Unit profits for the three products are

	UNIT PROFITS
X_1	$20
X_2	6
X_3	8

a. Set up the equations that can be solved to maximize the profit per week.
b. Solve these equations using the Excel Solver.
c. What is the optimal solution? How many of each product should be made, and what should the resultant profit be?

    d. What is this situation with respect to the machine groups? Would they work at capacity, or would there be unused available time? Will X_3 be at maximum sales capacity?

    e. Suppose that an additional 200 hours per week can be obtained from the milling machines by working overtime. The incremental cost would be $1.50 per hour. Would you recommend doing this? Explain how you arrived at your answer.

4   A diet is being prepared for the University of Arizona dorms. The objective is to feed the students at the least cost, but the diet must have between 1,800 and 3,600 calories. No more than 1,400 calories can be starch, and no fewer than 400 can be protein. The varied diet is to be made of two foods: A and B. Food A costs $0.75 per pound and contains 600 calories, 400 of which are protein and 200 starch. No more than two pounds of food A can be used per resident. Food B costs $0.15 per pound and contains 900 calories, of which 700 are starch, 100 are protein, and 100 are fat.

    a. Write the equations representing this information.

    b. Solve the problem graphically for the amounts of each food that should be used.

5   Repeat Problem 4 with the added constraint that not more than 150 calories shall be fat and that the price of food has escalated to $1.75 per pound for food A and $2.50 per pound for food B.

6   Logan Manufacturing wants to mix two fuels, A and B, for its trucks to minimize cost. It needs no fewer than 3,000 gallons to run its trucks during the next month. It has a maximum fuel storage capacity of 4,000 gallons. There are 2,000 gallons of fuel A and 4,000 gallons of fuel B available. The mixed fuel must have an octane rating of no less than 80.

    When fuels are mixed, the amount of fuel obtained is just equal to the sum of the amounts put in. The octane rating is the weighted average of the individual octanes, weighted in proportion to the respective volumes.

    The following is known: Fuel A has an octane of 90 and costs $1.20 per gallon. Fuel B has an octane of 75 and costs $0.90 per gallon.

    a. Write the equations expressing this information.

    b. Solve the problem using the Excel Solver, giving the amount of each fuel to be used. State any assumptions necessary to solve the problem.

7   You are trying to create a budget to optimize the use of a portion of your disposable income. You have a maximum of $1,500 per month to be allocated to food, shelter, and entertainment. The amount spent on food and shelter combined must not exceed $1,000. The amount spent on shelter alone must not exceed $700. Entertainment cannot exceed $300 per month. Each dollar spent on food has a satisfaction value of 2, each dollar spent on shelter has a satisfaction value of 3, and each dollar spent on entertainment has a satisfaction value of 5.

    Assuming a linear relationship, use the Excel Solver to determine the optimal allocation of your funds.

8   C-town brewery brews two beers: Expansion Draft and Burning River. Expansion Draft sells for $20 per barrel, while Burning River sells for $8 per barrel. Producing a barrel of Expansion Draft takes 8 pounds of corn and 4 pounds of hops. Producing a barrel of Burning River requires 2 pounds of corn, 6 pounds of rice, and 3 pounds of hops. The brewery has 500 pounds of corn, 300 pounds of rice, and 400 pounds of hops. Assuming a linear relationship, use Excel Solver to determine the optimal mix of Expansion Draft and Burning River that maximizes C-town's revenue.

9   BC Petrol manufactures three chemicals at their chemical plant in Kentucky: BCP1, BCP2, and BCP3. These chemicals are produced in two production processes known as zone and man. Running the zone process for an hour costs $48 and yields three units of BCP1, one unit of BCP2, and one unit of BCP3. Running the man process for one hour costs $24 and yields one unit of BCP1 and one unit of BCP2. To meet customer demands, at least 20 units of BCP1, 10 units of BCP2, and 6 units of BCP3 must be produced daily. Assuming a linear relationship, use Excel Solver to determine the optimal mix of processes zone and man to minimize costs and meet BC Petrol daily demands.

10 A farmer in Wood County has 900 acres of land. She is going to plant each acre with corn, soybeans, or wheat. Each acre planted with corn yields a $2,000 profit; each with soybeans yields $2,500 profit; and each with wheat yields $3,000 profit. She has 100 workers and 150 tons of fertilizer. The table below shows the requirement per acre of each of the crops. Assuming a linear relationship, use Excel Solver to determine the optimal planting mix of corn, soybeans, and wheat to maximize her profits.

	CORN	SOYBEANS	WHEAT
Labor (workers)	0.1	0.3	0.2
Fertilizer (tons)	0.2	0.1	0.4

SELECTED BIBLIOGRAPHY

Anderson, D. R.; D. J. Sweeney; and T. A. Williams. *An Introduction to Management Science*. 11th ed. Mason, OH. South-Western, 2005.

Kelly, Julia, and Curt Simmons. *The Unofficial Guide to Microsoft Excel 2007*. New York: John Wiley & Sons, 2007.

Winston, W. L., and S. C. Albright. *Practical Management Science*. 3rd ed. Mason, OH: South-Western, 2006.

FOOTNOTE

1 The slope of the objective function is -2. If P = profit, $P = \$2H + \$4C$; $\$2H = P + \$4C$; $H = P/2 - 2C$. Thus, the slope is -2.

OPERATIONS TECHNOLOGY

Much of the recent growth in productivity has come from the application of operations technology. In services this comes primarily from soft technology—information processing. In manufacturing it comes from a combination of soft and hard (machine) technologies. Given that most readers of this book have covered information technologies in services in MIS courses, our focus in this supplement is on manufacturing.

TECHNOLOGIES IN MANUFACTURING

Some technological advances in recent decades have had a significant, widespread impact on manufacturing firms in many industries. These advances, which are the topic of this section, can be categorized in two ways: hardware systems and software systems.

Hardware technologies have generally resulted in greater automation of processes; they perform labor-intensive tasks originally performed by humans. Examples of these major types of hardware technologies are numerically controlled machine tools, machining centers, industrial robots, automated materials handling systems, and flexible manufacturing systems. These are all computer-controlled devices that can be used in the manufacturing of products. Software-based technologies aid in the design of manufactured products and in the analysis and planning of manufacturing activities. These technologies include computer-aided design and automated manufacturing planning and control systems. Each of these technologies will be described in greater detail in the following sections.

Hardware Systems   *Numerically controlled (NC) machines* are comprised of (1) a typical machine tool used to turn, drill, or grind different types of parts and (2) a computer that controls the sequence of processes performed by the machine. NC machines were first adopted by U.S. aerospace firms in the 1960s, and they have since proliferated to many other industries. In more recent models, feedback control loops determine the position of the machine tooling during the work, constantly compare the actual location with the programmed location, and correct as needed. This is often called *adaptive control*.

Machining centers represent an increased level of automation and complexity relative to NC machines. Machining centers not only provide automatic control of a machine, they also may carry many tools that can be automatically changed depending on the tool required for each operation. In addition, a single machine may be equipped with a shuttle system so that a finished part can be unloaded and an unfinished part loaded while the machine is working on a part. To help you visualize a machining center, we have included a diagram in Exhibit B.1A.

Industrial robots are used as substitutes for workers for many repetitive manual activities and tasks that are dangerous, dirty, or dull. A robot is a programmable, multifunctional machine that may be equipped with an end effector. Examples of end effectors include a gripper to pick things up or a tool such as a wrench, a welder, or a paint sprayer. Exhibit B.1B examines the human motions a robot can reproduce. Advanced capabilities have been designed into robots to allow vision, tactile sensing, and hand-to-hand coordination. In addition, some models can be "taught" a sequence of motions in a three-dimensional pattern. As a worker moves the end of the robot arm through the required motions, the robot records this pattern in its memory and repeats it on command. Newer robotic systems can conduct

A. The CNC Machining Center

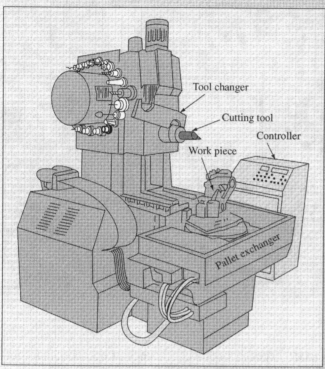

SOURCE: J. T. BLACK, *THE DESIGN OF THE FACTORY WITH A FUTURE* (NEW YORK: MCGRAW-HILL, 1991), P. 39, WITH PERMISSION OF THE MCGRAW-HILL COMPANIES.

B. Typical Robot Axes of Motion

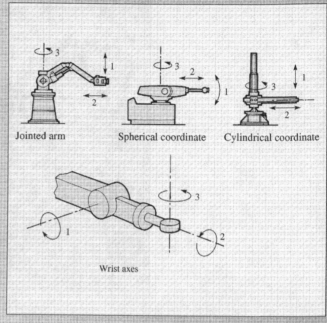

SOURCE: L. V. OTTINGER, "ROBOTICS FOR THE IE: TERMINOLOGY, TYPES OF ROBOTS," *INDUSTRIAL ENGINEERING*, NOVEMBER 1981, P. 30.

quality control inspections and then transfer, via mobile robots, those parts to other robots downstream. As shown in the box "Formula for Evaluating a Robot Investment," robots are often justified based on labor savings.

FORMULA FOR EVALUATING A ROBOT INVESTMENT

Many companies use the following modification of the basic payback formula in deciding if a robot should be purchased:

$$P = \frac{I}{L - E + q(L + Z)}$$

where

- P = Payback period in years
- I = Total capital investment required in robot and accessories
- L = Annual labor costs replaced by the robot (wage and benefit costs per worker times the number of shifts per day)
- E = Annual maintenance cost for the robot
- q = Fractional speedup (or slowdown) factor
- Z = Annual depreciation

Example:

I = $50,000

L = $60,000 (two workers × $20,000 each working one of two shifts; overhead is $10,000 each)

E = $9,600 ($2/hour × 4,800 hours/year)

q = 1.5 (robot works 150 percent as fast as a worker)

Z = $10,000

then

$$P = \frac{\$50,000}{\$60,000 - \$9,600 + 1.5(\$60,000 + \$10,000)}$$

$$= 1/3 \text{ year}$$

ONE OF THE FOUR LARGE MACHINING CENTERS (SEE EXHIBIT B.2) THAT ARE PART OF THE FLEXIBLE MANUFACTURING SYSTEMS AT CINCINNATI MILACRON'S MT. ORAB, OHIO, PLANT.

Automated materials handing (AMH) systems improve efficiency of transportation, storage, and retrieval of materials. Examples are computerized conveyors and automated storage and retrieval systems (AS/RS) in which computers direct automatic loaders to pick and place items. Automated guided vehicle (AGV) systems use embedded floor wires to direct driverless vehicles to various locations in the plant. Benefits of AMH systems include quicker material movement, lower inventories and storage space, reduced product damage, and higher labor productivity.

These individual pieces of automation can be combined to form *manufacturing cells* or even complete *flexible manufacturing systems (FMS)*. A manufacturing cell might consist of a robot and a machining center. The robot could be programmed to automatically insert and remove parts from the machining center, thus allowing unattended operation. An FMS is a totally automated manufacturing system that consists of machining centers with automated loading and unloading of parts, an automated guided vehicle system for moving parts between machines, and other automated elements to allow unattended production of parts. In an FMS, a comprehensive computer control system is used to run the entire system.

A good example of an FMS is the Cincinnati Milacron facility in Mt. Orab, Ohio, which has been in operation for over 25 years. Exhibit B.2 is a layout of this FMS. In this system, parts are loaded onto standardized fixtures (these are called "risers"), which are mounted on pallets that can be moved by the AGVs. Workers load and unload tools and parts onto the standardized fixtures at the workstations shown on the right side of the diagram. Most of this loading and unloading is done during a single shift. The system can operate virtually unattended for the other two shifts each day.

Within the system there are areas for the storage of tools (Area 7) and for parts (Area 5). This system is designed to machine large castings used in the production of the machine tools made by Cincinnati Milacron. The machining is done by the four CNC machining centers (Area 1). When the machining has been completed on a part, it is sent to the parts washing station (Area 4), where it is cleaned. The part is then sent to the automated inspection station (Area 6) for a quality check. The system is capable of producing hundreds of different parts.

The Cincinnati Milacron Flexible Manufacturing System

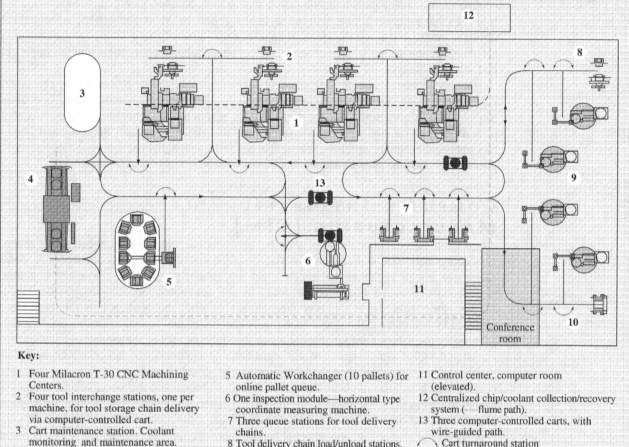

Key:

1 Four Milacron T-30 CNC Machining Centers.
2 Four tool interchange stations, one per machine, for tool storage chain delivery via computer-controlled cart.
3 Cart maintenance station. Coolant monitoring and maintenance area.
4 Parts wash station, automatic handling.

5 Automatic Workchanger (10 pallets) for online pallet queue.
6 One inspection module—horizontal type coordinate measuring machine.
7 Three queue stations for tool delivery chains.
8 Tool delivery chain load/unload stations.
9 Four part load/unload stations.
10 Pallet/fixture build station.

11 Control center, computer room (elevated).
12 Centralized chip/coolant collection/recovery system (— flume path).
13 Three computer-controlled carts, with wire-guided path.
⌒ Cart turnaround station (up to 360° around its own axis)

SOURCE: TOUR BROCHURE FROM THE PLANT.

Software Systems *Computer-aided design (CAD)* is an approach to product and process design that utilizes the power of the computer. CAD covers several automated technologies, such as *computer graphics* to examine the visual characteristics of a product and *computer-aided engineering (CAE)* to evaluate its engineering characteristics. Rubbermaid used CAD to refine dimensions of its ToteWheels to meet airline requirements for checked baggage. CAD also includes technologies associated with the manufacturing process design, referred to as *computer-aided process planning (CAPP)*. CAPP is used to design the computer part programs that serve as instructions to computer-controlled machine tools and to design the programs used to sequence parts through the machine centers and other processes (such as the washing and inspection) needed to complete the part. These programs are referred to as *process plans*. Sophisticated CAD systems also are able to do on-screen tests, replacing the early phases of prototype testing and modification.

CAD has been used to design everything from computer chips to potato chips. Frito-Lay, for example, used CAD to design its O'Grady's double-density, ruffled potato chip. The problem in designing such a chip is that if it is cut improperly, it may be burned on the outside and soggy on the inside, be too brittle (and shatter when placed in the bag), or display other characteristics that make it unworthy for, say, a guacamole dip. However, through the use of CAD, the proper angle and number of ruffles were determined mathematically; the O'Grady's model passed its stress test in the infamous Frito-Lay "crusher" and made it to your grocer's shelf. But despite some very loyal fans, O'Grady's has been discontinued, presumably due to lack of sales.

CAD is now being used to custom design swimsuits. Measurements of the wearer are fed into the CAD program, along with the style of suit desired. Working with the customer, the designer modifies the suit design as it appears on a human-form drawing on the computer screen. Once the design is decided upon, the computer prints out a pattern, and the suit is cut and sewn on the spot.

Automated manufacturing planning and control systems (MP&CS) are simply computer-based information systems that help plan, schedule, and monitor a manufacturing operation. They obtain information from the factory floor continuously about work status, material arrivals, and so on, and they release production and purchase orders. Sophisticated manufacturing and planning control systems include order-entry processing, shop-floor control, purchasing, and cost accounting.

COMPUTER-INTEGRATED MANUFACTURING (CIM)

All of these automation technologies are brought together under *computer-integrated manufacturing (CIM)*. CIM is the automated version of the manufacturing process, where the three major manufacturing functions—product and process design, planning and control, and the manufacturing process itself—are replaced by the automated technologies just described. Further, the traditional integration mechanisms of oral and written communication are replaced by computer technology. Such highly automated and integrated manufacturing also goes under the names *total factory automation* and the *factory of the future*.

All of the CIM technologies are tied together using a network and integrated database. For instance, data integration allows CAD systems to be linked to *computer-aided manufacturing (CAM)*, which consists of numerical-control parts programs; and the manufacturing planning and control system can be linked to the automated material handling systems to facilitate parts pick list generation. Thus, in a fully integrated system, the areas of design, testing, fabrication, assembly, inspection, and material handling are not only automated but also integrated with each other and with the manufacturing planning and scheduling function.

Evaluation of Technology Investments   Modern technologies such as flexible manufacturing systems or computerized order processing systems represent large capital investments. Hence, a firm has to carefully assess its financial and strategic benefits from a technology before acquiring it. Evaluating such investments is especially hard because the purpose of acquiring new technologies is not just to reduce labor costs but also to increase product quality and variety, to shorten production lead times, and to increase the flexibility of an operation. Some of these benefits are intangible relative to labor cost reduction, so justification becomes difficult. Further, rapid technological change renders new equipment obsolete in just a few years, making the cost–benefit evaluation more complex.

But never assume that new automation technologies are always cost-effective. Even when there is no uncertainty about the benefits of automation, it may not be worthwhile to adopt it. For instance, many analysts predicted that integrated CAD/CAM systems would be the answer to all manufacturing problems. But a number of companies investing in such systems lost money in the process. The idea was to take a lot of skilled labor out of the process of tooling up for new or redesigned products and to speed up the process. However, it can take less time to mill complex, low-volume parts than to program the milling machine, and programmer time is more expensive than the milling operator time. Also, it may not always be easy to transfer all the expert knowledge and experience that a milling operator has gained over the years into a computer program. CAD/CAM integration software has attained sufficient levels of quality and cost effectiveness that it is now routinely utilized even in high-variety low-volume manufacturing environments.

Benefits of Technology Investments   The typical benefits from adopting new manufacturing technologies are both tangible and intangible. The tangible benefits can be used in traditional modes of financial analysis such as discounted cash flow to make sound investment decisions. Specific benefits can be summarized as follows:

COST REDUCTION

Labor costs.   Replacing people with robots, or enabling fewer workers to run semiautomatic equipment.

Material costs.   Using existing materials more efficiently, or enabling the use of high-tolerance materials.

Inventory costs.   Fast changeover equipment allowing for JIT inventory management.

Quality costs.   Automated inspection and reduced variation in product output.

Maintenance costs.   Self-adjusting equipment.

OTHER BENEFITS

Increased product variety.   Scope economies due to flexible manufacturing systems.

Improved product features.   Ability to make things that could not be made by hand (e.g., microprocessors).

Shorter cycle times.   Faster setups and changeovers.

Greater product output.

Risks in Adopting New Technologies   Although there may be many benefits in acquiring new technologies, several types of risk accompany the acquisition of new technologies. These risks have to be evaluated and traded off against the benefits before the technologies are adopted. Some of these risks are described next.

TECHNOLOGICAL RISKS

An early adopter of a new technology has the benefit of being ahead of the competition, but he or she also runs the risk of acquiring an untested technology whose problems could disrupt the firm's operations. There is also the risk of obsolescence, especially with electronics-based technologies where change is rapid and when the fixed cost of acquiring new technologies or the cost of upgrades is high. Also, alternative technologies may become more cost-effective in the future, negating the benefits of a technology today.

OPERATIONAL RISKS

There also could be risks in applying a new technology to a firm's operations. Installation of a new technology generally results in significant disruptions, at least in the short run, in the form of plantwide reorganization, retraining, and so on. Further risks are due to the delays and errors introduced in the production process and the uncertain and sudden demands on various resources.

ORGANIZATIONAL RISKS

Firms may lack the organizational culture and top management commitment required to absorb the short-term disruptions and uncertainties associated with adopting a new technology. In such organizations, there is a risk that the firm's employees or managers may quickly abandon the technology when there are short-term failures or will avoid major changes by simply automating the firm's old, inefficient process and therefore not obtain the benefits of the new technology.

ENVIRONMENTAL OR MARKET RISKS

In many cases, a firm may invest in a particular technology only to discover a few years later that changes in some environmental or market factors make the investment worthless. For instance, in environmental issues, auto firms have been reluctant to invest in technology for making electric cars because they are uncertain about future emission standards of state and federal governments, the potential for decreasing emissions from gasoline-based cars, and the potential for significant improvements in battery technology. Typical examples of market risks are fluctuations in currency exchange rates and interest rates.

SUMMARY

Technology has played the dominant role in the productivity growth of most nations and has provided the competitive edge to firms that have adopted it early and implemented it successfully. Although each of the manufacturing and information technologies described here is a powerful tool by itself and can be adopted separately, their benefits grow exponentially when they are integrated with each other. This is particularly the case with CIM technologies.

With more modern technologies, the benefits are not entirely tangible and many benefits may be realized only on a long-term basis. Thus, typical cost accounting methods and standard financial analysis may not adequately capture all the potential benefits of technologies such as CIM. Hence, we must take into account the strategic benefits in evaluating such investments. Further, because capital costs for many modern technologies are substantial, the various risks associated with such investments have to be carefully assessed.

Implementing flexible manufacturing systems or complex decision support systems requires a significant commitment for most firms. Such investments may even be beyond the reach of small to medium-size firms. However, as technologies continue to improve and are adopted more widely, their costs may decline and place them within the reach of smaller firms. Given the complex, integrative nature of these technologies, the total commitment of top management and all employees is critical for the successful implementation of these technologies.

REVIEW AND DISCUSSION QUESTIONS

1 Do robots have to be trained? Explain.
2 How does the axiom used in industrial selling "You don't sell the product; you sell the company" pertain to manufacturing technology?
3 List three analytical tools (other than financial analysis) covered elsewhere in the book that can be used to evaluate technological alternatives.
4 The Belleville, Ontario, Canada, subsidiary of Atlanta-based Interface Inc., one of the world's largest makers of commercial flooring, credits much of its profitability to "green manufacturing" or "eco-efficiency." What do you believe these terms mean, eh? And how could such practices lead to cost reduction?
5 Give two examples each of recent process and product technology innovations.
6 What is the difference between an NC machine and a machining center?
7 The major auto companies are planning to invest millions of dollars in developing new product and process technologies required to make electric cars. Describe briefly why they are investing in these technologies. Discuss the potential benefits and risks involved in these investments.

SELECTED BIBLIOGRAPHY

Black, J. T. *The Design of the Factory with a Future.* New York: McGraw-Hill, 1991.

Groover, M. P. *Fundamentals of Modern Manufacturing.* 3rd ed. New York: Wiley, 2006.

Groover, M. P. *Automation, Production Systems, and Computer-Integrated Manufacturing.* 3rd ed. Upper Saddle River, NJ: Prentice Hall, 2007.

Hyer, N., and U. Wemmerlöv. *Reorganizing the Factory: Competing through Cellular Manufacturing.* Portland: OR; Productivity Press, 2002.

Kalpakjian, S., and S. Schmid. *Manufacturing, Engineering & Technology.* 5th ed. Upper Saddle River, NJ: Prentice Hall, 2005.

Melnyk, S. A., and R. Narasimhan. *Computer Integrated Manufacturing.* Homewood, IL: Irwin Professional Publishing, 1992.

FINANCIAL ANALYSIS

In this appendix we review basic concepts and tools of financial analysis for OSCM. These include the types of cost (fixed, variable, sunk, opportunity, avoidable), risk and expected value, and depreciation (straight line, sum-of-the-years'-digits, declining balance, double-declining balance, and depreciation-by-use). We also discuss activity-based costing and cost-of-capital calculations. Our focus is on capital investment decisions.

CONCEPTS AND DEFINITIONS
We begin with some basic definitions.

Fixed Costs   A *fixed cost* is any expense that remains constant regardless of the level of output. Although no cost is truly fixed, many types of expense are virtually fixed over a wide range of output. Examples are rent, property taxes, most types of depreciation, insurance payments, and salaries of top management.

Variable Costs   *Variable costs* are expenses that fluctuate directly with changes in the level of output. For example, each additional unit of sheet steel produced by USx requires a specific amount of material and labor. The incremental cost of this additional material and labor can be isolated and assigned to each unit of sheet steel produced. Many overhead expenses are also variable because utility bills, maintenance expense, and so forth, vary with the production level.

Exhibit C.1 illustrates the fixed and variable cost components of total cost. Note that total cost increases at the same rate as variable costs because fixed costs are constant.

Sunk Costs   *Sunk costs* are past expenses or investments that have no salvage value and therefore should not be taken into account in considering investment alternatives. Sunk costs also could be current costs that are essentially fixed such as rent on a building. For example, suppose an ice cream manufacturing firm occupies a rented building and is considering making sherbet in

Fixed and Variable Cost Components of Total Cost

exhibit C.1

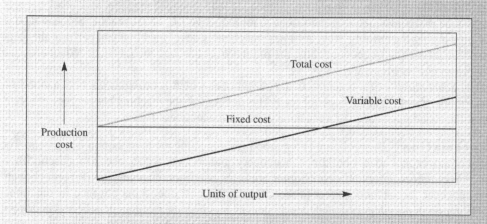

the same building. If the company enters sherbet production, its cost accountant will assign some of the rental expense to the sherbet operation. However, the building rent remains unchanged and therefore is not a relevant expense to be considered in making the decision. The rent is *sunk*; that is, it continues to exist and does not change in amount regardless of the decision.

Opportunity Costs   *Opportunity cost* is the benefit *forgone*, or advantage *lost*, that results from choosing one action over the *best-known alternative* course of action.

Suppose a firm has $100,000 to invest and two alternatives of comparable risk present themselves, each requiring a $100,000 investment. Investment A will net $25,000; Investment B will net $23,000. Investment A is clearly the better choice, with a $25,000 net return. If the decision is made to invest in B instead of A, the opportunity cost of B is $2,000, which is the benefit forgone.

Avoidable Costs   *Avoidable costs* include any expense that is *not* incurred if an investment is made but that *must* be incurred if the investment is *not* made. Suppose a company owns a metal lathe that is not in working condition but is needed for the firm's operations. Because the lathe must be repaired or replaced, the repair costs are avoidable if a new lathe is purchased. Avoidable costs reduce the cost of a new investment because they are not incurred if the investment is made. Avoidable costs are an example of how it is possible to "save" money by spending money.

Expected Value   Risk is inherent in any investment because the future can never be predicted with absolute certainty. To deal with this uncertainty, mathematical techniques such as expected value can help. Expected value is the expected outcome multiplied by the probability of its occurrence. Recall that in the preceding example the expected outcome of Alternative A was $25,000 and B, $23,000. Suppose the probability of A's actual outcome is 80 percent while B's probability is 90 percent. The expected values of the alternatives are determined as follows:

$$\text{Expected outcome} \times \text{Probability that actual outcome will be the expected outcome} = \text{Expected value}$$

Investment A: $25,000 \times 0.80 = \$20,000$
Investment B: $23,000 \times 0.90 = \$20,700$

Investment B is now seen to be the better choice, with a net advantage over A of $700.

Economic Life and Obsolescence   When a firm invests in an income-producing asset, the productive life of the asset is estimated. For accounting purposes, the asset is depreciated over this period. It is assumed that the asset will perform its function during this time and then be considered obsolete or worn out, and replacement will be required. This view of asset life rarely coincides with reality.

Assume that a machine expected to have a productive life of 10 years is purchased. If at any time during the ensuing 10 years a new machine is developed that can perform the same task more efficiently or economically, the old machine has become obsolete. Whether or not it is "worn out" is irrelevant.

The *economic life* of a machine is the period over which it provides the best method for performing its task. When a superior method is developed, the machine has become obsolete. Thus, the stated *book value* of a machine can be a meaningless figure.

Depreciation   Depreciation is a method for allocating costs of capital equipment. The value of any capital asset—buildings, machinery, and so forth—decreases as its useful life is expended. *Amortization* and *depreciation* are often used interchangeably. Through convention, however, *depreciation* refers to the allocation of cost due to the physical or functional deterioration of *tangible* (physical) assets such as buildings or equipment, whereas *amortization* refers to the allocation of cost over the useful life of *intangible* assets such as patents, leases, franchises, and goodwill.

Depreciation procedures may not reflect an asset's true value at any point in its life because obsolescence may at any time cause a large difference between true value and book value. Also, because depreciation rates significantly affect taxes, a firm may choose a particular method from the several alternatives with more consideration for its effect on taxes than its ability to make the book value of an asset reflect the true resale value.

Next we describe five commonly used methods of depreciation.

STRAIGHT-LINE METHOD

Under this method, an asset's value is reduced in uniform annual amounts over its estimated useful life. The general formula is

$$\text{Annual amount to be depreciated} = \frac{\text{Cost} - \text{Salvage value}}{\text{Estimated useful life}}$$

A machine costing $10,000 with an estimated salvage value of $0 and an estimated life of 10 years would be depreciated at the rate of $1,000 per year for each of the 10 years. If its estimated salvage value at the end of the 10 years is $1,000, the annual depreciation charge is

$$\frac{\$10,000 - \$1,000}{10} = \$900$$

SUM-OF-THE-YEARS'-DIGITS (SYD) METHOD

The purpose of the SYD method is to reduce the book value of an asset rapidly in early years and at a lower rate in the later years of its life.

Suppose that the estimated useful life is five years. The numbers add up to 15: $1 + 2 + 3 + 4 + 5 = 15$. Therefore, we depreciate the asset by $5 \div 15$ after the first year, $4 \div 15$ after the second year, and so on, down to $1 \div 15$ in the last year.

DECLINING-BALANCE METHOD

This method also achieves an accelerated depreciation. The asset's value is decreased by reducing its book value by a constant percentage each year. The percentage rate selected is often the one that just reduces book value to salvage value at the end of the asset's estimated life. In any case, the asset should never be reduced below estimated salvage value. Use of the declining-balance method and allowable rates are controlled by Internal Revenue Service regulations. As a simplified illustration, the preceding example is used in the next table with an arbitrarily selected rate of 40 percent. Note that depreciation is based on full cost, *not* cost minus salvage value.

YEAR	DEPRECIATION RATE	BEGINNING BOOK VALUE	DEPRECIATION CHARGE	ACCUMULATED DEPRECIATION	ENDING BOOK VALUE
1	0.40	$17,000	$6,800	$ 6,800	$10,200
2	0.40	10,200	4,080	10,880	6,120
3	0.40	6,120	2,448	13,328	3,672
4	0.40	3,672	1,469	14,797	2,203
5		2,203	203	15,000	2,000

In the fifth year, reducing book value by 40 percent would have caused it to drop below salvage value. Consequently, the asset was depreciated by only $203, which decreased book value to salvage value.

DOUBLE-DECLINING-BALANCE METHOD

Again, for tax advantages, the double-declining-balance method offers higher depreciation early in the life span. This method uses a percentage twice the straight line for the life span of the item but applies this rate to the undepreciated original cost. The method is the same as the declining-balance method, but the term *double-declining balance* means double the straight-line rate. Thus, equipment with a 10-year life span would have a straight-line depreciation rate of 10 percent per year and a double-declining-balance rate (applied to the undepreciated amount) of 20 percent per year.

DEPRECIATION-BY-USE METHOD

The purpose of this method is to depreciate a capital investment in proportion to its use. It is applicable, for example, to a machine that performs the same operation many times. The life of the machine is estimated not in years but rather in the total number of operations it may reasonably be expected to perform before wearing out. Suppose that a metal-stamping press has an estimated life of one million stamps and costs $100,000. The charge for depreciation per stamp is then $100,000 ÷ 1,000,000, or $0.10. Assuming a $0 salvage value, the depreciation charges are as shown in the following table:

YEAR	TOTAL YEARLY STAMPS	COST PER STAMP	YEARLY DEPRECIATION CHARGE	ACCUMULATED DEPRECIATION	ENDING BOOK VALUE
1	150,000	0.10	$15,000	$15,000	$85,000
2	300,000	0.10	30,000	45,000	55,000
3	200,000	0.10	20,000	65,000	35,000
4	200,000	0.10	20,000	85,000	15,000
5	100,000	0.10	10,000	95,000	5,000
6	50,000	0.10	5,000	100,000	0

The depreciation-by-use method is an attempt to gear depreciation charges to actual use and thereby coordinate expense charges with productive output more accurately. Also, because a machine's resale value is related to its remaining productive life, it is hoped that book value will approximate resale value. The danger, of course, is that technological improvements will render the machine obsolete, in which case book value will not reflect true value.

ACTIVITY-BASED COSTING

To know the costs incurred to make a certain product or deliver a service, some method of allocating overhead costs to production activities must be applied. The traditional approach is to allocate overhead costs to products on the basis of direct labor dollars or hours. By dividing the total estimated overhead costs by total budgeted direct labor hours, an overhead rate can be established. The problem with this approach is that direct labor as a percentage of total costs has fallen dramatically over the past decade. For example, introduction of advanced manufacturing technology and other productivity improvements has driven direct labor to as low as 7 to 10 percent of total manufacturing costs in many industries. As a result, overhead rates of 600 percent or even 1,000 percent are found in some highly automated plants.

This traditional accounting practice of allocating overhead to direct labor can lead to questionable investment decisions; for example, automated processes may be chosen over labor-intensive processes based on a comparison of projected costs. Unfortunately, overhead does not disappear when the equipment is installed and overall costs may actually be lower with the labor-intensive process. It also can lead to wasted effort because an inordinate amount of time is spent tracking direct labor hours. For example, one plant spent 65 percent of computer costs tracking information about direct labor transactions even though direct labor accounted for only 4 percent of total production costs.[1]

Activity-based costing techniques have been developed to alleviate these problems by refining the overhead allocation process to more directly reflect actual proportions of overhead consumed by the production activity. Causal factors, known as *cost drivers*, are identified and used as the means for allocating overhead. These factors might include machine hours, beds occupied, computer time, flight hours, or miles driven. The accuracy of overhead allocation, of course, depends on the selection of appropriate cost drivers.

Activity-based costing involves a two-stage allocation process, with the first stage assigning overhead costs to *cost activity pools*. These pools represent activities such as performing machine setups, issuing purchase orders, and inspecting parts. In the second stage, costs are assigned from these pools to activities based on the number or amount of pool-related activity required in their completion. Exhibit C.2 compares traditional cost accounting and activity-based costing.

Consider the example of activity-based costing in Exhibit C.3. Two products, A and B, are produced using the same number of direct labor hours. The same number of direct labor

Traditional and Activity-Based Costing

exhibit C.2

Traditional Costing

Total overhead

↓ Labor-hour allocation

End product cost

Activity-Based Costing

Total overhead

↓ Pooled based on activities

Cost pools

↓ Cost-driver allocation

End product costs

Overhead Allocations by an Activity Approach

exhibit C.3

BASIC DATA

ACTIVITY	TRACEABLE COSTS	EVENTS OF TRANSACTIONS		
		TOTAL	PRODUCT A	PRODUCT B
Machine setups	$230,000	5,000	3,000	2,000
Quality inspections	160,000	8,000	5,000	3,000
Production orders	81,000	600	200	400
Machine-hours worked	314,000	40,000	12,000	28,000
Material receipts	90,000	750	150	600
Number of units produced		25,000	5,000	20,000
	$875,000			

OVERHEAD RATES BY ACTIVITY

ACTIVITY	(a) TRACEABLE COSTS	(b) TOTAL EVENTS OR TRANSACTIONS	(a) ÷ (b) RATE PER EVENT OR TRANSACTION
Machine setups	$230,000	5,000	$46/setups
Quality inspections	160,000	8,000	$20/inspection
Production orders	81,000	600	$135/order
Machine-hours worked	314,000	40,000	$7.85/hour
Material receipts	90,000	750	$120/receipt

OVERHEAD COST PER UNIT OF PRODUCT

	PRODUCT A		PRODUCT B	
	EVENTS OR TRANSACTIONS	AMOUNT	EVENTS OR TRANSACTIONS	AMOUNT
Machine setups, at $46/setup	3,000	$138,000	2,000	$92,000
Quality inspections, at $20/inspection	5,000	100,000	3,000	60,000
Product orders, at $135/order	200	27,000	400	54,000
Machine-hours worked, at $7.85/hour	12,000	94,200	28,000	219,800
Material receipts, at $120/receipt	150	18,000	600	72,000
Total overhead cost assigned		$377,200		$497,800
Number of units produced		5,000		20,000
Overhead cost per unit, $\frac{\text{Total overhead}}{\text{No. of units}}$		$75.44		$24.89

SEE R. GARRISON, *MANAGERIAL ACCOUNTING*, 12TH ED. (NEW YORK: McGRAW-HILL, 2007).

hours produces 5,000 units of Product A and 20,000 units of Product B. Applying traditional costing, identical overhead costs would be charged to each product. By applying activity-based costing, traceable costs are assigned to specific activities. Because each product required a different amount of transactions, different overhead amounts are allocated to these products from the pools.

As stated earlier, activity-based costing overcomes the problem of cost distortion by creating a cost pool for each activity or transaction that can be identified as a cost driver, and by assigning overhead cost to products or jobs on a basis of the number of separate activities required for their completion. Thus, in the previous situation, the low-volume product would be assigned the bulk of the costs for machine setup, purchase orders, and quality inspections, thereby showing it to have high unit costs compared to the other product.

Finally, activity-based costing is sometimes referred to as *transactions costing*. This transactions focus gives rise to another major advantage over other costing methods: It improves the traceability of overhead costs and thus results in more accurate unit cost data for management.

THE EFFECTS OF TAXES

Tax rates and the methods of applying them occasionally change. When analysts evaluate investment proposals, tax considerations often prove to be the deciding factor because depreciation expenses directly affect taxable income and therefore profit. The ability to write off depreciation in early years provides an added source of funds for investment. Before 1986, firms could employ an investment tax credit, which allowed a direct reduction in tax liability. But tax laws change, so it is crucial to stay on top of current tax laws and try to predict future changes that may affect current investments and accounting procedures.

CHOOSING AMONG INVESTMENT PROPOSALS

The capital investment decision has become highly rationalized, as evidenced by the variety of techniques available for its solution. In contrast to pricing or marketing decisions, the capital investment decision can usually be made with a higher degree of confidence because the variables affecting the decision are relatively well known and can be quantified with fair accuracy.

Investment decisions may be grouped into six general categories:

1. Purchase of new equipment or facilities.
2. Replacement of existing equipment or facilities.
3. Make-or-buy decisions.
4. Lease-or-buy decisions.
5. Temporary shutdowns or plant abandonment decisions.
6. Addition or elimination of a product or product line.

Investment decisions are made with regard to the lowest acceptable rate of return on investment. As a starting point, the lowest acceptable rate of return may be considered to be the cost of investment capital needed to underwrite the expenditure. Certainly an investment will not be made if it does not return at least the cost of capital.

Investments are generally ranked according to the return they yield in excess of their cost of capital. In this way, a business with only limited investment funds can select investment alternatives that yield the highest net returns. (*Net return* is the earnings an investment yields after gross earnings have been reduced by the cost of the funds used to finance the investment.) In general, investments should not be made unless the return in funds exceeds the marginal cost of investment capital. (*Marginal cost* is the incremental cost of each new acquisition of funds from outside sources.)

Determining the Cost of Capital   The cost of capital is calculated from a weighted average of debt and equity security costs. This average will vary depending on the financing strategy employed by the company. The most common sources of financing are short-term debt, long-term debt, and equity securities. A bank loan is an example of short-term debt. Bonds normally provide long-term debt. Finally, stock is a common form of equity financing. In the following, we give a short example of each form of financing, and then show how they are combined to find the weighted average cost of capital.

The cost of short-term debt depends on the interest rate on the loan and whether the loan is discounted. Remember that interest is a tax-deductible expense for a company.

$$\text{Cost of short-term debt} = \frac{\text{Interest paid}}{\text{Proceeds received}}$$

If a bank discounts a loan, interest is deducted from the face of the loan to get the proceeds. When a compensating balance is required (that is, a percentage of the face value of the loan is held by the bank as collateral), proceeds are also reduced. In either case, the effective or real interest rate on the loan is higher than the face interest rate owing to the proceeds received from the loan being less than the amount (face value) of the loan.

EXAMPLE OF SHORT-TERM DEBT

A company takes a $150,000, one-year, 13 percent loan. The loan is discounted, and a 10 percent compensating balance is required. The effective interest rate is computed as follows:

$$\frac{13\% \times \$150,000}{\$115,500} = \frac{\$19,500}{\$115,500} = 16.89\%$$

Proceeds received equal

Face of loan	$150,000
Less interest	(19,500)
Compensating balance (10% × $150,000)	(15,000)
Proceeds	$115,500

Notice how the effective cost of the loan is significantly greater than the stated interest rate.

Long-term debt is normally provided through the sale of corporate bonds. The real cost of bonds is obtained by computing two types of yield: simple (face) yield and yield to maturity (effective interest rate). The first involves an easy approximation, but the second is more accurate. The nominal interest rate equals the interest paid on the face (maturity value) of the bond and is always stated on a per-annum basis. Bonds are generally issued in $1,000 denominations and may be sold above face value (at a premium) or below (at a discount, termed original issue discount, or OID). A bond is sold at a discount when the interest rate is below the going market rate. In this case, the yield will be higher than the nominal interest rate. The opposite holds for bonds issued at a premium.

The issue price of a bond is the par (or face value) times the premium (or discount).

$$\text{Simple yield} = \frac{\text{Nominal interest}}{\text{Issue price of bond}}$$

$$\text{Yield to maturity} = \frac{\text{Nominal interest} + \dfrac{\text{Discount (or premium)}}{\text{Years}}}{\dfrac{\text{Issue price} + \text{Maturity value}}{2}}$$

EXAMPLE OF LONG-TERM DEBT

A company issues a $400,000, 12 percent, 10-year bond for 97 percent of face value. Yield computations are as follows:

$$\text{Nominal annual payment} = 12\% \times \$400,000$$
$$= \$48,000$$
$$\text{Bond proceeds} = 97\% \times \$400,000$$
$$= \$388,000$$

$$\text{Bond discount} = 3\% \times \$400,000$$

$$= \$12,000$$

$$\text{Simple yield} = \frac{12\% \times \$400,000}{97\% \times \$400,000} = \frac{\$48,000}{\$388,000} = 12.4\%$$

$$\text{Yield to maturity} = \frac{\$48,000 + \dfrac{\$12,000}{10}}{\dfrac{\$388,000 + \$400,000}{2}} = \frac{\$48,000 + \$1,200}{\$394,000} = 12.5\%$$

Note that because the bonds were sold at a discount, the yield exceeds the nominal interest rate (12 percent). Bond interest is tax deductible to the corporation.

The actual cost of equity securities (stocks) comes in the form of dividends, which are not tax deductible to the corporation.

$$\text{Cost of common stock} = \frac{\text{Dividends per share}}{\text{Value per share}} + \text{Growth rate of dividends}$$

Here the value per share equals the market price per share minus flotation costs (that is, the cost of issuing securities such as brokerage fees and printing costs). It should be noted that this valuation does not consider what the investor expects in market price appreciation. This expectation is based on the expected growth in earnings per share and the relative risk taken by purchasing the stock. The capital asset pricing model (CAPM) can be used to capture this impact.[2]

EXAMPLE OF THE COST OF COMMON STOCK
A company's dividend per share is $10, net value is $70 per share, and the dividend growth rate is 5 percent.

$$\text{Cost of the stock} = \frac{\$10}{\$70} + 0.05 = 19.3\%$$

To compute the weighted average cost of capital, we consider the percentage of the total capital that is being provided by each financing alternative. We then calculate the after-tax cost of each financing alternative. Finally, we weight these costs in proportion to their use.

EXAMPLE OF CALCULATING THE WEIGHTED AVERAGE COST OF CAPITAL
Consider a company that shows the following figures in its financial statements:

Short-term bank loan (13%)	$1 million
Bonds payable (16%)	$4 million
Common stock (10%)	$5 million

For our example, assume that each of the percentages given above represents the cost of the source of capital. In addition to the above, we need to consider the tax rate of the firm because the interest paid on the bonds and on the short-term loan is tax deductible. Assume a corporate tax rate of 40 percent.

	PERCENT	AFTER-TAX COST	WEIGHTED AVERAGE COST
Short-term bank loan	10%	13% × 60% = 7.8%	.78%
Bonds payable	40%	16% × 60% = 9.6%	3.84%
Common stock	50%	10%	5%
Total	100%		9.62%

Keep in mind that in developing this section we have made many assumptions in these calculations. When these ideas are applied to a specific company, many of these assumptions may change. The basic concepts, though, are the same; keep in mind that the goal is to simply calculate the after-tax cost of the capital used by the company. We have shown the cost of capital for the entire company, though often only the capital employed for a specific project is used in the calculation.

Interest Rate Effects   There are two basic ways to account for the effects of interest accumulation. One is to compute the total amount created over the time period into the future as the *compound value*. The other is to remove the interest rate effect over time by reducing all future sums to present-day dollars, or the *present value*.

Compound Value of a Single Amount   Albert Einstein was quoted as saying that compound interest is the eighth wonder of the world. After reviewing this section showing compound interest's dramatic growth effects over a long time, you might wish to propose a new government regulation: On the birth of a child, the parents must put, say, $1,000 into a retirement fund for that child, available at age 65. This might reduce the pressure on Social Security and other state and federal pension plans. Although inflation would decrease the value significantly, there would still be a lot left over. At a 14 percent return on investment, our $1,000 would increase to $500,000 after subtracting the $4.5 million for inflation. That is still a 500-fold increase. (Many mutual funds today have long-term performances in excess of 14 percent per year.)

Spreadsheets and calculators make such computation easy. The box titled "Using a Spreadsheet" shows the most useful financial functions. However, many people still refer to tables for compound values. Using Appendix I, Table I.1 (compound sum of $1), for example, we see that the value of $1 at 10 percent interest after three years is $1.331. Multiplying this figure by $10 gives $13.31.

Compound Value of an Annuity   An *annuity* is the receipt of a constant sum each year for a specified number of years. Usually an annuity is received at the end of a period and does not earn interest during that period. Therefore, an annuity of $10 for three years would bring in $10 at the end of the first year (allowing the $10 to earn interest if invested for the remaining two years), $10 at the end of the second year (allowing the $10 to earn interest for the remaining one year), and $10 at the end of the third year (with no time to earn interest). If the annuity receipts were placed in a bank savings account at 5 percent interest, the total or compound value of the $10 at 5 percent for the three years would be

YEAR	RECEIPT AT END OF YEAR		COMPOUND INTEREST FACTOR $(1 + i)^n$		VALUE AT END OF THIRD YEAR
1	$10.00	×	$(1 + 0.05)^2$	=	$11.02
2	10.00	×	$(1 + 0.05)^1$	=	10.50
3	10.00	×	$(1 + 0.05)^0$	=	10.00
					$31.52

The general formula for finding the compound value of an annuity is

$$S_n = R[(1 + i)^{n-1} + (1 + i)^{n-2} + \cdots + (1 + i)^1 + 1]$$

where

S_n = Compound value of an annuity

R = Periodic receipts in dollars

n = Length of the annuity in years

USING A SPREADSHEET

We hope that you are all doing these calculations using a spreadsheet program. Even though the computer makes these calculations simple, it is important that you understand what the computer is actually doing. Further, you should check your calculations manually to make sure that you have the formulas set up correctly in your spreadsheet. There are many stories of the terrible consequences of making a wrong decision based on a spreadsheet with errors!

For your quick reference, the following are the financial functions you will find most useful. These are from the Microsoft Excel help screens.

PV (rate, nper, pmt)—Returns the present value of an investment. The present value is the total amount that a series of future payments is worth now. For example, when you borrow money, the loan amount is the present value to the lender. Rate is the interest rate per period. For example, if you obtain an automobile loan at a 10 percent annual interest rate and make monthly payments, your interest rate per month is 10%/12, or .83%. You would enter 10%/12, or .83%, or .0083, in the formula as the rate. Nper is the total number of payment periods in an annuity. For example, if you get a four-year car loan and make monthly payments, your loan has 4*12 (or 48) periods. You would enter 48 into the formula for nper. Pmt is the payment made each period and cannot change over the life of the annuity. Typically, this includes principal and interest but no other fees or taxes. For example, the monthly payment on a $10,000, four-year car loan at 12 percent is $263.33. You would enter 263.33 into the formula as pmt.

FROM MICROSOFT® EXCEL. COPYRIGHT © 2001 MICROSOFT CORPORATION.

FV (rate, nper, pmt)—Returns the future value of an investment based on periodic, constant payments and a constant interest rate. Rate is the interest rate per period. Nper is the total number of payment periods in an annuity. Pmt is the payment made each period; it cannot change over the life of the annuity. Typically, pmt contains principal and interest but no other fees or taxes.

NPV (rate, value1, value2, . . .)—Returns the net present value of an investment based on a series of periodic cash flows and a discount rate. The net present value of an investment is today's value of a series of future payments (negative values) and income (positive values). Rate is the rate of discount over the length of one period. Value1, value2. . ., must be equally spaced in time and occur at the end of each period.

IRR(values)—Returns the internal rate of return for a series of cash flows represented by the numbers in *values*. (*Values* is defined below.) These cash flows do not have to be even, as they would be for an annuity. The internal rate of return is the interest rate received for an investment consisting of payments (negative values) and income (positive values) that occur at regular periods. *Values* is an array or a reference to cells that contain numbers for which you want to calculate the internal rate of return. Values must contain at least one positive value and one negative value to calculate the internal rate of return. IRR uses the order of values to interpret the order of cash flows. Be sure to enter your payment and income values in the sequence you want.

Applying this formula to the preceding example, we get

$$S_n = R[(1 + i)^2 + (1 + i) + 1]$$
$$= \$10[(1 + 0.05)^2 + (1 + 0.05) + 1] = \$31.52$$

In Appendix I, Table I.2 lists the compound value factor of $1 for 5 percent after three years as 3.152. Multiplying this factor by $10 yields $31.52.

In a fashion similar to our previous retirement investment example, consider the beneficial effects of investing $2,000 each year, just starting at the age of 21. Assume investments in AAA-rated bonds are available today yielding 9 percent. From Table I.2 in Appendix I, after 30 years (at age 51) the investment is worth 136.3 times $2,000, or $272,600. Fourteen years later (at age 65) this would be worth $963,044 (using a hand calculator, because the table goes only to 30 years, and assuming the $2,000 is deposited at the end of each year)! But what 21-year-old thinks about retirement?

Present Value of a Future Single Payment   Compound values are used to determine future value after a specific period has elapsed; present value (PV) procedures accomplish just the reverse. They are used to determine the current value of a sum or stream of receipts expected to be received in the future. Most investment decision techniques use present value concepts rather than compound values. Because decisions affecting the future are made in the present, it is better to convert future returns into their present value at the time the decision is being made. In this way, investment alternatives are placed in better perspective in terms of current dollars.

An example makes this more apparent. If a rich uncle offers to make you a gift of $100 today or $250 after 10 years, which should you choose? You must determine whether the $250 in 10 years will be worth more than the $100 now. Suppose that you base your decision on the rate of inflation in the economy and believe that inflation averages 10 percent per year. By deflating the $250, you can compare its relative purchasing power with $100 received today. Procedurally, this is accomplished by solving the compound formula for the present sum, P, where V is the future amount of $250 in 10 years at 10 percent. The compound value formula is

$$V = P(1 + i)^n$$

Dividing both sides by $(1 + i)^n$ gives

$$P = \frac{V}{(1 + i)^n}$$

$$= \frac{250}{(1 + 0.10)^{10}} = \$96.39$$

This shows that, at a 10 percent inflation rate, $250 in 10 years will be worth $96.39 today. The rational choice, then, is to take the $100 now.

The use of tables is also standard practice in solving present value problems. With reference to Appendix I, Table I.3, the present value factor for $1 received 10 years hence is 0.386. Multiplying this factor by $250 yields $96.50.

Present Value of an Annuity   The present value of an annuity is the value of an annual amount to be received over a future period expressed in terms of the present. To find the value of an annuity of $100 for three years at 10 percent, find the factor in the present value table that applies to 10 percent in *each* of the three years in which the amount is received and multiply each receipt by this factor. Then sum the resulting figures. Remember that annuities are usually received at the end of each period.

YEAR	AMOUNT RECEIVED AT END OF YEAR		PRESENT VALUE FACTOR AT 10%		PRESENT VALUE
1	$100	×	0.909	=	$ 90.90
2	100	×	0.826	=	82.60
3	100	×	0.751	=	75.10
Total receipts	$300		Total present value	=	$248.60

The general formula used to derive the present value of an annuity is

$$A_n = R\left[\frac{1}{(1 + i)} + \frac{1}{(1 + i)^2} + \cdots + \frac{1}{(1 + i)^n}\right]$$

where

A_n = Present value of an annuity of n years

R = Periodic receipts

n = Length of the annuity in years

Applying the formula to the preceding example gives

$$A_n = \$100 \left[\frac{1}{(1 + 0.10)} + \frac{1}{(1 + 0.10)^2} + \frac{1}{(1 + 0.10)^3} \right]$$

$$= \$100(2.487) = \$248.70$$

In Appendix I, Table I.4 contains present values of an annuity for varying maturities. The present value factor for an annuity of $1 for three years at 10 percent (from Table I.4) is 2.487. Given that our sum is $100 rather than $1, we multiply this factor by $100 to arrive at $248.70.

When the stream of future receipts is uneven, the present value of each annual receipt must be calculated. The present values of the receipts for all years are then summed to arrive at total present value. This process can sometimes be tedious, but it is unavoidable.

Discounted Cash Flow   The term *discounted cash flow* refers to the total stream of payments that an asset will generate in the future discounted to the present time. This is simply present value analysis that includes all flows: single payments, annuities, and all others.

Methods of Ranking Investments

Net Present Value   The net present value method is commonly used in business. With this method, decisions are based on the amount by which the present value of a projected income stream exceeds the cost of an investment.

A firm is considering two alternative investments. The first costs $30,000 and the second, $50,000. The expected yearly cash income streams are shown in this table:

	CASH INFLOW	
YEAR	ALTERNATIVE A	ALTERNATIVE B
1	$10,000	$15,000
2	10,000	15,000
3	10,000	15,000
4	10,000	15,000
5	10,000	15,000

To choose between Alternatives A and B, find which has the higher net present value. Assume an 8 percent cost of capital.

ALTERNATIVE A		ALTERNATIVE B	
3.993 (PV factor)		3.993 (PV factor)	
× $10,000	= $39,930	× $15,000	= $59,895
Less cost of investment =	30,000	Less cost of investment =	50,000
Net present value	= $ 9,930	Net present value	= $ 9,895

Investment A is the better alternative. Its net present value exceeds that of Investment B by $35 ($9,930 − $9,895 = $35).

Payback Period   The payback method ranks investments according to the time required for each investment to return earnings equal to the cost of the investment. The rationale is that the sooner the investment capital can be recovered, the sooner it can be reinvested in new revenue-producing projects. Thus, supposedly, a firm will be able to get the most benefit from its available investment funds.

Consider two alternatives requiring a $1,000 investment each. The first will earn $200 per year for six years; the second will earn $300 per year for the first three years and $100 per year for the next three years.

If the first alternative is selected, the initial investment of $1,000 will be recovered at the end of the fifth year. The income produced by the second alternative will total $1,000 after only four years. The second alternative will permit reinvestment of the full $1,000 in new revenue-producing projects one year sooner than the first.

Though the payback method is declining in popularity as the sole measure in investment decisions, it is still frequently used in conjunction with other methods to indicate the time commitment of funds. The major problems with payback are that it does not consider income beyond the payback period and it ignores the time value of money. A method that ignores the time value of money must be considered questionable.

Internal Rate of Return   The internal rate of return may be defined as the interest rate that equates the present value of an income stream with the cost of an investment. There is no procedure or formula that may be used directly to compute the internal rate of return—it must be found by interpolation or iterative calculation.

Suppose we wish to find the internal rate of return for an investment costing $12,000 that will yield a cash inflow of $4,000 per year for four years. We see that the present value factor sought is

$$\frac{\$12,000}{\$4,000} = 3.000$$

and we seek the interest rate that will provide this factor over a four-year period. The interest rate must lie between 12 and 14 percent because 3.000 lies between 3.037 and 2.914 (in the fourth row of Appendix I, Table I.4). Linear interpolation between these values, according to the equation

$$I = 12 + (14 - 12)\frac{(3.037 - 3.000)}{(3.037 - 2.914)}$$

$$= 12 + 0.602 = 12.602\%$$

gives a good approximation to the actual internal rate of return.

When the income stream is discounted at 12.6 percent, the resulting present value closely approximates the cost of investment. Thus, the internal rate of return for this investment is 12.6 percent. The cost of capital can be compared with the internal rate of return to determine the net rate of return on the investment. If, in this example, the cost of capital were 8 percent, the net rate of return on the investment would be 4.6 percent.

The net present value and internal rate of return methods involve procedures that are essentially the same. They differ in that the net present value method enables investment alternatives to be compared in terms of the dollar value in excess of cost, whereas the internal rate of return method permits comparison of rates of return on alternative investments. Moreover, the internal rate of return method occasionally encounters problems in calculation, as multiple rates frequently appear in the computation.

Ranking Investments with Uneven Lives   When proposed investments have the same life expectancy, comparison among them, using the preceding methods, will give a reasonable picture of their relative value. When lives are unequal, however, there is the question of how to relate the two different time periods. Should replacements be considered the same as the original? Should productivity for the shorter-term unit that will be replaced earlier be considered higher? How should the cost of future units be estimated?

No estimate dealing with investments unforeseen at the time of decision can be expected to reflect a high degree of accuracy. Still, the problem must be dealt with, and some assumptions must be made in order to determine a ranking.

SAMPLE PROBLEMS: INVESTMENT DECISIONS

EXAMPLE C.1: An Expansion Decision

William J. Wilson Ceramic Products, Inc., leases plant facilities in which firebrick is manufactured. Because of rising demand, Wilson could increase sales by investing in new equipment to expand output. The selling price of $10 per brick will remain unchanged if output and sales increase. Based on

Step by Step

engineering and cost estimates, the accounting department provides management with the following cost estimates based on an annual increased output of 100,000 bricks:

Cost of new equipment having an expected life of five years	$500,000
Equipment installation cost	20,000
Expected salvage value	0
New operation's share of annual lease expense	40,000
Annual increase in utility expenses	40,000
Annual increase in labor costs	160,000
Annual additional cost for raw materials	400,000

The sum-of-the-years'-digits method of depreciation will be used, and taxes are paid at a rate of 40 percent. Wilson's policy is not to invest capital in projects earning less than a 20 percent rate of return. Should the proposed expansion be undertaken?

SOLUTION

Compute the cost of investment:

Acquisition cost of equipment	$500,000
Equipment installation costs	20,000
Total cost of investment	$520,000

Determine yearly cash flows throughout the life of the investment.

The lease expense is a sunk cost. It will be incurred whether or not the investment is made and is therefore irrelevant to the decision and should be disregarded. Annual production expenses to be considered are utility, labor, and raw materials. These total $600,000 per year.

Annual sales revenue is $10 \times 100,000$ units of output, which totals $1,000,000. Yearly income before depreciation and taxes is thus $1,000,000 gross revenue, less $600,000 expenses, or $400,000.

Next, determine the depreciation charges to be deducted from the $500,000 income each year using the SYD method (sum-of-years'-digits $= 1 + 2 + 3 + 4 + 5 = 15$):

YEAR	PROPORTION OF $500,000 TO BE DEPRECIATED		DEPRECIATION CHARGE
1	5/15 × $500,000	=	$166,667
2	4/15 × 500,000	=	133,333
3	3/15 × 500,000	=	100,000
4	2/15 × 500,000	=	66,667
5	1/15 × 500,000	=	33,333
	Accumulated depreciation		$500,000

Find each year's cash flow when taxes are 40 percent. Cash flow for only the first year is illustrated:

Earnings before depreciation and taxes		$400,000
Deduct: Taxes at 40% (40% × 400,000)	$160,000	
Tax benefit of depreciation expense (0.4 × 166,667)	66,667	93,333
Cash flow (first year)		$306,667

Determine the present value of the cash flow. Because Wilson demands at least a 20 percent rate of return on investments, multiply the cash flows by the 20 percent present value factor for each year. The factor for each respective year must be used because the cash flows are not an annuity.

YEAR	PRESENT VALUE FACTOR		CASH FLOW		PRESENT VALUE
1	0.833	×	$306,667	=	$255,454
2	0.694	×	293,333	=	203,573
3	0.579	×	280,000	=	162,120
4	0.482	×	266,667	=	128,533
5	0.402	×	253,334	=	101,840
	Total present value of cash flows (discounted at 20%) =				$851,520

Now find whether net present value is positive or negative:

Total present value of cash flows	$851,520
Total cost of investment	520,000
Net present value	$331,520

Net present value is positive when returns are discounted at 20 percent. Wilson will earn an amount in excess of 20 percent on the investment. The proposed expansion should be undertaken. ●

EXAMPLE C.2: A Replacement Decision

For five years Bennie's Brewery has been using a machine that attaches labels to bottles. The machine was purchased for $4,000 and is being depreciated over 10 years to a $0 salvage value using straight-line depreciation. The machine can be sold now for $2,000. Bennie can buy a new labeling machine for $6,000 that will have a useful life of five years and cut labor costs by $1,200 annually. The old machine will require a major overhaul in the next few months at an estimated cost of $300. If purchased, the new machine will be depreciated over five years to a $500 salvage value using the straight-line method. The company will invest in any project earning more than the 12 percent cost of capital. The tax rate is 40 percent. Should Bennie's Brewery invest in the new machine?

Step by Step

SOLUTION

Determine the cost of investment:

Price of the new machine		$6,000
Less: Sale of old machine	$2,000	
Avoidable overhaul costs	300	2,300
Effective cost of investment		$3,700

Determine the increase in cash flow resulting from investment in the new machine:

Yearly cost savings = $1,200
Differential depreciation
  Annual depreciation on old machine:

$$\frac{\text{Cost} - \text{Salvage}}{\text{Expected life}} = \frac{\$4,000 - \$0}{10} = \$400$$

  Annual depreciation on new machine:

$$\frac{\text{Cost} - \text{Salvage}}{\text{Expected life}} = \frac{\$6,000 - \$500}{5} = \$1,100$$

  Differential depreciation = $1,100 − $400 = $700
Yearly net increase in cash flow into the firm:

Cost savings		$1,200
Deduct: Taxes at 40%	$480	
Add: Advantage of increase in depreciation (0.4 × $700)	280	200
Yearly increase in cash flow		$1,000

Determine total present value of the investment:
  The five-year cash flow of $1,000 per year is an annuity.
  Discounted at 12 percent, the cost of capital, the present value is
  3.605 × $1,000 = $3,605
  The present value of the new machine, if sold at its salvage value of $500 at the end of the fifth year, is
  0.567 × $500 = $284
  Total present value of the expected cash flows is
  $3,605 + $284 = $3,889

Determine whether net present value is positive:

Total present value	$3,889
Cost of investment	3,700
Net present value	$189

Bennie's Brewery should make the purchase because the investment will return slightly more than the cost of capital.

Note: The importance of depreciation has been shown in this example. The present value of the yearly cash flow resulting from operations is

$$(\text{Cost savings} - \text{Taxes}) \times (\text{Present value factor})$$

$$(\$1,200 - \$480) \quad \times \quad (3.605) \quad = \$2,596$$

This figure is $1,104 less than the $3,700 cost of the investment. Only a very large depreciation advantage makes this investment worthwhile. The total present value of the advantage is $1,009:

$$(\text{Tax rate} \times \text{Differential depreciation}) \times (\text{PV factor})$$

$$(0.4 \times \$700) \quad \times \quad (3.605) \quad = \$1,009$$

Step by Step

EXAMPLE C.3: A Make-or-Buy Decision

The Triple X Company manufactures and sells refrigerators. It makes some of the parts for the refrigerators and purchases others. The engineering department believes it might be possible to cut costs by manufacturing one of the parts currently being purchased for $8.25 each. The firm uses 100,000 of these parts each year. The accounting department compiles the following list of costs based on engineering estimates:

Fixed costs will increase by $50,000.
Labor costs will increase by $125,000.
Factory overhead, currently running $500,000 per year, may be expected to increase 12 percent.
Raw materials used to make the part will cost $600,000.

Given the preceding estimates, should Triple X make the part or continue to buy it?

SOLUTION

Find the total cost incurred if the part were manufactured:

Additional fixed costs	$ 50,000
Additional labor costs	125,000
Raw materials cost	600,000
Additional overhead costs = 0.12 × $500,000	60,000
Total cost to manufacture	$835,000

Find the cost per unit to manufacture:

$$\frac{\$835,000}{100,000} = \$8.35 \text{ per unit}$$

Triple X should continue to buy the part. Manufacturing costs exceed the present cost to purchase by $0.10 per unit.

SELECTED BIBLIOGRAPHY

Bodie, Z.; A. Kane; and A. Marcus. *Investments*. 6th ed. New York: McGraw-Hill/Irwin, 2004.

Helfert, E. *Techniques of Financial Analysis: A Modern Approach*. 11th ed. New York: Irwin/McGraw-Hill, 2002.

Poterba, J. M., and L. H. Summers. "A CEO Survey of U.S. Companies' Time Horizons and Hurdle Rates." *Sloan Management Review*, Fall 1995, pp. 43–53.

FOOTNOTES

1 T. Johnson and R. Kaplan, *Relevance Lost: The Rise and Fall of Management Accounting* (Boston: Harvard Business School Press, 1987), p. 188.

2 A description of capital asset pricing is included in many finance textbooks; see, for example, Z. Bodie, A. Kane, and A. Marcus, *Investments*, 6th ed. (New York: McGraw-Hill/Irwin, 2004).

APPENDIX D

ANSWERS TO SELECTED PROBLEMS

CHAPTER 2

4. Productivity (hours)

    Deluxe   0.20

    Limited   0.20

  Productivity (dollars)

    Deluxe   133.33

    Limited   135.71

CHAPTER 3

No solved problems.

CHAPTER 4

3. No. Must consider demand in fourth year.

5. Expected NPV—Small

    $4.8 million

  Expected NPV—Large

    $2.6 million

CHAPTER 4A

3. LR labor, 80%

  LR parts, 90%

  Labor = 11,556 hours

  Parts = $330,876

7. 4,710 hours

11. *a.* 3rd = 35.1 hours

   b. Average = 7.9 hours each; well worth it

CHAPTER 5

3. Traditional method 20 min. setup + 10 × 2 = 40 min. total scan/retrieve system. 1 min. setup + 10 × 5 = 51 min. total. Traditional method is best.

5. *a.* The market can be served only at 3 gals/hr. In 50 hours bathtub will overflow.

   b. The average amount being served is only 2.5 gal/hr, so that is the output rate.

CHAPTER 5A

2. *a.* 1.35 minutes

   b. 1.51 minutes

   c. $48. The worker would not make the bonus.

6. *a.* NT = 0.9286 minute/part

   b. ST = 1.0679 minutes/part

   c. Daily output = 449.50

     Day's wages = $44.49

CHAPTER 6

6. *a.* 20,000 books

   b. higher

   c. lower

12. 80 units/hour

CHAPTER 6A

3. *b.* 120 seconds

   d. 87.5%

9. *a.* 33.6 seconds

   b. 3.51, therefore 4 workstations

   d. AB, DF, C, EG, H

   e. Efficiency = 70.2%

   f. Reduce cycle time to 32 seconds and work $6\frac{2}{3}$ minutes overtime

   g. 1.89 hours overtime; may be better to rebalance

CHAPTER 7

No solved problems.

CHAPTER 7A

5. W_s = 4.125 minutes

  L_q = 4.05 cars

  L_s = 4.95 car

9. *a.* L = 0.22 waiting

   b. W = 0.466 hour

   c. D = 0.362

10. *a.* 2 people

   b. 6 minutes

   c. 0.2964

   d. 67%

   e. 0.03375 hour

18. *a.* 0.833

   b. 5 documents

   c. 0.2 hour

   d. 0.4822

   e. L_1 = tends to infinity

CHAPTER 8

No solved problems.

CHAPTER 9

No solved problems.

CHAPTER 9A

1. *a.* Not inspecting cost = \$20/hr. Cost to inspect = \$9/hr. Therefore, inspect.
   b. \$0.18 each
   c. \$0.22 per unit
6. $\overline{\overline{X}}$ = 999.1
   UCL = 1014.965
   LCL = 983.235
   $\overline{R}$ = 21.733
   UCL = 49.551
   LCL = 0
   Process is in control
9. *a.* n = 31.3 (round sample size to 32)
   b. Random sample 32; reject if more than 8 are defective.
12. $\overline{\overline{X}}$ = 0.499
   UCL = 0.520
   LCL = 0.478
   R = 0.037
   UCL = 0.078
   LCL = 0.000
   Process is in control

CHAPTER 10

5. *b.* A-C-F-G-I and A-D-F-G-I
   c. C: one week
   D: one week
   G: one week
   d. Two paths: A-C-F-G-I; and A-D-F-G-I; 16 weeks
10. *a.* Critical path is A-E-G-C-D
   b. 26 weeks
   c. No difference in completion date
11. *a.* Critical path is A-C-D-F-G

b.

Day	Cost	Activity
First	\$1,000	A
Second	1,200	C
Third	1,500	D (or F)
Fourth	1,500	F (or D)
	\$5,200	

CHAPTER 11

1. Taiwan \$84,442.11
   In-house \$149,427.14
   Purchase from Taiwanese supplier
3. Average inventory turn = 148.6
   Days of supply = 2.46 days

CHAPTER 12

1. C_X = 176.7
   C_Y = 241.5
2. C_X = 374
   C_Y = 357

CHAPTER 13

1. 5 kanban card sets
5. 5 kanban card sets

CHAPTER 13A

No solved problems.

CHAPTER 14

No solved problems.

CHAPTER 15

3. *a.* February 84
   March 86
   April 90
   May 88
   June 84
   b. MAD = 15

7.

Quarter	Forecast
9	232
10	281
11	239
12	231

11. *a.* April to September = 130, 150, 160, 170, 160, 150
   b. April to September = 136, 146, 150, 159, 153, 146
   c. Exponential smoothing performed better.
15. MAD = 104
   TS = 3.1
   The high TS value indicates the model is unacceptable.
19. *a.* MAD = 90
   TS = −1.67
   b. Model okay since tracking is −1.67.

CHAPTER 16

2. Total cost = \$413,600
5. Total cost = \$413,750

CHAPTER 17

5. q = 713
8. *a.* Q = 1,225
   R = 824
   b. q = 390 − Inventory on hand
12. *a.* Q = 89
   b. \$224.72
   c. \$222.50
14. *a.* A(4, 13, 18);
   B (2, 5, 8, 10, 11, 14, 16);
   C (remainder)
   b. Classify as A.
17. q = 691
26. 729 hamburgers
31. 5,000 pounds

CHAPTER 18

4.

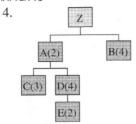

11. Least total cost method: Order 250 units in Period 1
    for Periods 1–8;
    Least unit cost method: Order 450 units in Period 1
    for Periods 1–9.

13. *c.* .A
    .B(2)
    .E(4)
    .F(3)
    .C(3)
    .D(3)
    .H(2)
    .E(5)
    .G(2)
    .D(1)

    d. Level 0   100 units of A
    Level 1   200 units of B
    300 units of C
    Level 2   600 units of F
    600 units of H
    1000 units of D
    Level 3   3800 units of E
    1200 units of G

CHAPTER 19

5. Job order: 5, 6, 7, 3, 1, 2, 4
7. A to 3, B to 1, C to 4, D to 2; cost = $17,000
8. Critical ratio schedule: 5, 3, 2, 4, 1
   Earliest due date, job priority: 2, 5, 3, 4, 1
   Shortest processing time (including delay time): 2, 1,
   4, 3, 5
9. E, A, B, D, C
14. C, B, D, F, E, A

CHAPTER 19A

2. Average customer waiting time = $\frac{1}{6}$ minute
   Average teller idle time = $\frac{4}{6}$ minute

7. *a.*

	Condition 1	Condition 2
(1)	Idle 18 min.	76 + 134 = 210 min.
(2)	Delay 87 min.	0 min.

b.

	Condition 1	Condition 2
Cost of repairperson	$ 38.80	$ 77.20
Cost of machine down	175.33	$117.33
	$214.13	$194.53 (Total Cost)

Lowest cost is Condition 2.

11. One car bypasses.

CHAPTER 20

1. Case I: X used = 933.3 hours
                 Y used = 700 hours
   Case II: Y = 700 hours
                 X = 933.3 hours
   Case III: X = 933.3 hours
                 Y = 700 hours
   Case IV: X = 933.3 hours
                 Y = 700 hours
   Otherwise:
   Case I: No problem
   Case II: Excess WIP
   Case III: Excess spare parts
   Case IV: Excess finished goods

8. *a.* Machine B is the constraint.
   b. All of M; as many N as possible
   c. $600 (100 M and 30 N)

APPENDIX A

2. Optimal combination is $B = 10$, $A = 15$, and $Z = 70$.
4. *a.* $600A + 900B \leq 3{,}600$
       $600A + 900B \geq 1{,}800$
       $200A + 700B \leq 1{,}400$
       $400A + 100B \geq 400$
       $A \leq 2$
       Minimize $.75A + .15B$

   b. $A = 0.54$
       $B = 1.85$
       $Obj = 0.68$

PRESENT VALUE TABLE

Present Value of $1

YEAR	1%	2%	3%	4%	5%	6%	7%	8%	9%	10%	12%	14%	15%
1	.990	.980	.971	.962	.952	.943	.935	.926	.917	.909	.893	.877	.870
2	.980	.961	.943	.925	.907	.890	.873	.857	.842	.826	.797	.769	.756
3	.971	.942	.915	.889	.864	.840	.816	.794	.772	.751	.712	.675	.658
4	.961	.924	.889	.855	.823	.792	.763	.735	.708	.683	.636	.592	.572
5	.951	.906	.863	.822	.784	.747	.713	.681	.650	.621	.567	.519	.497
6	.942	.888	.838	.790	.746	.705	.666	.630	.596	.564	.507	.456	.432
7	.933	.871	.813	.760	.711	.665	.623	.583	.547	.513	.452	.400	.376
8	.923	.853	.789	.731	.677	.627	.582	.540	.502	.467	.404	.351	.327
9	.914	.837	.766	.703	.645	.592	.544	.500	.460	.424	.361	.308	.284
10	.905	.820	.744	.676	.614	.558	.508	.463	.422	.386	.322	.270	.247
11	.896	.804	.722	.650	.585	.527	.475	.429	.388	.350	.287	.237	.215
12	.887	.788	.701	.625	.557	.497	.444	.397	.356	.319	.257	.208	.187
13	.879	.773	.681	.601	.530	.469	.415	.368	.326	.290	.229	.182	.163
14	.870	.758	.661	.577	.505	.442	.388	.340	.299	.263	.205	.160	.141
15	.861	.743	.642	.555	.481	.417	.362	.315	.275	.239	.183	.140	.123
16	.853	.728	.623	.534	.458	.394	.339	.292	.252	.218	.163	.123	.107
17	.844	.714	.605	.513	.436	.371	.317	.270	.231	.198	.146	.108	.093
18	.836	.700	.587	.494	.416	.350	.296	.250	.212	.180	.130	.095	.081
19	.828	.686	.570	.475	.396	.331	.276	.232	.194	.164	.116	.083	.070
20	.820	.673	.554	.456	.377	.312	.258	.215	.178	.149	.104	.073	.061
25	.780	.610	.478	.375	.295	.233	.184	.146	.116	.092	.059	.038	.030
30	.742	.552	.412	.308	.231	.174	.131	.099	.075	.057	.033	.020	.015

YEAR	16%	18%	20%	24%	28%	32%	36%	40%	50%	60%	70%	80%	90%
1	.862	.847	.833	.806	.781	.758	.735	.714	.667	.625	.588	.556	.526
2	.743	.718	.694	.650	.610	.574	.541	.510	.444	.391	.346	.309	.277
3	.641	.609	.579	.524	.477	.435	.398	.364	.296	.244	.204	.171	.146
4	.552	.516	.482	.423	.373	.329	.292	.260	.198	.153	.120	.095	.077
5	.476	.437	.402	.341	.291	.250	.215	.186	.132	.095	.070	.053	.040
6	.410	.370	.335	.275	.227	.189	.158	.133	.088	.060	.041	.029	.021
7	.354	.314	.279	.222	.178	.143	.116	.095	.059	.037	.024	.016	.011
8	.305	.266	.233	.179	.139	.108	.085	.068	.039	.023	.014	.009	.006
9	.263	.226	.194	.144	.108	.082	.063	.048	.026	.015	.008	.005	.003
10	.227	.191	.162	.116	.085	.062	.046	.035	.017	.009	.005	.003	.002
11	.195	.162	.135	.094	.066	.047	.034	.025	.012	.006	.003	.002	.001
12	.168	.137	.112	.076	.052	.036	.025	.018	.008	.004	.002	.001	.001
13	.145	.116	.093	.061	.040	.027	.018	.013	.005	.002	.001	.001	.000
14	.125	.099	.078	.049	.032	.021	.014	.009	.003	.001	.001	.000	.000
15	.108	.084	.065	.040	.025	.016	.010	.006	.002	.001	.000	.000	.000
16	.093	.071	.054	.032	.019	.012	.007	.005	.002	.001	.000	.000	
17	.080	.060	.045	.026	.015	.009	.005	.003	.001	.000	.000		
18	.069	.051	.038	.021	.012	.007	.004	.002	.001	.000	.000		
19	.060	.043	.031	.017	.009	.005	.003	.002	.000	.000			
20	.051	.037	.026	.014	.007	.004	.002	.001	.000	.000			
25	.024	.016	.010	.005	.002	.001	.000	.000					
30	.012	.007	.004	.002	.001	.000	.000						

Using Microsoft Excel®, these are calculated with the equation: $(1 + interest)^{-years}$.

NEGATIVE EXPONENTIAL DISTRIBUTION: VALUES OF e^{-x}

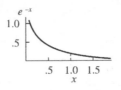

X	e^{-x} (VALUE)	X	e^{-x} (VALUE)	X	e^{-x} (VALUE)	X	e^{-x} (VALUE)
0.00	1.00000	0.50	0.60653	1.00	0.36788	1.50	0.22313
0.01	0.99005	0.51	.60050	1.01	.36422	1.51	.22091
0.02	.98020	0.52	.59452	1.02	.36060	1.52	.21871
0.03	.97045	0.53	.58860	1.03	.35701	1.53	.21654
0.04	.96079	0.54	.58275	1.04	.35345	1.54	.21438
0.05	.95123	0.55	.57695	1.05	.34994	1.55	.21225
0.06	.94176	0.56	.57121	1.06	.34646	1.56	.21014
0.07	.93239	0.57	.56553	1.07	.34301	1.57	.20805
0.08	.92312	0.58	.55990	1.08	.33960	1.58	.20598
0.09	.91393	0.59	.55433	1.09	.33622	1.59	.20393
0.10	.90484	0.60	.54881	1.10	.33287	1.60	.20190
0.11	.89583	0.61	.54335	1.11	.32956	1.61	.19989
0.12	.88692	0.62	.53794	1.12	.32628	1.62	.19790
0.13	.87809	0.63	.53259	1.13	.32303	1.63	.19593
0.14	.86936	0.64	.52729	1.14	.31982	1.64	.19398
0.15	.86071	0.65	.52205	1.15	.31664	1.65	.19205
0.16	.87514	0.66	.51685	1.16	.31349	1.66	.19014
0.17	.84366	0.67	.51171	1.17	.31037	1.67	.18825
0.18	.83527	0.68	.50662	1.18	.30728	1.68	.18637
0.19	.82696	0.69	.50158	1.19	.30422	1.69	.18452
0.20	.81873	0.70	.49659	1.20	.30119	1.70	.18268
0.21	.81058	0.71	.49164	1.21	.29820	1.71	.18087
0.22	.80252	0.72	.48675	1.22	.29523	1.72	.17907
0.23	.79453	0.73	.48191	1.23	.29229	1.73	.17728
0.24	.78663	0.74	.47711	1.24	.28938	1.74	.17552
0.25	.77880	0.75	.47237	1.25	.28650	1.75	.17377
0.26	.77105	0.76	.46767	1.26	.28365	1.76	.17204
0.27	.76338	0.77	.46301	1.27	.28083	1.77	.17033
0.28	.75578	0.78	.45841	1.28	.27804	1.78	.16864
0.29	.74826	0.79	.45384	1.29	.27527	1.79	.16696
0.30	.74082	0.80	.44933	1.30	.27253	1.80	.16530
0.31	.73345	0.81	.44486	1.31	.26982	1.81	.16365
0.32	.72615	0.82	.44043	1.32	.26714	1.82	.16203
0.33	.71892	0.83	.43605	1.33	.26448	1.83	.16041
0.34	.71177	0.84	.43171	1.34	.26185	1.84	.15882
0.35	.70469	0.85	.42741	1.35	.25924	1.85	.15724
0.36	.69768	0.86	.42316	1.36	.25666	1.86	.15567
0.37	.69073	0.87	.41895	1.37	.25411	1.87	.15412
0.38	.68386	0.88	.41478	1.38	.25158	1.88	.15259
0.39	.67706	0.89	.41066	1.39	.24908	1.89	.15107
0.40	.67032	0.90	.40657	1.40	.24660	1.90	.14957
0.41	.66365	0.91	.40252	1.41	.24414	1.91	.14808
0.42	.65705	0.92	.39852	1.42	.24171	1.92	.14661
0.43	.65051	0.93	.39455	1.43	.23931	1.93	.14515
0.44	.64404	0.94	.39063	1.44	.23693	1.94	.14370
0.45	.63763	0.95	.38674	1.45	.23457	1.95	.14227
0.46	.63128	0.96	.38289	1.46	.23224	1.96	.14086
0.47	.62500	0.97	.37908	1.47	.22993	1.97	.13946
0.48	.61878	0.98	.37531	1.48	.22764	1.98	.13807
0.49	.61263	0.99	.37158	1.49	.22537	1.99	.13670
0.50	.60653	1.00	.36788	1.50	.22313	2.00	.13534

Using Microsoft Excel®, these values are calculated with the equation: 1 − EXPONDIST(x, 1, TRUE).

AREAS OF THE CUMULATIVE STANDARD NORMAL DISTRIBUTION

An entry in the table is the proportion under the curve cumulated from the negative tail.

z	G(z)	z	G(z)	z	G(z)
−4.00	0.00003	−1.30	0.09680	1.40	0.91924
−3.95	0.00004	−1.25	0.10565	1.45	0.92647
−3.90	0.00005	−1.20	0.11507	1.50	0.93319
−3.85	0.00006	−1.15	0.12507	1.55	0.93943
−3.80	0.00007	−1.10	0.13567	1.60	0.94520
−3.75	0.00009	−1.05	0.14686	1.65	0.95053
−3.70	0.00011	−1.00	0.15866	1.70	0.95543
−3.65	0.00013	−0.95	0.17106	1.75	0.95994
−3.60	0.00016	−0.90	0.18406	1.80	0.96407
−3.55	0.00019	−0.85	0.19766	1.85	0.96784
−3.50	0.00023	−0.80	0.21186	1.90	0.97128
−3.45	0.00028	−0.75	0.22663	1.95	0.97441
−3.40	0.00034	−0.70	0.24196	2.00	0.97725
−3.35	0.00040	−0.65	0.25785	2.05	0.97982
−3.30	0.00048	−0.60	0.27425	2.10	0.98214
−3.25	0.00058	−0.55	0.29116	2.15	0.98422
−3.20	0.00069	−0.50	0.30854	2.20	0.98610
−3.15	0.00082	−0.45	0.32636	2.25	0.98778
−3.10	0.00097	−0.40	0.34458	2.30	0.98928
−3.05	0.00114	−0.35	0.36317	2.35	0.99061
−3.00	0.00135	−0.30	0.38209	2.40	0.99180
−2.95	0.00159	−0.25	0.40129	2.45	0.99286
−2.90	0.00187	−0.20	0.42074	2.50	0.99379
−2.85	0.00219	−0.15	0.44038	2.55	0.99461
−2.80	0.00256	−0.10	0.46017	2.60	0.99534
−2.75	0.00298	−0.05	0.48006	2.65	0.99598
−2.70	0.00347	0.00	0.50000	2.70	0.99653
−2.65	0.00402	0.05	0.51994	2.75	0.99702
−2.60	0.00466	0.10	0.53983	2.80	0.99744
−2.55	0.00539	0.15	0.55962	2.85	0.99781
−2.50	0.00621	0.20	0.57926	2.90	0.99813
−2.45	0.00714	0.25	0.59871	2.95	0.99841
−2.40	0.00820	0.30	0.61791	3.00	0.99865
−2.35	0.00939	0.35	0.63683	3.05	0.99886
−2.30	0.01072	0.40	0.65542	3.10	0.99903
−2.25	0.01222	0.45	0.67364	3.15	0.99918
−2.20	0.01390	0.50	0.69146	3.20	0.99931
−2.15	0.01578	0.55	0.70884	3.25	0.99942
−2.10	0.01786	0.60	0.72575	3.30	0.99952
−2.05	0.02018	0.65	0.74215	3.35	0.99960
−2.00	0.02275	0.70	0.75804	3.40	0.99966
−1.95	0.02559	0.75	0.77337	3.45	0.99972
−1.90	0.02872	0.80	0.78814	3.50	0.99977
−1.85	0.03216	0.85	0.80234	3.55	0.99981
−1.80	0.03593	0.90	0.81594	3.60	0.99984
−1.75	0.04006	0.95	0.82894	3.65	0.99987
−1.70	0.04457	1.00	0.84134	3.70	0.99989
−1.65	0.04947	1.05	0.85314	3.75	0.99991
−1.60	0.05480	1.10	0.86433	3.80	0.99993
−1.55	0.06057	1.15	0.87493	3.85	0.99994
−1.50	0.06681	1.20	0.88493	3.90	0.99995
−1.45	0.07353	1.25	0.89435	3.95	0.99996
−1.40	0.08076	1.30	0.90320	4.00	0.99997
−1.35	0.08851	1.35	0.91149		

Using Microsoft Excel®, these probabilities are generated with the NORMSDIST(z) function.

UNIFORMLY DISTRIBUTED
RANDOM DIGITS

56970	10799	52098	04184	54967	72938	50834	23777	08392
83125	85077	60490	44369	66130	72936	69848	59973	08144
55503	21383	02464	26141	68779	66388	75242	82690	74099
47019	06683	33203	29603	54553	25971	69573	83854	24715
84828	61152	79526	29554	84580	37859	28504	61980	34997
08021	31331	79227	05748	51276	57143	31926	00915	45821
36458	28285	30424	98420	72925	40729	22337	48293	86847
05752	96045	36847	87729	81679	59126	59437	33225	31280
26768	02513	58454	56958	20575	76746	40878	06846	32828
42613	72456	43030	58085	06766	60227	96414	32671	45587
95457	12176	65482	25596	02678	54592	63607	82096	21913
95276	67524	63564	95958	39750	64379	46059	51666	10433
66954	53574	64776	92345	95110	59448	77249	54044	67942
17457	44151	14113	02462	02798	54977	48340	66738	60184
03704	23322	83214	59337	01695	60666	97410	55064	17427
21538	16997	33210	60337	27976	70661	08250	69509	60264
57178	16730	08310	70348	11317	71623	55510	64750	87759
31048	40058	94953	55866	96283	40620	52087	80817	74533
69799	83300	16498	80733	96422	58078	99643	39847	96884
90595	65017	59231	17772	67831	33317	00520	90401	41700
33570	34761	08039	78784	09977	29398	93896	78227	90110
15340	82760	57477	13898	48431	72936	78160	87240	52710
64079	07733	36512	56186	99098	48850	72527	08486	10951
63491	84886	67118	62063	74958	20946	28147	39338	32109
92003	76568	41034	28260	79708	00770	88643	21188	01850
52360	46658	66511	04172	73085	11795	52594	13287	82531
74622	12142	68355	65635	21828	39539	18988	53609	04001
04157	50070	61343	64315	70836	82857	35335	87900	36194
86003	60070	66241	32836	27573	11479	94114	81641	00496
41208	80187	20351	09630	84668	42486	71303	19512	50277
06433	80674	24520	18222	10610	05794	37515	48619	62866
39298	47829	72648	37414	75755	04717	29899	78817	03509
89884	59651	67533	68123	17730	95862	08034	19473	63971
61512	32155	51906	61662	64430	16688	37275	51262	11569
99653	47635	12506	88535	36553	23757	34209	55803	96275
95913	11085	13772	76638	48423	25018	99041	77529	81360
55804	44004	13122	44115	01601	50541	00147	77685	58788
35334	82410	91601	40617	72876	33967	73830	15405	96554
57729	88646	76487	11622	96297	24160	09903	14047	22917
86648	89317	63677	70119	94739	25875	38829	68377	43918
30574	06039	07967	32422	76791	30725	53711	93385	13421
81307	13114	83580	79974	45929	85113	72268	09858	52104
02410	96385	79067	54939	21410	86980	91772	93307	34116
18969	87444	52233	62319	08598	09066	95288	04794	01534
87863	80514	66860	62297	80198	19347	73234	86265	49096
08397	10538	15438	62311	72844	60203	46412	65943	79232
28520	45542	58729	10854	99058	18260	38765	90038	94209
44285	09452	15867	70418	57012	72122	36634	97283	95943
86299	22510	33571	23309	57040	29285	67870	21913	72958
84842	05748	90894	61658	15001	94005	36308	41161	37341

INTEREST TABLES

Compound Sum of $1

table I.1

YEAR	1%	2%	3%	4%	5%	6%	7%	8%	9%
1	1.010	1.020	1.030	1.040	1.050	1.060	1.070	1.080	1.090
2	1.020	1.040	1.061	1.082	1.102	1.124	1.145	1.166	1.188
3	1.030	1.061	1.093	1.125	1.158	1.191	1.225	1.260	1.295
4	1.041	1.082	1.126	1.170	1.216	1.262	1.311	1.360	1.412
5	1.051	1.104	1.159	1.217	1.276	1.338	1.403	1.469	1.539
6	1.062	1.126	1.194	1.265	1.340	1.419	1.501	1.587	1.677
7	1.072	1.149	1.230	1.316	1.407	1.504	1.606	1.714	1.828
8	1.083	1.172	1.267	1.369	1.477	1.594	1.718	1.851	1.993
9	1.094	1.195	1.305	1.423	1.551	1.689	1.838	1.999	2.172
10	1.105	1.219	1.344	1.480	1.629	1.791	1.967	2.159	2.367
11	1.116	1.243	1.384	1.539	1.710	1.898	2.105	2.332	2.580
12	1.127	1.268	1.426	1.601	1.796	2.012	2.252	2.518	2.813
13	1.138	1.294	1.469	1.665	1.886	2.133	2.410	2.720	3.066
14	1.149	1.319	1.513	1.732	1.980	2.261	2.579	2.937	3.342
15	1.161	1.346	1.558	1.801	2.079	2.397	2.759	3.172	3.642
16	1.173	1.373	1.605	1.873	2.183	2.540	2.952	3.426	3.970
17	1.184	1.400	1.653	1.948	2.292	2.693	3.159	3.700	4.328
18	1.196	1.428	1.702	2.026	2.407	2.854	3.380	3.996	4.717
19	1.208	1.457	1.754	2.107	2.527	3.026	3.617	4.316	5.142
20	1.220	1.486	1.806	2.191	2.653	3.207	3.870	4.661	5.604
25	1.282	1.641	2.094	2.666	3.386	4.292	5.427	6.848	8.623
30	1.348	1.811	2.427	3.243	4.322	5.743	7.612	10.063	13.268

YEAR	10%	12%	14%	15%	16%	18%	20%	24%	28%
1	1.100	1.120	1.140	1.150	1.160	1.180	1.200	1.240	1.280
2	1.210	1.254	1.300	1.322	1.346	1.392	1.440	1.538	1.638
3	1.331	1.405	1.482	1.521	1.561	1.643	1.728	1.907	2.067
4	1.464	1.574	1.689	1.749	1.811	1.939	2.074	2.364	2.684
5	1.611	1.762	1.925	2.011	2.100	2.288	2.488	2.932	3.436
6	1.772	1.974	2.195	2.313	2.436	2.700	2.986	3.635	4.398
7	1.949	2.211	2.502	2.660	2.826	3.185	3.583	4.508	5.629
8	2.144	2.476	2.853	3.059	3.278	3.759	4.300	5.590	7.206
9	2.358	2.773	3.252	3.518	3.803	4.435	5.160	6.931	9.223
10	2.594	3.106	3.707	4.046	4.411	5.234	6.192	8.594	11.806
11	2.853	3.479	4.226	4.652	5.117	6.176	7.430	10.657	15.112
12	3.138	3.896	4.818	5.350	5.936	7.288	8.916	13.216	19.343
13	3.452	4.363	5.492	6.153	6.886	8.599	10.699	16.386	24.759
14	3.797	4.887	6.261	7.076	7.988	10.147	12.839	20.319	31.691
15	4.177	5.474	7.138	8.137	9.266	11.974	15.407	25.196	40.565
16	4.595	6.130	8.137	9.358	10.748	14.129	18.488	31.243	51.923
17	5.054	6.866	9.276	10.761	12.468	16.672	22.186	38.741	66.461
18	5.560	7.690	10.575	12.375	14.463	19.673	26.623	48.039	85.071
19	6.116	8.613	12.056	14.232	16.777	23.214	31.948	59.568	108.89
20	6.728	9.646	13.743	16.367	19.461	27.393	38.338	73.864	139.38
25	10.835	17.000	26.462	32.919	40.874	62.669	95.396	216.542	478.90
30	17.449	29.960	50.950	66.212	85.850	143.371	237.376	634.820	1645.5

Using Microsoft Excel®, these are calculated with the equation: $(1 + \text{interest})^{\text{years}}$.

appendix I   INTEREST TABLES

table I.2

Sum of an Annuity of $1 for *N* Years

YEAR	1%	2%	3%	4%	5%	6%	7%	8%
1	1.000	1.000	1.000	1.000	1.000	1.000	1.000	1.000
2	2.010	2.020	2.030	2.040	2.050	2.060	2.070	2.080
3	2.030	3.060	3.019	3.122	3.152	3.184	3.215	3.246
4	4.060	4.122	4.184	4.246	4.310	4.375	4.440	4.506
5	5.101	5.204	5.309	5.416	5.526	5.637	5.751	5.867
6	6.152	6.308	6.468	6.633	6.802	6.975	7.153	7.336
7	7.214	7.434	7.662	7.898	8.142	8.394	8.654	8.923
8	8.286	8.583	8.892	9.214	9.549	9.897	10.260	10.637
9	9.369	9.755	10.159	10.583	11.027	11.491	11.978	12.488
10	10.462	10.950	11.464	12.006	12.578	13.181	13.816	14.487
11	11.567	12.169	12.808	13.486	14.207	14.972	15.784	16.645
12	12.683	13.412	14.192	15.026	15.917	16.870	17.888	18.977
13	13.809	14.680	15.618	16.627	17.713	18.882	20.141	21.495
14	14.947	15.974	17.086	18.292	19.599	21.051	22.550	24.215
15	16.097	17.293	18.599	20.024	21.579	23.276	25.129	27.152
16	17.258	18.639	20.157	21.825	23.657	25.673	27.888	30.324
17	18.430	20.012	21.762	23.698	25.840	28.213	30.840	33.750
18	19.615	21.412	23.414	25.645	28.132	30.906	33.999	37.450
19	20.811	22.841	25.117	27.671	30.539	33.760	37.379	41.446
20	22.019	24.297	26.870	29.778	33.066	36.786	40.995	45.762
25	28.243	32.030	36.459	41.646	47.727	54.865	63.249	73.106
30	34.785	40.568	47.575	56.085	66.439	79.058	94.461	113.283

YEAR	9%	10%	12%	14%	16%	18%	20%	24%
1	1.000	1.000	1.000	1.000	1.000	1.000	1.000	1.000
2	2.090	2.100	2.120	2.140	2.160	2.180	2.200	2.240
3	3.278	3.310	3.374	3.440	3.506	3.572	3.640	3.778
4	4.573	4.641	4.770	4.921	5.066	5.215	5.368	5.684
5	5.985	6.105	6.353	6.610	6.877	7.154	7.442	8.048
6	7.523	7.716	8.115	8.536	8.977	9.442	9.930	10.980
7	9.200	9.487	10.089	10.730	11.414	12.142	12.916	14.615
8	11.028	11.436	12.300	13.233	14.240	15.327	16.499	19.123
9	13.021	13.579	14.776	16.085	17.518	19.086	20.799	24.712
10	15.193	15.937	17.549	19.337	21.321	23.521	25.959	31.643
11	17.560	18.531	20.655	23.044	25.733	28.755	32.150	40.238
12	20.141	21.384	24.133	27.271	30.850	34.931	39.580	50.985
13	22.953	24.523	28.029	32.089	36.786	42.219	48.497	64.110
14	26.019	27.975	32.393	37.581	43.672	50.818	59.196	80.496
15	29.361	31.772	37.280	43.842	51.660	60.965	72.035	100.815
16	33.003	35.950	42.753	50.980	60.925	72.939	87.442	126.011
17	36.974	40.545	48.884	59.118	71.673	87.068	105.931	157.253
18	41.301	45.599	55.750	68.394	84.141	103.740	128.117	195.994
19	46.018	51.159	63.440	78.969	98.603	123.414	154.740	244.033
20	51.160	57.275	72.052	91.025	115.380	146.628	186.688	303.601
25	84.701	93.347	133.334	181.871	249.214	342.603	471.981	898.092
30	136.308	164.494	241.333	356.787	530.312	790.948	1181.882	2640.916

Using Microsoft Excel®, these are calculated with the function: FV(interest, years, −1).

Present Value of $1

table I.3

YEAR	1%	2%	3%	4%	5%	6%	7%	8%	9%	10%	12%	14%	15%
1	.990	.980	.971	.962	.952	.943	.935	.926	.917	.909	.893	.877	.870
2	.980	.961	.943	.925	.907	.890	.873	.857	.842	.826	.797	.769	.756
3	.971	.942	.915	.889	.864	.840	.816	.794	.772	.751	.712	.675	.658
4	.961	.924	.889	.855	.823	.792	.763	.735	.708	.683	.636	.592	.572
5	.951	.906	.863	.822	.784	.747	.713	.681	.650	.621	.567	.519	.497
6	.942	.888	.838	.790	.746	.705	.666	.630	.596	.564	.507	.456	.432
7	.933	.871	.813	.760	.711	.665	.623	.583	.547	.513	.452	.400	.376
8	.923	.853	.789	.731	.677	.627	.582	.540	.502	.467	.404	.351	.327
9	.914	.837	.766	.703	.645	.592	.544	.500	.460	.424	.361	.308	.284
10	.905	.820	.744	.676	.614	.558	.508	.463	.422	.386	.322	.270	.247
11	.896	.804	.722	.650	.585	.527	.475	.429	.388	.350	.287	.237	.215
12	.887	.788	.701	.625	.557	.497	.444	.397	.356	.319	.257	.208	.187
13	.879	.773	.681	.601	.530	.469	.415	.368	.326	.290	.229	.182	.163
14	.870	.758	.661	.577	.505	.442	.388	.340	.299	.263	.205	.160	.141
15	.861	.743	.642	.555	.481	.417	.362	.315	.275	.239	.183	.140	.123
16	.853	.728	.623	.534	.458	.394	.339	.292	.252	.218	.163	.123	.107
17	.844	.714	.605	.513	.436	.371	.317	.270	.231	.198	.146	.108	.093
18	.836	.700	.587	.494	.416	.350	.296	.250	.212	.180	.130	.095	.081
19	.828	.686	.570	.475	.396	.331	.276	.232	.194	.164	.116	.083	.070
20	.820	.673	.554	.456	.377	.312	.258	.215	.178	.149	.104	.073	.061
25	.780	.610	.478	.375	.295	.233	.184	.146	.116	.092	.059	.038	.030
30	.742	.552	.412	.308	.231	.174	.131	.099	.075	.057	.033	.020	.015

YEAR	16%	18%	20%	24%	28%	32%	36%	40%	50%	60%	70%	80%	90%
1	.862	.847	.833	.806	.781	.758	.735	.714	.667	.625	.588	.556	.526
2	.743	.718	.694	.650	.610	.574	.541	.510	.444	.391	.346	.309	.277
3	.641	.609	.579	.524	.477	.435	.398	.364	.296	.244	.204	.171	.146
4	.552	.516	.482	.423	.373	.329	.292	.260	.198	.153	.120	.095	.077
5	.476	.437	.402	.341	.291	.250	.215	.186	.132	.095	.070	.053	.040
6	.410	.370	.335	.275	.227	.189	.158	.133	.088	.060	.041	.029	.021
7	.354	.314	.279	.222	.178	.143	.116	.095	.059	.037	.024	.016	.011
8	.305	.266	.233	.179	.139	.108	.085	.068	.039	.023	.014	.009	.006
9	.263	.226	.194	.144	.108	.082	.063	.048	.026	.015	.008	.005	.003
10	.227	.191	.162	.116	.085	.062	.046	.035	.017	.009	.005	.003	.002
11	.195	.162	.135	.094	.066	.047	.034	.025	.012	.006	.003	.002	.001
12	.168	.137	.112	.076	.052	.036	.025	.018	.008	.004	.002	.001	.001
13	.145	.116	.093	.061	.040	.027	.018	.013	.005	.002	.001	.001	.000
14	.125	.099	.078	.049	.032	.021	.014	.009	.003	.001	.001	.000	.000
15	.108	.084	.065	.040	.025	.016	.010	.006	.002	.001	.000	.000	.000
16	.093	.071	.054	.032	.019	.012	.007	.005	.002	.001	.000	.000	
17	.080	.060	.045	.026	.015	.009	.005	.003	.001	.000	.000		
18	.069	.051	.038	.021	.012	.007	.004	.002	.001	.000	.000		
19	.060	.043	.031	.017	.009	.005	.003	.002	.000	.000			
20	.051	.037	.026	.014	.007	.004	.002	.001	.000	.000			
25	.024	.016	.010	.005	.002	.001	.000	.000					
30	.012	.007	.004	.002	.001	.000	.000						

Using Microsoft Excel®, these are calculated with the equation: $(1 + interest)^{-years}$.

table I.4

Present Value of an Annuity of $1

YEAR	1%	2%	3%	4%	5%	6%	7%	8%	9%	10%
1	0.990	0.980	0.971	0.962	0.952	0.943	0.935	0.926	0.917	0.909
2	1.970	1.942	1.913	1.886	1.859	1.833	1.808	1.783	1.759	1.736
3	2.941	2.884	2.829	2.775	2.723	2.673	2.624	2.577	2.531	2.487
4	3.902	3.808	3.717	3.630	3.546	3.465	3.387	3.312	3.240	3.170
5	4.853	4.713	4.580	4.452	4.329	4.212	4.100	3.993	3.890	3.791
6	5.795	5.601	5.417	5.242	5.076	4.917	4.766	4.623	4.486	4.355
7	6.728	6.472	6.230	6.002	5.786	5.582	5.389	5.206	5.033	4.868
8	7.652	7.325	7.020	6.733	6.463	6.210	6.971	5.747	5.535	5.335
9	8.566	8.162	7.786	7.435	7.108	6.802	6.515	6.247	5.985	5.759
10	9.471	8.983	8.530	8.111	7.722	7.360	7.024	6.710	6.418	6.145
11	10.368	9.787	9.253	8.760	8.306	7.887	7.449	7.139	6.805	6.495
12	11.255	10.575	9.954	9.385	8.863	8.384	7.943	7.536	7.161	6.814
13	12.134	11.348	10.635	9.986	9.394	8.853	8.358	7.904	7.487	7.103
14	13.004	12.106	11.296	10.563	9.899	9.295	8.745	8.244	7.786	7.367
15	13.865	12.849	11.938	11.118	10.380	9.712	9.108	8.559	8.060	7.606
16	14.718	13.578	12.561	11.652	10.838	10.106	9.447	8.851	8.312	7.824
17	15.562	14.292	13.166	12.166	11.274	10.477	9.763	9.122	8.544	8.022
18	16.398	14.992	13.754	12.659	11.690	10.828	10.059	9.372	8.756	8.201
19	17.226	15.678	14.324	13.134	12.085	11.158	10.336	9.604	8.950	8.365
20	18.046	16.351	14.877	13.590	12.462	11.470	10.594	9.818	9.128	8.514
25	22.023	19.523	17.413	15.622	14.094	12.783	11.654	10.675	9.823	9.077
30	25.808	22.397	19.600	17.292	15.373	13.765	12.409	11.258	10.274	9.427

YEAR	12%	14%	16%	18%	20%	24%	28%	32%	36%
1	0.893	0.877	0.862	0.847	0.833	0.806	0.781	0.758	0.735
2	1.690	1.647	1.605	1.566	1.528	1.457	1.392	1.332	1.276
3	2.402	2.322	2.246	2.174	2.106	1.981	1.868	1.766	1.674
4	3.037	2.914	2.798	2.690	2.589	2.404	2.241	2.096	1.966
5	3.605	3.433	3.274	3.127	2.991	2.745	2.532	2.345	2.181
6	4.111	3.889	3.685	3.498	3.326	3.020	2.759	2.534	2.339
7	4.564	4.288	4.039	3.812	3.605	3.242	2.937	2.678	2.455
8	4.968	4.639	4.344	4.078	3.837	3.421	3.076	2.786	2.540
9	5.328	4.946	4.607	4.303	4.031	3.566	3.184	2.868	2.603
10	5.650	5.216	4.833	4.494	4.193	3.682	3.269	2.930	2.650
11	5.988	5.453	5.029	4.656	4.327	3.776	3.335	2.978	2.683
12	6.194	5.660	5.197	4.793	4.439	3.851	3.387	3.013	2.708
13	6.424	5.842	5.342	4.910	4.533	3.912	3.427	3.040	2.727
14	6.628	6.002	5.468	5.008	4.611	3.962	3.459	3.061	2.740
15	6.811	6.142	5.575	5.092	4.675	4.001	3.483	3.076	2.750
16	6.974	6.265	5.669	5.162	4.730	4.033	3.503	3.088	2.758
17	7.120	6.373	5.749	5.222	4.775	4.059	3.518	3.097	2.763
18	7.250	6.467	5.818	5.273	4.812	4.080	3.529	3.104	2.767
19	7.366	6.550	5.877	5.316	4.844	4.097	3.539	3.109	2.770
20	7.469	6.623	5.929	5.353	4.870	4.110	3.546	3.113	2.772
25	7.843	6.873	6.097	5.467	4.948	4.147	3.564	3.122	2.776
30	8.055	7.003	6.177	5.517	4.979	4.160	3.569	3.124	2.778

Using Microsoft Excel®, these are calculated with the function: PV(interest, years, −1).

CHAPTER 1 *p. 3*, The McGraw-Hill Companies, Inc./Andrew Resek, photographer; *p. 4*, Courtesy of L.L. Bean, Inc.; *p. 6*, Digital Vision/PunchStock; *p. 10*, Edgar R. Schoepal/ASSOCIATED PRESS; *p. 13*, Getty Images; *p. 14*, Library of Congress.

CHAPTER 2 *p. 21*, Getty Images; *p. 23*, Photodisc/Getty Images; *p. 25*, Louie Psihoyos/Science Faction/Corbis; *p. 28*, AFP/Getty Images; *p. 36*, Kim Kulish/CORBIS.

CHAPTER 3 *p. 39*, Courtesy of IDEO; *p. 41*, Associated Press; *p. 44*, Courtesy of W.L. Gore, Inc.; *p. 51*, Courtesy of Topspeed.com; *p. 53*, Courtesy of Stereolithography.com; *p. 56*, Tony Freeman/PhotoEdit; *p. 58*, Iain Masterton/Alamy.

CHAPTER 4 *p. 71*, Courtesy of Shouldice Hospital; *p. 74*, Star-Ledger Photographs/John O'Boyle © 2008 The Star-Ledger, Newark, NJ; *p. 83*, AFP/Getty Images.

CHAPTER 4A *p. 99*, AP Photo/Jamie-Andrea Yanak.

CHAPTER 5 *p. 107*, Courtesy of IDEO; *p. 109*, Axel M. Cipollini/Aurora/Getty Images; *p. 115*, Associated Press; *p. 117*, Jeff Greenberg/PhotoEdit; *p. 119*, Brand X Pictures/PunchStock; *p. 127*, Plush Studios/Bill Reitzel/Getty Images.

CHAPTER 5A *p. 140*, M. Freeman/PhotoLink/Getty Images; *p. 144*, Underwood & Underwood/CORBIS.

CHAPTER 6 *p. 159*, ROBYN BECK/AFP/Getty Images; *p. 162*, Courtesy of Dell Inc.; *p. 166*, (t) Digital Vision/Getty Images, (c) David Parker/Photo Researchers, Inc., (b) William Taufic/CORBIS; *p. 167*, Getty Images.

CHAPTER 6A *p. 181*, Courtesy of Nokia; *p. 183*, Courtesy of Group Lotus Plc.; *p. 187*, Photofest, Inc.

CHAPTER 7 *p. 217*, FoodPix/Jupiterimages/Getty Images; *p. 219*, Keith Brofsky/Getty Images; *p. 226*, Adam Crowley/Photodisc/Getty Images; *p. 227*, Associated Press; *p. 228*, Tim Boyle/Getty Images; *p. 232*, Courtesy of the Kimpton Boutique Hotels.

CHAPTER 7A *p. 239*, Yellow Dog Productions/Riser/Getty Images; *p. 241*, Associated Press.

CHAPTER 8 *p. 269*, © 2009 NCR Corporation. All rights reserved.; *p. 275*, Hulton Archive/Getty Images; *p. 278*, © 2009. Cardinal Health, Inc. or one of its subsidiaries. All rights reserved. Pyxis®, CUBIE®, MedStation® and Pyxis STARTERx® are registered trademarks and SpecialtyStation™ is a trademark of Cardinal Health, Inc. or one of its subsidiaries. 3PMP0588-02 (0309/1000); *p. 280*, © 2009 InTouch Technologies, Inc. All Rights Reserved. InTouch Technologies, InTouch Health, the Company logos and all other Company product or service names are trademarks of InTouch Technologies, Inc.

CHAPTER 9 *p. 285*, Courtesy of General Electric; *p. 286*, Courtesy of National Institute of Standards & Technology; *p. 289*, Courtesy of the Goodyear Tire and Rubber Company; *p. 291*, Courtesy of J.D. Power & Associates.

CHAPTER 9A *p. 307*, David Joel/Getty Images; *p. 309*, Tim Boyle/Getty Images; *p. 318*, Courtesy of Ford Motor Company; *p. 322*, Barry Willis/Taxi/Getty Images.

CHAPTER 10 *p. 335*, NASA Headquarters – GReatest Images of NASA (NASA-HQ-GRIN); *p. 339*, (t) Getty Images, (c) ELMER MARTINEZ/AFP/Getty Images, (b) Courtesy of Foster + Partners; *p. 347*, Thinkstock/Masterfile.

CHAPTER 11 *p. 375*, Li jianbin – Imaginechina/AP Worldwide Images; *p. 377*, Charlie Westerman/Stone/Getty Images; *p. 378*, Jeff Greenberg/Alamy; *p. 382*, Courtesy of Deutsche Post AG; *p. 384*, TWPhoto/Corbis; *p. 385*, Associated Press; *p. 387*, Associated Press.

CHAPTER 12 *p. 397*, Courtesy of Federal Express; *p. 398*, Courtesy of Deutsche Post AG; *p. 401*, Directphoto.org/Alamy; *p. 402*, Courtesy of Honda of America Mfg.

CHAPTER 13 *p. 417*, AFP/Getty Images; *p. 420*, Courtesy of Toyota Motor Sales, U.S.A., Inc.; *p. 421*, Courtesy of Dematic Corp.; *p. 423*, Courtesy of FKI Logistex®; *p. 428*, Courtesy of Kawasaki Motors Mfg., Corp., USA, Maryville Plant; *p. 435*, Dana Neely Photography/The Image Bank/Getty Images.

CHAPTER 13A *p. 451*, MEIGNEUX/SIPA/Associated Press; *p. 458*, Peter Yates/Time & Life Pictures/Getty Images; *p. 463*, Courtesy of Texas Instruments.

CHAPTER 14 *p. 472*, Jon Feingersh/Bland Images/Getty Images; *p. 476*, Jetta Productions/Iconica/Getty Images.

CHAPTER 15 *p. 483*, Courtesy of Walmart; *p. 484*, TRBfoto/Getty Images; *p. 493*, Courtesy of The Toro Company; *p. 509*, Courtesy of Gilmore Research Group – Seattle/Portland.

CHAPTER 16 *p. 529*, Ryan McVay/Getty Images; *p. 533*, RF/Corbis; *p. 535*, Courtesy of Finisar Corporation; *p. 545*, TravelStockCollection – Homer Sykes/Alamy.

CHAPTER 17 *p. 555*, Courtesy of Univted Parcel Service of America, Inc.; *p. 560*, Christoph Morlinghaus; *p. 569*, Associated Press; *p. 580*, AFP/Getty Images.

CHAPTER 18 *p. 597*, Ed Honowitz/Stone/Getty Images; *p. 598*, David R. Frazier Photolibrary, Inc./Alamy; *p. 601*, AFP/Getty Images; *p. 606*, John Zoiner/Workbook Stock/Getty Images.

CHAPTER 19 *p. 627*, Courtesy Oakwood Healthcare System, Inc.; *p. 629*, Courtesy of Intelligent Instrumentation, Inc.; *p. 641*, Flip Chalfant/Riser/Getty Images.

CHAPTER 20 *p. 681*, Tsuneo Yamashita/Taxi Japan/Getty Images; *p. 688*, Courtesy of United States Steel Corporation.

Note: Page numbers followed by *n* refer to footnotes.

Note: Page numbers followed by *n* refer to footnotes.